Supporting open minds since 2005

Modeling and Simulation in Engineering - Selected Problems
http://dx.doi.org/10.5772/intechopen.87734
Edited by Jan Valdman and Leszek Marcinkowski

Contributors
Cemil Koyunoğlu, Yuri Menshikov, Dmytro Yevdokymov, Jean-Luc Autran, Daniela Munteanu, Mikhail E. Belkin, Tatiana N. Bakhvalova, Vladislav Golovin, Yuri Tyschuk, Alexander S. Sigov, Anna Kapranova, Daria Bahaeva, Dmitry Stenko, Ivan Verloka, Anton Lebedev, Mikhail Tarshis, Syed Islam, Samira Shamsir, Omiya Hassan, Partha Sarathi Paul, Md. Razuan Hossain, Md Sakib Hasan, Saud Altaf, Shafiq Ahmad, Marek Werner, Kerstin Weinberg, Carola Bilgen, Tim Dally, Nencho Stanev Deliiski, Natalia Yordanova Tumbarkova, Ladislav Dzuranda, Mohamed Abdelsabour Abdelsabour Fahmy, Surya Prasada Rao Borra, Kongara Ramanjaneyulu, K Raja Rajeswari

First published in London, United Kingdom, 2020 by IntechOpen
IntechOpen is the global imprint of INTECHOPEN LIMITED, registered in England and Wales, registration number: 11086078, 5 Princes Gate Court, London, SW7 2QJ, United Kingdom
Printed in Croatia

British Library Cataloguing-in-Publication Data
A catalogue record for this book is available from the British Library

Additional hard and PDF copies can be obtained from orders@intechopen.com

Modeling and Simulation in Engineering - Selected Problems
Edited by Jan Valdman and Leszek Marcinkowski
p. cm.
Print ISBN 978-1-83968-249-0
Online ISBN 978-1-83968-250-6
eBook (PDF) ISBN 978-1-83968-251-3

For EU product safety concerns:
IN TECH d.o.o., Prolaz Marije Krucifikse Kozulić 3, 51000 Rijeka, Croatia, info@intechopen.com or visit our website at intechopen.com.

Meet the editors

Dr. Jan Valdman is an associate professor of applied mathematics at the Faculty of Science, University of South Bohemia in České Budějovice and a researcher at the Institute of Information Theory and Automation of the Czech Academy of Sciences in Prague. He obtained his MSc degrees from the Mathematical Research Institute in Utrecht, the Netherlands, and the University of West Bohemia in Pilsen, Czech Republic in 1998. He graduated from the University of Kiel, Germany with his PhD thesis on modeling of elastoplasticity in 2002. After spending further years at several foreign institutions (Linz, Bergen, Reykjavik, and Leipzig), he returned to Czech Republic and finished his habilitation at the Technical University of Ostrava in 2011. His areas of interest include computational nonlinear mechanics of solids and aposteriori error estimates for nonlinear problems. He has published several vectorized finite element codes in MATLAB.

Dr. Leszek Marcinkowski is an associate professor of applied mathematics at the Faculty of Mathematics, Informatics, and Mechanics, University of Warsaw. He obtained his MSc degree in 1994, his Ph.D. degree in 2000, and his habilitation in 2010 from the University of Warsaw. All degrees were obtained with distinctions. His Ph.D. thesis was on parallel solvers for partial differential equations discretizations. Later he was a post-doctoral fellow in the Department of Computer Science of the University of Colorado at Boulder, USA. He visited many foreign institutions, including the University of Colorado, Lawrence Livermore National Laboratory, and the University of Bergen, for shorter research visits. His research areas are focused on discretization methods and parallel solvers for partial differential equations. In particular, he is interested in discretizations built on nonmatching grids and domain decomposition methods.

Contents

Preface

The idea of editing this book together came at the conference PPAM 2019, in September 2019 in Białystok, Poland, which both editors attended. The actual work started in November 2019 and took a bit longer due to Covid-19; however, our online cooperation did not stop our activities. The general aim of this book was to present selected chapters of two types: chapters with more focus on modeling with some necessary simulation details and chapters with less focus on modeling but with more simulation details. During the selection process, many contributions were received, but some had to be rejected. These were mostly too theoretical and missing explanations of the algorithms or simulation details. Finally, we present eleven chapters divided into two sections according to areas of their applications:

1. Modeling in continuum mechanics

2. Modeling in electronics and engineering

We hope our book entitled "Modeling and Simulation in Engineering - Selected Problems" will serve as a useful reference to students, scientists, and engineers. We are thankful to each author for the technical effort presented in each book chapter and their patience when working on revisions.

Our biggest thanks go to Ms. Dolores Kuzelj, Author Service Manager from IntechOpen, who instructed us through all stages of the editorial process. Together, we did our best to ensure the book's high quality.

Dr. Jan Valdman
Institute of Mathematics,
České Budějovice and Institute of Information Theory
and Automation of the Czech Academy of Sciences,
University of South Bohemia,
Prague, Czech Republic

Dr. Leszek Marcinkowski
Faculty of Mathematics,
Informatics and Mechanics,
University of Warsaw,
Warsaw, Poland

Section 1

Modeling in Continuum Mechanics

Chapter 1

Cohesive Elements or Phase-Field Fracture: Which Method Is Better for Dynamic Fracture Analyses?

Tim Dally, Carola Bilgen, Marek Werner and Kerstin Weinberg

Abstract

Numerical techniques to simulate crack propagation can roughly be divided into sharp and diffuse interface methods. Two prominent approaches to quantitative dynamic fracture analysis are compared here. Specifically, an adaptive cohesive element technique and a phase-field fracture approach are applied to simulate Hopkinson bar experiments on the fracture toughness of high-performance concrete. The experimental results are validated numerically in the sense of an inverse analysis. Both methods allow predictive numerical simulations of crack growth with an a priori unknown path and determine the related material parameter in a quantitative manner. Reliability, precision, and numerical costs differ however.

Keywords: Split-Hopkinson bar experiment, UHPC, cohesive elements, phase-field fracture, inverse analysis, dynamic fracture, crack propagation, crack tracking algorithms

1. Introduction

One of the main challenges in computational mechanics is the prediction of cracks and fragmentation in dynamic fracture. There are high demands on the modeling side, but mainly the complicated structure and the nonregular behavior of the cracks turn numerical simulations into a difficult task. Every crack in a solid forms a new surface of a priori unknown position, which needs to be identified. Different discretization techniques have been developed to solve such problems, for example the cohesive element technique [1–3], the extended finite element method [4, 5], eroded finite elements or eigenfracture strategies [6, 7], and phase-field approaches [8–13].

The numerical techniques to treat the moving boundary problem of crack propagation can roughly be divided into two different strategies: sharp interface and diffuse interface modeling. The sharp interface approach describes a crack as a new boundary $\Gamma_C(t) \subset \partial\Omega$ in a solid of domain Ω undergoing a deformation $\chi(\boldsymbol{x}, t)$: $\Omega \times [0, t_{\text{total}}] \rightarrow \mathbb{R}^3$ in a time t_{total}. For a known crack path this is the natural way to capture the mechanics of fracture. In dynamic fracture, however, with a priori unknown ways of crack propagation, kinks, and branching, sophisticated tracking methods need to be employed to localize the boundaries by the position and to enforce (free) boundary conditions along the moving crack. Unfortunately, such surface tracking methods require a high numerical effort and tend to fail for great changes in the topology of the solid, such as the fragmentation into small particles and their further movement.

An alternative way to describe moving boundaries are diffuse interface models where the cracks are smeared over a small but finite length ε. Here an additional field $s(\boldsymbol{x}, t) : \Omega \times [0, t_{\text{total}}] \to \mathbb{R}$ characterizes the state of the material and marks the intact or broken state. The set of evolving crack surfaces is replaced by a crack-surface density γ, which is typically a function of the marker field s and its gradient. This crack-surface density function allows an approximation of the moving crack boundaries over the body's domain,

$$\int_{\Gamma_C(t)} \mathrm{d}\Gamma \approx \int_{\Omega} \gamma(t)\, \mathrm{d}\Omega. \tag{1}$$

By γ being not only a function of field $s(\boldsymbol{x}, t)$ but also its gradient ∇s, it regularizes (or *diffuses*) the local jump of a crack. The net effect of this regularization is to eliminate spurious mesh-dependencies that afflict naive damage schemes. The potential energy of such a regularized cracking body corresponds to the well-known Ambrosio-Tortorelli functional of continuum damage mechanics [14]. Therefore, the diffuse interface approach can be seen as a gradient damage model with the major difference that the order parameter s indicates the material to be either intact ($s = 1$) or broken ($s = 0$). Intermediate states are not physically meaningful. However, it is still an open question how reliable such a diffuse approach can quantify the mechanics of fracture.

Here we compare a sharp interface method with crack tracking algorithm and a diffuse interface method for its usability in material identification. Background for our comparison are our experimental investigations on the fracture toughness of ultra-high performance concrete (UHPC). Specifically, we use the cohesive element technique and the phase-field fracture approach to simulate spalling experiments performed with concrete specimen in a Hopkinson-Bar (HB) setup.

UHPC is a class of advanced cementitious-based composites whose mechanical strength and durability surpass classical concrete. Typically, UHPC composites are fine grained, almost homogeneous mixtures of small aggregates of cement, a certain amount of silica, other supplements, and a low water content—and so they are more similar to brittle ceramics than to construction concrete. UHPCs are still under development and in order to optimize their composition mechanical tests have to provide material data. Hereby classical experiments determine the concrete's elasticity as well as its compressive and flexural strength under static loading conditions. For the dynamic properties, however, such as dynamic tensile resistance and fracture energy, it is more complicated to ensure reproducible test conditions. Here numerical simulations in the sense of an inverse analysis are helpful to evaluate the reliability of the obtained material data.

HB spalling experiments are test arrangements to determine the failure strength of brittle materials, see [15–19]. In these tests the experimental setup of a classical HB is modified in such a way, that the induced pressure impulse is transmitted via an incident bar into the specimen, see **Figure 1**. Within the specimen a superposition of transmitted and reflected waves determines the stress state. For details of the experimental work we refer to another work [20], here we just use the experimental setup to compare two numerical techniques employed for *quantitative* analysis. Specifically, for fracture parameter identification we need: (i) numerical methods that are able to find the crack position dependent on the external load and the material parameter of the specimen; (ii) the pressure wave and the stress

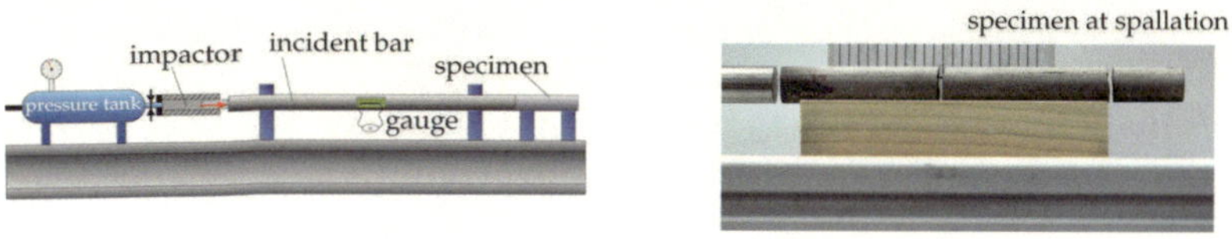

Figure 1.
Illustration of the HB-spallation test setup where the pressure tank accelerates the impactor and the impact-induced wave propagates trough the specimen (left) and UHPC specimen cracked after wave reflection (right).

distribution in the fast (cracking) specimen; and (iii) we need to quantify the fracture energy and the critical energy release rate of the material.

The remaining paper is organized as follows. In the next section we provide shortly the governing equations of elasto-dynamics and fracture mechanics. Then we introduce the cohesive element technique in Section 3 and the phase-field fracture method in Section 4. Both sections conclude with a short study on the influence of the relevant model parameters. In Section 5 the simulations of the HB spalling experiment are described in detail and a range of values for the fracture parameters is derived. The inverse analysis is presented in Section 6. Here we provide several numerical simulations and evaluate both methods. Such a quantitative comparison is new and has not yet been presented before. In particular, predictive applications of the phase-field approach to fracture are not common by now. A summary of the pros and cons of both methods in Section 7 concludes the paper.

2. Governing equations

We consider a body of domain $\Omega \subset \mathbb{R}^3$ with external boundary $\Gamma \equiv \partial\Omega$. The body's displacement field at point $\boldsymbol{x}$ and time t is denoted by $\boldsymbol{u}(\boldsymbol{x}, t)$; its velocity and acceleration fields are $\boldsymbol{v} = \dot{\boldsymbol{u}}$ and $\boldsymbol{a} = \ddot{\boldsymbol{u}}$. A crack splits the body into subbodies $\Omega^+ \cup \Omega^- = \Omega$ and induces a displacement jump on Γ_C as $[\![\boldsymbol{u}]\!] = \boldsymbol{u}^+ - \boldsymbol{u}^-$. The displacements satisfy the Dirichlet boundary conditions $\boldsymbol{u} = \overline{\boldsymbol{u}}$ at Γ_1. The body is loaded with traction $\overline{\boldsymbol{t}}$ at boundary Γ_2; it holds $\Gamma_1 \cup \Gamma_2 \subset \Gamma \backslash \Gamma_C$.

2.1 Elasto-dynamics

Linear-elastic material is presumed to follow Hooke's law with elastic strain energy density,

$$\Psi^e = \frac{1}{2}\ \lambda(\mathrm{tr}\boldsymbol{\varepsilon})^2 + \mu\boldsymbol{\varepsilon} : \boldsymbol{\varepsilon} = \frac{1}{2}\ \boldsymbol{\varepsilon} : \mathbb{C} : \boldsymbol{\varepsilon} \tag{2}$$

where the Lamé material parameters $\lambda = E\nu/((1+\nu)(1-2\nu))$ and $\mu = E/(2(1+\nu))$ are formulated with Young's modulus E and Poisson number ν. Equivalently we use the Hookean material tensor $\mathbb{C}$ with components $C_{ijkl} = \lambda\delta_{ij}\delta_{kl} + \mu(\delta_{ik}\delta_{jl} + \delta_{il}\,\delta_{jk})$. The strain tensor $\boldsymbol{\varepsilon}$ describes small deformations $\boldsymbol{\varepsilon}(\boldsymbol{u}) = 1/2(\nabla\boldsymbol{u} + \nabla\boldsymbol{u}^T)$; the mechanical stress tensor follows as $\boldsymbol{\sigma} = \partial\boldsymbol{\varepsilon}\,\Psi^e = \mathbb{C}\boldsymbol{\varepsilon}$. It holds the balance of linear momentum,

$$\mathrm{div}\boldsymbol{\sigma} + \overline{\boldsymbol{b}} = \rho\boldsymbol{a} \quad \text{in } \Omega \tag{3}$$

where ρ is the mass density and $\overline{\boldsymbol{b}}$ a prescribed body force density. Boundary conditions are prescribed as

$$\boldsymbol{u} = \bar{\boldsymbol{u}} \, \text{on} \, \Gamma_1, \qquad \boldsymbol{\sigma n} = \bar{\boldsymbol{t}} \, \text{on} \, \Gamma_2, \qquad [\![\boldsymbol{\sigma n}]\!] = [\![\boldsymbol{t}]\!] = \mathbf{0} \, \text{on} \, \Gamma_C, \tag{4}$$

with normal vector $\boldsymbol{n}$ and traction $\boldsymbol{t}$; $[\![\cdot]\!]$ denotes a jump. Eq. $(4)_3$ corresponds to traction-free crack boundaries. Additional initial conditions may apply.

2.2 Fracture mechanics

Let the evolving internal cracks be represented by a set of boundaries $\Gamma_C(t)$. According to the linear-elastic fracture theory of Griffith and Irwin [21, 22], a material fails upon attainment of a critical surface-energy density. The crack growth corresponds to the creation of new surfaces and hence the internal work of the body is composed of

$$W_{\text{int}}(\boldsymbol{u}, t) = \int_{\Omega} \Psi^e(\boldsymbol{u}) \, \mathrm{d}\Omega + \int_{\Gamma(t)} \mathcal{G}_c \, \mathrm{d}\Gamma, \tag{5}$$

where $\mathcal{G}_c$ is commonly known as Griffith's critical energy release rate (Griffith energy). An optimum of Eq. (5) corresponds to crack growth.

The specific energy $\mathcal{G}$ corresponds to the energy W dissipated per unit newly created surface area A, $\mathcal{G} = \mathrm{d}W/\mathrm{d}A$. The Griffith fracture criterion states that a crack will grow when the available energy release rate is greater than or equal to a critical value, $\mathcal{G} \geq \mathcal{G}_c$, which is related to the classical stress intensity factors of linear-elastic fracture mechanics given by $\mathcal{G} = (K_I^2 + K_{II}^2)/E' + K_{III}^2/(2\mu)$ with $E' = E$ regarding the plane stress state and otherwise $E' = E/(1 - \nu^2)$. Thus, Griffith's criterion can also be written with the critical stress intensity factor K_c as $\mathcal{G}_c = K_c^2/E'$. The single summands of $\mathcal{G}$ may also be understood as mode-dependent Griffith energy densities $\mathcal{G}_I$, $\mathcal{G}_{II}$, and $\mathcal{G}_{III}$. The indices denote the fracture modes of crack opening, in-plane and out-of-plane sliding. For a brittle elastic material the $\mathcal{J}$-integral is equal to the strain energy release rate, that is, it holds the identity $\mathcal{J}_c = \mathcal{G}_c$.

Another fracture criterion is the crack tip opening displacement with critical value δ_c. The underlying theory of Dugdale [23] and Barenblatt [24] explains crack growth as loss of cohesion in a cohesive zone. If the decohesion is modeled in a nonlinear way, that is, for a given relation between the vector of cohesive traction $\boldsymbol{t}$ and crack opening $\boldsymbol{\delta}$, a standard application of the $\mathcal{J}$-integral will establish a link between the critical energy release rate and the critical crack opening displacement. Starting with the relation $\boldsymbol{t}(\boldsymbol{\delta})$ and choosing a contour Γ for the evaluation of the $\mathcal{J}$-integral that surrounds the cohesive zone gives for an effective crack opening $\delta = |\boldsymbol{\delta}|$,

$$\mathcal{G}_c = \int_{\Gamma} \boldsymbol{t} \cdot \boldsymbol{\delta} \;\, \mathrm{d}\Gamma = \int_0^{\delta_c} \boldsymbol{t} \;\, \mathrm{d}\delta. \tag{6}$$

2.3 Weak form of the problem and finite element discretization

The motions of a solid can be characterized by recourse to Hamilton's principle of stationary action. The action of a motion within a closed time interval $[t_0, t]$ defines a functional $\mathcal{I}[\boldsymbol{u}] = \int_{t_0}^{t} \mathcal{L} \, \mathrm{d}t$ with the Lagrangian function as the difference of kinetic and potential energy, $\mathcal{L}(\boldsymbol{u}, \boldsymbol{v}) = \mathcal{K}(\boldsymbol{v}) - \Pi(\boldsymbol{u})$. Stationarity demands the first variation to vanish,

$$\delta\mathcal{I} = \delta \int_{t_0}^{t} \mathcal{L}(\boldsymbol{u}, \boldsymbol{v}) \, \mathrm{d}t = \int_{t_0}^{t} \delta\mathcal{K}(\boldsymbol{v}) - \delta\Pi(\boldsymbol{u}) \, \mathrm{d}t = 0 \qquad \forall t \geq t_0, \tag{7}$$

and with $\delta\Pi = \delta W_{\text{int}} - \delta W_{\text{ext}}$ and Eqs. (2)–(4) we obtain

$$\int_{t_0}^{t} \left(\int_{\Omega} \rho \boldsymbol{v} \cdot \delta \boldsymbol{v} + \delta \Psi^e(\boldsymbol{u}) - \delta \boldsymbol{u} \cdot \overline{\boldsymbol{b}} \, \mathrm{d}\Omega - \int_{\Gamma_C} \delta [\![\boldsymbol{u}]\!] \cdot \boldsymbol{t} \, \mathrm{d}\Gamma - \int_{\Gamma_2} \delta \boldsymbol{u} \cdot \overline{\boldsymbol{t}} \, \mathrm{d}\Gamma \right) \mathrm{d}t = 0 \tag{8}$$

for all admissible test functions $\delta\boldsymbol{u} \in \mathfrak{U}$ with $\mathfrak{U} = \{\delta\boldsymbol{u} \in H^1(\Omega) | \delta\boldsymbol{u} = 0 \text{ on } \Gamma_1\}$; H^1 denotes the Hilbert space of weak square-integrable functions and its first derivatives. Eq. (8) must hold for all times $t \geq t_0$, which leads to the weak momentum balance. For a body with stationary crack it is equivalent to

$$\int_{\Omega} \delta \boldsymbol{u} \cdot \rho \boldsymbol{a} + \delta \boldsymbol{\varepsilon} : \boldsymbol{\sigma} - \delta \boldsymbol{u} \cdot \overline{\boldsymbol{b}} \, \mathrm{d}\Omega = \int_{\Gamma_2} \delta \boldsymbol{u} \cdot \overline{\boldsymbol{t}} \, \mathrm{d}\Gamma \qquad \forall \delta \boldsymbol{u} \in \mathfrak{U}. \tag{9}$$

For discretization the domain Ω is subdivided into a finite set of nonoverlapping elements. We make use of a conforming ansatz and approximate the displacement field and its variation with

$$\boldsymbol{u} \approx \sum_{i=1}^{n_k} N_i \boldsymbol{u}_i = \mathbf{N}\hat{\mathbf{u}}, \qquad \delta \boldsymbol{u} \approx \sum_{i=1}^{n_k} N_i \boldsymbol{w}_i = \mathbf{N}\hat{\mathbf{w}}, \tag{10}$$

where N_i are the piecewise ansatz functions collected in a matrix $\mathbf{N}$ and the vectors $\hat{\mathbf{u}}$, $\hat{\mathbf{w}}$ contain all unknown nodal displacements $\boldsymbol{u}_i$ of the n_k nodes and its nodal variations $\boldsymbol{w}_i$, respectively. Plugging Eq. (10) into Eq. (8) and a straightforward calculation gives the global system of equations

$$\overline{\mathbf{M}}\ddot{\hat{\mathbf{u}}} + \overline{\mathbf{K}}\hat{\mathbf{u}} = \overline{\mathbf{f}} \tag{11}$$

where $\overline{\mathbf{M}}$ and $\overline{\mathbf{K}}$ denote the mass and stiffness matrix of the finite element discretization, and $\overline{\mathbf{f}}$ is the vector of external forces. The Hookean tensor $\mathbb{C}$ is reformulated in a matrix $\overline{\mathbb{C}}$, and we specify

$$\overline{\mathbf{M}} = \bigcup_{e=1}^{n_e} \int_{\Omega_e} \rho \mathbf{N}\mathbf{N}^T \, \mathrm{d}\Omega_e, \quad \overline{\mathbf{K}} = \nabla \bigcup_{e=1}^{n_e} \int_{\Omega_e} \mathbf{N}\overline{\mathbb{C}}\nabla\mathbf{N}^T \, \mathrm{d}\Omega_e,$$

$$\overline{\mathbf{f}} = \bigcup_{e=1}^{n_e} \int_{\Omega_e \cap \Gamma_1} \mathbf{N}\overline{\mathbf{b}} + \mathbf{N}\overline{\mathbf{t}} \mathrm{d}\Omega + \int_{\Gamma_1} \mathbf{N}\overline{\mathbf{t}} \, \mathrm{d}\Gamma.$$

Discretization in time is performed by an implicit Euler method, that is, with time step $\Delta t = t_{n+1} - t_n$ and, thus, velocity and acceleration are approximated by

$$\dot{\hat{\mathbf{u}}}^{n+1} \approx \left(\hat{\mathbf{u}}^{n+1} - \hat{\mathbf{u}}^{n}\right)(\Delta t)^{-1} \text{ and } \ddot{\hat{\mathbf{u}}}^{n+1} \approx \left(\hat{\mathbf{u}}^{n+1} - 2\hat{\mathbf{u}}^{n} + \hat{\mathbf{u}}^{n-1}\right)(\Delta t)^{-2}. \tag{12}$$

3. The cohesive element technique

The nucleation and the propagation of cracks are efficiently modeled through the cohesive zone model where fracture is assumed to happen along an extended crack tip triggered by tractions on the crack flanks, [23, 24]. A particularly appealing aspect of the cohesive zone model is that it fits naturally in the framework of finite element analysis and leads directly to the cohesive element technique introduced by Needleman, Ortiz, and co-workers [25–27]. The main idea of this approach is to add cohesive interfaces between the continuum elements that are able to model crack growth, see **Figure 2**. We employ this classical cohesive element

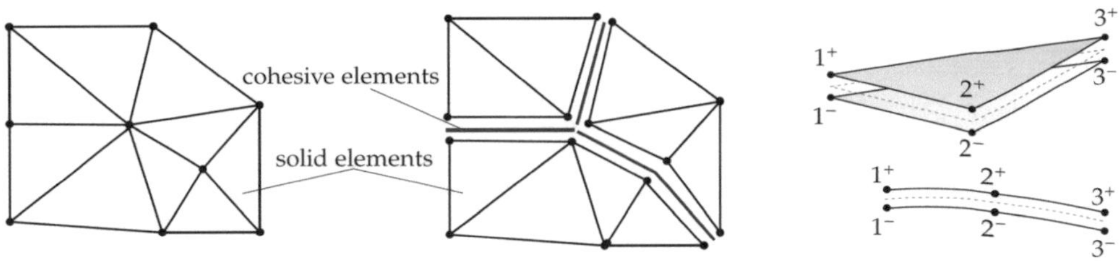

Figure 2.
Discretization of a solid with the cohesive element technique (left) and geometry of a 2D and 3D cohesive element, respectively (right). The surfaces Γ_C^- and Γ_C^+ coincide if the element is closed.

approach combined with an automatic fragmentation and cohesive surface insertion procedure. The method has proven to be reliable and efficient for numerous applications, see among others [2, 28–30].

3.1 Fundamentals

In cohesive theories, the displacement jump across a cohesive surface Γ_C

$$\boldsymbol{\delta} = [\![\boldsymbol{u}]\!] = \boldsymbol{u}^+ - \boldsymbol{u}^- \tag{13}$$

plays the role of a deformation measure while the tractions $\boldsymbol{t}$ furnish the work-conjugate stress measure. They follow a traction separation law—the cohesive law—which models locally the loss of material resistance during cracking. If the cohesive element has attained a critical opening displacement δ_c, no tractions can be transfered and the adjacent continuum elements are de-facto disconnected.

Typically, isotropic and anisotropic materials behave differently in crack opening (mode-I separation) and sliding (mode-II and mode-III separation) and, therefore, normal and tangential components of the displacement jump across the surface Γ_C have to be treated differently. Given a vector field $\boldsymbol{u}$ over Γ_C, its normal and tangential components are $u_n = \boldsymbol{u}\cdot\boldsymbol{n}$, and $u_t = |\boldsymbol{u}_\Gamma| = |\boldsymbol{u} - u_n\boldsymbol{n}| = |(\boldsymbol{I} - \boldsymbol{n}\otimes\boldsymbol{n})\boldsymbol{u}|$, and, the corresponding jump components $\delta_n = u_n^+ - u_n^-$ and $\delta_t = u_t^+ - u_t^-$ follow from Eq. (13). To further simplify the formulation of mixed-mode cohesive laws, we follow [25] and introduce an effective opening displacement

$$\delta = |\boldsymbol{\delta}| = \left(\beta^2\delta_t + \delta_n\right)^{1/2}. \tag{14}$$

Here the parameter β assigns different weights to the sliding and normal opening components. This allows us to formulate the traction as a function of the effective opening displacement δ only.

3.2 Cohesive laws

A cohesive law defines the relation between crack opening displacements d and tractions on the crack flanks $\boldsymbol{t}$. Generally, a cohesive law can be stated in the general form $\boldsymbol{t} = \partial_{\boldsymbol{\delta}}\mathcal{G}$, where $\mathcal{G}$ is the specific fracture energy describing the dissipation in the cohesive zone. It is subject to the restrictions imposed by material frame indifference, material symmetry, and the isotropy of sliding. The most general dependence of $\mathcal{G}$ has the form $\mathcal{G} = \mathcal{G}(\delta_n, \boldsymbol{\delta}\cdot\boldsymbol{u}) = \mathcal{G}(\delta_n, \delta_t)$ and with Eq. (14) follows $\mathcal{G}(\delta)$. Thus, a key benefit of the potential structure of the cohesive law is that it reduces the identification of the cohesive law from the three components of **t** to a single scalar function. Then an effective traction $|\boldsymbol{t}| = \hat{t} = \hat{t}_{\text{eff}}$ follows,

$$\hat{t}_{\text{eff}} = \left(\hat{t}_n + \beta^{-2}|\boldsymbol{t}_t|\right)^{1/2}. \tag{15}$$

An appropriate choice of cohesive variable is the maximum attained (effective) crack opening displacement $\delta_{\max}$. Loading of the cohesive surface is then characterized by the conditions $\delta = \delta_{\max}$ and $\dot{\delta} \geq 0$; all other states correspond to unloading. **Figure 3** shows different common loading envelopes, whereas unloading is commonly assumed to be linear in δ to the origin,

$$\hat{t}(\delta) = \frac{\hat{t}_{\max}}{\delta_{\max}}\,\delta, \quad \text{if } \delta < \delta_{\max} \text{ or } \dot{\delta} < 0. \tag{16}$$

The simplest cohesive law for brittle materials has a linear loading envelope

$$\hat{t}(\delta) = \sigma_c\left(1 - \frac{\delta}{\delta_c}\right). \tag{17}$$

The two parameter cohesive strength σ_c and critical opening displacement δ_c determine via Eq. (6) the specific fracture energy

$$\mathcal{G}_c = 1/2\ \sigma_c\ \delta_c. \tag{18}$$

There are several modifications of Eq. (17), for example bilinear laws for concrete [31] or convex cohesive laws for ductile materials [32]. A cohesive law that can be adapted to brittle and ductile behavior is the universal binding law of Smith and Ferrante [33].

$$\hat{t}(\delta) = \sigma_c\,\frac{\delta}{\delta_0}\,\exp\left(1 - \frac{\delta}{\delta_0}\right), \tag{19}$$

where δ_0 is the position of the maximal traction. Note that here the cohesive stress does not vanish at the critical separation δ_c. The corresponding fracture energy is $\mathcal{G}_c = \sigma_c\delta_0(\exp(1) - (1 + \delta_c/\delta_0)\exp(1 - \delta_c/\delta_0))$. Unloading at $\hat{t} < \hat{t}_{\max}$ follows a linear relation of the form Eq. (16). Upon closure, the cohesive surfaces are subject to unilateral contact constraints, including friction. Therefore, suitable contact conditions have to be applied under compression. Friction in the cohesive zone is regarded as an independent phenomena, which is not modeled here.

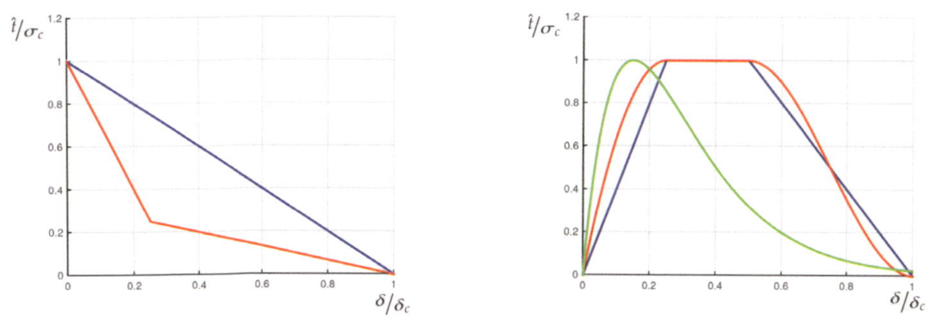

Figure 3.
Typical cohesive laws: (left) linear cohesive envelope (blue) of Eq. (17); concave bilinear envelope (red) with $\delta_1 = \delta_c/4, \sigma_1 = \sigma_c/4$; and (right) convex trilinear envelope (blue), modification with smooth transitions (red), both with $\delta_1 = \delta_c/4, \delta_2 = \delta_c/2$, and exponential law (green) of Eq. (19) with $\delta_0 = 3\delta_c/20$.

3.3 Finite element implementation

The class of cohesive elements considered here consists of two surface elements, which coincide in the reference configuration of the solid. Each surface element has n_{coh} nodes; the total number of nodes of the cohesive element is $2n_{\text{coh}}$. The particular triangulation depicted in **Figure 2** is compatible with edge or line elements of four nodes.

Basis of the finite element implementation is Hamilton's principle given in Eq. (7). Inserting the balance of linear momentum and the static boundary conditions gives the deformation power with variation

$$\delta W_{\text{int}}(\boldsymbol{u}) = \int_{\Omega} \delta\boldsymbol{\varepsilon} : \mathbb{C} : \boldsymbol{\varepsilon}\, \mathrm{d}\Omega + \delta W_{\text{int}}^{\text{coh}}(\boldsymbol{u}) \;\text{ with }\; \delta W_{\text{int}}^{\text{coh}}(\boldsymbol{u}) := \int_{\Gamma_{\text{coh}}} \delta[\![\boldsymbol{u}]\!] \cdot \boldsymbol{t}\, \mathrm{d}\Gamma \tag{20}$$

where Γ_{coh} are the total cohesive surfaces and $\delta[\![\boldsymbol{u}]\!]$ is the variation of the separation vector given in Eq. (13). The first term of Eq. $(20)_1$ as well as the remaining energy contributions correspond to standard finite element forms and will not be repeated here. The variation of the cohesive energy leads with ansatz Eq. (10) in Eq. $(20)_2$ for one cohesive element to

$$\delta W_{\text{int},e}^{\text{coh}}(\boldsymbol{u}) = \int_{\Gamma_{\text{coh},e}} \delta\left(\mathbf{N}\,[\![\hat{\mathbf{u}}]\!]_e\right)^T \mathbf{t}\, \mathrm{d}\Gamma = \delta[\![\hat{\mathbf{u}}]\!]_e{}^T \int_{\Gamma_{\text{coh},e}} \mathbf{N}^T \mathbf{t}\, \mathrm{d}\Gamma. \tag{21}$$

The kinetic energy does not have any support in the cohesive element and only the external virtual work has to be determined. For one cohesive element it is

$$\delta W_{\text{ext},e}^{\text{coh}}(\boldsymbol{u}) = \delta W_{\text{int},e}^{\text{coh}} = \delta[\![\hat{\mathbf{u}}]\!]_e{}^T \mathbf{f}_{\text{coh},e}^{\pm} \quad \text{with} \quad \mathbf{f}_{\text{coh},e}^{\pm} = \mp \int_{\Gamma_{\text{coh},e}} \mathbf{N}^T \mathbf{t}\, \mathrm{d}\Gamma. \tag{22}$$

The tangent stiffness matrix follows by its consistent linearization, with the result $\mathbf{K}_{\text{coh},e} = \int_{\Gamma_{\text{coh},e}} \mathbf{N}^T \partial\mathbf{t}/\partial[\![\boldsymbol{u}]\!] \mathbf{N}\, \mathrm{d}\Gamma$. To avoid singularities at $\delta \to 0$ in the derivatives of Eq. (17) some numerical modifications are required, cf. [34]. Finally, the equations added by the cohesive elements to the system Eq. (11) can be formulated as $\mathbf{K}_{\text{coh}} \cdot \Delta[\![\hat{\mathbf{u}}]\!] = \Delta\mathbf{f}_{\text{coh}}$ with $\mathbf{K}_{\text{coh}} = \bigcup_{e=1}^{n_{\text{coh}}} \mathbf{K}_{\text{coh},e}$, $\mathbf{f}_{\text{coh}} = \bigcup_{e=1}^{n_{\text{coh}}} \mathbf{f}_{\text{coh},e}$, where Δ symbolizes the incremental solution procedure, which is required for the nonlinear crack-opening problem.

3.4 Adaptive meshing

Since in most problems the expected crack path is not known the decision where the cohesive elements should be inserted has to be made during the simulation. The analysis proceeds incrementally in time. Our decision criterion is based on the effective tensile stress given in Eq. (15), which has to exceed a threshold. This means, in every time step of the calculations, this condition is checked for each internal face. The faces that met the criterion are flagged for subsequent processing. A cohesive element will be inserted at the flagged face and in this manner, the shape and location of a successive crack front is itself an outcome of the calculations.

Within the finite element mesh the insertion of cohesive elements requires topological changes. The local sequential numbering of the corner-nodes defines the orientation; the mid-side node is subsequently duplicated. Owing to the variable environment of the edges in the triangulation, the data structure has to be adapted as illustrated in **Figure 4** with case 1: the marked edge with nodes k_1 and k_2 is inside

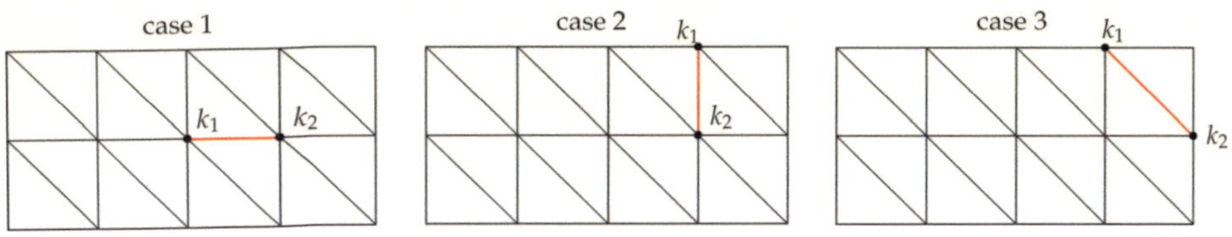

Figure 4.
Classification according to whether the fractured segment has zero (case 1), one (case 2), or two (case 3) nodes on the boundary.

of the body, the edge with all nodes will be duplicated: $\overline{k_1 k_2} \cap (\partial\Omega \cup \Gamma(t)) = \emptyset$; case 2: one of the marked nodes is on the boundary, one node will be duplicated: $k_1 \in \partial\Omega \cup \Gamma(t) \veebar k_2 \in \partial\Omega \cup \Gamma(t)$; and case 3: both nodes are on the boundary, two nodes (all nodes) will be duplicated: $k_1 \in \partial\Omega \cup \Gamma(t) \wedge k_2 \in \partial\Omega \cup \Gamma(t)$, for the two-dimensional situation. In three dimensions the situation consists of four cases but the main idea is the same. However, loops over all facets, edges, and nodes of the mesh are computationally expensive and require very efficient search and insertion algorithms, cf. [35].

3.5 Effect of the crack initiation criteria in the cohesive model

Here we illustrate the influence of the cohesive strength σ_c and critical opening displacement δ_c on the cohesive element simulations. Exemplarily we investigate a plane mode-I tension test under quasistatic conditions; however, the observations have been confirmed also in other models.

The test specimen with material data $E = 60$ GPa, $\nu = 0.2$ has a unit domain $[0, 1] \times [0, 1]$; all lengths are given in meter. On the vertical boundaries the displacements in x-direction are constrained and on the lower and upper side $y = 0$ and $y = 1$, a traction boundary condition is prescribed, $\bar{t}_y = 15$ MPa. A crack is predefined in the area $x \in [0, 0.2]$, $y = 0.5$, by including cohesive elements that are completely open. We employ a cohesive law with linear envelope given in Eq. (17), set the cohesive strength $\sigma_c = 20$ MPa and the critical crack opening displacement $\delta_c = 10^{-4}$. Following Eq. (18) this corresponds to a critical energy release rate of $\mathcal{G}_c = 1$ N/mm.

During the simulation a cohesive element will be added if the effective traction Eq. (15), here $\hat{t} = \hat{t}_{\text{eff}}(\beta \to \infty)$, exceeds a critical value, $\hat{t} \geq \sigma_i$. We identify the insertion criterium σ_i with the cohesive strength σ_c. Because the specimen is pulled with constant load, the computation is stopped at a crack length of 0.7 m.

Figure 5 demonstrates the crack evolution in a mesh of 25 × 25 squares, each divided into eight triangular finite elements with linear shape functions. The computed stresses σ_y in **Figure 5** correspond very well to the analytical solution.

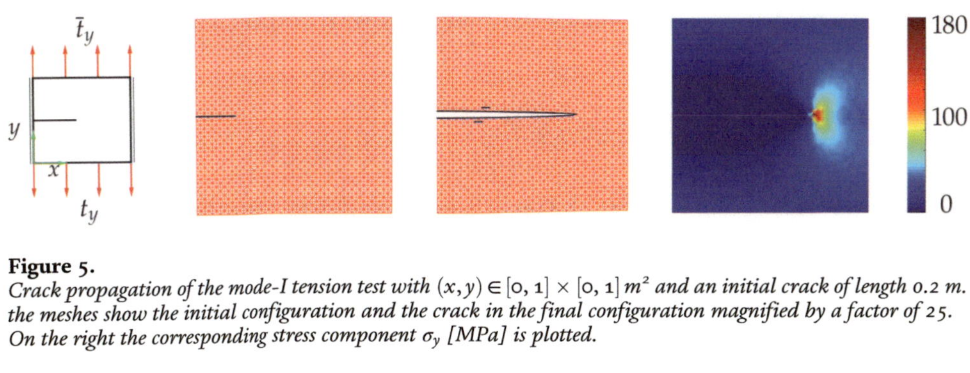

Figure 5.
Crack propagation of the mode-I tension test with $(x, y) \in [0, 1] \times [0, 1]$ m^2 and an initial crack of length 0.2 m. the meshes show the initial configuration and the crack in the final configuration magnified by a factor of 25. On the right the corresponding stress component σ_y [MPa] is plotted.

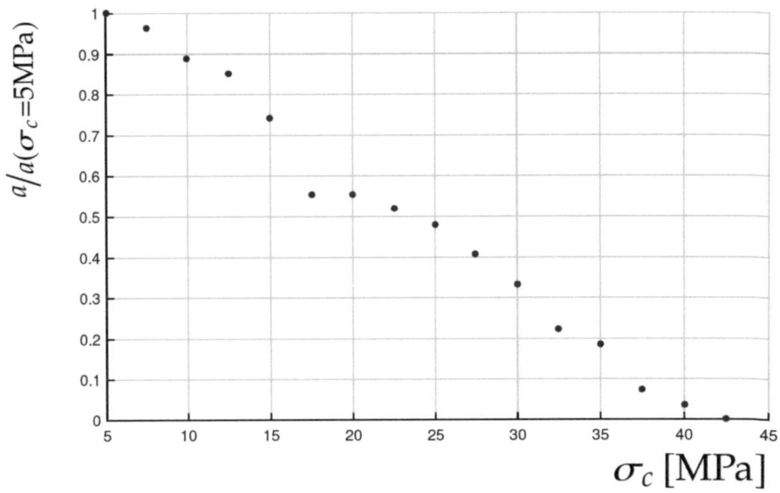

Figure 6.
Normalized crack growth versus the critical cohesive stress.

They disappear at the crack flanks and are maximal at the crack tip with the typical butterfly shape.

At next we apply the traction $\bar{t}_y = 15$MPa as a linearly increasing load within 200 load steps. A cohesive element will be added if the effective tensile stress exceeds $\sigma_i = \sigma_c$. The crack length is determined via $a := (\max\{x \in [0,1] : \delta_n(x) > \delta_c\} - 0.2)$. **Figure 6** shows the crack growth normalized to the crack growth at $\sigma_c = 5$ MPa. Obviously, the insertion criteria has an influence on the appearance of cohesive elements and so—indirectly—on the crack propagation. In consequence, the insertion stress σ_i should correspond to the cohesive strength σ_c to avoid artificial numerical stiffness.

4. The phase-field fracture approach

The evolving crack in a solid with potential energy of Eq. (5) is represented in the phase-field fracture approach by an additional continuous field $s(\boldsymbol{x}, t) \in [0,1]$, $\forall \boldsymbol{x} \in \Omega, \quad t \in \mathbb{R}$. It has a value of $s = 1$ in the intact material and indicates for $s = 0$ the *cracked zones*. Continuity requires a transition zone between both phases. Such a transition zone cannot reflect the sharp boundary of a crack but models a diffuse interface instead. Thus, in a phase-field approach the crack set $\Gamma_C(t)$ is replaced by a regularizing crack-surface density function $\gamma(t)$ and the corresponding boundary integral in Eq. (5) is approximated by Eq. (1).

The crack-surface density function can be chosen in different ways. If a second-order phase-field approach is considered (like originally proposed in [36, 37]) it has the form

$$\gamma(s, \nabla s) = \frac{(1-s)^2}{4\varepsilon} + \varepsilon |\nabla s|^2. \tag{23}$$

The parameter ε has the unit of a length and is a measure for the width of the diffuse interface zone, see **Figure 7**. Moreover, this parameter weights the influence of the linear and the gradient term whereby the gradient enforces a regularization of the sharp interface. Another ansatz for the crack-surface density function is the fourth-order form

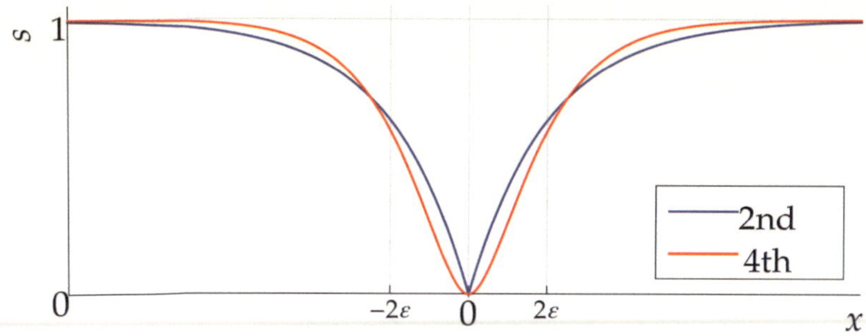

Figure 7.
Analytic solution of a crack in a second- and a fourth-order phase-field.

$$\gamma(s, \nabla s, \nabla \cdot \nabla s) = \frac{(1-s)^2}{4\varepsilon} + \frac{\varepsilon |\nabla s|^2}{2} + \frac{\varepsilon^3 (\nabla \cdot \nabla s)^2}{4} \tag{24}$$

which has been used, for example, in [38, 39]. However, in a finite element discretization ansatz given in Eq. (24) requires C^1-continuous basis functions. In [40] we investigated this formulation in more detail, applied quadratic NURBS-ansatz functions, and found that a smoother crack and a better convergence rate can be achieved.

Here we use the ansatz of Eq. (23) and the corresponding total potential energy reads

$$W(\boldsymbol{u}, s) = \int_\Omega \Psi^e(\boldsymbol{u}) + \mathcal{G}_c \gamma(s)\, \mathrm{d}\Omega = \int_\Omega \frac{1}{2}\ \boldsymbol{\varepsilon} : \mathbb{C}^* : \boldsymbol{\varepsilon} + \mathcal{G}_c \left(\frac{(1-s)^2}{4\varepsilon} + \varepsilon |\nabla s|^2 \right) \mathrm{d}\Omega \tag{25}$$

The tensor $\mathbb{C}^*$ in the elastic strain energy density is derived from Eq. (2) by means of a substitute-material approach, $\mathbb{C}^* = g(s)\mathbb{C}$, where $g(s)$ is a degradation function, which is here of the form $g(s) = s^2 + s_0$, with $s_0 \ll 1$ being a small parameter introduced for numerical reasons only. With $s = 0$ tensor $\mathbb{C}^*$ models the *empty* crack.

At this point the evolution equation for the phase-field parameter s is stated in a general Allen-Cahn form,

$$\dot{s} = -\overline{M} \delta_s \Psi. \tag{26}$$

where the nonnegative function $\overline{M}$ is the mobility with unit [mm^2/Ns]; δ_s denotes the variational or total derivative of Ψ wrt. s. With Eq. (25) it follows

$$\dot{s} = -\overline{M} \delta_s \Psi = -\overline{M} \left[\boldsymbol{\varepsilon} : \mathbb{C} : \boldsymbol{\varepsilon} s - \frac{\mathcal{G}_c}{2\varepsilon} \left(1 - s + 4\varepsilon^2\ \nabla \cdot \nabla s \right) \right]. \tag{27}$$

This evolution equation can also be deduced in a fully variational manner from energy dissipation, cf. [41]. For more theoretical details we also refer to our recent works [42, 43].

4.1 Elastic strain energy split

The quadratic form of the elastic strain energy density does not distinguish between tensile and pressure states in the material. A direct use of the formulations

Eq. (25) or Eq. (27) would allow a crack to grow also in a compressive regime, which clearly contradicts the physics of the underlying problem. For that reason a split of the elastic strain energy into a tensile and a compressive part is necessary. We use the degradation function $g(s)$ and state $\Psi^e(\boldsymbol{\varepsilon}, s) = g(s)\Psi^{e+} + \Psi^{e-}$. This split is based on the spectral decomposition of the strain tensor $\boldsymbol{\varepsilon} = \sum_{a=1}^{3} \varepsilon_a \boldsymbol{n}_a \otimes \boldsymbol{n}_a$, where ε_a denote the principal strains and $\boldsymbol{n}_a$ the corresponding principal directions, $a = 1, 2, 3$. Based on this representations and using the Macaulay brackets

$$\langle x \rangle^+ = \begin{cases} 0, & x < 0 \\ x, & x \geq 0, \end{cases} \qquad \langle x \rangle^- = \begin{cases} x, & x < 0 \\ 0, & x \geq 0, \end{cases}$$

we define the positive and the negative parts of the strain tensor as $\boldsymbol{\varepsilon}^{\pm} = \sum_{a=1}^{3} \langle \varepsilon_a \rangle^{\pm} \boldsymbol{n}_a \otimes \boldsymbol{n}_a$. The positive parts contain contributions due to positive dilatation and contributions due to positive principal strains. Only this part of the strain energy is responsible for crack growth. A similar decomposition can be deduced for the stress tensor $\boldsymbol{\sigma}$. This finally leads to an elastic energy density function, which only accounts for tension, $\Psi^{e+} = 1/2 \langle \boldsymbol{\sigma} \rangle^+ : \langle \boldsymbol{\varepsilon} \rangle^+ = 1/2 \langle \boldsymbol{\varepsilon} \rangle^+ : \mathbb{C}^* : \langle \boldsymbol{\varepsilon} \rangle^+$.

Furthermore, the irreversibility of the crack growth has to be considered. This can be done by Dirichlet constraints on the phase-field parameter, that is $\dot{s} = 0$ if $s = 0$. The same effect has a product of s with the mobility parameter $M = \overline{M} \mathcal{G}_c / 2\varepsilon$, where we additionally formulate the evolution Eq. (26) in a dimensionless form, $\dot{s} = -M \delta_s \Psi = -M[\Psi^{e+} - (1 - s) - 4\varepsilon^2 \ \nabla \cdot \nabla s]$.

4.2 Discretization

The numerical solution of the phase-field fracture model within the finite element framework leads to a coupled-field problem. The weak formulation of the mechanical field is derived in the usual way with the result given in Eq. (9). The weak formulation of the phase-field equation is set up analogously

$$\int_{\Omega} \left(\frac{\dot{s}}{\overline{M}} \delta s + \partial_s \Psi^{e+} \delta s + 4\mathcal{G}_c \varepsilon \nabla s \nabla \delta s - \frac{\mathcal{G}_c}{2\varepsilon} (1 - s) \delta s \right) \mathrm{d}\Omega = 0 \quad \forall \delta s \in \mathfrak{V} \tag{28}$$

with test functions $\delta s \equiv v$ and $\mathfrak{V} = \left\{ v \in H^1(\Omega) | \nabla v \cdot \boldsymbol{n} = 0 \ \text{ on } \ \partial\Omega, v = 0 \ \text{ on } \ \Gamma_1 \right\}$.

The shape and test functions given in Eq. (10) are inserted in Eq. (9) to obtain the discrete mechanical problem of Eq. (11). For the phase-field we approximate

$$s \approx \sum_{i=1}^{n_k} N_i s_i = \mathbf{N}\hat{\mathbf{s}}, \qquad \delta s \approx \sum_{i=1}^{n_k} N_i v_i = \mathbf{N}\hat{\mathbf{v}} \tag{29}$$

with ansatz functions $N_1, \ldots, N_{n_k}$ for n_k nodes. Plugging this ansatz into Eq. (28) leads after a straightforward calculation to a finite element system of equations. Additionally we specify the phase-field driving force $\partial_s \Psi^e = 2s\Psi^{e+} = s\langle \boldsymbol{\varepsilon}(\boldsymbol{u}) \rangle^+ : \mathbb{C} : \langle \boldsymbol{\varepsilon}(\boldsymbol{u}) \rangle^+$.

In short hand notation we get for the mechanical problem the matrix Eq. (11), whereby now the Hookean matrix $\mathbb{C}^* (\boldsymbol{u}, s)$ depends on the phase-field. For Eq. (28) the approximation leads to $\overline{\mathbf{M}}\dot{\mathbf{s}} + (\overline{\mathbf{A}} + \overline{\mathbf{C}} + \overline{\mathbf{D}})\mathbf{s} = \overline{\mathbf{f}}$ with $\mathbf{s} = [s_i]$ and

$$\overline{\mathbf{M}} = \bigcup_{e=1}^{n_e} \frac{1}{M} \int_{\Omega} \mathbf{N}\mathbf{N}^T \, \mathrm{d}\Omega, \qquad \overline{\mathbf{C}} = \bigcup_{e=1}^{n_e} \int_{\Omega} \mathbf{N}\mathbf{N}^T \, \mathrm{d}\Omega, \qquad \overline{\mathbf{f}} = \bigcup_{e=1}^{n_e} \int_{\Omega} \mathbf{N}\mathbf{N}^T \mathbf{1} \, \mathrm{d}\Omega$$

$$\overline{\mathbf{A}} = \bigcup_{e=1}^{n_e} 4\varepsilon^2 \int_{\Omega} \nabla\mathbf{N}(\nabla\mathbf{N})^T \, \mathrm{d}\Omega, \qquad \overline{\mathbf{D}} = \bigcup_{e=1}^{n_e} \frac{4\varepsilon}{\mathcal{G}_c} \int_{\Omega} \Psi^{e+}(\boldsymbol{u}, s)\mathbf{N}\mathbf{N}^T \, \mathrm{d}\Omega.$$

Here we assumed the same ansatz functions for $\boldsymbol{u}$ and s for the ease of writing.

After the discretization in time by using Eq. (12) the following system of global equations is obtained:

$$\left[\overline{\mathbf{M}}(\Delta t)^{-1} + \overline{\mathbf{A}} + \overline{\mathbf{C}} + \overline{\mathbf{D}}\right]\mathbf{s}^{n+1} = \overline{\mathbf{f}} + (\Delta t)^{-1}\overline{\mathbf{M}}\mathbf{s}^{n} \tag{30}$$

Note that the coupled problem of Eq. (11) and Eq. (30) is nonlinear. The solution of the implicit problem is obtained with recourse to a Newton-Raphson method. The necessary linearization (tangent stiffness matrix) can be calculated monolithically or by recourse to a staggered scheme. For the HB experiment we employ an explicit time discretization, which simplifies the solution.

4.3 Effect of the coefficients M and ε

With the problem formulation at hand we now illustrate the influence of the parameter mobility M and regularization length ε in the phase-field fracture model. To this end we again investigate a plane mode-I tension test of unit length $[0,1] \times [0,1]$, with a predefined crack at $x \in [0, 0.5]$, $y = 0.5$, and boundary conditions as depicted in **Figure 8**. The finite element mesh of $100 \times 100 \times 4$ triangular elements has a uniform size of $h = 0.005$. The simulation is quasistatic with a prescribed, linearly increasing displacement up to $\overline{u} = \pm 1.2 \cdot 10^{-3}$.

The kinematic mobility parameter $M = \overline{M}\mathcal{G}_c/(2\varepsilon)$ is responsible for the rate of phase-field evolution. For higher values of M the crack will show (and propagate) faster. In **Figure 8** the crack growth for different values of M normalized with the crack length for $M = 1$ is demonstrated. We see a steady state for $M \geq 50$ mm²sN. In this case the crack length is defined as $a := \max\{x \in [0,1] : s(x, 0.5) \leq 0.05\} - 0.5$. The mobility M [s] can be seen as the inverse of a kinematic viscosity η [s^{-1}], $M = 1/\eta$, which illustrates its effect on the crack evolution within a phase-field fracture computation. Large values of M correspond to a small viscosity, that is, the material will crack fast, whereas a highly viscous material retards crack growth. In this sense, low values of M correspond a high dissipation. However, in the case of quasi-static brittle fracture there exist no local material dissipation because energy is only stored by elastic deformations and in the surface energy of the crack. Consequently, the mobility parameter M has to be sufficiently large for meaningful computations, it is only limited by the numerics.

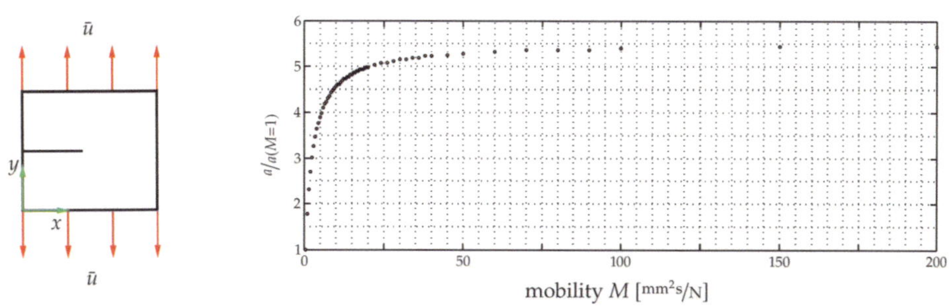

Figure 8.
Mode-I tension-test with $(x,y) \in [0, 1] \times [0, 1]$, an initial crack of length 0.5, and a prescribed total displacement of $\overline{u} = \pm 1.2 \cdot 10^{-3}$. Plotted is the normalized crack length a *versus the kinematic mobility* M.

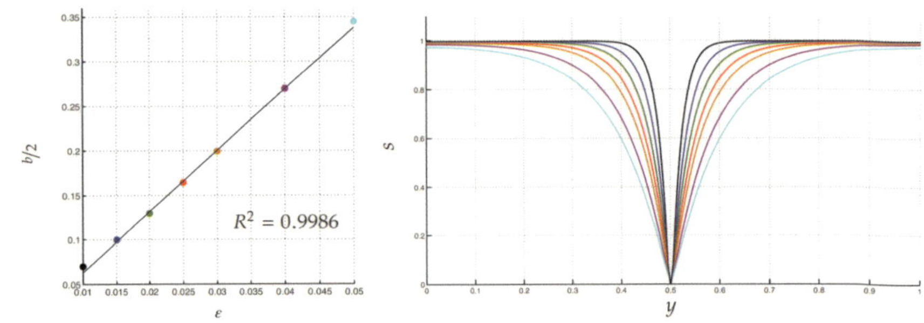

Figure 9.
Influence of the length-scale parameter ε on the crack width in the converged state of the mode-I-tension-test of **Figure 8**. *In the left panel the half crack width b/2 is plotted versus ε, the linear regression coefficient is* $R^2 = 0.9986$, *and the right plot demonstrates the phase-field s in the diffuse interface zone to the crack in corresponding colors.*

The influence of the length-scale parameter ε on the crack is now demonstrated. For definiteness, the domain where the phase-field parameter s is larger than 0.95 is called crack-free. Hence the width of the crack is defined as

$$b := \left|\{y \in [0,1] : s(0.9, y) \leq 0.95\}\right|_e, \tag{31}$$

whereby the Lebesgue-measure of a set is denoted with $|\cdot|_e$ and the diffuse interface zone is included in the relevant set.

Please note, that the effect of the length-scale parameter ε is two-fold. On one hand, it enters the material because, in the sense of Griffith's criteria for crack growth, the fracture energy density $\mathcal{G}_c/\varepsilon$ competes with the elastic energy density Ψ^{e+} determined by E, ν or combinations thereof. Here ε has the effect of a material parameter. On the other hand, ε is determined by the mesh size h because it has to be large enough to enable the approximation of a diffuse interface. This clearly requires an adaption on the mesh size, $\varepsilon > h$.

In **Figure 9** the crack width b is plotted over different values of ε. The computation starts with $\varepsilon = 0.01$, which is the smallest possible parameter for the chosen mesh size, that is $\varepsilon \approx h$. A clear proportionality between the length-scale parameter ε and the width of the crack can be seen, and we set $b/2 = c\varepsilon$ with constant $c > 1$. The exact value of c depends on the model via definition of Eq. (31). At any case it is greater than one and so it is obvious that ε is smaller than the diffuse crack width, see also **Figure 7**. Therefore, to approximate a sharp crack the length-scale parameter ε should be as small as possible. Based on some parameter studies we propose to choose $\varepsilon = 1 \ldots 3h$ for linear shape functions, which is similar to other author's suggestion of $l_c = 2\varepsilon > 2h$, [12].

5. Simulation of the HB-spalling experiment

A classical Split-Hopkinson-Pressure Bar consists of a steel projectile (striker), an incident bar and a transmission bar. The specimen is placed between the bars and an analysis of the propagating waves allows to deduce its Young's modulus. For our UHPC mixture the result is $E = 59\,\mathrm{GPa}$; details of the experiments can be found in [20, 44]. For the *spalling experiment* the HB setup is modified; we have a striker, an incident bar and a cylindrical specimen but no transmission bar. The impact of the striker generates a compressive stress pulse traveling through the incident bar. When the pulse reaches the end of the incident bar, a part of the stress is transmitted into the specimen. This stress pulse σ_T is of interest for us. At the free end of the specimen it is reflected as a tensile pulse and spalling occurs if the superposition of both pulses is beyond the cohesive strength, cf. **Figure 10**. Please note that with the formation of a crack boundary the wave propagation and reflection continue, which may result in several further cracks; this can be seen in the specimen of **Figure 1**.

The aim of spalling experiments is to determine a material's resistance to fracture, specifically its fracture energy W_c or specific energy $\mathcal{G}_c$ and/or its tensile resistance R^t_m. The spalling test presumes brittle materials which can sustain compression but fails under tension. Plastic deformations do not matter, neither do temperature effects; all tests are conducted under ambient conditions.

5.1 Finite element discretization

The UHPC specimen has a length of 200 mm and a diameter of 20 mm. Because of the cylindrical symmetry of the problem we can use an axialsymmetric finite element model. This model maps a fully three-dimensional material behavior with the reduced effort of a plane mesh, which allows us to do extensive parametric studies.

A first challenge was the correct reproduction of the incident and reflected stress pulses in the specimen. From the strain pulse measured in the incident bar, the difference in impedance, and a low-amplitude pulse measured in the specimen we conclude on the shape of the transmitted wave. It is applied on the (left) boundary as a pressure impulse of trapezoidal form $\overline{q} = \sigma_{\max} f(t)$ with $f(0 \le t \le t_1) = t/t_1$, $f(t_1 < t \le t_2) = 1$, and, $f(t_2 < t \le t_3) = t_3 - t/t_3 - t_2$, where $t_1 = 12\,\mu s$ and $t_2 = 47\,\mu s$ and $t_3 = 62\,\mu s$ and $\sigma_{\max} = -17\,\text{MPa}$. Within the 80μs of simulation time the stress wave travels through the specimen, is reflected and reaches the left end again. Further propagation (and further cracks) are not considered. The average velocity of the specimen before spallation is $v_{\text{spec}} = 6.8\text{m/s}$. For time discretization we use a special central difference scheme with a weighted displacement field, which results in stress pulses that largely correspond to the measured data, see **Figure 10**; for numerical details we refer to [34, 45].

5.2 Fracture parameter

The dynamic tensile resistance of a brittle material R^t_m is usually defined as the maximum tension a material can sustain. A higher stress results in fracture—in our experiments in spallation. There are several attempts but no established way to deduce the tensile resistance directly from the data measured in the experiments, see [46] for a discussion. One way is to measure the incident and reflected waves, "shift" them to the position of fracture z_c, and determine the superposed elastic

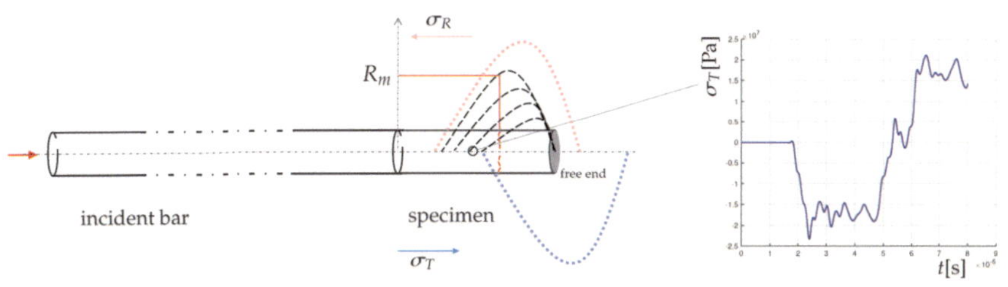

Figure 10.
Schematics of the HB-spalling experiment and typical incoming stress wave in the middle of the specimen with $t_1 = 0$ and $t_2 = t_3 = 30\,\mu s$.

stress state there. The dynamic tensile strength is then defined as the level of the tensile stress reached at the location of fracture. In this sense we identify R_m^t with the cohesive strength σ_c and try to capture it by adaptive insertion of cohesive elements.

5.2.1 Cohesive element technique

Our specimen is meshed uniformly with triangular finite elements (2560 elements) and a mixed-mode cohesive law is employed. We start with the linear envelope given in Eq. (17) and an effective opening displacement $\delta_c = 10\,\mu\text{m}$ for $\sigma_c = 15\,\text{MPa}$, $G_c = 75\,\text{N/m}$, $\beta = 1$. As outlined in Section 3.5 a cohesive element will be added if the effective tensile stress given in Eq. (15) exceeds the value of σ_c. In tension, the elements can subsequently open, in compression contact conditions apply. Once the opening has exceeded δ_c, a crack has formed. The simulation stops after a spallation plane has built or after 120 μs.

Figure 11 shows one symmetry half of the specimen at the end of the simulation for different values of σ_c. At first, with $\sigma_c = 20\,\text{MPa}$, the cohesive stress is obviously too high, no elements are inserted and no crack can grow. For $\sigma_c = 17\,\text{MPa}$ a small, localized crack zone develops. Lowering $\sigma_c = 14 \ldots 8\,\text{MPa}$ gives a wider zone and, moreover, the cracked zone moves toward the free end. This follows from the fact that the superposed pulse $\sigma_R + \sigma_I$ reaches the value of σ_c earlier. However, this position does not correspond to the measured crack position. In all our experiments the crack appeared at $z_c = 120 \ldots 130\,\text{mm}$, with coordinate z starting at the free end.

Obviously, the cohesive stress σ_c plays a significant role in the simulation of crack growth with cohesive elements. If it is too low, an unrealistic scattered crack zone will be computed, which does not give fully opened cracks (assuming a fixed fracture energy). However, some energy is dissipated here and the crack plane cannot appear at the right position anymore.

We further studied the influence of the critical crack opening displacement δ_c. Here we observe for higher values of δ_c a longer time of crack opening whereas δ_c has no influence on the position of the crack. Studies with the exponential cohesive law given in Eq. (19) show a very similar behavior in variations of σ_c and δ_0, cf. **Figure 12**.

5.2.2 Phase-field fracture

In phase-field simulations the fracture energy is the essential parameter for crack growth. Other parameter, like the mobility, are of numerical nature and can be calibrated. Further, the length-scale parameter ε is responsible for the width of the diffuse interface. Because of the fact, that ε depends on the mesh size, the mesh

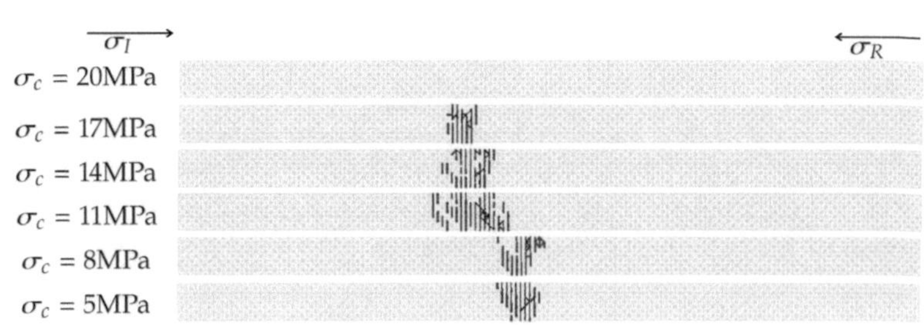

Figure 11.
Finite element mesh of the specimen with adaptively inserted cohesive elements. A variation of the critical cohesive stress leads to different positions of the crack. Here the inserted but not yet fully open elements are purple, the cracks (open elements) are black.

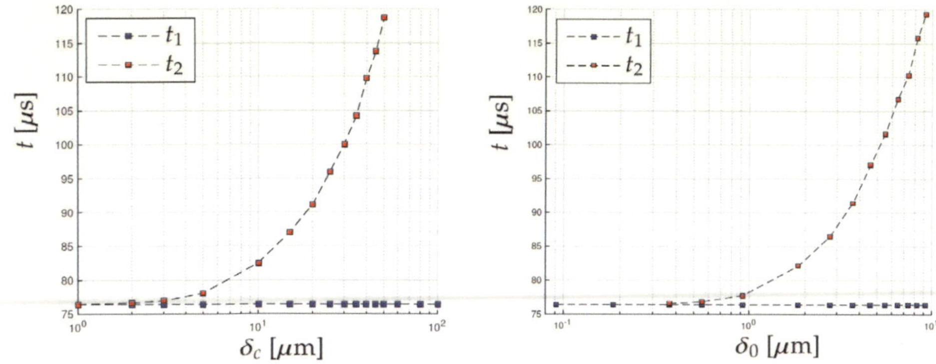

Figure 12.
Influence of the critical crack opening displacement on the time of crack initiation t_1 *and of total crack opening* t_2 *for* $\sigma_c = 15\,MPa$ *with (left)* δ_c *in the linear cohesive law Eq. (17) and (right)* δ_0 *in the exponential form with* $\delta_c = 30\,\mu m$ *Eq. (19).*

has to be very fine in the domain of a potential crack. To avoid numerical artifacts we chose here a uniform mesh of 5760 triangular elements; the mesh size is $h = 5/6\,\text{mm}$. We set $\varepsilon = 3h$ and $\tilde{M} = 200,000\ \text{s}^{-1}$ and define regions with phase-field parameter $s < 0.2$ as cracked.

For a large critical energy release rate, $\mathcal{G}_c > 150\,\text{N/m}$, no crack is computed. Obviously, here such values are too high. Reducing the value leads to the appearance of a zone with $s < 1$; however, it depends on the defining threshold if this is already considered to be a crack. For $\mathcal{G}_c = 90\,\text{N/m}$ a sharp crack zone appears at the expected position. Smaller values, for example $\mathcal{G}_c = 30\,\text{N/m}$ in **Figure 13(left)**, show a wider cracked zone but the position of the crack is nearly the same, see **Figure 13(right)**. Specifically we define the diffuse zone as

$$b_{\text{trans}} := \left|\{z \in [0, 200] : 0.2 \leq s(0, z) \leq 0.8\}\right|_e \tag{32}$$

and the cracked zone is given by $s(0, z) \leq 0.8$.

Figure 14 shows the effect of the specific fracture energy on the time of crack evolution. In opposite to the cohesive model the time difference between crack formation and final state grows linearly with $\mathcal{G}_c$. Similar is the situation for an decrease of parameter ε. A value of $\varepsilon < 6h$ increases the time of crack formation at constant $\mathcal{G}_c$.

Further studies have been performed to simulate the experiments, cf. [34], and with the collected knowledge we conclude, that for UHPC the tensile strength R_m^t,

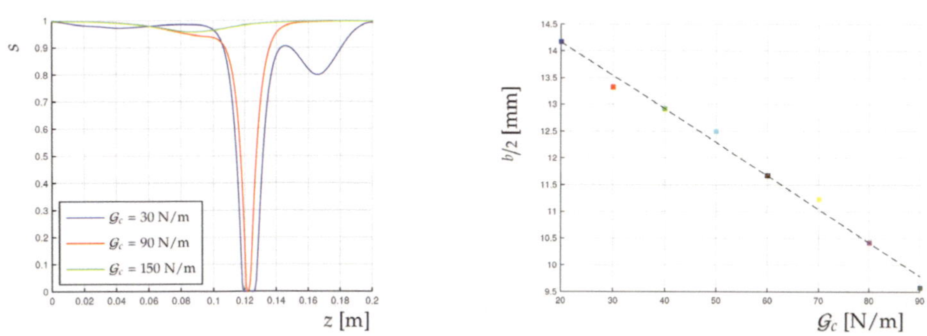

Figure 13.
Influence of the specific fracture energy $\mathcal{G}_c$ *on the width given in Eq. (32) of the crack; left plot shows the phase-field parameter at crack position in longitudinal direction and right plot shows width b as function of* $\mathcal{G}_c$*, approximated with R-coefficient* $R^2 \approx 0.9894$.

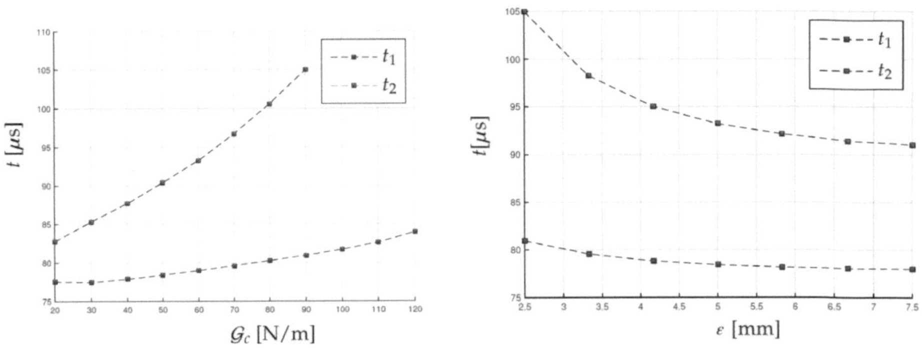

Figure 14.
Influence of the specific fracture energy $\mathcal{G}_c$ is shown in left plot and the length parameter ε on the time of crack initiation t_1 and of total crack opening t_2 is shown in the right plot, computed with $M = 0.2\,\mu s^{-1}$ and $\varepsilon = 3h$ (left), $G_c = 90 N/m$ (right).

the critical opening displacement δ_c, and the specific fracture energy $\mathcal{G}_c$ are in the ranges $12 < R_m^t\,[\text{MPa}] < 18, 5 < \delta_c\,[\mu\text{m}] \leq 17.5,$ and $40 \leq \mathcal{G}_c\,[\text{N/m}] \leq 105.$

6. Inverse analysis: determination of the $\mathcal{G}_c$

The aim of our study was to evaluate the two fracture simulation methods for the use in an inverse analysis where the measured data of the experiment are used to deduce fracture parameters and the obtained results are used to simulate the experiment. The deduced parameters are considered “correct” when the difference between experiment and simulation is small.

6.1 Derivation of the specific fracture energy from spallation

After spallation two fragments result with the crack located at the position where the stress exceeds the tensile resistance first. Depending on the energy of the incoming wave the same process may continue in both fragments with the results of additional cracks. The total fracture energy W_c corresponds to the amount of work necessary to form such a new surface. In order to determine W_c we balance the energy before and after crack initiation, that is, at time t_1 right before cracking and at time t_2 immediately after the crack opened. In the simple case of two fragments, cf. **Figure 15**, with masses $m_{\text{fra},1}$, $m_{\text{fra},2}$, and $m_{\text{spec}} = m_{\text{fra},1} + m_{\text{fra},2}$ it follows for the difference of kinetic energy:

$$\Delta\mathcal{K} = \frac{1}{2}m_{\text{spec}}\left(v_{\text{spec}}\left(t_1\right)\right)^2 - \frac{1}{2}m_{\text{fra},1}\left(v_{\text{fra},1}\left(t_2\right)\right)^2 - \frac{1}{2}m_{\text{fra},2}\left(v_{\text{fra},2}\left(t_2\right)\right)^2 \qquad (33)$$

where $v_{\text{fra},1}$, $v_{\text{fra},2}$ refer to the velocities of the fragments 1 and 2. Because we presume the UHPC to behave linear elastically, the loss of kinetic energy between initial and spalled state will completely be related to the fracturing process. Consequently, we state $\Delta\mathcal{K} = W_c$ to be the fracture energy of the specimen.

In order to deduce $\mathcal{G}_c$ the fracture energy Eq. (33) needs to be referred to the fractured surface A_c of the specimen. Ideally, the crack is smooth and perpendicular to the specimen’s axis. Then the specific fracture energy simply follows as $\mathcal{G}_c = W_c/A_c$ with $A_c = 2\pi r_{\text{spec}}^2$. In practice, there may be spalled and rough crack surfaces and so we replaced A_c by the measured surface size.

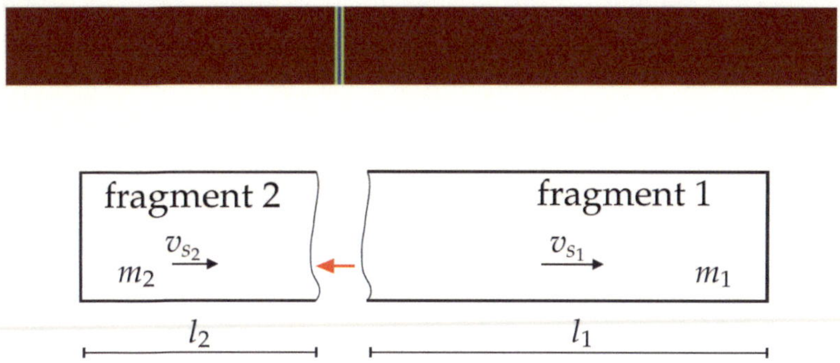

Figure 15.
Cracked specimen in a phase-field simulation and fragments after spallation.

For the inverse analysis we proceed as follows: we use the data obtained in our previous simulations to define a range of input data $\mathcal{G}_c^{\text{inp}}$, simulate the spallation experiment, and from the computed velocities and masses we deduce via Eq. (33) the "measured" value $\mathcal{G}_c^{\text{sim}}$. To this end we determine the velocities of the fragments by $v_{\text{spec}} = \left(2\sum_e \mathcal{K}_e / m_{\text{spec}}\right)^{1/2}$, $v_{\text{fra},1} = \left(2\sum_{e(\text{fra},1)} \mathcal{K}e / m_{\text{fra},1}\right)^{1/2}$, and, $v_{\text{fra},2} = \left(2\sum_{e(\text{fra},2)} \mathcal{K}_e / m_{\text{fra},2}\right)^{1/2}$, with the kinetic energy of the finite elements, $\mathcal{K}_e = \frac{1}{2} m_e |\boldsymbol{v}_e|^2$.

6.2 Cohesive element technique

We mesh the specimen uniformly with 2560 elements and employ the linear cohesive law from Eq. (17) with parameter $\beta = 1$. The cohesive stress is $\sigma_c = 15\text{MPa}$ to ensure crack formation at the expected position and we vary the critical opening displacement δ_c to obtain values of $\mathcal{G}_c$ between 20 N/m and 150 N/m. All computations result in similar fragments with masses $m_{\text{fra},1} \in [895, 905]\text{g}$ and $m_{\text{fra},2} \in [572, 582]\text{g}$. Also the fractured surfaces show little variations, $A_c \in [9.5, 11.5]\text{cm}^2$.

In **Figure 16** the computed specific fracture energy $\mathcal{G}_c^{\text{sim}}$ is shown. In the optimal case is $\mathcal{G}_c^{\text{inp}} = \mathcal{G}_c^{\text{sim}}$, this is marked with a dotted line. The computed values show a clear proportionality between $\mathcal{G}_c^{\text{inp}}$ and its simulated counterpart $\mathcal{G}_c^{\text{sim}}$. This generally validates the chosen method of energy balance. However, the value of $\mathcal{G}_c$ deduced from the simulation is higher than the real one. This corresponds to a higher difference in the kinetic energy, that is, for the given initial velocity the velocity of the fragments is underestimated, that is there is too much energy dissipated. This likely results from the fact that some of the adaptively inserted cohesive elements are "useless," they are inserted in a wrong place and do not fully open. This partial opening costs energy, which is dissipated but does not contribute to spallation. Therefore we observe $\mathcal{G}_c^{\text{inp}} < \mathcal{G}_c^{\text{sim}}$ with discrepancies between 30 and 60%, see **Figure 16**.

6.3 Phase-field fracture

For phase-field simulations we use a finer mesh of 5760 elements, $h = 5/6$ mm and set $\varepsilon = 2.5$ mm and $M = 0.6\ \mu\text{s}^{-1}$. At first we accelerate the specimen to $v_{\text{spec}} = 6.8\,\text{m/s}$, then the actual simulation starts. Again, during spallation the velocity of the fragments develops differently, the first fragment moves faster then the second one. The time of fracture depends on the input value $\mathcal{G}_c^{\text{inp}}$, the lower it is the easier both fragments split, cf. **Figure 14**.

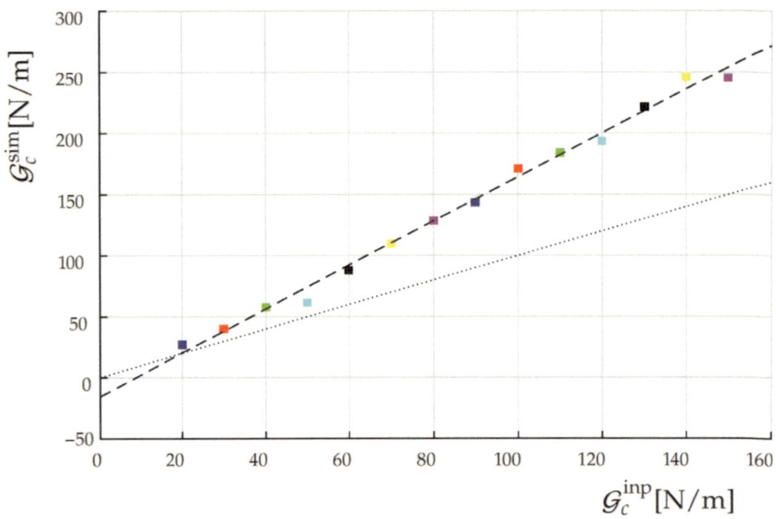

Figure 16.
Determination of the specific fracture energy with the cohesive element technique: displayed are the values $\mathcal{G}_c^{\text{sim}}$ derived from the velocity and mass data obtained in the simulation versus the input parameter $\mathcal{G}_c^{\text{inp}}$ of the experiment. The dotted line marks the identity $\mathcal{G}_c^{\text{sim}} = \mathcal{G}_c^{\text{inp}}$; the dashed line is approximated with $R^2 \approx 0.9928$ and corresponds roughly to $\mathcal{G}_c^{\text{sim}} = 1.5\mathcal{G}_c^{\text{inp}}$.

Since the phase-field model is a diffuse interface approach, which does give a discrete distinction between the both states, it is necessary to specify tolerances for the states $s(t_1)$ and $s(t_2)$. Here we consider $s(t_1)$ and set for symmetry $s(t_2) = 1 - s(t_1)$. A lower "crack initiation" point $s(t_1)$ clearly needs less time and energy to open the crack. On the one hand, if crack initiation equals crack opening, $s(t_1) = s(t_2) = 0.5$, that is the crack appears immediately after initiation and the dissipated energy $\mathcal{G}_c^{\text{sim}}$ will be close to zero. The input value $\mathcal{G}_c^{\text{inp}}$ would work only as a threshold for the fragments to loose contact and (almost) no dissipation will take place. On the other hand, if we raise $s(t_1) > 0.95$, $s(t_2) > 0.05$ the crack may not fully open, which gives

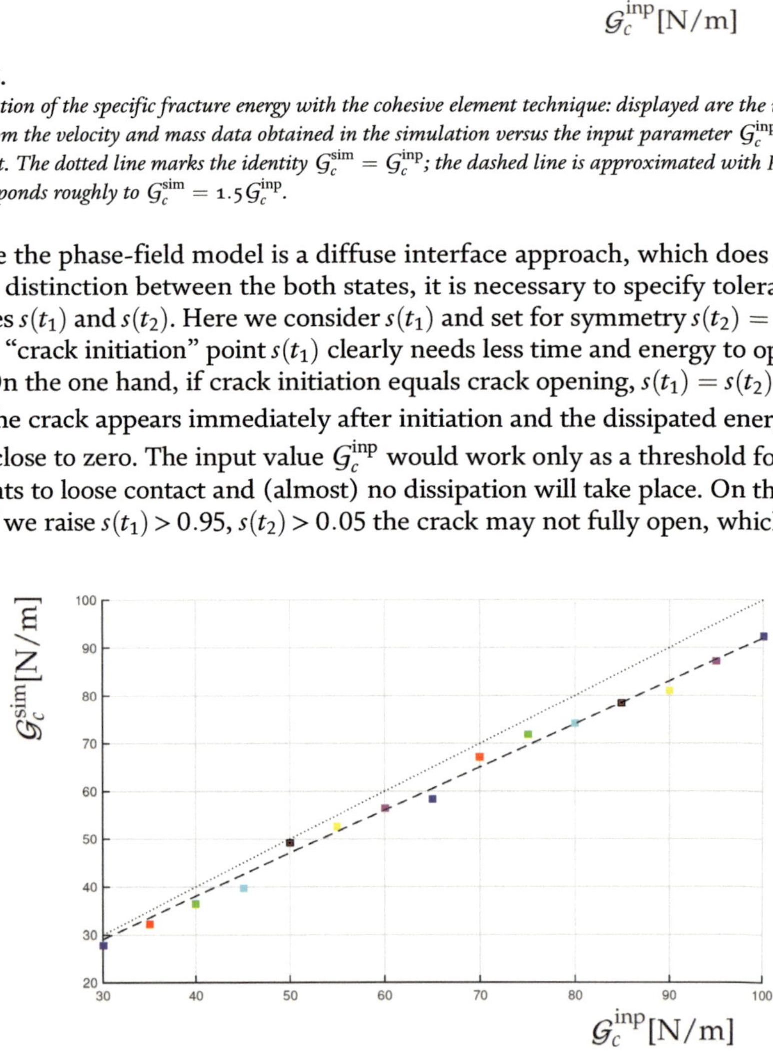

Figure 17.
Determination of the specific fracture energy with the phase-field fracture approach: displayed are the values $\mathcal{G}_c^{\text{sim}}$ derived from the velocity and mass data obtained simulations with $\varepsilon = 5/2$ mm, $s(t_1) = 0.8$, $s(t_2) = 0.2$ versus the input parameter $\mathcal{G}_c^{\text{inp}}$ of the experiment. The dotted line marks the identity $\mathcal{G}_c^{\text{sim}} = \mathcal{G}_c^{\text{inp}}$; the dashed line is approximated with $R^2 \approx 0.9969$ and corresponds well to $\mathcal{G}_c^{\text{sim}} = 0.9\mathcal{G}_c^{\text{inp}}$.

inaccurate fragment velocities. A stable state we found for $s(t_1) \in [0.75, 0.9]$ and so we set $s(t_1) = 0.8$ and $s(t_2) = 0.2$.

In **Figure 17** the computed specific fracture energy $\mathcal{G}_c^{\text{sim}}$ over the input value $\mathcal{G}_c^{\text{inp}}$ is shown. Again, the optimal case $\mathcal{G}_c^{\text{inp}} = \mathcal{G}_c^{\text{sim}}$ is marked with a dotted line and the computed values show a clear proportionality between $\mathcal{G}_c^{\text{inp}}$ and $\mathcal{G}_c^{\text{sim}}$. The value of $\mathcal{G}_c^{\text{sim}}$ is now lower than the input value $\mathcal{G}_c^{\text{inp}}$ with relative difference less than 10%. Reason for this is basically the definition of crack initiation with $s < 1$, which attributes the beginning of the crack still to the full specimen. Please note that for very small values of $\mathcal{G}_c^{\text{inp}} < 20\,\text{N/m}$ the specimen cracks basically without dissipation whereas too high values of $\mathcal{G}_c^{\text{inp}}$ prevent any crack. In the range of interest, $\mathcal{G}_c^{\text{inp}} = 30 \dots 100\,\text{N/m}$ both values $\mathcal{G}_c^{\text{sim}}$ and $\mathcal{G}_c^{\text{inp}}$ correlate very well with an R-coefficient of 0.9969. Specifically we have $\mathcal{G}_c^{\text{sim}} \approx 0.9\mathcal{G}_c^{\text{inp}}$. Therefore, it is possible and useful to employ a phase-field fracture simulation for a quantitative analysis of the experiments.

7. Conclusions

In the previous we compared the possibilities of a sharp interface method and a diffuse interface method for crack nucleation and quantitative dynamic fracture analysis. Exemplarily, we validated investigations on the fracture toughness of high-performance concrete in a Hopkinson bar spallation experiment whereby, in particular, the fracture energy values have been determined. Both methods, the cohesive element technique and the phase-field fracture approach, allow numerical simulations of crack growth with an a priori unknown path, and both methods allow to determine the related material parameter in a quantitative manner. Reliability, precision, and numerical costs differ however. Pros and cons of both methods are summarized in the following.

7.1 Model parameters

The core of the cohesive zone model is a cohesive law, $\boldsymbol{t}(\boldsymbol{\delta})$, which describes the forces between the crack flanks as a function of separation. Such cohesive laws allow for pure mode-I cracks in the sense of Griffith as well as for mixed-mode cracks, for example by using the effective traction and separation. Essential cohesive parameters are the critical cohesive stress σ_c, the critical separation δ_c, and the weight β, which relates shear and tension. These parameters depend on the specific material and can be determined experimentally whereby δ_c is implicitly given via the specific crack energy $\mathcal{G}_c$. Further specifications of the cohesive law may require additional material parameters, for example, in the classical exponential Rose-Ferrante law an additional parameter δ_0 needs to be set. All these parameters have a clear physical meaning.

Sensitive for the cohesive element technique is the critical traction for adaptive insertion of the cohesive elements, which has no direct physical background but strongly influences energy dissipation and numerical efficiency. Wrongly inserted elements may dissipate energy but do not contribute to fracture and skew the simulation results.

The phase-field approach to fracture is based on an evolution equation that essentially refers to the elastic strain energy density $\Psi^e(\boldsymbol{u}, s)$ of the material. The remaining relevant parameters are the mobility M, the specific crack energy $\mathcal{G}_c$, and the length-scale parameter ε. The mobility has only numerical character and controls the rate of phase-field decrease during crack formation. The critical length-scale parameter ε is a measure for the width of the diffuse interface, which relates to both, the finite element mesh size and the material properties. The latter enters the crack growth criteria via the term $\mathcal{G}_c/\varepsilon$ in the crack resistance and therefore ε needs to be calibrated carefully. The only material parameter in the phase-field model with a clear physical background is the Griffith energy $\mathcal{G}_c$.

7.2 Numerical implementation and computation

In the cohesive zone model cohesive elements are adaptively inserted between the continuum elements to describe the crack opening. The continuum elements themselves are not directly affected and the crack can only propagate along the element boundaries, which results in a certain mesh dependence. The adaptive insertion of cohesive elements require a continuous update of the data structure, which leads to a significant programming effort and also increases the costs of computation. Additionally, the cohesive zone has to be equipped with contact constraints in order to prevent penetration in case of unloading. In total, the numerical implementation of an adaptive cohesive zone model becomes very complex.

In contrast, the structure of the finite element mesh in the phase-field approach remains constant during the simulation. The phase-field parameter can decrease to zero at each node and the crack is able to propagate theoretically everywhere in the whole domain. Essential requirement is a very fine mesh with $\varepsilon > h$.

For numerical computation of the coupled fields $\boldsymbol{u}, s$ there exist two different types of solution. On the one hand it is possible to determine the displacements $\boldsymbol{u}$ and the phase-field parameter s successive such that two system of equations have to be built up—this method is called staggered scheme; on the other hand a fully coupled system of equations can be constructed. In general the implementation effort is much larger for the coupled approach and the staggered scheme converges (when implemented correctly) to the same solution so that this method is usually preferred. Much more relevant than the rise in the degrees of freedom by the additional field is, however, the required fine mesh size. The resolution of the mesh needs to be $h < \varepsilon$ everywhere where the crack will be able to form. This can be solved by adaptive mesh refinement—which results in a similar effort like the insertion of cohesive elements—or by an a priori fine mesh in the relevant zones, which, in turn, raises the numerical costs tremendously.

7.3 Constraints and driving forces

The major advantage of the cohesive zone model is that the crack properties can be mapped exactly. The local opening is known, the crack width is the separation δ of the crack flanks, and the corresponding normal and tangential forces follow from the cohesive law. Since the loading and unloading processes are distinguished, compressive forces do not contribute to crack growth. The irreversibility of crack propagation is guaranteed and although the separation can decrease during the simulation the crack will not "heal." Regarding mixed-mode problems it is positive that the normal and tangential traction components are weighted by a parameter so that different crack opening modes can be realized for each specific material under consideration.

In phase-field fracture by definition a continuous function s and a diffuse interface with width $\varepsilon \propto \delta$ models the crack. The values $0 < s < 1$ can not be interpreted physically so that threshold values have to be chosen. Crack closure needs to be prevented by explicit local constraints, for example $\dot{s} < 0$, or by a modified mobility.

In order to ensure that only tensile stresses contribute to crack growth the strain energy function needs to be decomposed in tensile and compressive components, which is by no means unique, cf. [47], and also influences the resulting crack.

Summarizing we state that both methods are mechanically consistent and have a clear variational structure. The cohesive element technique is difficult to implement but provides a strong physical background. For static computations with expected way of crack propagation it is definitely preferred because it allows cohesive laws, which may consider anisotropy, friction, and other material specific properties. In general dynamic applications of unknown crack path, however, its numerical drawbacks, together with the fact that a suboptimal insertion may lead to wrong predictions, dominate. Here the phase-field approach to fracture is clearly the better choice. Unknown crack paths can simply be followed—as long as the mesh resolution is fine enough. The major drawback of phase-field fracture is its parameter sensitivity. Also, extensions to more complex fracture models, which account, for example, for sliding, anisotropy, and interlocking, contradict the original variational derivation and are still an open problem.

Author details

Tim Dally†, Carola Bilgen†, Marek Werner*† and Kerstin Weinberg†
Lehrstuhl für Festkörpermechanik, Fakultät IV, Department Maschinenbau, Institut für Mechanik und Regelungstechnik - Mechatronik, Siegen, Germany

*Address all correspondence to: marek.werner@uni-siegen.de

† These authors contributed equally.

References

[1] Pandolfi A, Ortiz M. Solid modeling aspects of three-dimensional fragmentation. Engineering with Computers. 1998;**14**:287-308

[2] Scheider I, Brocks W. Cohesive elements for thin-walled structures. Computational Materials Science. 2006; **37**(1–2):101-109

[3] Xu XP, Needleman A. Numerical simulations of dynamic interfacial crack growth allowing for crack growth away from the bond line. International Journal of Fracture. 1995;**74**:253-275

[4] Moës N, Belytschko T. Extended finite element method for cohesive crack growth. Engineering Fracture Mechanics. 2002;**69**(7):813-833

[5] Stazi FL, Budyn E, Chessa J, Belytschko T. An extended finite element method with higher-order elements for curved cracks. Computational Mechanics. 2003;**31**: 38-48

[6] Pandolfi A, Ortiz M. An eigenerosion approach to brittle fracture. International Journal for Numerical Methods in Engineering. 2012;**92**: 694-714

[7] Schmidt B, Fraternali F, Ortiz M. Eigenfracture: An eigen deformation approach to variational fracture. SIAM Journal on Multiscale Modeling and Simulation. 2009;7:1237-1266

[8] Borden MJ, Verhoosel CV, Scott MA, Hughes TJR, Landis CM. A phase-field description of dynamic brittle fracture. Computer Methods in Applied Mechanics and Engineering. 2012;**217–220**:77-95

[9] Bourdin B. The variational formulation of brittle fracture: Numerical implementation and extensions. In: Volume 5 of IUTAM Symposium on Discretization Methods for Evolving Discontinuities, IUTAM Bookseries, Chapter 22; Springer, Netherlands. 2007. pp. 381-393

[10] Henry H, Levine H. Dynamic instabilities of fracture under biaxial strain using a phase field model. Physics Review Letters. 2004;**93**:105505

[11] Karma A, Kessler DA, Levine H. Phase-field model of mode III dynamic fracture. Physical Review Letters. 2001; **81**:045501

[12] Miehe C, Hofacker M, Welschinger F. A phase field model for rate-independent crack propagation: Robust algorithmic implementation based on operator splits. Computer Methods in Applied Mechanics and Engineering. 2010;**199**:2765-2778

[13] Verhoosel CV, de Borst R. A phase-field model for cohesive fracture. International Journal for Numerical Methods in Engineering. 2013. In press

[14] Ambrosio L, Tortorelli VM. Approximation of functional depending on jumps by elliptic functional via γ-convergence. Communications on Pure and Applied Mathematics. 1990;**348–349**:13-16

[15] Diaz-Rubio FG, Perez JR, Galvez VS. The spalling of long bars as a reliable method of measuring the dynamic tensile strength of ceramics. International Journal of Impact Engineering. 2002;**27**:161-177

[16] Klepaczko JR, Brara A. An experimental method for dynamic tensile testing of concrete by spalling. International Journal of Impact Engineering. 2001;**25**(4):387-409

[17] Schuler H, Mayrhofer C, Thoma K. Spall experiments for the measurement

of the tensile strength and fracture energy of concrete at high strain rates. International Journal of Impact Engineering. 2006;**32**(10):1635-1650

[18] Weerheijma J, Van Doormaal JCAM. Tensile failure of concrete at high loading rates: New test data on strength and fracture energy from instrumented spalling tests. International Journal of Impact Engineering. 2007;**34**:609

[19] Zhang L, Hu S-S, Chen D-X, Yu Z-Q, Liu F. An experimental technique for spalling of concrete. Experimental Mechanics. 2009;**49**(4): 523-532

[20] Khosravani MR, Wagner P, Fröhlich D, Weinberg K. Dynamic fracture investigations of ultra-high performance concrete by spalling tests. Engineering Structures. 2019;**201**: 109844

[21] Griffith AA. The phenomena of rupture and flow in solids. Philosophical Transactions of the Royal Society of London. 1921;**221**:163-198

[22] Irwin GR. Elasticity and plasticity: Fracture. In: Függe S, editor. Encyclopedia of Physics. 1958

[23] Dugdale DS. Yielding of steel sheets containing clits. Journal of the Mechanics and Physics of Solids. 1960;**8**: 100-104

[24] Barenblatt GI. The mathematical theory of equilibrium of cracks in brittle fracture. Advances in Applied Mechanics. 1962;7:55-129

[25] Camacho GT, Ortiz M. Computational modelling of impact damage in brittle materials. International Journal of Solids and Structures. 1996;**33**:2899-2938

[26] Ortiz M, Pandolfi A. A class of cohesive elements for the simulation of three-dimensional crack propagation. International Journal for Numerical Methods in Engineering. 1999;**44**: 1267-1282

[27] Xu XP, Needleman A. Numerical simulations of fast crack growth in brittle solids. Journal of the Mechanics and Physics of Solids. 1994;**42**: 1397-1434

[28] Ferrara A, Pandolfi A. Numerical modelling of fracture of human arteries. Computer Methods in Biomechanics and Biomedical Engineering. 2008;**11**: 553-567

[29] Pandolfi A, Weinberg K. A numerical approach to the analysis of failure modes in anisotropic plates. Engineering Fracture Mechanics. 2011; **78**:2052-2069

[30] Yu C, Pandolfi A, Ortiz M, Coker D, Rosakis AJ. Three-dimensional modeling of intersonic shear-crack growth in asymmetrically loaded unidirectional composite plates. International Journal of Solids and Structures. 2002;**39**:6135-6157

[31] Bazant ZP. Concrete fracture models: Testing and practice. Engineering Fracture Mechanics. 2002; **69**:165-205

[32] Tvergaard V, Hutchinson JW. The relation between crack growth resistance and fracture process parameters in elastic-plastic solids. Journal of the Mechanics and Physics of Solids. 1992;**40**:1377-1397

[33] Rose JH, Ferrante J, Smith JR. Universal binding energy curves for metals and bimetallic interfaces. Physical Review Letters. 1981;**47**: 675-678

[34] Dally T. Vergleich von Kohäsivelement-Methode und Phasenfeld-Methode anhand ausgewählter Probleme der Bruchmechanik. Technical Report at Universität Siegen; 2017

[35] Pandolfi A, Ortiz M. An efficient adaptive procedure for three-dimensional fragmentation simulations. Engineering with Computers. 2002;**18**: 48-159

[36] Bourdin B, Francfort GA, Marigo JJ. The variational approach to fracture. Journal of Elasticity. 2008;**9**:5-148

[37] Francfort GA, Marigo J-J. Revisiting brittle fracture as an energy minimization problem. Journal of the Mechanics and Physics of Solids. 1998; **46**:1319-1342

[38] Borden MJ, Hughes TJR, Landis CM, Verhoosel CV. A higher-order phase-field model for brittle fracture: Formulation and analysis within the isogeometric analysis framework. Computer Methods in Applied Mechanics and Engineering. 2014; **273**(0):100-118

[39] Hesch C, Stefan S, Dittmann M, Franke M, Weinberg K. Isogeometric analysis and hierarchical refinement for higher-order phase-field models. Computer Methods in Applied Mechanics and Engineering. 2016;**303**: 185-207

[40] Weinberg K, Hesch C. A high-order finite-deformation phase-field approach to fracture. Continuum Mechanics and Thermodynamics. 2017;**29**:935-945

[41] Miehe C, Welschinger F, Hofacker M. Thermodynamically consistent phase-field models of fracture: Variational principles and multi-field FE implementations. International Journal for Numerical Methods in Engineering. 2010;**83**: 1273-1311

[42] Bilgen C, Kopanicakova A, Krause R, Weinberg K. A phase-field approach to conchoidal fracture. Meccanica. 2018;**53**:1203-1219

[43] Weinberg K, Dally T, Schuß S, Werner M, Bilgen C. Modeling and numerical simulation of crack growth and damage with a phase field approach. GAMM-Mitteilungen. 2016;**39**(1):55-77

[44] Weinberg K, Khosravani MR. On the tensile resistance of UHPC at impact. The European Physical Journal Special Topics. 2018;**227**:167-177

[45] Park KC, Lim SJ, Huh H. A method for computation of discontinuous wave propagation in heterogeneous solids: Basic algorithm description and application to one-dimensional problems. International Journal for Numerical Methods in Engineering. 2012;**91**:622-643

[46] Erzar B, Forquin P. An experimental method to determine the tensile strength of concrete at high rates of strain. Experimental Mechanics. 2010;**50**(7):941-955

[47] Bilgen C, Weinberg K. On the crack-driving force of phase-field models in linearized and finite elasticity. Computer Methods in Applied Mechanics and Engineering. 2019; **353**(15):348-372

Chapter 2

Methods of Nonequilibrium Statistical Mechanics in Models for Mixing Bulk Components

Anna Kapranova, Daria Bahaeva, Dmitry Stenko, Ivan Verloka, Anton Lebedev and Mikhail Tarshis

Abstract

When describing the mechanics of the behavior of bulk materials during their mixing, a theoretical basis for the design of the specified equipment is formed. In recent years, the most well-known methods of modeling this process include the stochastic approach, in the framework of which models of the following types are actively developing: cell, managerial, with time series, energy, etc. Moreover, as a rule, predicting the quality of the finished mixture according to the selected criterion is achieved by using numerical calculation methods based on the generated cyber system. Of particular interest is the use of the energy method from the statistical mechanics of nonequilibrium processes due to the possibility of obtaining analytical simulation results. The paper describes the motion models of bulk components in rarefied flows, which are built on the basis of the energy method and take into account the main characteristics of the studied mixing process.

Keywords: apparatus, process, mixing, bulk material, rarefied flow, stochastic model

1. Introduction

Mixing of bulk materials belongs to the category of mechanical processes in the field of chemical technology in a variety of manufacturing enterprises, including paint and varnish, glass, construction, food, pharmaceutical, chemical, etc. The result of this technological operation is a loose mixture with a regulated degree of homogeneity, the quality of which is influenced by many factors. Moreover, factors that have a decisive influence on the quality of the final product can be conditionally divided into several types:

- Properties of components—physical, mechanical (particle-size distribution, tendency to adhesion, agglomeration, degree of moisture, etc.), and chemical.

- Features of the behavior of different-sized particles when moving in the working chamber of the apparatus under the established modes of its operation (segregation, classification).

- The features of mixing equipment are structural (the presence or absence of additional mixing elements, the nature of these elements, the dimensions of the working chamber, etc.) and operational (rotation speed of the apparatus elements, conveyor speed, consumable characteristics of materials).

- Features of the operating conditions of the mixer (dosing method, the presence or absence of a combination of mechanical, vibrational, and pneumatic types of mixing).

The multifactorial nature of the task of describing the behavior of particles of mixed components [1], as the basis for the formation of a cyber-physical system [2], requires, when choosing a method for modeling this mixing process, to take into account the possibility of evaluating the quality of the mixture [3], for example, from the standpoint of the average statistical deviation of the content of the key component in her samples. Moreover, analytical dependences (in comparison with numerical) between the heterogeneity coefficient of the resulting mixture and the selected parameter of the studied mixing process are preferred [4]. The significance of the formation of a theoretical platform for the design of mixing apparatuses based on system-structural analysis [5, 6] increases with the combination (sequential implementation) of several technological operations within the same apparatus [7]. The indeterminacy of the behavior of bulk components during their mixing allows us to choose stochastic approaches as appropriate modeling methods [8]. The aim of the work is to describe the main features of the application of the energy method [9, 10] from the statistical mechanics of nonequilibrium processes in modeling the motion of bulk components in rarefied flows during their mixing in various working volumes of chemical technology apparatuses, for example, constructions [11–13]

2. On modern methods of stochastic modeling of the process of mixing bulk solids

In contrast to the deterministic approach [14], when there is ambiguity between the given input parameters of the mathematical model of mixing bulk solids and the desired indicator of this process, in stochastic models [15, 16] there is ambiguity of correspondence between the initial and final states of the macrosystems of particles of each component. Currently, there is an active development of indeterministic methods built on various theoretical platforms, for example, statistical thermodynamics and information theory [15, 17]; principles of cybernetics [18, 19]; description of time series [20–22]; the A.A. Markov circuit theory [15, 23–29], including on the basis of the energy approach [9, 10] from the statistical mechanics of nonequilibrium processes, etc. Briefly Section 2 describes the main features of these methods of stochastic modeling.

2.1 General provisions of entropy-informational models of mixing bulk solids

The use of entropy-informational models is typical for the preparation of bulk mixtures with a ratio of components of 1: 100 or more [15, 17]. From the standpoint of information theory, the process of mixing granular media as a studied information system is characterized by an indicator of its disorder (uncertainty)—information entropy. At the same time, it is believed that obtaining all the useful information means bringing this system to zero uncertainty. On the other hand, this mixing operation can be considered as a thermodynamic system described by a change in the Boltzmann entropy. A decrease in the latter leads to the transition of this system from a more probable state to a less probable one. Then, when applied to the process of mixing bulk materials, the maximum value of information entropy is determined by a logarithmic dependence on the number of components to be mixed with equal mass fractions and associated with the mixing efficiency parameter taking into account the specific fractions of each component in the selected sample of their many samples [17]. However, taking into account the peculiarities of the motion of the particles that make up the mixed components is difficult when using the specified entropy-information approach.

2.2 The main difficulties of using cybernetic models of granular media

Another variety of methods for mathematical modeling of the process of mixing bulk materials is the construction of models based on control theory [18, 19]. The cybernetic model describes the operation of the "input disturbance-mixer-output signal" system, in which the mixing apparatus plays the role of a "converter." In this case, the residence time distribution function (DFID) of the particles of bulk components in the working volume of the apparatus is simulated depending on the response curve. Usually, perfect mixing is characterized by an exponential decrease of a given function from the specified argument with a mathematical expectation inversely proportional to the normalization coefficient. At the same time, the difficulties of using such a cybernetic model are associated with an experimental estimation of the model constants, scaling of the results obtained when the values of the structural and operating parameters of the process under study are changed, and the behavior of particles of mixed components is taken into account.

2.3 To the statement of the problem of identifying a trend class for a random mixing process

The next method for modeling the random process of mixing bulk solids relates to models of the theory of time series [20–22], which involve the construction of a set of correlation functions and other probabilistic characteristics. In this case, mixed flows of granular media are modeled as classes of elementary components of "trends" (components), depending on the time parameter and having a general systematically linear or nonlinear character, in contrast to another class of time series theory—the "seasonal component" with a periodically repeating component. In particular, superpositions of polynomial or trigonometric dependencies are used to ensure trend highlighting by fitting functions when modeling mixed flows with an explicit monotonic nonlinear component. However, the application of the theory of time series to the indicated technological operation of mixing bulk media involves not only solving the problem of identifying the model, in particular by the fitting method, but also forecasting with an appropriate estimate of the parameters of the random process. Note that the latter is achieved quite laboriously and the result is difficult to analyze for widespread use in the design of mixing equipment.

2.4 On the variety of descriptions of mixing using A.A. Markov chains

In the framework of the A.A. Markov circuit theory [23–27], there are many models for mixing bulk components, which are the basis for the design of mixers of various types and operating modes, with conditional classification in the form of the following stochastic descriptions: diffusion [28], kinetic [23], birth-death [15], etc. [29]. It is known that random processes are divided into two main classes from the standpoint of causality of the relationship between the states of the probability system (events): (a) without correlations between events, when there is complete independence between the values, and (b) A.A. Markov processes, for which only the instantaneous states of the system are significant. In the latter case, the weight fraction of the key component of the granular mixture has the meaning of the probability density of a continuous random mixing process depending on the state and time parameter. For example, simulation of the share of a key component of a jump-like nature is used when layer-by-layer material splitting into cells or by postulating a matrix type of mass distribution of the mixed components with elements, as the probabilities of moving particles of materials from one selected area to another. In particular, in kinetic models [23], differential equations for the weight fractions of bulk components with spatiotemporal coordinates take into account their dispersion concentrations and mixing rate constants. In the birth-death models [15], these equations additionally contain a power-law dependence on spatial coordinates, and in diffusion models [28], there is a diffusion parameter along a given direction, and the influence of the acting force fields is taken into account. An active application of the A.A. Markov circuit method in his various interpretations with a cellular approach allows us to solve practical problems both with continuous and periodic operations of mixers. However, the difficulties that arise associated with the choice of the method of separation into cells and the calculation of the duration of the transition of the system to the boundary state are often solved by postulation. As a rule, two types of equations are used to describe continuous random mixing processes [25]: the Kolmogorov diffusion equation (e.g., for transverse and longitudinal displacements of component particles) and the Fokker-Planck kinetic equation for the probability density of the mixing process, as a consequence of the Chapman-Kolmogorov-Smoluchowski equation with a macrodiffusion coefficient and in the absence of a drift. In addition, cell models based on the Boltzmann equation [29] are known that allow the calculation of multidimensional combined processes of grinding, classification, and mixing of bulk materials. However, this modeling method in the case of forming torches of rarefied flows is difficult due to the complicated description of their behavior, for example, in a cylindrical coordinate system. Another variation in the use of A.A. Markov chains refers to the energy method [9, 10], which can be developed in two directions: with a description of the equilibrium (Ornstein-Uhlenbeck process) [4, 30, 31] and nonequilibrium [2, 32–34] distribution functions of the number of particles of mixed components in selected phase volume. Let us dwell on this method in more detail.

3. Features of the application of the energy method in stochastic modeling of the process of mixing bulk solids in rarefied flows

3.1 On the conditions for the formation of rarefied flows of bulk components in the working volumes of the apparatus

The principles of stochastic modeling of random processes are described in Yu. L. Klimontovich [9, 10], initially proved their effectiveness for equilibrium cases when studying shock processes in liquid-dispersed media [35], and then were successfully adapted in the analysis of the technological operation of separation of suspensions [36]. Studies of the random process of mixing bulk materials in different working volumes [11–13] with a set of additional mixing elements in the form of flexible bills [11], brushes [12], or elastic blades [13], as well as fenders [12, 13], showed the possibility of applying the energy method [9, 10]. This method of Yu. L. Klimontovich [9, 10] was used in two versions: for equilibrium [9] and nonequilibrium [10] random processes for obtaining a bulk mixture in rarefied streams of constituent components.

The formation of these flows occurs when the bulk materials are scattered by mixing elements of the above types, which are fixed on the cylindrical surfaces of rotating drums, for example, along a helical line [11], on counter helical lines [12], and in tangent planes to these surfaces [13]. It should be noted that the main advantage of this mechanical method of mixing bulk solids is, first of all, the ability to control the effect of segregation, virtually eliminating its manifestations in the working volume of the apparatus by identifying and selecting rational ranges of changes in the design and operating parameters of the process under study. In this regard, the main task of modeling is to describe the mechanism of behavior of particles of bulk components when they are mixed in rarefied streams, followed by prediction of effective mixing conditions.

Consider the behavior of particles of mixed components $\left(i = \overline{1, n_k}\right)$ in the working volume of the apparatus with the possibility of their scattering by mixing elements $\left(j = \overline{1, n_b}\right)$ (**Figure 1**).

Let the grading composition by particle size of these components be known. The average values over fractions $\left(\nu = \overline{1, n_f}\right)$ for the diameter and mass of particles of the components i are determined by the expressions $D_i = \sum_{\nu=1}^{n_f} d_{i\nu}$; $M_i = \sum_{\nu=1}^{n_f} m_{i\nu}$. It is believed that the speed of their centers of mass has correspondingly components $\left(V_{xij}, V_{yij}\right)$ and $\left(V_{rij}, V_{\theta ij}\right)$ in Cartesian (x, y) and polar (r, θ) coordinate systems in the projection onto the plane of the cross section of a mixing drum rotating at an angular speed ω. The choice of centers of coordinate systems depends on the geometry of the working area of the mixing apparatus (**Figure 1**).

Let random scattering by mixing elements $\left(j = \overline{1, n_b}\right)$ specified particles from sets $\left(i = \overline{1, n_k}\right)$ can occur according to two schemes: (A) in the absence of their collisions, when particle motion is observed in practically combined flows i with one direction of distribution, and (B) in the presence of collisions of particles from intersecting flows i. Conditional images of the described circuits A and B are presented at **Figure 2** in the case of mixing two streams of bulk components $(i = 1, 2)$ from one (**Figure 2A**) and two (**Figure 2B**) point sources C_0 for circuit A and points C_1, C_2 for Scheme B.

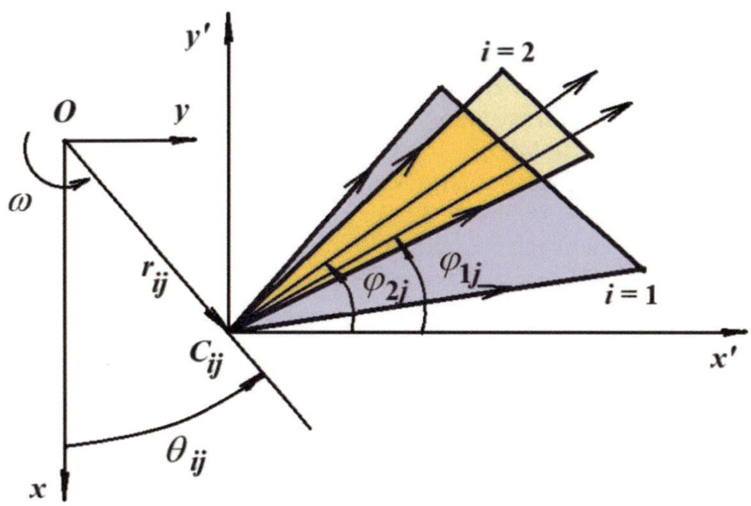

Figure 1.
Conditional coordinate system selection scheme.

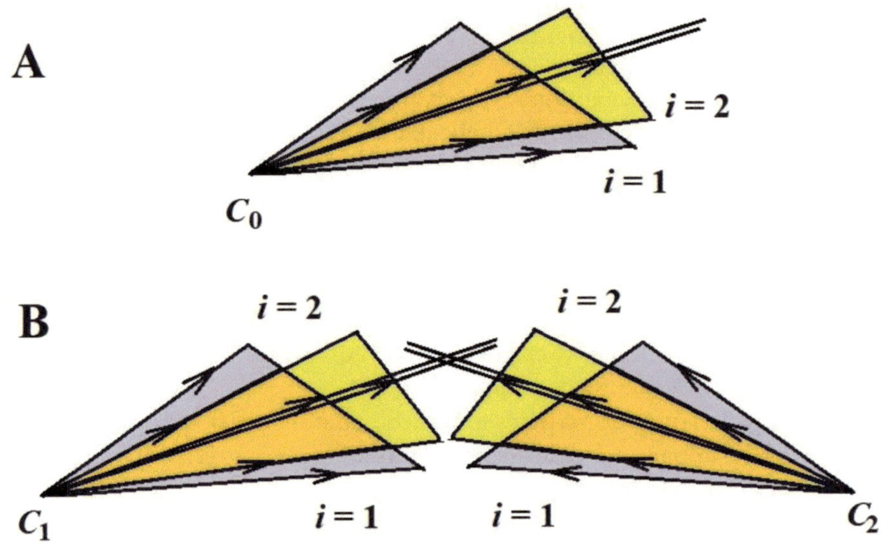

Figure 2.
Scattered images of loose components $(i = 1, 2)$ *sources of* $C_\varepsilon, \varepsilon = 0, 1, 2$*: (A) scheme A; (B) scheme B.*

Each Scheme A and B needs its own stochastic description, taking into account the presence or absence of large-scale fluctuations in the states of the macrosystem, as a set of particles for a component i.

3.2 The case of combining rarefied flows of bulk materials

Scheme A (**Figure 2A**) implies the constancy of the average energy value over the Gibbs ensemble for each macrosystem (bulk component i) in the approximation of the same microsystems (particles of one component i). Coordinate $\left(x_{ij}, y_{ij}\right)$ and impulse $\left(M_{ij}V_{xij}, M_{ij}V_{yij}\right)$ component mass centers i after spreading with a mixing element j in this case play the role of Hamilton parameters. Then, the state of the macrosystem i obeys the principle of maximum entropy, i.e., an increase in entropy characterizes the evolution of a macrosystem to an equilibrium state, and its conservation means the achievement of this equilibrium. Therefore, the random process of mixing granular media according to Scheme A is characterized by instantaneous states of macrosystems i and can be modeled as a homogeneous and stationary process A.A. Markov [9, 10, 25]. In addition, taking into account the approximations of the absence of large-scale particle collisions, a continuous, homogeneous, stationary random Gaussian process is considered. This process obeys the Ornstein-Uhlenbeck formalism [9, 35]; then when choosing an element of the phase volume in the Cartesian and polar coordinate systems

$$d\Omega_{ij} = dV_{xij}dV_{yij} = \omega^2 r_{ij}dr_{ij}d\theta_{ij} \tag{1}$$

Fokker-Planck type kinetic equation for distribution functions $U_{Aij}\left(V_{xij}, V_{yij}, t\right)$ or $u_{Aij}\left(r_{ij}, \theta_{ij}, t\right)$ for the state of macrosystems of particles of mixed components, it has diffusion and drift components. According to Eq. (1) and relations from [34] for phase variables in various coordinate systems

$$\partial\theta_{ij}/\partial V_{xij} = -\left(\omega r_{ij}\right)^{-1}\sin\theta_{ij}, \partial\theta_{ij}/\partial V_{yij} = \left(\omega r_{ij}\right)^{-1}\cos\theta_{ij} \tag{2}$$

we have the following forms of the Fokker-Planck equation for Scheme A of mixing bulk solids (**Figure 2A**):

$$\frac{\partial U_{Aij}(V_{xij}, V_{yij}, t)}{\partial t} = D_{1ij}\frac{\partial^2 U_{Aij}}{\partial V_{xij}{}^2} + D_{2ij}\frac{\partial^2 U_{Aij}}{\partial V_{yij}{}^2} + q_{1ij}\frac{\partial (V_{xij} U_{Aij})}{\partial V_{xij}} + q_{2ij}\frac{\partial (V_{yij} U_{Aij})}{\partial V_{yij}}, \tag{3}$$

$$\begin{aligned}\frac{\partial u_{Aij}(r_{ij}, \theta_{ij}, t)}{\partial t} &= D_{1ij}\left\{\cos^2\theta_{ij}\frac{\partial^2 u_{Aij}}{\partial r_{ij}{}^2} + \frac{\sin^2\theta_{ij}}{r_{ij}}\left[\frac{\partial u_{Aij}}{\partial r_{ij}} + \frac{1}{r_{ij}}\frac{\partial^2 u_{Aij}}{\partial \theta_{ij}{}^2}\right] - \frac{\sin 2\theta_{ij}}{r_{ij}} \times \right.\\ &\left.\times\left[\frac{\partial^2 u_{Aij}}{\partial r_{ij}\partial\theta_{ij}} - \frac{1}{r_{ij}}\frac{\partial u_{Aij}}{\partial \theta_{ij}}\right]\right\} + D_{2ij}\left\{\sin^2\theta_{ij}\frac{\partial^2 u_{Aij}}{\partial r_{ij}{}^2} + \frac{\cos^2\theta_{ij}}{r_{ij}}\left[\frac{\partial u_{Aij}}{\partial r_{ij}} + \frac{1}{r_{ij}}\frac{\partial^2 u_{Aij}}{\partial \theta_{ij}{}^2}\right] + \right.\\ &\left.\frac{\sin 2\theta_{ij}}{r_{ij}}\left[\frac{\partial^2 u_{Aij}}{\partial r_{ij}\partial\theta_{ij}} - \frac{1}{r_{ij}}\frac{\partial u_{Aij}}{\partial \theta_{ij}}\right]\right\} + \left(q_{1ij} + q_{2ij}\right)u_{Aij} + q_{1ij}\left[\cos\theta_{ij}\frac{\partial u_{Aij}}{\partial r_{ij}} - \frac{\sin\theta_{ij}}{r_{ij}}\frac{\partial u_{Aij}}{\partial \theta_{ij}}\right] + \\ &+ q_{2ij}\left[\sin\theta_{ij}\frac{\partial u_{Aij}}{\partial r_{ij}} - \frac{\cos\theta_{ij}}{r_{ij}}\frac{\partial u_{Aij}}{\partial \theta_{ij}}\right].\end{aligned} \tag{4}$$

In Eq. (3), four designations are accepted: D_{1ij}, D_{2ij}, diffusion parameters in the directions of the vectors of the Cartesian velocity components; q_{1ij}, q_{2ij}, drop rates by the mixing element j component particles i; and t, time parameter.

Besides, in Eq. (4) it is advisable to lead to an energy representation regarding the distribution function $u_{Aij}(E_{ij}, t)$:

$$\frac{\partial u_{Aij}(E_{ij}, t)}{\partial t} = \Psi_{A0ij}\left[\frac{\partial}{\partial E_{ij}}\left(E_{ij}\frac{\partial u_{Aij}}{\partial E_{ij}}\right) + \frac{1}{E_{A0ij}}\frac{\partial (E_{ij} u_{Aij})}{\partial E_{ij}}\right], \tag{5}$$

where E_{ij} is the energy of the stochastic motion of the particles of the component i after spreading with a mixing element j; t_0 is the time moment, when there was stochastization of the macrosystems of the particles of each component, i.e., particle motion paths and solutions of dynamic equations acquire a probabilistic nature; and $E_{A0ij} = E_{ij}(t_0)$ is the stationary value of energy E_{ij} at the time of stochastization t_0. The semantic load of the parameter $\Psi_{A0ij} \equiv (dE_{ij}/dt)\big|_{t_0}$ in Eq. (5) corresponds to the flow of energy at the time of stochastization of each of these macrosystems. According to the data of [34], the species in Eqs. (4) and (5) allow us to take the approximation $\Psi_{A0ij} = 4\lambda_{1ij}D_{1ij} = 4\lambda_{2ij}D_{2ij}$, if the energy of the stochastic motion of the particles of the component i in accordance with Eq. (1) is defined by the expression:

$$E_{ij} = \lambda_{1ij} V_{xij}{}^2 + \lambda_{2ij} V_{yij}{}^2 \tag{6}$$

where $\lambda_{1ij}, \lambda_{2ij}$ are the coefficients depending on the structural and operational parameters of the apparatus, as well as the physico-mechanical properties of the mixed bulk materials. The stationary solution of the kinetic equation of the Fokker-Planck type in Eq. (5) subject to Eq. (6) represented in the form of an exponential dependence on energy E_{ij}:

$$u_{Aij}(E_{ij}, t_0) = \alpha_{Aij}\exp\left(-E_{ij}/E_{A0ij}\right) \tag{7}$$

where the normalization parameter α_{Aij} according to Eq. (1) depends on the selected element of the phase volume and is calculated using the equation: $\int_{\Omega_{ij}} u_{Aij} d\Omega_{ij} = 1$.

Thus, the choice of Scheme A (**Figure 2A**) leads to the following form for $u_{1Aij}\left(\varphi_j\right)$, differential particle number distribution function N_{Aij} each component i after spreading with a mixing element j by the selected parameter, for example, the spreading angle φ_j (**Figure 1**), whose reference is determined by the coordinate system used and the geometry of the working volume of the apparatus

$$u_{1Aij}\left(\varphi_j\right) = \left(dN_{Aij}/d\varphi_j\right)/N_{Aij}, \tag{8}$$

if the calculation of the number of particles in the phase volume element $d\Omega_{ij}$ is performed by the formula:

$$dN_{Aij} = \alpha_{1Aij} \exp\left(-E_{ij}/E_{1A0ij}\right)d\Omega_{ij}. \tag{9}$$

In this form $u_{1Aij}\left(\varphi_j\right)$ from Eq. (7) allows to describe $w_{1Ai}\left(\varphi_j\right)$—full functional dependencies for the distribution of the number of particles of the component i after scattering by all deformed mixing elements of the drum according to the selected characteristic of the mixing process φ_j:

$$w_{1Ai}\left(\varphi_j\right) = \prod\nolimits_{j=1}^{n_b} u_{1Aij}\left(\varphi_j\right). \tag{10}$$

So, for use $w_{1Ai}\left(\varphi_j\right)$ in Scheme A (**Figure 2A**), two sets of parameters need to be calculated: normalization parameter α_{1Aij} and stationary value of the energy of stochastic particle motion of the component i after spreading with a mixing element j at the time of stochastization E_{1A0ij}.

3.3 The case of crossing rarefied flows of bulk components

Scheme B (**Figure 2B**) for the random process of mixing bulk solids has a number of significant differences. Taking into account the principles of the energy method of stochastic modeling [10], it is believed that in the case of crossing rarefied flows of loose components, large-scale fluctuations of the states of the corresponding macrosystems are observed, such as collisions of particles that are scattered by two sources symmetrically located at points C_1, C_2. In this case, the small-scale fluctuations of the states of these macrosystems of particles related to their collisions during scattering from each source separately, i.e., in combined rarefied streams. Then, the macrosystems of particles are not energetically closed, and to describe the evolution of their states, it is proposed to apply the formalism of random sources of Langevin in the Fokker-Planck kinetic equation according to the energy approach from [10]. In this case, the ordering of the states of the macrosystems of the components is characterized by the S-theorem for the Lyapunov function, given by the change in the values of the Boltzmann-Gibbs-Shannon entropy for different states of each macrosystem when the energy index is averaged. The decisive role in finding the control parameters of the random mixing process to achieve the state of ordering of the component macrosystems belongs to the operation of renormalization of the Boltzmann-Gibbs-Shannon entropy.

Therefore, with the introduction g_{1ij}, g_{2ij}—collision coefficients as large-scale fluctuations—the presence of Langevin sources leads to the following changes in the notation of the Fokker-Planck kinetic equation with respect to the distribution function $U_{Bij}(V_{xij}, V_{yij}, t)$ or $u_{Bij}(r_{ij}, \theta_{ij}, t)$ in contrast to the species in Eq. (3) according to Eq. (2):

$$\begin{aligned}\frac{\partial U_{Bij}(V_{xij}, V_{yij}, t)}{\partial t} = D_{1ij}\frac{\partial^2 U_{Bij}}{\partial V_{xij}{}^2} + D_{2ij}\frac{\partial^2 U_{Bij}}{\partial V_{yij}{}^2} + q_{1ij}\frac{\partial (V_{xij}U_{Bij})}{\partial V_{xij}} + q_{2ij}\frac{\partial (V_{yij}U_{Bij})}{\partial V_{yij}} \\ + g_{1ij}\frac{\partial (V_{xij}E_{ij}U_{Bij})}{\partial v_{xij}} + g_{2ij}\frac{\partial (V_{yij}E_{ij}U_{Bij})}{\partial v_{yij}},\end{aligned} \tag{11}$$

$$\begin{aligned}\frac{\partial u_{Bij}(r_{ij}, \theta_{ij}, t)}{\partial t} &= D_{1ij}\left\{\cos^2\theta_{ij}\frac{\partial^2 u_{Bij}}{\partial r_{ij}{}^2} + \frac{\sin^2\theta_{ij}}{r_{ij}}\left[\frac{\partial u_{Bij}}{\partial r_{ij}} + \frac{1}{r_{ij}}\frac{\partial^2 u_{Bij}}{\partial \theta_{ij}{}^2}\right] - \frac{\sin 2\theta_{ij}}{r_{ij}}\times\right. \\ &\times\left.\left[\frac{\partial^2 u_{Bij}}{\partial r_{ij}\partial\theta_{ij}} - \frac{1}{r_{ij}}\frac{\partial u_{Bij}}{\partial \theta_{ij}}\right]\right\} + D_{2ij}\left\{\sin^2\theta_{ij}\frac{\partial^2 u_{Bij}}{\partial r_{ij}{}^2} + \frac{\cos^2\theta_{ij}}{r_{ij}}\left[\frac{\partial u_{Bij}}{\partial r_{ij}} + \frac{1}{r_{ij}}\frac{\partial^2 u_{Bij}}{\partial \theta_{ij}{}^2}\right] + \right. \\ &\left.\frac{\sin 2\theta_{ij}}{r_{ij}}\left[\frac{\partial^2 u_{Bij}}{\partial r_{ij}\partial\theta_{ij}} - \frac{1}{r_{ij}}\frac{\partial u_{Bij}}{\partial \theta_{ij}}\right]\right\} + \left(q_{1ij} + q_{2ij}\right)u_{Bij} + q_{1ij}\left[\cos\theta_{ij}\frac{\partial u_{Bij}}{\partial r_{ij}} - \frac{\sin\theta_{ij}}{r_{ij}}\frac{\partial u_{Bij}}{\partial \theta_{ij}}\right] + \\ &+ q_{2ij}\left[\sin\theta_{ij}\frac{\partial u_{Bij}}{\partial r_{ij}} - \frac{\cos\theta_{ij}}{r_{ij}}\frac{\partial u_{Bij}}{\partial \theta_{ij}}\right] + g_{1ij}\left[\cos\theta_{ij}\frac{\partial (E_{ij}u_{Bij})}{\partial r_{ij}} - \frac{\sin\theta_{ij}}{r_{ij}}\frac{\partial (E_{ij}u_{Bij})}{\partial \theta_{ij}}\right] + \\ &+ g_{2ij}\left[\sin\theta_{ij}\frac{\partial (E_{ij}u_{Bij})}{\partial r_{ij}} - \frac{\cos\theta_{ij}}{r_{ij}}\frac{\partial (E_{ij}u_{Bij})}{\partial \theta_{ij}}\right].\end{aligned} \tag{12}$$

Similar to Eq. (5), it is convenient in the future to use the energy representation of the Fokker-Planck equation with respect to the distribution function $u_{Bij}(E_{ij}, t)$

$$\frac{\partial u_{Bij}(E_{ij}, t)}{\partial t} = \left(\Psi_{B0ij}\Psi_{fij}\right)^{1/2}\left[\frac{\partial}{\partial E_{ij}}\left(E_{ij}\frac{\partial u_{Bij}}{\partial E_{ij}}\right) + \frac{1}{E_{B0ij}}\frac{\partial (E_{ij}u_{Bij})}{\partial E_{ij}} + \frac{1}{E_{fij}{}^2}\frac{\partial (E_{ij}{}^2 u_{Bij})}{\partial E_{ij}}\right], \tag{13}$$

where $E_{B0ij} = E_{ij}(t_0)$; $\Psi_{B0ij} \equiv \left(dE_{ij}/dt\right)\big|_{t_0}$ have the same physical meaning as in Eq. (5); $E_{fij} \equiv E_{ij}(\Delta t)$, particle energy loss of each component i after spreading with a mixing element j in collisions, as macroscale fluctuations of the states of the system over a period of time Δt; and $\Psi_{fij} \equiv \left(dE_{ij}/dt\right)\big|_{\Delta t}$, changes in these energy losses over Δt.

In particular, on the basis of the approach [10], the parameters were identified in [34] $\mu_{ijk}, k = 0, 1, 2, 3$ for the random process of mixing bulk materials: manager $\mu_{ij0} = \left(\Psi_{B0ij}\Psi_{fij}\right)^{1/2}/E_{B0ij}$ and optimizing $\mu_{ij1} = \left(\Psi_{B0ij}\Psi_{fij}\right)^{1/2}$; $\mu_{ij2} = \left(\Psi_{B0ij}\Psi_{fij}\right)^{1/2}/E_{B0ij}{}^2$; $\mu_{ij3} = \Psi_{fij}/E_{fij}$. Note that, if necessary, estimates of diffusion parameters in the directions of the vectors of the Cartesian velocity components D_{1ij}, D_{2ij} can be used through the method proposed in the work [37].

In addition, the main stages of the formation of rarefied flows corresponding to various states of component macrosystems were identified in [34]:

- Smoothing out small-scale fluctuations of the states of macrosystems during the dropping of particles from deformed mixing elements in the region of combining rarefied flows, when $\mu_{ij0} = 0$ and $\Psi_{B0ij} << 1$ rightly for Eq. (7)

- Nucleation of large-scale fluctuations in the states of macrosystems of mixed components at the boundary of the regions of overlapping and crossing of their rarefied flows, if the state of the regeneration threshold is realized $\mu_{ij0} = \mu_{ij3}$ with a solution of the form $u_{ABij} = \alpha_{ABij} \exp\left[-E_{ij}{}^2 (2E_{AB0ij})^{-1}\right]$ for Eq. (13)

- An increase in energy losses with an increasing intensity of large-scale fluctuations in the states of macrosystems of mixed components i in the area of crossing of their rarefied flows, when the regeneration mode can be implemented, a transition to a new stationary state in a certain range of variation of the control parameter μ_{ij0}

In the latter case, the solution Eq. (13) corresponds to the regime of advanced regeneration, when the relations $\mu_{ij0}\mu_{ij3}{}^{-1} < <1$ and $\mu_{ij1}\mu_{ij2}\mu_{ij0}{}^{-2} < <1$ are true

$$u_{Bij} = \alpha_{Bij} \exp\left[-E_{ij}/E_{B0ij} + E_{ij}{}^2/(2E_{fij})\right] \tag{14}$$

where α_{Bij} is the normalization parameter taking into account Eq. (1) determined from the equation $\int_{\Omega_{ij}} u_{Bij} d\Omega_{ij} = 1$.

Therefore, the choice of Scheme B (**Figure 2B**) allows according to Eq. (14) to build dependencies $u_{1Bij}(\varphi_j)$ for differential distribution functions of the number of particles N_{Bij} of each component i after spreading by the mixing element j, for example, by the spread angle φ_j (**Figure 1**), in this case, similar to Eq. (8), (9) we have

$$u_{1Bij}(\varphi_j) = (dN_{Bij}/d\varphi_j)/N_{Bij}, \tag{15}$$

$$dN_{Bij} = \alpha_{1Bij} \exp\left(-E_{ij}/E_{1B0ij}\right) d\Omega_{ij}. \tag{16}$$

Then, when describing the complete differential distribution functions of the number of particles of the components after scattering by all deformed mixing elements of the drum in the corner φ_j, as in Eq. (10), dependencies are used $u_{1Bij}(\varphi_j)$ from Eq. (15):

$$w_{1Bi}(\varphi_j) = \prod_{j=1}^{n_b} u_{1Bij}(\varphi_j) M_i V_{r\theta ij}^2/2L_{ij}{}^2/(2I_i)k_u\theta_{ij}{}^2/2. \tag{17}$$

So for analysis $u_{1Bij}(\varphi_j)$ in Scheme B (**Figure 2B**), it is necessary to carry out the calculation of three sets of parameters: normalization parameter α_{1Bij}; stationary value of the energy of stochastic motion of the particles of the component i after spreading with mixing element j at the time of stochastization E_{1B0ij}; and particle energy loss of each component after interacting with the mixing element j in interparticle collisions E_{fij}.

4. The results of stochastic modeling of the motion of bulk components in rarefied flows during their mixing

We give some examples of the application of stochastic mixing models built on the basis of the energy method [9, 10] according to the two motion schemes of rarefied flows of bulk components considered in paragraph 3. Initially, we set the type of energy of the stochastic motion of particles of mixed components $i = 1, 2$

after spreading with a mixing element j. As the working volumes of the mixing apparatus, we will choose the elements of a number of designs, for example, [11–13]. In all three cases, rarefied flows are ensured by the spreading of particles of bulk materials i with the help of mixing elements fixed on rotating drums in the form of flexible bills located along a helical line [11]; brushes installed with multidirectional screw coils [12]; and elastic blades in tangent planes to the surface of the drum [13]. In designs [11, 13], the mixing process is carried out on a movable tape, in the apparatus [12]—on the tray of gravity equipment. The geometry features of drum mixing devices [11, 13] allow the mixing process to be carried out according to Scheme A when combining rarefied flows (**Figure 2A**) and for the apparatus [12] according to Scheme B when they are crossed (**Figure 2B**). Let the energy E_{ij} consists of three components, taking into account the translational movement of the particle of the component in the transverse plane of the cross section of the mixing drum i together with its center of mass $(M_i V^2_{r\theta ij}/2)$, rotational motion relative to it $({L_{ij}}^2/(2I_i))$, and elastic interaction with a deformed mixing element $(k_u {\theta_{ij}}^2/2)$. Here, in addition to the notation from paragraph 2, the following are additionally introduced: L_{ij}, random moments of impulses; I_i, axial moments of inertia; and k_u, angular stiffness of the mixing element. According to Eq. (1), (6) dependence $E_{ij}\left(r_{ij}, \theta_{ij}\right)$ with averaged values $\theta_{im} = (1/n_b)\sum_{j=1}^{n_b}\theta_{ij}$ by the number of deformed mixing elements has a general view $E_{ij} = \varepsilon_{1ij}(\theta_{im}){r_{ij}}^2 + \varepsilon_2{\theta_{ij}}^2$.

Without dwelling in detail on the analysis of the features of each model for the indicated types of mixing apparatuses, we present some of their results to illustrate the possibility of a preliminary assessment of the effectiveness of the process of mixing bulk components. Note that the model parameters are the design and operating parameters of the mixer, as well as the physical and mechanical characteristics of the working media and mixing elements (in particular, angular stiffness $k_u = 1.6 \times 10^{-4}$kg × m/rad). The working bulk materials include natural sand GOST 8736-93 ($D_i = 1.5 \times 10^{-4}$ m, $\rho_i = 1.525 \times 10^3$ kg/m^3) and soda ash GOST 5100-85 ($D_i = 1.75 \times 10^{-4}$ m, $\rho_i = 1.08 \times 10^3$ kg/m^3). The calculations were performed using the software xwMaxima18.02.0; for visualization, the gnuplot 5.2 environment was used.

An example of the results of stochastic modeling of obtaining a granular mixture in the presence of natural sand GOST 8736-93 in combined rarefied flows (Scheme A; **Figure 2A**) [4, 30, 31] when they are scattered from a movable belt by flexible bills located along a helix on the surface of a rotating drum in a mixer [11] on **Figure 3** shows a family of surfaces for dependencies $u_{1A2j}\left(\varphi_j, \Delta\right)$ and $w_{1A2}\left(\varphi_j, \Delta\right)$ according to Eq. (1) (7)-(10). An analysis of these functions shows a significant effect of the complex parameter $\Delta = h_0/l_b$, characterizing the degree of deformation of flexible bill length l_b after leaving the height gap h_0 between the tape and the drum on the distribution of the number of component particles ($i = 2$) after elastic interaction with the bills j. Therefore, in addition to the operational parameter (angular velocity of rotation of the drum), there are other significant factors affecting the process under study. As was shown earlier [4, 30, 31], the design parameters of the apparatus can be attributed to such factors: step of screw winding h_s for the flexible bill. Note that the radius also belongs to the set of design parameters r_b and length L_b of drum. The classes of parameters of this mixing process are discussed in more detail in [4, 30, 31].

An example of the implementation of the conditions for mixing bulk components with crossed rarefied streams (Scheme B; **Figure 2B**) is the operation of the gravitational apparatus when scattering mixed materials from its tray with brush elements mounted with multidirectional screw windings on a rotating drum [12].

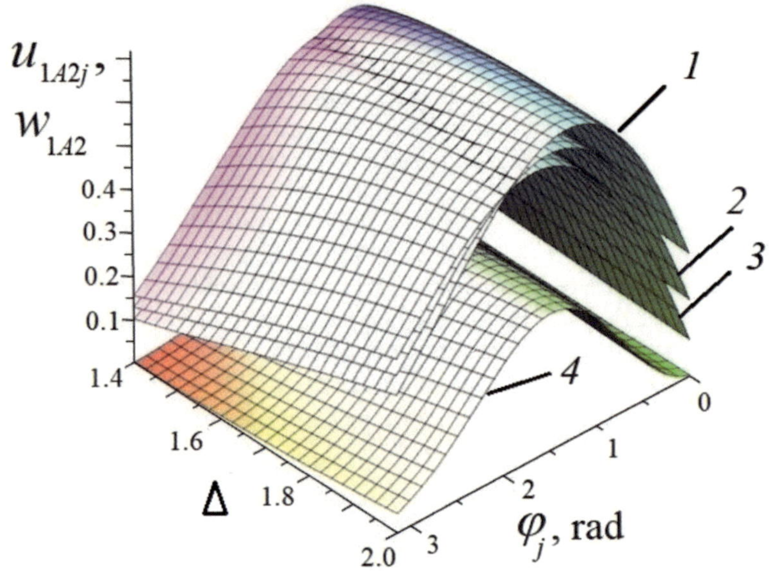

Figure 3.
Dependencies $u_{1A2j}(\varphi_j, \Delta), w_{1A2}(\varphi_j, \Delta)$ *for natural sand GOST 8736-93*$(i = 2)$ *when scattering from a movable belt with flexible bills located along a helix on the surface of a rotating drum (Scheme A):* $\omega = 52.36\,c^{-1}$; $h_s = 1.6 \times 10^{-2}$ *m;* $r_b = 3.0 \times 10^{-2}$ *m;* $L_b = 1.85 \times 10^{-1}$ *m;* $l_b = 4.5 \times 10^{-2}$ *m; 1,* $j = 1$*; 2,* $j = 2$*; 3,* $j = 3$ *for* $u_{1A2j}(\varphi_j, \Delta)$*; and 4, for* $w_{1A2}(\varphi_j, \Delta)$.

According to the stochastic modeling performed by the authors [2, 32–34] in accordance with Eq. (1), (14)-(17), we give the dependencies $u_{1B2j}(\varphi_j, \Delta)$ for soda ash GOST 5100-85$(i = 2)$ (**Figure 4**).

In this case, a detailed analysis of the simulation results given in [2, 34] revealed the conditions for the effective mixing of bulk components, as a result of the convergence of the spreading angles corresponding to the extrema for each working solid-dispersed medium. The obtained dependencies for distribution functions

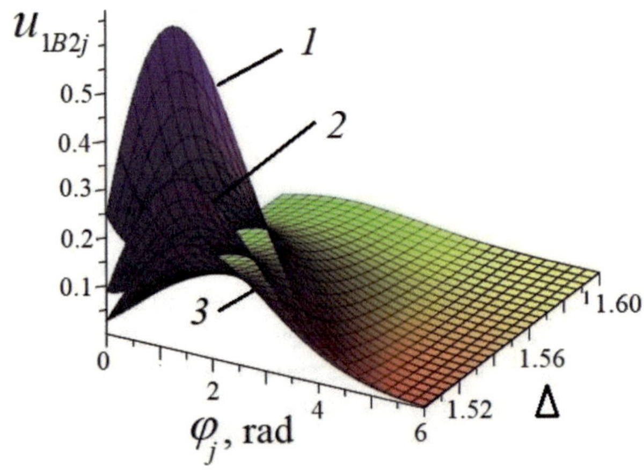

Figure 4.
Dependencies $u_{1B2j}(\varphi_j, \Delta)$ *for soda ash GOST 5100-85*$(i = 2)$ *when scattering the gravitational apparatus from the tray with brush elements installed with multidirectional screw windings on a rotating drum (scheme B):* $\omega = 52.36\,c^{-1}$; $h_s = 1.6 \times 10^{-2}$ *m;* $r_b = 3.0 \times 10^{-2}$ *m;* $L_b = 1.85 \times 10^{-1}$ *m;* $l_b = 4.5 \times 10^{-2}$ *m; 1,* $j = 1$*; 2,* $j = 2$*; and 3,* $j = 3$.

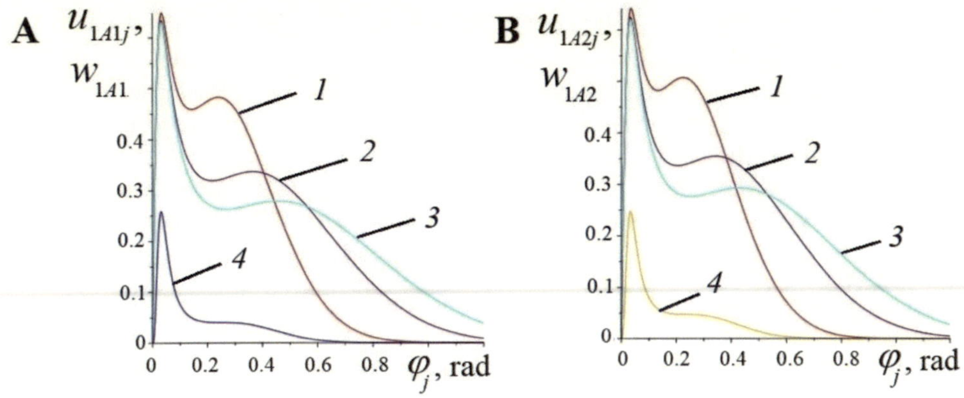

Figure 5.
Dependencies when scattering loose components from a movable belt with elastic blades in tangent planes to the surface of the mixing drum (scheme A): A, soda ash GOST 5100-85 ($i = 1$); B, natural sand GOST 8736-93 ($i = 2$); $\omega = 52.36\ c^{-1}$; $r_b = 3.0 \times 10^{-2}$ m; $L_b = 1.85 \times 10^{-1}$ m; $l_b = 4.5 \times 10^{-2}$ m; 1, $j = 1$; 2, $j = 2$; 3, $j = 3$ for $u_{1Aij}(\varphi_j)$; and 4, for $w_{1A2}(\varphi_j)$.

$u_{1A2j}(\varphi_j, \Delta)$ and $u_{1B2j}(\varphi_j, \Delta)$ shown on **Figures 3** and **4** have a general character with a pronounced maximum of the operating ranges of parameter changes and are confirmed experimentally [2, 34] with a relative error not exceeding 18% for scheme A and 12% for scheme B.

Let us show that in the case of scattering of loose components from the moving tape by elastic blades fixed in tangent planes to the surface of the mixing drum [13], the result of the implementation of scheme A (**Figure 2A, Figure 5**) may not be inferior in its efficiency to the operation of scheme B (**Figure 2B**) for rational choice of design and operational parameters of the device.

In particular, when modeling in the plane of the cross section of the drum the equations of motion of the end points of the elastic blades using the Archimedes spiral equation, the application in Eq. (1) (7)-(9) allows you to get dependencies

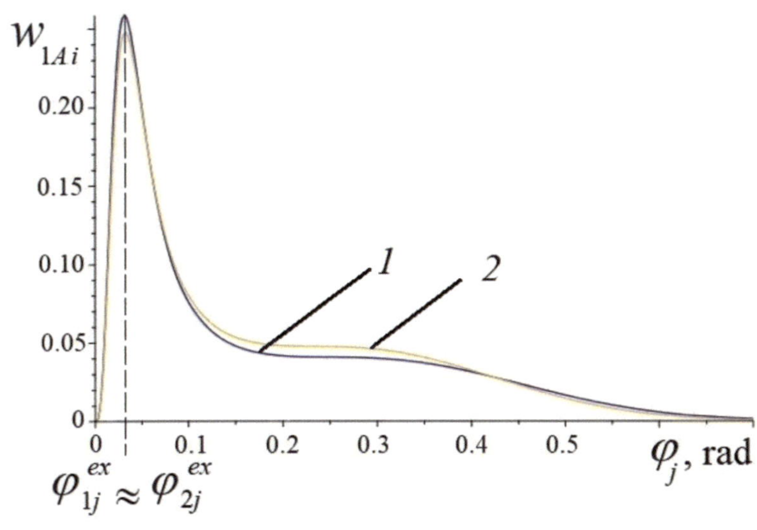

Figure 6.
Comparison of dependencies when scattering loose components from a moving tape with elastic blades in tangent planes to the surface of the mixing drum (scheme A): 1, soda ash GOST 5100-85 ($i = 1$); 2, natural sand GOST 8736-93 ($i = 2$); $\omega = 52.36\ c^{-1}$; $r_b = 3.0 \times 10^{-2}$ m; $L_b = 1.85 \times 10^{-1}$ m; $l_b = 4.5 \times 10^{-2}$ m.

$u_{1Aij}\left(\varphi_j\right)$ or soda ash GOST 5100-85 (**Figure 5A**) and natural sand GOST 8736-93 (**Figure 5B**). The presented families of curves show that the bulk of each bulk material when they are mixed is scattered with elastic blades at the initial angles of rotation of the drum (see the first burst on the graphs *1–3*; **Figure 5A**, **Figure 5B**). Moreover, there is the possibility of subsequent self-cleaning of the deformed mixing elements when the angular coordinate of the ends is less than 0.758 rad (see the second surge in the charts *1–3*; **Figure 5A**, **Figure 5B**). Benchmarking dependencies $w_{1Ai}\left(\varphi_j\right)$ (**Figure 6**) showed preferably the cleaning of the blades at the initial stage of restoration of their geometric shape.

In addition, according to **Figure 6**, the conditions for efficient mixing of bulk components are observed. $i = 1, 2$ due to the approach of not only extreme angular values $\varphi_{1j}^{ex} \approx \varphi_{2j}^{ex}$ for scattering angles of mixed materials but also the behavior of functional dependencies $w_{1A1}\left(\varphi_j\right)$ and $w_{1A2}\left(\varphi_j\right)$ (see bends of curves 1 and 2; **Figure 6**), in particular, the attitude $w_{1A2}\left(\varphi_{2j}^{ex}\right)/w_{1A1}\left(\varphi_{1j}^{ex}\right) \approx 0.94$.

5. Conclusions

The paper provides a brief analysis of the current state of the current direction of mathematical modeling of the process of mixing bulk components—stochastic methods for describing this technological operation. Moreover, for these purposes, the feasibility of applying the energy method proposed by Klimontovich [9, 10], due to the possibility of obtaining analytical dependences for the distribution functions of bulk components according to the selected characteristic indicator of the random process under study, takes into account the peculiarities of the state of macrosystems of mixed particles. The energy approach has been adapted to describe the mechanism of behavior of particles of loose components during their mixing in rarefied flows according to the two schemes: in combination (scheme A, neglecting collisions of different particles) and crossing (scheme B, taking into account their collisions) of rarefaction areas of mixed solid-dispersed media.

As an illustration of the work of the energy method, a generalization of the results of stochastic modeling of the formation of rarefied flows of bulk components in various working volumes of mechanical type mixers obtained on the basis of author's models that have passed verification is given. In particular, cases are considered when scattering particles of bulk materials using mixing elements fixed on rotating drums in the form of flexible bills located along a helix, according to the results of models [4, 30, 31], and brushes installed with multidirectional screw windings, according to models [2, 32–34].

Additionally, results of the stochastic model of the formation of rarefied flows of granular media when they are scattered by elastic blades mounted in tangent planes to the surface of the mixing drum are presented [13]. In particular, for this case, the analysis of the application of the described modeling method for scheme A was performed when smoothing small-scale fluctuations in the state of the macrosystems of these components due to the approximation of the unidirectional motion of different-sized particles in combined flows. It was found that at an angular rotation speed of the mixing drum of 52.36 s^{-1}, the range of variation of the spread angle for mixed bulk materials (soda ash GOST 5100-85 and natural sand GOST 8736-93) is limited by 0.758 rad excluding dispersion intervals. In particular, a pronounced discharge of particles by deformable mixing elements is observed at the initial rotation angles of the drum. Theoretical confirmation of the possible implementation of the conditions for the effective mixing of bulk components when scattering with elastic blades on the example of obtaining a mixture of soda ash GOST 5100-85 and natural sand GOST 8736-93, reflecting the convergence of the distribution curves for the number of particles of different grades according to their scattering angle, when the following relations of values are obtained $w_{1A2}\left(\varphi_{2j}^{ex}\right)/w_{1A1}\left(\varphi_{1j}^{ex}\right)\approx 0.94$; $\varphi_{2j}^{ex}/\varphi_{1j}^{ex}\approx 1$.

The obtained analytical differential functions of the distribution of the number of particles according to the characteristic indicator of the random process under study according to the author's models [4, 34] are used to preliminarily limit the limits of variation of the design and operating parameters [31], evaluate the quality of the mixture [4, 38] and the performance of the device [39], and predict effective equipment operation modes [30]; the selection of rational ranges of parameter changes [2, 33].

Conflict of interest

The authors declare that the research was conducted in the absence of any commercial or financial relationships that could be construed as a potential conflict of interest.

Author contributions

All authors contributed to manuscript revision, read, and approved the submitted version.

Author details

Anna Kapranova*, Daria Bahaeva, Dmitry Stenko, Ivan Verloka, Anton Lebedev and Mikhail Tarshis
Yaroslavl State Technical University, Yaroslavl, Russian Federation

*Address all correspondence to: kapranova_anna@mail.ru

References

[1] Shaul S, Rabinovich E, Kalman H. Generalized flow regime diagram of fluidized beds based on the height to bed diameter ratio. Powder Technology. 2012;**228**:264-271. DOI: 10.1016/j.powtec.2012.05.029

[2] Kapranova AB, Verloka II, Bahaeva DD. About preparation of the analytical platform for creation of a cyber-physical system of industrial mixture of loose components. In: Kravets A, Bolshakov A, Shcherbakov M, editors. Monograph: Cyber-Physical Systems: Advances in Design & Modelling. Studies in Systems, Decision and Control. Vol. 259. Cham: Springer; 2020. pp. 81-91. DOI: 10.1007/978-3-030-32579-4_7

[3] Bauman I, Curic D, Boban M. Mixing of solids in different mixing devices. Sadhana. 2008;**33**(6):721-731. DOI: 10.1007/s12046-008-0030-5

[4] Kapranova AB, Bakin MN, Verloka II. Simulation of the quality criterion of a mixture in a drum-belt apparatus. Chemical and Petroleum Engineering. 2018;**54**(5):287-297. DOI: 10.1007/s10556-018-0477-0. More about changing the spelling of the author's name. 2018;**54**(7-8):618. DOI: 10.1007/s10556-018-0524-x

[5] Rosato AD, Zuo L, Blackmore D, et al. Tapped granular column dynamics: Simulations, experiments and modeling. Computational Particle Mechanics. 2016;**3**(3):333-348. DOI: 10.1007/s40571-015-0075-2

[6] Anchal J, Matthew JM, Benjamin J. Effect of particle size distribution on segregation in vibrated systems. Powder Technology. 2013;**237**:543-553. DOI: 10.1016/j.powtec.2012.12.044

[7] Kapranova AB. Stochastic model of parallel or sequential processes of deaeration and mixing of granular media using the operation of a centrifugal device as an example. Theoretical Foundations of Chemical Engineering. 2018;**53**(2):292-304. DOI: 10.1134/S004057951901007X

[8] Lim KS, Zhu JX, Grace JR. Hydrodynamics of gas-solid fluidization. International Journal of Multiphase Flow. 1995;**21**:141-193. DOI: 10.1016/0301-9322(95)00038-Y

[9] Klimontovich Yu L. Turbulent Motion and the Structure of Chaos. Series: Fundamental Theories of Physics. Vol. 42. Netherlands: Springer; 1991. p. 401. DOI: 10.1007/978-94-011-3426-2

[10] Klimontovich Yu L. Turbulent Motion and the Structure of Chaos: A New Approach to the Statistical Theory of Open Systems. 4th ed. Moscow: Lenand; 2014. p. 328

[11] Zaitzev AI, Lebedev AE, Bakin MN, Petrov AA, Volkov AN. Unit for mixing bulk materials. Pat. 2506208. IPC 65 V 1/36. Bull. No. 4. Publ. 02.10.2014; Russian Federation. February 2014

[12] Zaitzev AI, Lebedev AE, Kapranova AB, Verloka II. Gravity-type bulk solids mixer. Patent 2586126. IPC B01F3/18. Bull. No. 16. Publ. 06.10.2016. Russian Federation; June 2016

[13] Lebedev AE, Vatagin AA, Borisovsky ME, Romanova MN, Badaeva NV, Sheronina IS. Unit for mixing and compaction of loose materials. Utility Model Patent: 2624698. B01F3/18. Bull. No. 19. Publ. 07.05.2017. Russian Federation; July 2017

[14] Protodyakonov IO, Lyublinskaya IE, Ryzhkov AE. Hydrodynamics and Mass Transfer in

Dispersed Liquid-Solid Systems. Leningrad: Chemistry; 1987. p. 336

[15] Leonchik BI, Mayakin VP. Measurements in Dispersed Flows. Moscow: Energy; 1985. p. 248

[16] Dehling HG, Gottschalk T, Hoffmann AC. Stochastic Modeling in Process Technology. London: Elsevier Science; 2007. p. 279

[17] Kordas M, Pluskota D, Rakoczy R. The characterization of the residence time distribution in a fluid mixer by means of the information entropy. In: Practical Aspects of Chemical Engineering. 2018. pp. 201-216. DOI: 10.1007/978-3-319-73978-6_14

[18] Geng T, Sau LL, Ya X, Moo SHA. Dimensionless analysis of residence time distributions for continuous powder mixing. Powder Technology. 2017;**315**:332-338. DOI: 10.1016/j.powtec.2017.04.007

[19] Sen M, Barrasso D, Singh R, Ramachandran R. A multi-scale hybrid CFD-DEM-PBM description of a fluid-bed granulation process. Processes. 2014;**2**(1):89-111. DOI: 10.3390/pr2010089

[20] Kendall MG, Stuart A. The Advanced Theory of Statistics, Vol. 2. Inference and Relationship. 4th ed. New York: Haffner; 1967. p. 690

[21] Johnson N, Kendall M, Stuart A. Review (The Advanced Theory of Statistics: Volume I (1958): Distribution Theory; The Advanced Theory of Statistics. Volume II (1961): Inference and Relationship. by M. G. Kendall; A. Stuart). Journal of the Royal Statistical Society Series D (The Statistician). 1962;**12**(2):138-142. DOI: 10.2307/2987065

[22] Ghaderi A. Continuous mixing of particulate materials. In: Proceedings of the 4th International Conference for Conveying and Handling of Particulate Solids, at Budapest, Hungary, Vol. 2. January 2003. DOI: 10.13140/2.1.3487.6801

[23] Bharucha-Reid AT. Elements of the Theory of Markov Processes and Their Applications. New York: McGraw-Hill; 1960

[24] Papoulis A. Brownian movement and Markoff processes. In: Ch. 15 in Probability, Random Variables, and Stochastic Processes. 2nd ed. New York: McGraw-Hill; 1984. pp. 515-553

[25] Röpke G. Statistical Mechanics for Non-Equilibrium. Berlin: German Publishing House of Sciences; 1987

[26] Mizonov V, Balagurov I, Berthiaux H, Gatumel C. Gatumel Markov chain model of mixing kinetics for ternary mixture of dissimilar particulate solids. Particuology. 2016;**31**: 80-86. DOI: 10.1016/j.partic.2016.05.006

[27] Zhuang Y, Chen X, Liu D. Stochastic bubble developing model combined with Markov process of particles for bubbling fluidized beds. Chemical Engineering Journal. 2016;**291**:206-214. DOI: 10.1016/j.cej.2016.01.095

[28] Kafarov VV, Dorokhov IN, Arutyunov SY. System analysis of chemical technology processes. In: The Processes of Grinding and Mixing Bulk Materials. Moscow: Nauka; 1985. p. 440

[29] Zhukov VP, Belyakov AN. Simulation of combined heterogeneous processes based on discrete models of the Boltzmann equation. Theoretical Foundations of Chemical Engineering. 2017;**51**(1):88-93. DOI: 10.1134/S0040579517010158

[30] Kapranova AB, Bakin MN, Zaitzev AI. Taking into account the granulometric composition of media when describing their mixing in an

apparatus with a moving tape. Bulletin of Tamb. State Technical University. 2014;**20**(4):754-757. DOI: 10.0000/cyberleninka.ru/article/n/uchet-granulometricheskogo-sostava-sred-pri-opisanii-ih-smeshivaniya-v-apparate-s-podvizhnoy-lentoy

[31] Kapranova AB, Bakin MN, Verloka II, Zaitzev AI. Influence of the moisture content of granular media on their distribution in the working volume of a mixer with a movable belt. Bulletin of Tamb. State Technical University. 2015;**21**(1):97-104. DOI: 10.17277/vestnik.2015.01.pp.097-104. ISSN: 0136-5835

[32] Kapranova AB, Verloka II, Lebedev AE, Zaitzev AI. The model of dispersion of particles during their flow from chipping the surface. Czasopismo Techniczne. Mechanika Krakov, Poland. 2016;**113**(2):145-150. Available from: http://www.ejournals.eu/sj/index.php/Cz/article/view/6714/pdf_835

[33] Verloka I, Kapranova A, Tarshis M, Cherpitsky S. Stochastic modeling of bulk components batch mixing process in gravity apparatus. International Journal of Mechanical Engineering & Technology (IJMET). 2018;**9**(2): 438-444. Article ID: IJMET_09_02_045. Available online at http://www.iaeme.com/IJMET/issues.asp?JType=IJMET&VType=9&IType=2

[34] Kapranova AB, Verloka II. Stochastic description of the formation of flows of particulate components in apparatuses with brush elements. The oretical Foundations of Chemical Eng ineering. 2018;**52**(6):1004-1018. DOI: 10.1134/S0040579518050330

[35] Zaitsev AI, Bytev DO. Impact Processes in the Dispersion-Film Systems. Moscow: Chemistry; 1994. p. 176

[36] Kapranova AB, Lebedev AE, Bytev DO, Zaitzev AI. Stochastic description of the motion of the clarified fraction of a suspension of powders. News of Higher Educational Institutions. Chemistry and Chemical Technology–Ivanovo. 2004;**47**(6): 99-101. Available from: https://www.elibrary.ru/author_items.asp?authorid=337327&titleid=7726

[37] Kapranova AB. Method for determining the coefficient of macrodiffusion in the process of mixing solid dispersed media in a centrifugal apparatus. Mathematical Modeling. 2009;**21**(3):83-94. Available from: http://www.mathnet.ru/php/archive.phtml?wshow=paper&jrnid=mm&paperid=2749&option_lang=rus; https://www.elibrary.ru/item.asp?id=21276331

[38] Kapranova AB, Verloka II, Yakovlev PA, Bahaeva DD. Investigation of the quality of mixture at the first stage of work of the gravitational type apparatus. Russian Chemical Journal (Journal of the Chemical Society named after D. I. Mendeleev). 2018;**62**(4):48-50. Available from: https://www.elibrary.ru/item.asp?id=36290375

[39] Kapranova A, Verloka I, Bahaeva D, Tarshis M. Factors of increasing the performance of the bulk material mixer of the gravity type. In: Anatolijs B, Nikolai V, Vitalii S, editors. Proceedings of EECE 2019. EECE 2019: Lecture Notes in Civil Engineering. Vol. 70. Cham: Springer; 2020. pp. 337-347. DOI: 10.1007/978-3-030-42351-3_30

Chapter 3

Mathematical Modelling and Numerical Simulation of Diffusive Processes in Slow Changing Domains

Dmytro V. Yevdokymov and Yuri L. Menshikov

Abstract

Nowadays, diffusion and heat conduction processes in slow changing domains attract great attention. Slow-phase transitions and growth of biological structures can be considered as examples of such processes. The main difficulty in numerical solutions of correspondent problems is connected with the presence of two time scales. The first one is time scale describing diffusion or heat conduction. The second time scale is connected with the mentioned slow domain evolution. If there is sufficient difference in order of the listed time scale, strong computational difficulties in application of time-stepping algorithms are observed. To overcome the mentioned difficulties, it is proposed to apply a small parameter method for obtaining a new mathematical model, in which the starting parabolic initial-boundary-value problem is replaced by a sequence of elliptic boundary-value problems. Application of the boundary element method for numerical solution of the obtained sequence of problems gives an opportunity to solve the whole considered problem in slow time with high accuracy specific to the mentioned algorithm. Besides that, questions about convergence of the obtained asymptotic expansion and correspondence between initial and obtained formulations of the problem are considered separately. The proposed numerical approach is illustrated by several examples of numerical calculations for relevant problems.

Keywords: moving boundary problem, Stefan problem, biological tissue growth, asymptotic method, heat conduction equation, diffusion equation, Laplace equation, boundary element method

1. Introduction

Processes in moving boundary domains are commonly known starting from antiquity. Freezing of water with ice creation and an inverse process, when ice melts, evidently show how important this class of phenomena for environmental sciences. Similar processes of solidification and melting create physical background for most technologies of metal or other material productions. Even the mentioned two examples are enough to understand an urgency of the considered problems. However, beside of that, free surface fluid flows, shock wave propagations in gases, growing processes in biological tissues, virus dynamics can be classified as moving boundary problems too. Thus, a number of relevant problems are so many, that they require huge efforts for their mathematical modeling and numerical simulation in different fields of sciences and industries. As a result, the specific direction in numerical analysis was developed to satisfy to numerous demands of practical applications. First of all, the mentioned demands concern accuracy and effectiveness of the correspondent computational schemes.

Let us consider the specific computational difficulties arising in moving boundary problems, in details. There exist, at least, one physical evolutionary field inside the solution domain, which determines the considered process of boundary motion. This field is described by some mathematical model with specific parameters, some of which would be grouped into dimensionless complexes like Fourier number. At least, one of such parameters must be connected with dimensionless time for evolutionary problem. Motion of solution domain boundary is completely another process, determined by different mathematical model. The mathematical model of boundary motion includes time too and allows its conversion into dimensionless time. Thus, the general problem includes, at least, two-time scales, connected with the governing physical field and with the boundary motion. Since there are not any restrictions on time scales or even connections between them, a relation of the considered time scales can have any value, including extremely small or extremely large. In last case, one of the considered processes can be defined as "slow" and other as "fast". As a rule, the boundary motion is "slow" and the field governing equation time is "fast" in the practical applications, like phase transitions in industrial technologies. To obtain an accurate solution using traditional step-by-step approximation in time, it is necessary to use extremely small-time step (to avoid sufficient approximation errors) during enough large time interval in "slow" time. Since such computational procedure requires a huge number of time steps, it is undesirable due to high-consumed computer resources and possible accumulation of computational errors. To overcome the described difficulty, an asymptotic analysis can be applied to the considered problem. A relation of dimensionless "fast" time to dimensionless "slow" time is dimensionless time-independent constant, which is enough small. It is suitable to use this value as a small parameter in correspondent asymptotic expansions. As a result, the obtained asymptotic sequence of problems gives an opportunity to solve the general problem in "slow" time instead "fast" time, what provides more effective tools of numerical or approximate analytical analysis. For example, heat conduction equation in well-known Stefan problem is replaced by sequence of Laplace equations in two-dimensional and three-dimensional in space cases and by sequence of second order ordinary differential equations in one-dimensional in space case. As a rule, the last one-dimensional case allows analytical integration of the problem.

Generally speaking, arbitrary shapes of domains and their boundaries can arise in the moving boundary problems, what is connected with rebuilding of computational grid at every time step. It means very serious computational difficulties for applications of finite difference and finite element methods, because of their computational opportunities are sufficiently determined by the grid parameters. Beside of that, transfer process of the computed solutions from nodes of old grid into the nodes of new built grid generates hard for checking errors. Boundary element method is often used for such problem because the rebuilding of boundary element grid is sufficiently simpler than similar procedure for finite element and finite difference methods.

At last, moving boundary problems are connected with specific kind of nonlinearity, which restricts a set of effective tools for the problem analysis. Beside of that, the governing equations describing temperature fields inside the phases can be nonlinear too. Fortunately, asymptotic approach described above provides linearization of obtained boundary-value problems.

Taking into account all circumstances and requirements, the following conclusion can be made: only the boundary element method would be effective approach to numerical solution of the obtained asymptotic sequence of elliptic boundary-value problems, constructed for moving boundary problems with the governing parabolic equation.

Two practically important problems are used as examples in the present work. The first one is well-known and mentioned above Stefan problem, in particular, case of slow phase transition will be considered below, because the condition, that Stefan number is less than 1, provides an effective applicability of asymptotic approach. The second considered problem is biological tissue growth problem, describing specific processes, which are investigated in biological, medical and agricultural sciences.

Physical theory of phase transformations on microscopic and macroscopic levels were good developed and, as a result, there are not sufficient unsolved questions, what can arise during solution of most of applied heat and mass transfer problems including phase transition [1]. However, there is not so good situation from the point of view of computational mathematics, because phase transition problems contain specific kind of nonlinearity connected with motion of phase transition boundary. As a rule, time-stepping algorithms are used for numerical solution of phase transition problems and the domain shape is fixed on the time step, that is, there is an implicit splitting of the process by the field evolution and interphase boundary motion. Thus such algorithms provide "jumping" domain shape and time step must be enough small to guarantee small domain shape "jump" and high accuracy of the field calculation. Beside of additional time step restriction, there is an additional error source, concerning the domain boundary motion. Any full review of numerical methods of Stefan problem solution requires a special investigation and cannot be included in restricted amount of the present paper. However, the following general conclusion can be made: all mentioned numerical algorithms of Stefan problem solution, based on finite element or finite difference approaches, are rather directed to fast phase transformations, because under restricted time step they require a lot of time steps for slow phase transformations. Then they are found noneffective in the case of slow phase transitions.

The quasi-stationary approximation (called Leybenzon approximation in Russian literature) is used to apply for numerical calculations of such processes [1]. However, the number of similar works was very restricted, and they were devoted to engineering design. This approach becomes popular in problems of freezing (melting) of soil, for investigation of phase transitions in solid body, in some evaporation (condensation) problems. The situation in numerical modeling of slow phase transitions was sharply changed in connection with three new problems. The first problem was simple attempt to build more accurate mathematical models for environment processes, for example, in meteorology or soil investigations. The second problem is phase transitions in microgravity conditions, which became important with starting of intensive space explorations. And finally, the third problem was connected with attempts to obtain a material with minimal residual stresses during material production or during phase transitions in solid body, what was important in material sciences. An experience of application of traditional finite difference and finite element approach to the mentioned problems was rather unsuccessful, because their numerical solution required huge computer resources and therefore their research opportunities were strongly restricted. Beside of that, the traditional methods often could not provide necessary accuracy of the numerical solution. On the other hand, the quasi-stationary approximation had difficulties too, because it is related to asymptotically slow processes and doesn't take into account initial conditions. Beside of that, elliptical boundary-value problems, which must be numerically solved at every time step of quasi-stationary problem solution, are rather inconvenient for finite difference method. As a result, using of quasi-stationary approximation was very restricted last decades.

Velocity of phase transition is described by dimensionless parameter called Stefan number [2], which is relation of thermal energy, spent in heating (cooling) of some phase, to energy spent in phase transformation process. The term "slow" means that the Stefan number is small and therefore there are two different time scales in the problem. Asymptotic approaches give an opportunity to build a mathematical model excluding "fast" time. The first work in this direction was paper [2], where the small parameter method was applied to Stefan problem.

After the first original works of Chuang and Szekely [3, 4] a lot of papers were devoted to boundary element method application to Stefan problem. However general effectiveness of boundary element method for parabolic problems is less than similar effectiveness of finite difference method, what was shown in many papers, see, for example, [5]. Of course, using of some special boundary element method algorithms can improve the situation, but any time-stepping numerical method cannot enough effectively solve the problem of slow phase transition.

Boundary element method [6, 7] has become powerful tool for numerical solution of linear boundary-value problems. It is especially effective in comparison with traditional finite difference method and finite element method for elliptical problems in domains of complex geometrical shape. The main idea of the present paper, concerning the numerical approach, is using of boundary element method for solution of elliptical boundary-value problems, which arise for every approximation on every time step. As a result, an effective computational algorithm is developed, because of well-known advantages of boundary element method such as analysis boundary alone and high accuracy of computations. First time, the idea to use asymptotic approach to a wide class of slow phase transition problems was formulated in the paper [8], but the work [8] was mainly devoted to quasi-stationary approximation and the following terms in asymptotic expansion were not considered there. The approach was developed in the article [9], where application of boundary element method in order to solve the obtained elliptic boundary-value problems was proposed. However, the paper [9] was restricted by quasi-stationary approximation too. Full idea of boundary element application to the considered problem was briefly described in the conference paper [10]. The authors of the present work have to reproduce some results of articles [8, 9], including the initial problem statement and asymptotic formulations, because they are practically unknown for modern scientific community.

Problem of biological tissue growth [11] became very actual item at the present stage of biological science development, because a lot of processes used in agriculture and biotechnology are determined by growth of biological tissue. Beside of that, problem of tumor growth is one of the most important in medicine [11, 12]. Two kinds of circumstances determine the growth process, the first one is genetic properties of tissue and the second one is environmental conditions, for example, nutrition, temperature and so on. Most of investigations concerning a biological growth are based on phenomenological approach, considering biological tissues as a "black box" with experimentally determined properties. The growth is one of such properties of biological tissue. Full review of mathematical modeling in biological sciences requires a separate investigation, which must be sufficiently more than the present paper. Since the growth of biological tissue is the object of the present work, let us consider specific features of the mathematical models of the given processes. General simplifying assumptions must be made to formulate a mathematical model.

It is commonly known that any biological tissue consists of cells. Process of cell reproduction is caution of multicellular tissue growth. The growth process consists of two parts: growth of individual cells and fission of cells, that is the growth process has evidently discrete behavior. Since cells are very small and number of them is very large, consideration of each individual cell is impossible and therefore some averaging is necessary. As a rule, averaging process used in biology is similar to well-known continuous approach in mechanics. According to this approach a multicellular biological tissue is assumed as continues media with distributed sources and some diffusive properties. In fact, cells create a porous media, but pressure difference enough for filtration flow is very seldom presence in the biological tissues, therefore transport phenomena due to filtration flow can be neglected and they are provided by diffusive mechanisms. There is no single quantitative measure of biological tissue metabolism, because a lot of chemical reactions mutually interact. However, the simplest way to formulate a mathematical model for metabolism process is to introduce some numerical value called metabolism intensity and to assume, that any chemical reaction and consequently heat and mass transfer process rate is determined by (in the simplest case it is proportional to) metabolism intensity. As a rule, metabolism intensity is connected by linear relation with velocity of tissue growth. This rule is almost always right for simplest organisms, but metabolism of highest animals is more complex. All mathematical models, which will be developed in the present paper below, will be based on this assumption. Of course, it is phenomenological approach and relation function connecting metabolism intensity and consuming of nutrient substances (excrement production) must be determined experimentally. An evident advantage of such mathematical models (so-called one-parametrical models) is their flexibility and opportunity to take into account different number of concentration fields on different levels of consideration.

There are two possible mechanisms of biological tissue growth. The first one is the surface growth and the second one is the volume growth. The intensive cell fission takes place in relatively thin layer near the tissue surface in the case of surface growth. Cells situated inside the tissue have stable metabolism without intensive fission in this case, then their total volume remains constant. Reproduction of all cells takes place in the case of volume growth, although the most intensive fission, as a rule, takes place near the surface.

All considered above mathematical models are reduced to initial-boundary-value problems for system of diffusion equations with nonlinear sources in moving boundary domain. Motion of the domain boundary is caused by tissue growth, what is described in the work [13], which immediately preceded to the present work; however, the main attention in this paper was paid to the analytical solution of the problem. Boundary element method application for numerical solution of the obtained asymptotic problems, was, rather, pointed out briefly. Nevertheless, the problem statement from the paper [13] is reproduced in the present work.

The main aim of the present paper is to develop a universal effective numerical approach for solution of two physically different diffusive problems in slow moving boundary domains and to show a mathematical and computational similarity of the considered problems.

2. Mathematical model of slow-phase transition

2.1 Stefan problem formulation

Stefan problem is traditionally considered as a successful mathematical model of phase transition process in immovable media. Usually, the Stefan problem does not

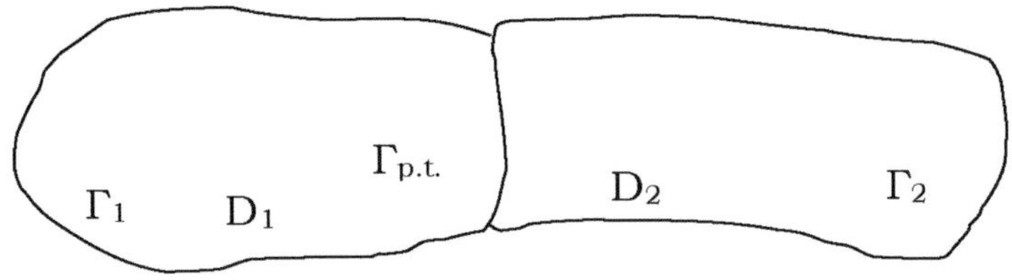

Figure 1.
Two-phase Stefan problem. The first phase occupies the domain D_1 with boundary Γ_1, and the second phase is situated in the domain D_2 with boundary Γ_2. The boundary part $\Gamma_{p.t.} = \Gamma_1 \cap \Gamma_2$ is moving phase transition boundary.

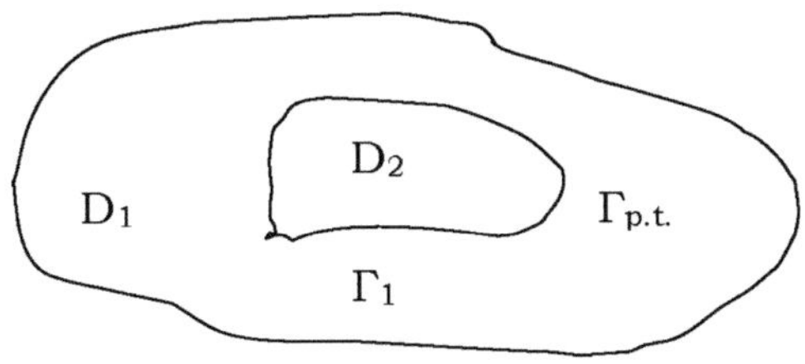

Figure 2.
The most widespread one-phase Stefan problem. The first phase occupies the domain D_1 with boundary Γ_1, and it surrounds the second phase, which is situated in the domain D_2 with boundary $\Gamma_2 = \Gamma_{p.t.} \subset \Gamma_1$. The second phase is kept under phase transition temperature $T_2 = T_{p.t.}$.

take into account a change of the substance density under phase transition, what is the main difference between Stefan problem and real phase transition processes. A density change stimulates specific flows in liquid and gaseous phases and it causes an appearing of specific additional stress fields under solid-state phase transitions. However, influence of the mentioned phenomena often can be enough small in comparison with heat conduction processes. Stefan problems can be classified by number of phases (see **Figures 1** and **2**). In particular, one-phase and two-phase Stefan problems are considered in the present work. The term "one-phase problem" does not mean that the second phase is absent, it only points out, that the second phase is kept under constant temperature of phase transition. Generally speaking, one-phase Stefan problem is particular case of two-phase problem, therefore all following formulations will be presented for two-phase problem.

Let consider a classical two-phase Stefan problem. Let the first phase occupies the domain D_1 and the second phase occupies the domain D_2. The boundary $\Gamma_{p.t.}$ separates mentioned domains, it is a phase transition boundary and has a constant temperature $T_{p.t.}$. Let domains D_1 and D_2 are bounded by finite or infinite curves Γ_1 and Γ_2, correspondingly. For the sake of simplicity, restrict the following consideration by the cases of first and second kind boundary conditions on the outside parts of curves Γ_1 and Γ_2. Thus, assuming thermophysical properties of materials as constant, we obtain the following mathematical model [1, 2].

$$\frac{\partial T_1}{\partial \tau} = a_1 \Delta T_1, \tag{1}$$

$$\frac{\partial T_2}{\partial \tau} = a_2 \Delta T_2, \tag{2}$$

Here Eqs. (1) and (2) describe the temperature fields inside the first phase and the second phase correspondingly. Boundary conditions of the first or second kinds must be prescribed on the outside parts of curves Γ_1 and Γ_2:

In particular, first kind

$$T_1|_{\Gamma_1} = T_{1s}, \tag{3}$$

$$T_2|_{\Gamma_2} = T_{2s}, \tag{4}$$

or second kind

$$\lambda_1 \frac{\partial T_1}{\partial n}\bigg|_{\Gamma_1} = q_1, \tag{5}$$

$$\lambda_2 \frac{\partial T_2}{\partial n}\bigg|_{\Gamma_2} = q_2, \tag{6}$$

and boundary conditions on the phase transition boundary

$$T_1|_{\Gamma_{p.t.}} = T_{p.t.}, \tag{7}$$

$$T_2|_{\Gamma_{p.t.}} = T_{p.t.}, \tag{8}$$

$$\lambda_1 \frac{\partial T_1}{\partial n}\bigg|_{\Gamma_{p.t.}} - \lambda_2 \frac{\partial T_2}{\partial n}\bigg|_{\Gamma_{p.t.}} = \rho\sigma V_{p.t.}, \tag{9}$$

where a_1, a_2 are thermal diffusivity coefficients of phases, T_{1s}, T_{2s}, q_1, q_2 are temperatures and thermal fluxes on the outside parts of curves Γ_1 and Γ_2, λ_1, λ_2 are heat conduction coefficients, ρ is density of some phase (as a rule, incompressible phase, if the both phases are incompressible, the density of initial phase is chosen), $V_{p.t.}$ is phase transition boundary propagation velocity. Condition (9) is called Stefan condition, and it describes the motion of the phase transition boundary in dependence on balance of thermal fluxes. Note, that the phase transformation temperature $T_{p.t.}$ is constant of the material. To complete the formulation, add the initial conditions:

$$T_1(0, x) = T_{10}(x), \tag{10}$$

$$T_2(0, x) = T_{20}(x). \tag{11}$$

Let us become to dimensionless variables in the problem, using following representation

$$\theta_1 = \frac{T_1 - T_{p.t.}}{T_n - T_{p.t.}}, \tag{12}$$

where value T_n is chosen as one from following values $\max\{T_{1s}, T_{2s}\}$ or $\min\{T_{1s}, T_{2s}\}$ (but sometimes it is possible to use $\max\{T_{10}, T_{20}\}$ or $\min\{T_{10}, T_{20}\}$) in dependence on the particular problem. The temperature field in the second phase is transformed by similar way. Thus, Eqs. (1) and (2) have forms

$$\frac{\partial \theta_1}{\partial Fo_1} = \Delta^* \theta_1, \tag{13}$$

$$\frac{\partial \theta_2}{\partial Fo_2} = \Delta^* \theta_2, \tag{14}$$

where

$$Fo_1 = \frac{\tau a_1}{L^2}. \tag{15}$$

The asterisk "*" in Laplace operator means the differentiation with respect to dimensionless coordinates

$$X^* = x/L. \tag{16}$$

It will be omitted in following. Dimensionless forms of the boundary and initial conditions are

$$\theta_1|_{\Gamma_1} = \theta_{1s}, \tag{17}$$

$$\theta_2|_{\Gamma_2} = \theta_{2s}, \tag{18}$$

$$\theta_1|_{\Gamma_{p.t.}} = 0, \tag{19}$$

$$\theta_2|_{\Gamma_{p.t.}} = 0, \tag{20}$$

$$\theta_1(0, x) = \theta_{10}, \tag{21}$$

$$\theta_2(0, x) = \theta_{20}. \tag{22}$$

The dimensionless Stefan condition must be considered in details. Let

$$V_{p.t.} = \frac{\partial n}{\partial \tau}, \tag{23}$$

where $\frac{\partial n}{\partial \tau}$ means the normal velocity of the phase transformation boundary motion. If $n^* = n/L$, we have following dimensionless relation

$$\frac{\partial \theta_1}{\partial n} - f_\lambda \frac{\partial \theta_2}{\partial n} = \frac{\partial n^*}{\partial \tau_{st}}, \tag{24}$$

where

$$f_\lambda = \lambda_2/\lambda_1, \tag{25}$$

and

$$\tau_{st} = \frac{\tau \lambda_1 (T_n - T_{p.t.})}{L^2 \sigma \rho}, \tag{26}$$

τ_{st} is dimensionless time, connected with the phase transformation process.

Thus there three dimensionless time Fo_1, Fo_2 and τ_{st} in the problem, however it is desirable to use only one time scale. Since the main interest on the problem is phase transition process, choose the Stefan time τ_{st} as the main time scale. Beside of that, as a rule, τ_{st} is the "most slow" dimensionless time. Then Eq. (13) must be replaced by

$$\frac{\partial \theta_1}{\partial \tau_{st}} St = \Delta \theta_1, \tag{27}$$

where St is the Stefan number determined as

$$\mathrm{St} = \frac{\tau_{st}}{\mathrm{Fo}_1} = \frac{\frac{\tau\lambda_1\left(T_n - T_{p.t.}\right)}{L^2\sigma\rho}}{\frac{\tau a_1}{L^2}} = \frac{\lambda_1\left(T_n - T_{p.t.}\right)}{a_1\sigma\rho} = \frac{C\left(T_n - T_{p.t.}\right)}{\sigma}, \tag{28}$$

Eq. (14) is transformed by following way:

$$\frac{\partial\theta_2}{\partial\tau_{st}} f_a \mathrm{St} = \Delta\theta_2, \tag{29}$$

where

$$f_a = \frac{\mathrm{Fo}_1}{\mathrm{Fo}_2} = \frac{a_1}{a_2}. \tag{30}$$

Physical sense of the Stefan number is quite simple; it is equal to relation of heat, spent to heating (cooling) of the phase, to heat spent to phase transition. But in the same time, it can be considered as relation of two-time scales, concerning heating (cooling) and phase transition boundary motion. Since, as a rule, the latent heat of phase transformation σ is quite large value, $\mathrm{St} < 1$.

Formulated above Stefan problem can be easy generalized for any number of phases, but one-phase Stefan problem (see **Figure 2**) has special importance for the theory. This particular case of general Stefan problem physically corresponds to situation, when one phase has temperature equal to the phase transformation temperature and it undergoes the phase transformation due to heat conduction of the another phase. The phase under constant temperature must be excluded from the consideration. Thus

$$\frac{\partial\theta}{\partial\tau_{st}} \mathrm{St} = \Delta\theta, \tag{31}$$

$$\theta|_{\Gamma_1} = \theta_s, \tag{32}$$

$$\theta|_{\Gamma_{p.t.}} = 0, \tag{33}$$

$$\theta(0, x) = \theta_0, \tag{34}$$

$$\frac{\partial\theta}{\partial n} = \frac{\partial n}{\partial\tau_{st}}. \tag{35}$$

2.2 Asymptotic approach to Stefan problem

As it was noted earlier, the considered Stefan problem is nonlinear, because of complicated dependence between the temperature field and shape (motion) of the phase transition boundary. Although the question on existence and uniqueness of Stefan problem solution is still far from a complete clearness [1], the continuous dependency of Stefan problem solution on Stefan number is evident. It could be clear shown, if an integral formulation for temperature field is considered (see [6, 7]), besides of that, it is seen from the same integral formulation, that the solution can be continuously differentiated with respect to Stefan number any number of times. Then the temperature field can represented as a series of Stefan number orders, which must converge for $\mathrm{St} < 1$, and in the case of slow phase transformation $\mathrm{St} < < 1$ it must converge quickly.

On the base of above conclusions on the solution properties we shall search solution in a form of series

$$\theta_1 = \theta_1{}^0(x, \tau) + \sum_{k=1}^{\infty} St^k \theta_1{}^k(x, \tau), \tag{36}$$

$$\theta_2 = \theta_2{}^0(x, \tau) + \sum_{k=1}^{\infty} St^k \theta_2{}^k(x, \tau). \tag{37}$$

As a result of using of expansions (36) and (37), the initial problem is reduced to determination of function series $\theta_1^0, \ldots, \theta_1^k, \ldots; \theta_2^0, \ldots, \theta_2^k, \ldots$.

Let substitute expansions (36) and (37) into Eqs. (27) and (29) and obtain

$$St\frac{\partial}{\partial \tau}\theta_1{}^0(x, \tau) + St\frac{\partial}{\partial \tau}\sum_{k=1}^{\infty} St^k \theta_1{}^k(x, \tau) = \Delta\theta_1{}^0(x, \tau) + \Delta\sum_{k=1}^{\infty} St^k \theta_1{}^k(x, \tau), \tag{38}$$

$$f_a St\frac{\partial}{\partial \tau}\theta_2{}^0(x, \tau) + f_a St\frac{\partial}{\partial \tau}\sum_{k=1}^{\infty} St^k \theta_2{}^k(x, \tau) = \Delta\theta_2{}^0(x, \tau) + \Delta\sum_{k=1}^{\infty} St^k \theta_2{}^k(x, \tau).$$

If the functions θ_1^k, θ_2^k are bounded, the series (36) and (37) absolutely converge; therefore, correspondent series can be differentiated term by term. Thus

$$St\frac{\partial \theta_1{}^0}{\partial \tau} + \sum_{k=1}^{\infty} St^{k+1}\frac{\partial \theta_1{}^k}{\partial \tau} = \Delta\theta_1{}^0 + \sum_{k=1}^{\infty} St^k \Delta\theta_1{}^k, \tag{39}$$

$$f_a St\frac{\partial \theta_2{}^0}{\partial \tau} + f_a\sum_{k=1}^{\infty} St^{k+1}\frac{\partial \theta_2{}^k}{\partial \tau} = \Delta\theta_2{}^0 + \sum_{k=1}^{\infty} St^k \Delta\theta_2{}^k.$$

Since the value of Stefan number is, generally speaking, arbitrary, equality (39) takes place only in case of equality of factors at equal orders of Stefan number. Hence

$$\Delta\theta_1{}^0 = 0, \tag{40}$$

$$\Delta\theta_1{}^1 = \frac{\partial \theta_1{}^0}{\partial \tau}, \tag{41}$$

$$\Delta\theta_1{}^i = \frac{\partial \theta_1{}^{i-1}}{\partial \tau}, \tag{42}$$

$$\Delta\theta_2{}^0 = 0, \tag{43}$$

$$\Delta\theta_2{}^1 = f_a\frac{\partial \theta_2{}^0}{\partial \tau}, \tag{44}$$

$$\Delta\theta_1{}^i = f_a\frac{\partial \theta_1{}^{i-1}}{\partial \tau}, \tag{45}$$

Let prescribe boundary conditions for Eqs. (40)–(45)

$$\theta_1{}^0\big|_{\Gamma_1} = \theta_{1s}, \tag{46}$$

$$\theta_1{}^0\big|_{\Gamma_{p.t.}} = 0, \tag{47}$$

$$\theta_1{}^i\big|_{\Gamma_1} = 0, \tag{48}$$

$$\theta_1{}^i\big|_{\Gamma_{p.t.}} = 0, \tag{49}$$

$$\theta_2{}^0\big|_{\Gamma_2} = \theta_{2s}, \tag{50}$$

$$\theta_2{}^0\big|_{\Gamma_{p.t.}} = 0, \tag{51}$$

$$\theta_2{}^i\big|_{\Gamma_2} = 0, \tag{52}$$

$$\theta_2{}^i\big|_{\Gamma_{p.t.}} = 0. \tag{53}$$

Let consider the Stefan condition (24) separately. If the series of boundary-value problems (40)–(45) are solved, the relation (24) can be considered as ordinary differential equation, what describes motion of phase transformation boundary. If Eq. (24) is integrated analytically (it is very seldom case, because the right hand part of relation (24) depends on phase boundary position in a complicated way), the general problem could be considered as completely solved. In general case Cauchy problem for Eq. (24) can be solved numerically by some numerical method. However, the most successful approach is method proposed in the paper [2] and based on expansion of left-hand side of Eq. (24) into a series with respect to Stefan number.

$$\begin{aligned} &\frac{\partial\theta_1{}^0(x,\tau)}{\partial n} + \sum_{k=1}^{\infty} St^k \frac{\partial\theta_1{}^k(x,\tau)}{\partial n} = f_a\left(\frac{\partial\theta_2{}^0(x,\tau)}{\partial n} + \sum_{k=1}^{\infty} St^k \frac{\partial\theta_2{}^k(x,\tau)}{\partial n}\right) = \\ &= \left(\frac{\partial\eta^0(x,\tau)}{\partial\tau} + \sum_{k=1}^{\infty} St^k \frac{\partial\eta^k(x,\tau)}{\partial\tau}\right). \end{aligned} \tag{54}$$

By the same reasons as earlier let equate factors at equal orders of Stefan number and obtain

$$\frac{\partial\theta_1{}^0}{\partial n} - f_\lambda \frac{\partial\theta_2{}^0}{\partial n} = \frac{\partial\eta^0}{\partial\tau}, \tag{55}$$

$$\frac{\partial\theta_1{}^i}{\partial n} - f_\lambda \frac{\partial\theta_2{}^i}{\partial n} = \frac{\partial\eta^i}{\partial\tau}, \tag{56}$$

where functions η^k are subjects to determination. The relationships (56) must be complemented by some initial conditions and can be considered as series of Cauchy problems for phase transition boundary position. The first equations and boundary conditions in (40)–(53), which describes the temperature approximations indicated by index "0", coincide with well-known quasi-stationary approximation. Note that for one-dimensional (in space) case for any Stefan problems the boundary-value problems indicated by "0" and "1" can be integrated analytically but the following approximations requires some numerical method for solution of mentioned Cauchy problem. Such solutions were built for one-phase and two-phase one-dimensional (in ordinary Cartesian, polar and spherical coordinate systems) Stefan problems with different boundary conditions on the outer boundaries. There are particular cases of one-dimensional Stefan problems, analytical solutions of which are known. The mentioned analytical solutions were used to check the approach accuracy. As a result, it is shown that accuracy of test problem solutions is enough high.

The presented series of problem (40)–(53), (55), and (56) is equivalent to the initial Stefan problem (1)–(4), (7)–(11). Under restrictions imposed on functions, included into the formulation, concerning their physical sense, (for example, requirement of piecewise smooth boundary of the finite domain D, where the problem is solved, and requirement of boundedness of temperatures and thermal fluxes) the temperature functions inside domains D_1 and D_2 are differentiable infinite number of times [2]. Moreover, temperature derivatives with respect to time are finite too. Last assumption has physical sense, if the moment of phase creation is excluded from the consideration, because thermal fluxes can be enough large (asymptotically infinite) in this case. Under mentioned restrictions the following theorem takes place.

Theorem 1. If the boundary and initial conditions in the boundary-value problems (27), (17), (19), (21) and (29), (18), (20), (22) are such that their solutions are differentiable infinite number of times and these derivatives are restricted, series (36) and (37) converge under any Stefan number less than 1 (St < 1), and order of the remainder term is $O\left(St^{j+1}M_{j+1}\right)$, where $M_{j+1} = \max_{j+1 \le m < \infty} \theta^m$ (it is assumed that the series is cut off after j-th term).

The proof of the Theorem 1 is evident and based on majorizing sequence, built by replacing of functions θ^i by M_i. This sequence is geometrical progression with factor St, which is less than 1, according to the theorem conditions. Therefore, the series converge.

It is necessary to note, that the Theorem 1 proves convergence of asymptotic expansions and thus it grounds an application of asymptotic approach to the considered class of Stefan problems. More than that, an error of such approach can be estimated analytically, however such estimations, as a rule, are found useless for determination of computation error in whole, because there are other error sources in the general computational scheme.

Let consider one-phase Stefan problem, which is a particular case of above formulated problem:

$$\Delta\theta^0 = 0, \tag{57}$$

$$\Delta\theta^1 = \frac{\partial\theta^0}{\partial\tau}, \tag{58}$$

$$\Delta\theta^i = \frac{\partial\theta^{i-1}}{\partial\tau} \tag{59}$$

with boundary conditions

$$\theta^0\big|_{\Gamma_1} = \theta_s, \tag{60}$$

$$\theta^0\big|_{\Gamma_{p.t.}} = 0, \tag{61}$$

$$\theta^i\big|_{\Gamma_1} = 0, \tag{62}$$

$$\theta^i\big|_{\Gamma_{p.t.}} = 0, \tag{63}$$

Stefan condition

$$\frac{\partial\theta^0}{\partial n} = \frac{\partial\eta^0}{\partial\tau} \tag{64}$$

$$\frac{\partial\theta^i}{\partial n} = \frac{\partial\eta^i}{\partial\tau} \tag{65}$$

3. Boundary element method application to slow phase transition calculations

However, the temperature fields must be determined numerically in two-dimensional and three-dimensional cases. Boundary element method [6, 7] is used in the present work. It supposes transformation of Eqs. (40)–(45) into boundary integral equations

$$C(x_0)\theta_1^0(x_0) = \int\limits_{\Gamma_1 \cup \Gamma_{p.t.}} \phi_0(x, x_0)\frac{\partial\theta_1^0}{\partial n}ds - \int\limits_{\Gamma_1 \cup \Gamma_{p.t.}} \theta_1^0\frac{\partial\phi_0(x, x_0)}{\partial n}ds, \tag{66}$$

$$C(x_0)\theta_2^0(x_0) = \int\limits_{\Gamma_2 \cup \Gamma_{p.t.}} \phi_0(x, x_0)\frac{\partial\theta_2^0}{\partial n}ds - \int\limits_{\Gamma_2 \cup \Gamma_{p.t.}} \theta_2^0\frac{\partial\phi_0(x, x_0)}{\partial n}ds, \tag{67}$$

$$C(x_0)\theta_1^i(x_0) = \int\limits_{\Gamma_1 \cup \Gamma_{p.t.}} \phi_0(x, x_0)\frac{\partial\theta_1^i}{\partial n}ds - \int\limits_{\Gamma_1 \cup \Gamma_{p.t.}} \theta_1^i\frac{\partial\phi_0(x, x_0)}{\partial n}ds + \int\limits_{D_1} \phi_0(x, x_0)\frac{\partial\theta_1^{i-1}}{\partial \tau}dx, \tag{68}$$

$$C(x_0)\theta_2^i(x_0) = \int\limits_{\Gamma_2 \cup \Gamma_{p.t.}} \phi_0(x, x_0)\frac{\partial\theta_2^i}{\partial n}ds - \int\limits_{\Gamma_2 \cup \Gamma_{p.t.}} \theta_2^i\frac{\partial\phi_0(x, x_0)}{\partial n}ds + \int\limits_{D_2} \phi_0(x, x_0)\frac{\partial\theta_2^{i-1}}{\partial \tau}dx, \tag{69}$$

where ϕ_0 is fundamental solution of Laplace equation, $C(x_0)$ is special function reflecting control point x_0 position with respect to the boundary and shape of the boundary. Eqs. (66)–(69) are solved numerically by well-known boundary element algorithm [6, 7]. According to that algorithm, the boundaries of phases are fragmented by boundary elements; the temperatures and thermal fluxes are assumed constant on every boundary element. Thus, the system of linear algebraic equations with respect to unknown values of temperature or thermal flux on elements is formed.

Solving mentioned systems of linear algebraic equations, corresponding to every boundary integral Eqs. (66)–(69) we can obtain the temperature distribution with required accuracy at some instant of time, that is under specific shape of interphase boundary. Then new position of interphase boundary must be determined using the Stefan condition (55) and (56). To build new interphase boundary relations (55) and (56) must be considered as an ordinary differential equation, and correspondent Cauchy problems must be solved numerically. The Euler method is used for this aim in the present work. If it is necessary, the problems (66)–(69) can be solved by boundary element method for new shape of the interphase boundary. Such time-stepping process can be continued during any time interval. The simplest algorithm of the boundary element method with approximation of boundary elements by straight lines segments and approximation of known and unknown function values on boundary elements by constants [6, 7] is used in the present work. Of course, using of improved boundary element method algorithm and methods of numerical solution of Cauchy problem can make the solution procedure more effective; however their applications require special investigation.

The main advantage of proposed time-stepping approach in comparison with time-stepping finite difference and finite element methods is time discretization with respect to slow time scale determined by interphase boundary motion unlike finite difference and finite element methods, which requires time discretization with respect to fast time scale determined by heat conduction process.

4. Results of slow phase transition calculations

The restricted amount of the present paper doesn't give an opportunity to analyze a lot of calculation results, therefore the proposed approach is illustrated by only several following examples of numerical calculations. Melting process of cylinder, which had initial circular shape, is shown in **Figures 3** and **4** under different conditions of heating.

It is easy to see from comparison of **Figures 3** and **4** that the way of heating sufficiently affects shape of phase transition boundary, in particular, side heating leads to oval shape of the second phase domain, but nearly circular second phase domain takes place under multilateral heating. The times of calculations are relatively small in comparison with known finite difference and finite element calculations.

Since there is not any known analytical solution of Stefan problem to check accuracy of the obtained numerical solutions, the authors of the present work had to change numbers of boundary elements and compare correspondent numerical results. For example, the presented above numerical calculations were made under following parameters: phase transition boundary is approximated by 40 boundary elements at every time step of calculation and outer boundaries of the domain were approximated by 4×40 boundary elements. Checking calculations with 80 and 4×80 and 160 and 4×160 boundary elements and dimensionless time step varying from $\Delta\tau = 0,1$ to $\Delta\tau = 0,001$, correspondingly, shows change of the obtained results no more than 1%. The authors made a conclusion about satisfactory accuracy of the considered numerical approach.

Some conclusions can be made here. It is evident that the above proposed approach is more general and has more opportunities than earlier existing computational methods for slow phase transitions. It gives an opportunity to effectively calculate of the processes in broader interval of Stefan numbers. Enough high accuracy of the proposed algorithms is confirmed by the above-mentioned series of

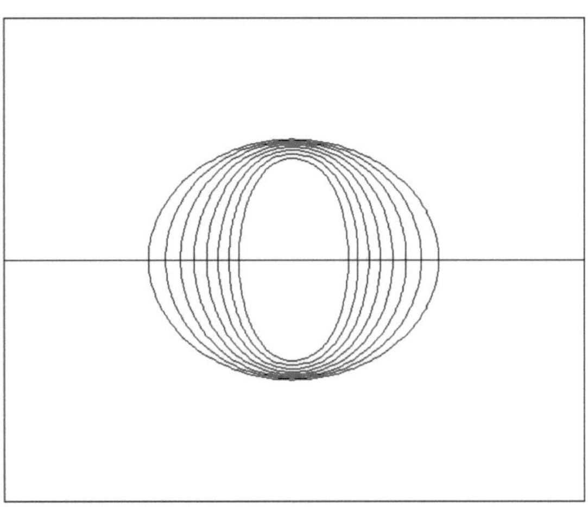

Figure 3.
Sequence of phase transformation boundary positions under side heating.

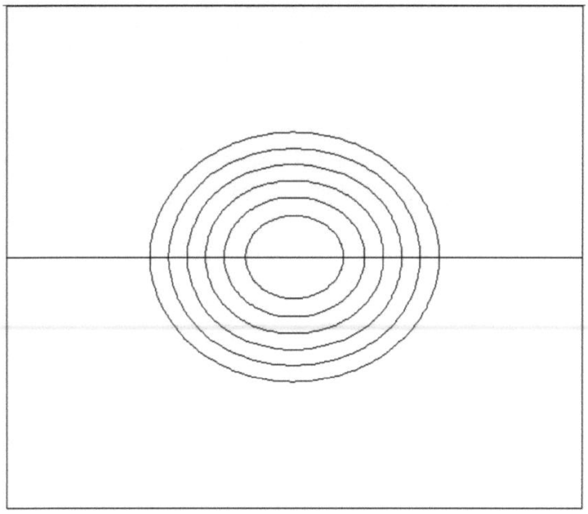

Figure 4.
Sequence of phase transformation boundary positions under multilateral heating.

test calculations. The results of calculations can be used in investigations of a number of processes, first of all, in investigations of slow phase transformations in microgravity and in environment. They also can be used in design of space-rocket technique.

5. Mathematical model of biological tissue growth

Let consider D_1 filled by some biological structures (in the simplest case by homogeneous or nondifferentiated cellular mass). Let restrict the following consideration by the case of homogeneous cellular structures. The tissue in the domain D_1 is porous media where cells form a frame and intercellular space is porosity. Let assume that pores are filled by same liquid, which is complex solution of nutrient substances and excrements of cells. There is an intensive heat and mass transfer between the frame and the liquid in pores, what is very important specific feature of the described structure. Let the domain D_1 is partially or completely surrounded by the domain D_2, filled by the same solution completely. In general case there may be a convective transfer in the domain D_2 and filtration flow in the domain D_1. Thus, a general mathematical model of heat and mass transfer processes is considered system is following:

$$\frac{\partial T_1}{\partial \tau} + (V_f \cdot \nabla) \cdot T_1 = a_1 \Delta T_1 + q_{T1}, \tag{70}$$

$$\frac{\partial C_{i1}}{\partial \tau} + (V_f \cdot \nabla) \cdot C_{i1} = d_{i1} \Delta C_{i1} + q_{i1}, i = \overline{1, N}, \tag{71}$$

$$\frac{\partial T_2}{\partial \tau} + (V_C \cdot \nabla) T_2 = a_2 \Delta T_2, \tag{72}$$

$$\frac{\partial C_{i2}}{\partial \tau} + (V_C \cdot \nabla) C_{i2} = d_{i2} \Delta C_{i2}, i = \overline{1, N}, \tag{73}$$

where T_1 is temperature in the domain D_1 (the one-temperature model, assuming the temperatures of frame and solution in pores are equal, is used here), V_f is filtration velocity, a_1 is thermal diffusivity of porous media, q_{T1} is heat source, concerning the metabolism of cells, c_{i_1} is concentration of the i-th component in porous media, d_{i_1} is diffusion coefficient of i-th component in the porous media, q_{i_1} is source (sink) of the i-th component in porous media, concerning the metabolism of cells, T_2 is temperature in the domain D_2, V_2 is flow velocity in the domain D_2, a_2 is thermal diffusivity of solution, c_{i_2} is concentration of i-th component in the domain D_2, d_{i_2} is diffusion coefficient of i-th component in the domain D_2, N_{i_2} number of components, participating of heat and mass transfer process, τ is time, Δ is Laplace operator.

Restrict the following consideration by the case:

$$V_f = 0, \tag{74}$$

$$V_c = 0, \tag{75}$$

what corresponds to conventional multicellular structure, formed by independent cells, that is simple colony of one-cellular organisms in immovable fluid. Then:

$$\frac{\partial T_1}{\partial \tau} = a_1 \Delta T_1 + q_{T1}, \tag{76}$$

$$\frac{\partial C_{i1}}{\partial \tau} = d_{i1} \Delta C_{i1} + q_{i1}, i = \overline{1, N}, \tag{77}$$

$$\frac{\partial T_2}{\partial \tau} = a_2 \Delta T_2, \tag{78}$$

$$\frac{\partial C_{i2}}{\partial \tau} = d_{i2} \Delta C_{i2}, i = \overline{1, N}. \tag{79}$$

If the condition (75) is not realized, it could be better to not consider the system (72) and (73), but to take into account a convective transfer using boundary conditions for Eqs. (76) and (77). This assumption is quite proved, since the system (76) and (77) describes enough slow processes.

Let prescribe boundary conditions for the systems (76)–(79). Note the common boundary of the domain D_1 and D_2 as Γ and reminder part as Γ_1 and Γ_2 correspondingly. The first kind boundary conditions can be prescribed on the boundaries Γ_1 and Γ_2

$$T_1|_{\Gamma 1} = T_{1e}, \tag{80}$$

$$C_{i1}|_{\Gamma 1} = C_{i1e}, \tag{81}$$

$$T_2|_{\Gamma 2} = T_{2e}, \tag{82}$$

$$C_{i2}|_{\Gamma 2} = C_{i2e}, \tag{83}$$

or the second kind boundary condition

$$\lambda_1 \frac{\partial T_1}{\partial n}\bigg|_{\Gamma 1} = q_{1e}, \tag{84}$$

$$d_{1i} \frac{\partial C_{i1}}{\partial n}\bigg|_{\Gamma 1} = q_{i1e}, \tag{85}$$

$$\lambda_2 \frac{\partial T_2}{\partial n}\bigg|_{\Gamma 2} = q_{2e}, \tag{86}$$

$$d_{i2} \frac{\partial C_{i2}}{\partial n}\bigg|_{\Gamma 2} = q_{i2e}, \tag{87}$$

or the third boundary condition

$$\lambda_1 \frac{\partial T_1}{\partial n}\bigg|_{\Gamma 1} + \alpha_1 \left(T_1|_{\Gamma 1} - T_{1e}\right) = 0, \tag{88}$$

$$d_{i1} \frac{\partial C_{i1}}{\partial n}\bigg|_{\Gamma 1} + \alpha_{i1} \left(C_{i1}|_{\Gamma 1} - C_{i1e}\right) = 0, \tag{89}$$

$$\lambda_2 \frac{\partial T_2}{\partial n}\bigg|_{\Gamma 2} + \alpha_2 \left(T_2|_{\Gamma 2} - T_{2e}\right) = 0, \tag{90}$$

$$d_{i2} \frac{\partial C_{i2}}{\partial n}\bigg|_{\Gamma 2} + \alpha_{i2} \left(C_{i2}|_{\Gamma 2} - C_{i2e}\right) = 0, \tag{91}$$

where $T_{1e}, C_{i1e}, T_{2e}, C_{i2e}, q_{1e}, q_{i1e}, q_{2e}, q_{i2e}$ are known functions, all coefficients in boundary conditions (80)–(91) are understood in conventional sense. Let consider boundary conditions on the boundary Γ. It is evident that

$$T_1|_\Gamma = T_2|_\Gamma, \tag{92}$$

$$C_{i1}|_\Gamma = C_{i2}|_\Gamma. \tag{93}$$

It is possible to formulate the second condition as a forth kind boundary condition.

$$\lambda_1 \frac{\partial T_1}{\partial n}\bigg|_\Gamma = \lambda_2 \frac{\partial T_2}{\partial n}\bigg|_\Gamma, \tag{94}$$

$$d_{i1} \frac{\partial C_{i1}}{\partial n}\bigg|_\Gamma = d_{i2} \frac{\partial C_{i2}}{\partial n}\bigg|_\Gamma. \tag{95}$$

Conditions (94) and (95) correspond to the case of cell fission in whole domain D_1. However, it is possible the situation, when the fission of cells takes place only on the boundary Γ, then condition (94) is saved, but condition (95) must be replaced by following condition

$$d_{i1} \frac{\partial C_{i1}}{\partial n}\bigg|_\Gamma - d_{i2} \frac{\partial C_{i2}}{\partial n}\bigg|_\Gamma = \chi_i \frac{\partial n}{\partial \tau}, \tag{96}$$

here $\frac{\partial n}{\partial \tau}$ is velocity of the boundary Γ propagation (velocity of biological structure growth), χ_i is "expenditure" coefficient of the i-th component during growth of biological structure. Note that condition (96) is not conventional Stefan condition (nevertheless its form coincides with Stefan condition), because right hand part of condition (96) is determined by fission process, that is by parameters determining the fission process such as the temperature, concentrations and possibly the histories, therefore right hand part of the condition (96) is prescribed. It means that the given problem is similar to phase transition problem under prescribed velocity of phase boundary motion. The moving boundary velocity is determined in the considered problem as a function of metabolism intensity.

The case, when cellular mass growth takes place in whole domain D_1 is more complex than previous one. Consider a function describing metabolism intensity. As it is noted earlier, metabolism intensity is assumed proportional to a cellular mass growth (nevertheless the cell fission is very complex process with possibly enough large delay time that is with sufficient influence of previous history of the process). Let metabolism intensity function $\omega(T_1, c_{i_1})$ is defined, then correspondent source terms are following

$$q_{i1} = \chi_i \omega, \tag{97}$$

$$q_{\Gamma 1} = \chi_\Gamma \omega. \tag{98}$$

The function ω is determined experimentally. Let ω_i is function of influence of the i-th parameter on the metabolism velocity function. It is evident that

$$\omega = \prod_{i=1}^{N+1} \omega_i. \tag{99}$$

As it is noted earlier the growth of cellular mass is proportional to metabolism intensity

$$q_s = \chi_s \omega - \chi_0 \omega_0. \tag{100}$$

Terms indicated by ″0″ in last relationship correspond to regular metabolism, which is specific for tissues of highest animals.

Let consider a problem about motion of the boundary Γ again, in particular, let consider the case, when local volume change is determined by relation (100). The velocity (deformation) field depends on mechanical links between cells. If cells are "free" in intercellular solution the model of distributed sources in incompressible fluid can be applied, according to which the velocity of the boundary Γ is determined as

$$V_n(x_\circ) = \frac{\partial}{\partial n} \int_{D_1} q_s(x) \phi_\circ(x, x_\circ) dx, \tag{101}$$

where x_i is arbitrary point of the curve-line Γ.

If the cells are linked mechanically between themselves, to determine the motion of the boundary Γ it is necessary to solve an elastoplastic problem, as a rule, under large strains. Consideration of such problems requires especial investigation and will not be made in the present work.

However, the another case is possible in biological structures; a biological structure grows saving its shape in this case. Thus, change of the structure volume can be referred to the boundary Γ uniformly:

$$\delta\Omega_{D_1} = \int_{D_1} q_s(x) dx. \tag{102}$$

The replacement of the boundary Γ is determined by the following relation

$$\delta\Gamma = \frac{\delta\Omega_{D_1}}{S}, \tag{103}$$

here S is square of surface Γ (length of curve line Γ in the plane case).

If for simplest organism's linear dependence of growth velocity on metabolism intensity defined by relationship (100) is intrinsic, a tissue existence during an enough long time without growth, but under nonzero metabolism intensity, restricted by some limits, is possible for more complex multicellular organisms.

6. Boundary element method application to biological tissue growth

The above-developed algorithm cannot be directly applied to the two-dimensional and three-dimensional problems because boundary-value problems for partial differential equations arise in the mentioned cases instead boundary-value problems for ordinary differential equations as above. Thus two- and three-dimensional cases require some numerical method for solution of elliptic boundary-value problems in moving boundary domain. The most powerful tool for such problems is boundary element method [6, 7], which requires a reformulation of the considered problems as boundary integral equations.

Let consider the initial boundary value problem (76)–(96). Small parameter method application to this problem is, generally speaking, similar to above one-dimensional case application (see, for example, [8, 9]). Restrict the following consideration by plane case and by zero approximation of small parameter method, what corresponds to very small value of the Stefan number analogue. Thus

$$\Delta T_1^0 = -\frac{q_{T1}}{a_1}, \tag{104}$$

$$\Delta C_{i1}^0 = -\frac{q_{i1}}{d_{i1}}, i = \overline{1, N}, \tag{105}$$

$$\Delta T_2^0 = 0, \tag{106}$$

$$\Delta C_{i2}^0 = 0, i = \overline{1, N}. \tag{107}$$

Boundary conditions for the system (104)–(107) coincide with boundary conditions for the initial system. Let apply methods of potential theory to the system (104)–(107).

$$\chi(x_0)T_1^0(x_0) = \int_{\Gamma_1} \phi_0(x, x_0)\frac{\partial T_1^0}{\partial n} ds - \int_{\Gamma_1} T_1^0 \frac{\partial \phi_0(x, x_0)}{\partial n} ds + \\ + \int_D \phi_0(x, x_0)\frac{q_{T_1}}{a_1} dxdy, \tag{108}$$

$$\chi(x_0)C_{i1}^0(x_0) = \int_{\Gamma_1} \phi_0(x, x_0)\frac{\partial C_{i1}^0}{\partial n} ds - \int_{\Gamma_1} C_{i1}^0 \frac{\partial \phi_0(x, x_0)}{\partial n} ds + \\ + \int_D \phi_0(x, x_0)\frac{q_{i1}}{d_{i1}} dxdy, \tag{109}$$

$$\chi(x_0)T_2^0(x_0) = \int_{\Gamma_2} \phi_0(x, x_0)\frac{\partial T_2^0}{\partial n} ds - \int_{\Gamma_2} T_2^0 \frac{\partial \phi_0(x, x_0)}{\partial n} ds, \tag{110}$$

$$\chi(x_0)C_{i2}^0(x_0) = \int_{\Gamma_2} \phi_0(x, x_0)\frac{\partial C_{i2}^0}{\partial n} ds - \int_{\Gamma_2} C_{i2}^0 \frac{\partial \phi_0(x, x_0)}{\partial n} ds. \tag{111}$$

Here the function $\phi_0(x, x_0)$ is well-known fundamental solution of Laplace equation, which is in plane case

$$\varphi_0(x, x_0) = \frac{1}{2\pi} \ln\left(\frac{1}{\sqrt{(x - x_0)^2 + (y - y_0)^2}}\right),$$

and function χ is determined by the observation point position:

$$\chi(x_0) = \begin{cases} 0, (x_0) \notin D, (x_0) \notin \Gamma \\ 1/2, (x_0) \in \Gamma \\ 1, (x_0) \in D. \end{cases}$$

The system (108)–(111) can be easy solved by conventional boundary element method. A specific feature of the problem is boundary condition on the boundary $\Gamma = \Gamma_1 \cap \Gamma_2$, that is boundary of growth. If the forth kind boundary conditions are prescribe on the Γ (volume growth), then correspondent integral equations are simply coupled on the curve-line Γ. If correspondent fluxes on the curve-line Γ are discontinuous, then the gap value on previous time step is used.

A quite natural problem of calculation of last domain integrals in Eqs. (108) and (109) arise during the numerical solution. As a rule, it leads to serious computational difficulties, however since the time scale of growth process is enough large and the source terms in the initial Eqs. (104) and (105) are understood as averaged in time, the considered source terms are often constant with respect to space variables. The case of constant source is considered in the present work. The domain integrals can be easy transformed in this case

$$\int_{D_1} \phi_0(x, x_0) q dx dy = q \int_{D_1} \operatorname{div} \operatorname{grad} \phi_1 dx dy = q \int_{\Gamma_1} \frac{\partial \phi_1}{\partial n} ds, \tag{112}$$

where $\Delta\phi_1 = \phi_0$, that is $\phi_1 = -\frac{r^2}{8\pi}(\ln r - 1)$.

7. Results of biological tissue growth calculations

The results of numerical calculations of model problems of growth of one-cell organism colony are shown in **Figures 5** and **6** and in **Tables 1** and **2**.

Growth in direction of maximum concentration of nutrition is evident in both cases. Note only that the structure shown in **Figures 5** and **6** initially were the same structure and only nutrition concentrations were different.

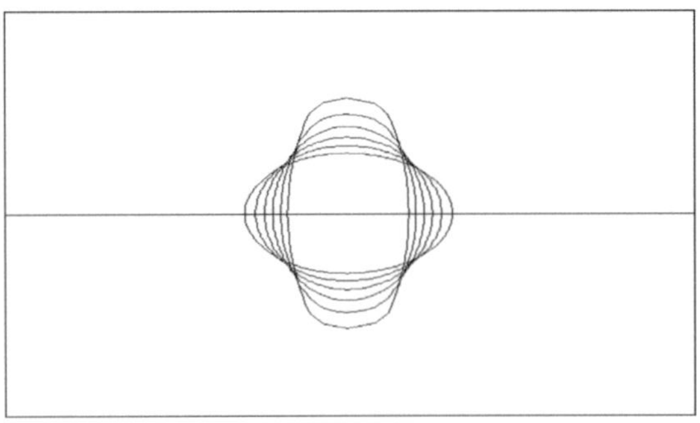

Figure 5.
Growth of biological structure, which was circular at the beginning; nutritions are going into the domain from above and from below [13].

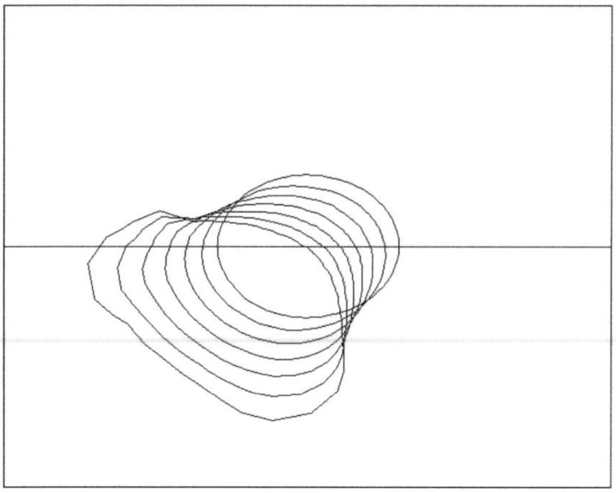

Figure 6.
Growth of biological structure, which was circular at the beginning; nutritions are going into the domain from left and from below [13].

Time (h)	Mass of biological structure
0	0.28378030
1	0.28792960
2	0.29541710
3	0.30700770
4	0.32328381
5	0.34431560
6	0.37013320
7	0.40161840

Table 1.
*Mass of growing biological structure shown in **Figure** 5.*

As it can be seen from **Table 2**, the growth process is accelerated with time. A caution of such acceleration is approaching of the boundary of growing biological structure to the outer boundaries of the domain, where high nutrition concentrations are prescribed according to boundary conditions (82) and (83); as a result, correspondent diffusive fluxes are increasing, what is accelerating the growth process. However, effect of nutrition consumption by more massive increased biological structure decelerates the growth process.

Similarly to above considered case of Stefan problem, since there is not any known analytical solution of biological growth problem to check accuracy of the obtained numerical solutions, the authors of the present work had to change numbers of boundary elements and compare correspondent numerical results. For example, the presented above numerical calculations were made under following parameters: phase transition boundary is approximated by 40 boundary elements at every time step of calculation and outer boundaries of the domain were approximated by 4x40 boundary elements. Checking calculations with 80 and 4x80 and 160 and 4x160 boundary elements and dimensionless time step varying from $\Delta\tau = 0,1$ to $\Delta\tau = 0,001$, correspondingly, shows change of the obtained results no more than 1%. The authors made a conclusion about satisfactory accuracy of the considered numerical approach.

Time (h)	Mass of biological structure
0	0.28751980
1	0.30294060
2	0.32969960
3	0.36981910
4	0.42709790
5	0.50863440
6	0.63095590

Table 2.
Mass of growing biological structure shown in ***Figure 6****.*

8. Conclusions

Beside formulated above conclusions, some additional conclusions can be made concerning the whole investigation. As it is mentioned above, the proposed approach is more general and has more opportunities than earlier existing computational methods for slow-phase transitions. It gives an opportunity to effectively calculate of the processes in more broad interval of Stefan numbers in domains of complex geometrical shapes. Nevertheless, an accuracy of the proposed approach has not been investigated theoretically by a proper way, and enough high accuracy of the proposed algorithms is confirmed by the series of test calculations. The proposed approach can be recommended for calculations of relevant phenomena of slow phase transformations in microgravity and in environment. They also can be used in design of space-rocket techniques. The proposed approach is the only way of calculation for a lot of practically interesting cases. It is necessary to note that the phase transition process is mainly determined by zeroth approximation; another approximations starting from the first one have small influences on the process, especially for small Stefan numbers.

The main idea of the second part of the present paper is to develop a computational method for the problem of biological structure growth, based on the fact that biological growth is relatively very slow process. Considered circumstance leads to asymptotic analysis based on smallness of relation of correspondent time scales. Nevertheless the problem was formulated in quite general form, as a result of asymptotic analysis by small parameter method it is managed to build an analytical solution in one-dimensional case (what was made in previous publications, see, for example [13]) and to propose effective boundary element algorithm for numerical solution described above. Note that the above consideration is restricted only by zero-th approximation in the asymptotic expansion of the solution.

Calculations of specific biological structures did not concern the aim of the present work. However, the examples of calculations of special model problems show workability and effectiveness of the proposed method.

There is a quite natural question about applicability of the algorithm to the very important problem of tumor growth. The answer remains unclear at the moment, because it is unclear whether the used metabolism model can describe a tumor growth process or not. However there is no mathematical insuperable hindrance but only biological.

Author details

Dmytro V. Yevdokymov and Yuri L. Menshikov*
Mechanical and Mathematical Faculty, Oles Honchar Dnipro National University, Ukraine

*Address all correspondence to: menshikov2003@mail.ru

References

[1] Rubinstein L. The Stefan Problem. Translations of Mathematical Monographs. Vol. 27. Providence, R.L.: American Mathematical Society; 1971. pp. 347-419

[2] Lock G, Gunderson J, Quon D, Donnelly J. International Journal of Heat and Mass Transfer. 1969;**12**(11):130-145

[3] Chuang YK, Szekely J. International Journal of Heat and Mass Transfer. 1971; **14**:1285-1294

[4] Chuang Y, Szekely J. International Journal of Heat and Mass Transfer. 1972; **15**:1171-1174

[5] Khrutch V, Yevdokymov D. Bulletin of Dnipropetrovsk University. Series: Mechanics. 2002;**6**(1):9-16. (in Russian)

[6] Brebbia C, Telles J, Wrobel LC. Boundary Element Techniques. Berlin, New York: Springer-Verlag; 1984. p. 345

[7] Banerjee P, Butterfield R. Boundary Element Methods in Engineering Science. London, New York: McGraw-Hill; 1981. p. 452

[8] Bevza E, Yevdokymov D, Kochubey O. Bulletin of Donetsk National University. Series A: Natural Sciences. 2002;**12**:249-253. (in Russian)

[9] Bevza E, Yevdokymov D, Kochubey O. Bulletin of Kharkov National University. 2003;**590**:26-31. (in Russian)

[10] Brazaluk I, Yevdokymov D. Asymptotic approach and boundary element method for calculation of slow phase transitions. In: Proceedings of the 4th International Conference on Computational Methods for Thermal Problems; Georgia Tech, Atlanta, USA. 2016. pp. 286-289. Available from: http://www.thermacomp.com/public/index.php?node=6&nm=ThermaComp

[11] Greenspan H. Journal of Theoretical Biology. 1976;**56**:229-242

[12] Byrne H, Chaplin M. Mathematical Biosciences. 1995;**130**:151-181

[13] Brazaluk I, Gubin O, Yevdokymov D. Bulletin of Dnipropetrovsk University. Series: Mechanics. 2015:96-114

Chapter 4

Modeling of the Two-Dimensional Thawing of Logs in an Air Environment

Nencho Deliiski, Ladislav Dzurenda and Natalia Tumbarkova

Abstract

A two-dimensional mathematical model has been created, solved, and verified for the transient nonlinear heat conduction in logs during their thawing in an air environment. For the numerical solution of the model, an explicit form of the finite-difference method in the computing medium of Visual FORTRAN Professional has been used. The chapter presents solutions of the model and its validation towards own experimental studies. During the validation of the model, the inverse task of the heat transfer has been solved for the determination of the logs' heat transfer coefficients in radial and longitudinal directions. This task has been solved also in regard to the logs' surface temperature, which depends on the mentioned coefficients. The results from the experimental and simulative investigation of 2D nonstationary temperature distribution in the longitudinal section of poplar logs with a diameter of 0.24 m, length of 0.48 m, and an initial temperature of approximately –30°C during their many hours thawing in an air environment at room temperature are presented, visualized, and analyzed.

Keywords: heat conduction, modeling, logs, thawing, heat transfer coefficients, surface temperature

1. Introduction

The duration and the energy consumption of the thermal treatment of frozen logs aimed at their thawing and plasticizing for the production of veneer in winter are very high [1–9]. For example, thawing and plasticizing of poplar and pine logs with an initial temperature of –10°C and moisture content of 0.6 $kg{\cdot}kg^{-1}$ about 53 $kWh{\cdot}m^{-3}$ and 64 $kWh{\cdot}m^{-3}$ thermal energy, respectively, are needed [9].

In the specialized literature, there are few reports about the temperature fields subjected to thawing in agitated water or steam frozen logs [7–21], and there is very scarce information about research of the temperature distribution in frozen logs during their thawing in an air environment given by the authors only [22].

The computation of the temperature field in logs during their thawing in water or steam is carried out using mathematical models, which solve the so-called direct task of the heat transfer. This is the task when all variables in the model are known, and this allows computing the temperature field in the body [23, 24].

The computation of the temperature field in logs during their thawing in an air environment requires solving of the so-called inverse task of the heat transfer. This is the task when the model of the studied object and the experimentally obtained temperature field in it are known, but one or more variables in the model need to be determined during the solving and validation of the model [24].

The results from investigations of the temperature change subjected to thawing frozen logs only at conductive boundary conditions (i.e., at prescribed surface temperature) have been reported [2, 7–21].

The modeling and the multiparameter study of the thawing process of logs in air environment is of considerable scientific and practical interest. For example, as a result of such a study, it is possible to determine the real initial temperature of logs depending on their dimensions, wood species, moisture content, and the temperature of the air near the logs during their many days staying in an open warehouse before the thermal treatment in the production of veneer. The information about the real value of that immeasurable parameter can be used for scientifically based computing of the optimal, energy saving regimes for thermal treatment of each specific batch of logs.

This chapter presents the creation, numerical solving and validation of a two-dimensional nonlinear mathematical model of the transient heat conduction in frozen logs during their thawing at convective boundary conditions in an air environment. A validation of the models towards own experimentally determined 2D temperature distribution in poplar logs with a diameter of 0.24 m, length of 0.48 m, initial temperature of approximately –30°C, and moisture content above the hygroscopic range during their 70 h thawing at room temperature has been carried out.

During the validation of the model, the inverse task has been solved for the determination of the unknown logs' heat transfer coefficients in radial and longitudinal directions. This task has been solved also in regard to the logs' surface temperature, which depends on the mentioned coefficients.

2. Mechanism of 2D heat distribution in logs during thawing

2.1 Mathematical model of the 2D temperature distribution in frozen logs during their thawing in an air environment

In [8] the following common form of a model, which describes the 2D nonstationary temperature distribution subjected to thawing frozen logs in an air environment, has been suggested:

$$c_{\text{we-1,2,3}} \cdot \rho_{\text{w}} \frac{\partial T(r,z,\tau)}{\partial \tau} = \lambda_{\text{wr}} \left[\frac{\partial^2 T(r,z,\tau)}{\partial r^2} + \frac{1}{r} \cdot \frac{\partial T(r,z,\tau)}{\partial r} \right] + \frac{\partial \lambda_{\text{wr}}}{\partial T} \left[\frac{\partial T(r,z,\tau)}{\partial r} \right]^2 + \\ + \lambda_{\text{wp}} \frac{\partial^2 T(r,z,\tau)}{\partial z^2} + \frac{\partial \lambda_{\text{wp}}}{\partial T} \left[\frac{\partial T(r,z,\tau)}{\partial z} \right]^2 \qquad (1)$$

with an initial condition

$$T(r,z,0) = T_{\text{w0-avg}} \qquad (2)$$

and boundary conditions for convective heat transfer:

- Along the radial coordinate r on the logs' frontal surface during thawing

$$\frac{\partial T(r,0,\tau)}{\partial r} = -\frac{\alpha_{\text{wp}}(r,0,\tau)}{\lambda_{\text{wp}}(r,0,\tau)} [T(r,0,\tau) - T_{\text{m}}(\tau)] \qquad (3)$$

- Along the longitudinal coordinate z on the logs' cylindrical surface during thawing

$$\frac{\partial T(0,z,\tau)}{\partial z} = -\frac{\alpha_{\mathrm{wr}}(0,z,\tau)}{\lambda_{\mathrm{wr}}(0,z,\tau)}\left[T(0,z,\tau) - T_{\mathrm{m}}(\tau)\right] \tag{4}$$

In [8] solutions of Eq. (1) only at conductive boundary conditions for the case of autoclave steaming of logs aimed at their plasticizing in the production of veneer have been realized and graphically presented.

An approach for solving Eq. (1) at much more complicated convective boundary conditions and verification of model (1) to (4) is considered below.

2.2 Mathematical description of the thermophysical characteristics of logs

In **Figure 1** the three temperature ranges are presented, at which the process of the logs' thawing above the hygroscopic range is carried out, i.e., when $u > u_{\mathrm{fsp}}$.

There thermophysical characteristics of the logs and of both the frozen and nonfrozen free and bound water in them during the separate temperature ranges are also shown. The information on these characteristics is very important for the solving of the model given above.

The mathematical descriptions of the thermal conductivities of nonfrozen wood, $\lambda_{\text{w-nfr}}$, and frozen wood, $\lambda_{\text{w-fr}}$, and also of the specific heat capacities of nonfrozen wood, $c_{\text{w-nfr}}$, frozen wood, $c_{\text{w-fr}}$, and frozen free and bound water in the wood, c_{fw} and c_{bwm}, have been suggested in [8, 9, 18] using the experimentally determined data in the dissertations by Kanter [25] and Chudinov [2] for their change as a function of t and u. According to the suggested in [8, 9, 18] approach, the wood thermal conductivity during thawing of logs with moisture content u above the hygroscopic range can be calculated with the help of the following equations for $\lambda_{\mathrm{w}}(T, u, \rho_{\mathrm{b}}, u_{\mathrm{fsp}})$:

$$\lambda_{\mathrm{w}} = \lambda_{\mathrm{w0}} \cdot \gamma \cdot [1 + \beta \cdot (T - 273.15)], \tag{5}$$

$$\lambda_{\mathrm{w0}} = K_{\mathrm{ad}} \cdot v \cdot \left[0.165 + (1.39 + 3.8u) \cdot \left(3.3 \cdot 10^{-7}\rho_{\mathrm{b}}^{2} + 1.015 \cdot 10^{-3}\rho_{\mathrm{b}}\right)\right], \tag{6}$$

$$v = 0.1284 - 0.013u. \tag{7}$$

The coefficients γ and β in Eq. (5) are calculated using the next equations:

- For nonfrozen wood at $u > u_{\mathrm{fsp}}^{272.15}$ and $272.15\mathrm{K} < T \leq 423.15\mathrm{K}$

$$\gamma = 1.0, \tag{8}$$

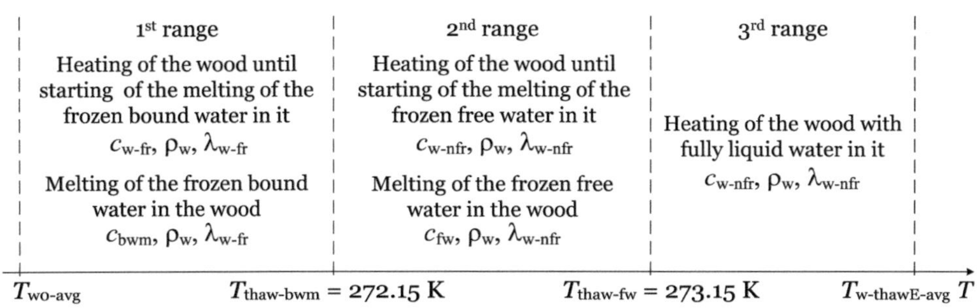

Figure 1.
Temperature ranges of the logs' thawing process at u > u_{fsp} *and thermophysical characteristics of the wood and of the frozen and nonfrozen bound and free water in it.*

$$\beta = 3.65\left(\frac{579}{\rho_b} - 0.124\right) \cdot 10^{-3}. \tag{9}$$

- For frozen wood at $u > u_{fsp}^{272.15}$ and $213.15K \le T \le 272.15K$

$$\gamma = 1 + 0.34\left[1.15\left(u - u_{fsp}\right)\right], \tag{10}$$

$$\beta = 0.002\left(u - u_{fsp}\right) - 0.0038\left(\frac{579}{\rho_b} - 0.124\right). \tag{11}$$

The fiber saturation points of the wood species, u_{fsp} and $u_{fsp}^{272.15}$, are calculated according to following Eqs. [9]:

$$u_{fsp} = u_{fsp}^{293.15} - 0.001(T - 293.15), \tag{12}$$

and consequently

$$u_{fsp}^{272.15} = u_{fsp}^{293.15} + 0.021, \tag{13}$$

where $u_{fsp}^{293.15}$ is the standardized fiber saturation point of the wood at T = 293.15 K (i.e., at t = 20°C), kg·kg^{-1}, and $u_{fsp}^{272.15}$ is the fiber saturation point at T = 272.15 K (i.e., at t = –1°C), kg·kg^{-1}. At t = –1°C, the melting of the frozen bound water in the wood is fully completed, and the melting of the free water in the wood starts [22, 26].

The effective specific heat capacities of the logs during the pointed three ranges of the thawing process, $c_{\text{we-1,2,3}}$, which participate in Eq. (1), are equal to the following:

$$\text{First range}: c_{\text{we-1}} = c_{w-fr} + c_{bwm}, \tag{14}$$

$$\text{Second range}: c_{\text{we-2}} = c_{w-nfr} + c_{fw}, \tag{15}$$

$$\text{Third range}: c_{\text{we-3}} = c_{w-nfr}. \tag{16}$$

According to the suggested in [8, 9, 22] mathematical description, the effective specific heat capacities of the logs during their thawing can be calculated with the help of the following equations for $c_{\text{we-1,2,3}}(T, u, u_{fsp})$:

$$c_{\text{we-1,2,3}} = \left\{\begin{array}{l} \left[1.06 + 0.04u + \dfrac{0.00075(T - 272.15)}{u_{fsp}^{272.15}}\right] \cdot \\ \cdot \dfrac{526 + 2.95T + 0.0022T^2 + 2261u + 1976u_{fsp}^{272.15}}{1 + \text{u}} + \\ +1.8938 \cdot 10^4\left(u_{fsp}^{272.15} - 0.12\right) \cdot \dfrac{\exp\left[0.0567(T - 272.15)\right]}{1 + u} \\ @u > u_{fsp}^{272.15} \& 213.15\text{K} \le T \le 272.15\text{K} \quad (1^{\text{st}}\ \text{range}) \\ \\ \dfrac{2862u + 555}{1 + u} + \dfrac{5.42u + 2.95}{1 + u}T + \dfrac{0.0036}{1 + u}T^2 + \\ +3.34 \cdot 10^5 \dfrac{u - u_{fsp}^{272.15}}{1 + u} \\ @u > u_{fsp}^{272.15}\ \& 272.15\text{K} < T < 273.15\text{K} \quad (2^{\text{nd}}\ \text{range}) \\ \\ \dfrac{2862u + 555}{1 + u} + \dfrac{5.42u + 2.95}{1 + u}T + \dfrac{0.0036}{1 + u}T^2 \\ @u > u_{fsp}^{272.15}\ \& 273.15\text{K} \le T \le 413.15\text{K} \quad (3^{\text{rd}}\ \text{range}) \end{array}\right\} \tag{17}$$

The wood density, ρ_w, which participates in Eq. (1), is determined above the hygroscopic range according to the following Equation [1–22, 27]:

$$\rho_w = \rho_b \cdot (1 + u). \tag{18}$$

2.3 Mathematical description of the heat transfer coefficients of logs

For solving of the 2D mathematical model given above, it is needed to have values for the heat transfer coefficients of the logs in radial and longitudinal directions, α_{wr} and α_{wp}, respectively, which participate in Eqs. (3) and (4).

As it was mentioned in the Introduction, the values of α_{wr} and α_{wp} can be computed by solving the inverse task of the heat transfer between the logs and surrounding air environment.

The calculation of α_{wr} and α_{wp} can be carried out with the help of the following equations of the similarity theory, which are valid for the cases of heating of horizontally situated cylindrical bodies in conditions of free air convection [28]:

$$\alpha_{wr} = \frac{Nu_r \cdot \lambda_a}{L}, \tag{19}$$

$$\alpha_{wp} = \frac{Nu_p \cdot \lambda_a}{D}, \tag{20}$$

$$Nu_r = f\left[(Gr_r \cdot Pr_a)^{0.25} \cdot \left(\frac{Pr_a}{Pr_s}\right)^{0.25}\right], \tag{21}$$

$$Nu_p = f\left[(Gr_p \cdot Pr_a)^{0.25} \cdot \left(\frac{Pr_a}{Pr_s}\right)^{0.25}\right], \tag{22}$$

$$Gr_r = \frac{g \cdot \beta_a \cdot L^3}{w_a^2} \cdot [T_m(\tau) - T_s(\tau)], \tag{23}$$

$$Gr_p = \frac{g \cdot \beta_a \cdot D^3}{w_a^2} \cdot [T_m(\tau) - T_s(\tau)], \tag{24}$$

$$Pr_a = \frac{w_a(T_a)}{a_a(T_a)}, \tag{25}$$

$$Pr_s = \frac{w_a(T_s)}{a_a(T_s)}, \tag{26}$$

For the usage of Eqs. (19)–(26), it is needed to have a mathematical description of the thermophysical characteristics of the air, λ, β, w, and a, depending on T and φ. The temperature of the air near the logs subjected to thawing during our experiments described below changes in the range from 243.15 to 303.15 K (i.e., from –30°C to 30°C), and φ changes from 40–100% (see **Figures 2** and **3**).

For the calculation of λ_a, β_a, w_a, and a_a, the temperature of the air, T_a, must be used, but for the calculation of w_s and a_s in Eq. (26), the temperature of the surface of the logs, T_s, has to be used.

In the accessible specialized sources, we did not find suitable mathematical descriptions of λ, β, w, and a of the air, depending on T and φ, which could be applied for the precise determination of α_{wr} and α_{wp} according to Eqs. (19)–(26).

Our further study has shown that for solving the inverse task of the heat transfer between the logs and surrounding air, i.e., for the calculation of the heat transfer coefficients of the logs, which participate in the boundary conditions (3) and (4) of the model, the following equations are suitable [29]:

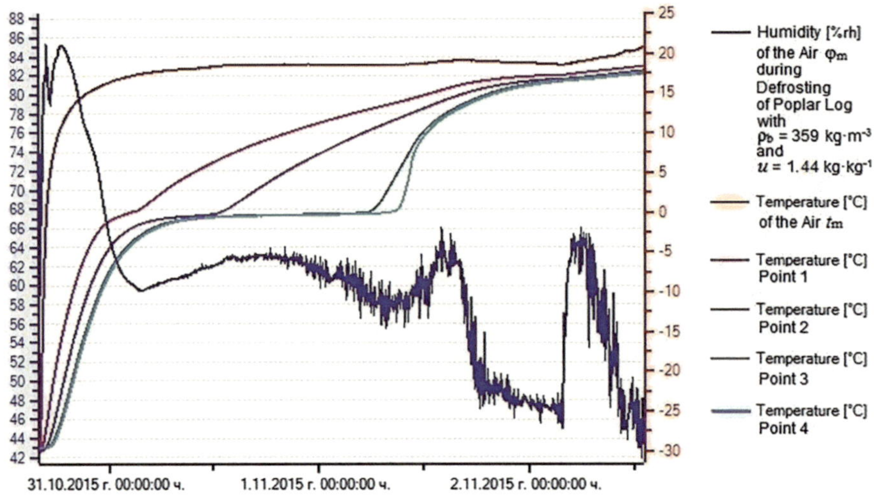

Figure 2.
Experimentally determined change in t_m, φ_m, and t in four points of the studied poplar log P1 during its 70 h thawing.

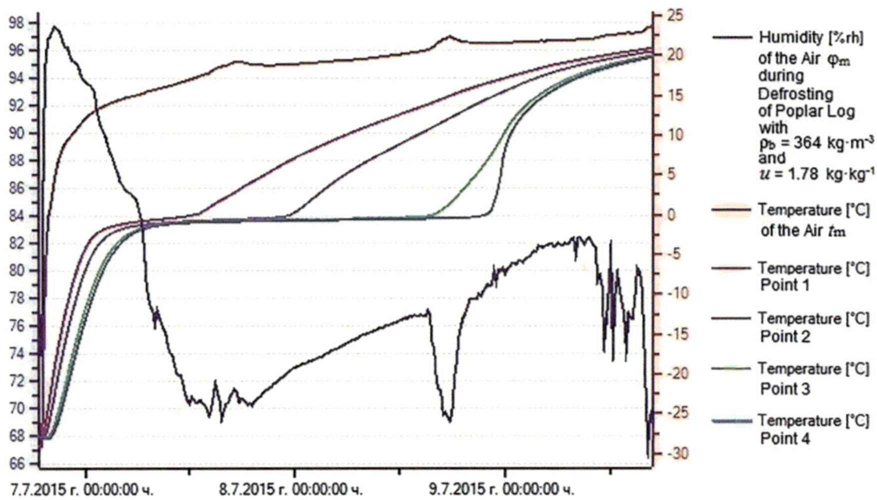

Figure 3.
Experimentally determined change in t_m, φ_m, and t in four points of the studied poplar log P2 during its 70 h thawing.

- In the radial direction on the cylindrical surface of the logs

$$\alpha_{\text{wr}} = 1.123[T(0, z, \tau) - T_{\text{m}}(\tau)]^x \tag{27}$$

- In the longitudinal direction on the frontal surface of the logs

$$\alpha_{\text{wp}} = 2.56[T(r, 0, \tau) - T_{\text{m}}(\tau)]^x \tag{28}$$

where x is an exponent, whose values are determined during the solving and validation of the model through the minimization of the root-square-mean error

(RSME) between the calculated model and experimentally obtained results about the change of the temperature fields subjected to thawing logs.

3. Experimental research of the thawing process of logs

3.1 Experimental research of the 2D temperature distribution in poplar logs during their thawing

For solving the inverse task of the heat transfer aimed at validation of the suggested above mathematical model, it is necessary to have experimentally obtained data about the 2D temperature distribution in logs during their thawing. That is why we realized such experiments using poplar (*Populus nigra* L.) logs with $D = 0.24$ m, $L = 0.48$ m, and $u > u_{fsp}$ [26].

In **Figure 4** the coordinates of four representative points of the logs, in which the 2D change in the temperature was measured and registered during the logs' thawing, are shown.

For the freezing of the logs before their thawing, a horizontal freezer was used with adjustable temperature range from –1 to –30°C. Sensors Pt100 with long metal casings were positioned in the drilled four holes of the logs. After 50 h separately freezing each logs, the freezer was switched off. Then its lid was opened, and 70 h thawing of the log at room temperature was carried out.

The automatic measurement and record of t_m, φ_m, and t in the representative points of the logs during the experiments was accomplished by Data Logger type HygroLog NT3 produced by the Swiss firm ROTRONIC AG.

In **Figures 2** and **3**, the change in the temperature of the processing air medium, t_m, and in its humidity, φ_m, and also in the temperature in four representative points of two poplar logs, named below as P1 and P2, respectively, during their separate 70 h thawing is presented.

All curves of the experimentally obtained data on these figures are drawn using the licensed software HW4 of the Data Logger. The left coordinate axis on the figures is graduated at % of φ_m, and the right one is graduated at °C of t.

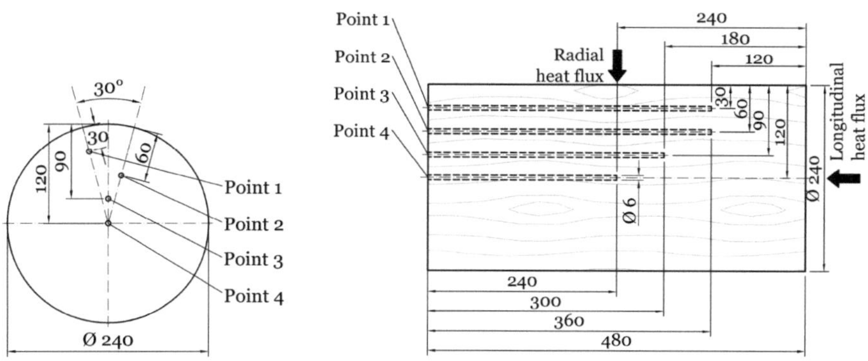

Figure 4.
Radial (left) and longitudinal (right) coordinates of four characteristic points for the measurement of the temperature in logs subjected to thawing.

3.2 Mathematical description of the air medium temperature during logs' thawing

The change shown in **Figures 2** and **3** air medium temperature T_m during the logs' thawing with correlation 0.98 and root-square-mean error, $\sigma < 1.5°C$, has been approximated with the help of the software package Table Curve 2D by the following equation:

$$T_m = \frac{a + c \cdot \tau^{0.5}}{1 + b \cdot \tau^{0.5}}, \tag{29}$$

whose coefficients are equal to:

- For log P1: a = 293.3637194, b = −0.00236425, c = −0.69281743.
- For log P2: a = 299.2738855, b = −0.00245303, c = −0.73047119.

and τ is the sum of the time of logs' freezing, equal to 50 h = 180,000 s, and the current time of the subsequent thawing of the logs, s.

Eq. (29) was used for solving Eqs. (3) and (4) of the model.

4. Numerical solution of the mathematical model of the logs' thawing process

The mathematical descriptions of the thermophysical characteristics of the logs and also of T_m considered above were introduced in the mathematical model (1) to (4). An explicit form of the finite-difference method was used for solving of the model without any simplifications [7, 8].

4.1 Presentation of the model in a form suitable for programming

4.1.1 Presentation of Eq. (1) of the model

The presentation of Eq. (1) of the model suitable for programming discrete analogue has been carried out using the given in **Figures 5** and **6** coordinate system.

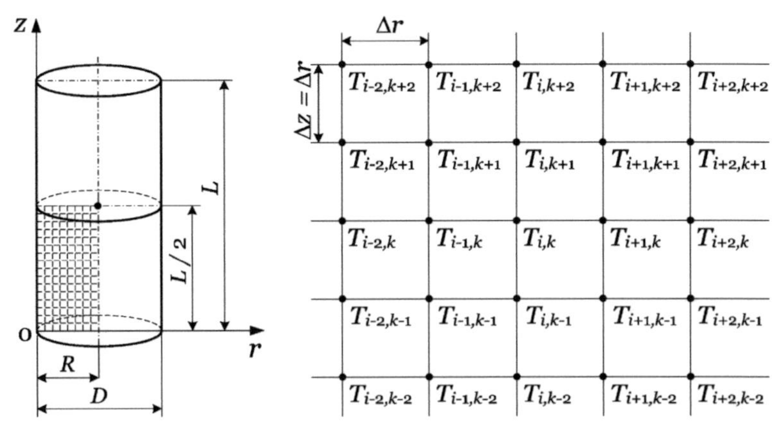

Figure 5.
Positioning of the knots of 2D calculation mesh on ¼ of longitudinal section of a log subjected to thawing (left) and calculation mesh for solving of the model (right).

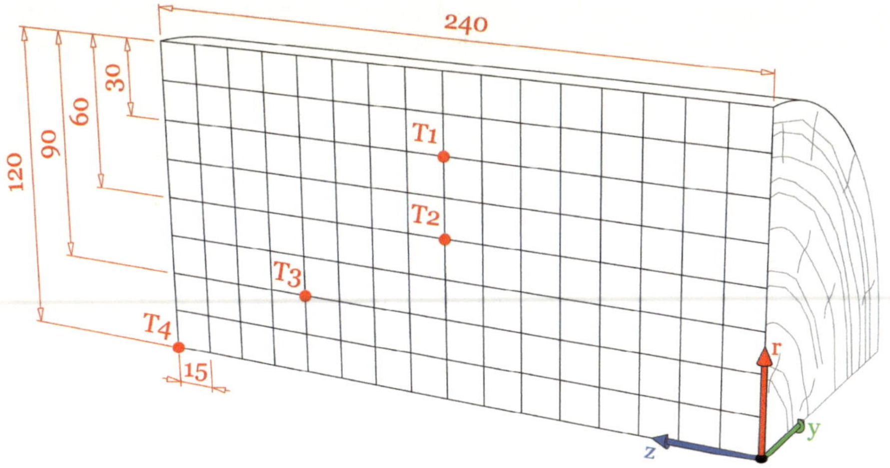

Figure 6.
Calculation mesh and representative points T1, T2, T3, and T4 on ¼ of the longitudinal section subjected to thawing log.

These figures show the positioning of the knots of the calculation mesh and four representative points, in which the nonstationary 2D distribution of the temperature in the longitudinal section subjected to thawing log has been calculated. The mesh has been built on ¼ of the longitudinal section of the log due to the fact that this ¼ is mirrored symmetrical towards the remaining ¾ of the same section.

Taking into consideration Eqs. (5) and (6), it can be written that

$$\lambda_{\mathrm{w}} = \lambda_{\mathrm{w0r,p}} \cdot \gamma \cdot [1 + \beta \cdot (T - 273.15)] \tag{30}$$

$$\lambda_{\mathrm{w0r}} = K_{\mathrm{wr}} \cdot v \cdot \left[0.165 + (1.39 + 3.8u) \cdot \left(3.3 \cdot 10^{-7} \rho_{\mathrm{b}}^2 + 1.015 \cdot 10^{-3} \rho_{\mathrm{b}}\right)\right] \tag{31}$$

$$\lambda_{\mathrm{w0p}} = K_{\mathrm{wp}} \cdot v \cdot \left[0.165 + (1.39 + 3.8u) \cdot \left(3.3 \cdot 10^{-7} \rho_{\mathrm{b}}^2 + 1.015 \cdot 10^{-3} \rho_{\mathrm{b}}\right)\right] \tag{32}$$

and using the coefficient

$$K_{\mathrm{wp/wr}} = \frac{K_{\mathrm{wp}}}{K_{\mathrm{wr}}} \tag{33}$$

The discrete finite-difference analogue of the left-hand part of Eq. (1), which is suitable for programming in FORTRAN, has the following form [7, 30]:

$$c_{\mathrm{we-1,2,3}} \cdot \rho_{\mathrm{w}} \frac{\partial T(r,z,\tau)}{\partial \tau} \approx c_{\mathrm{we-1,2,3}}^{n} \cdot \rho_{\mathrm{w}} \frac{T_{i,k}^{n+1} - T_{i,k}^{n}}{\Delta \tau}. \tag{34}$$

Taking into account Eqs. (30), (31), and (32), the discrete analogue of the right-hand part of Eq. (1) has the following form:

$$\begin{aligned} &\lambda_{\mathrm{wr}} \left[\frac{\partial^2 T(r,z,\tau)}{\partial r^2} + \frac{1}{r} \cdot \frac{\partial T(r,z,\tau)}{\partial r}\right] + \frac{\partial \lambda_{\mathrm{wr}}}{\partial T}\left[\frac{\partial T(r,z,\tau)}{\partial r}\right]^2 + \\ &+\lambda_{\mathrm{wp}} \frac{\partial^2 T(r,z,\tau)}{\partial z^2} + \frac{\partial \lambda_{\mathrm{wp}}}{\partial T}\left[\frac{\partial T(r,z,\tau)}{\partial z}\right]^2 = \left\{\lambda_{\mathrm{w0r}} \cdot \gamma \cdot \left[1 + \beta \cdot \left(T_{i,k}^{n} - 273.15\right)\right]\right\} \cdot \\ &\cdot \left[\frac{T_{i-1,k}^{n} - 2T_{i,k}^{n} + T_{i+1,k}^{n}}{\Delta r^2} + \frac{1}{(i-1) \cdot \Delta r} \cdot \frac{T_{i-1,k}^{n} - T_{i,k}^{n}}{\Delta r}\right] + \beta \cdot \left(\frac{T_{i-1,k}^{n} - T_{i,k}^{n}}{\Delta r^2}\right)^2 + \\ &+\left\{\lambda_{\mathrm{w0p}} \cdot \gamma \cdot \left[1 + \beta \cdot \left(T_{i,k}^{n} - 273.15\right)\right]\right\} \cdot \frac{T_{i,k-1}^{n} - 2T_{i,k}^{n} + T_{i,k+1}^{n}}{\Delta z^2} + \beta \cdot \left(\frac{T_{i,k-1}^{n} - T_{i,k}^{n}}{\Delta z^2}\right)^2. \end{aligned} \tag{35}$$

After alignment of Eq. (34) with Eq. (35) and taking into account Eq. (33), at $\Delta z = \Delta r$, it is obtained that Eq. (1) is transformed into the following system of algebraic equations:

$$T_{i,k}^{n+1} = T_{i,k}^{n} + \frac{\lambda_{\text{w0r}} \cdot \gamma \cdot \Delta\tau}{c_{\text{we-1,2,3}}^{n} \cdot \rho_{\text{w}} \cdot \Delta r^{2}} \cdot \left\{ \begin{array}{l} \left[1 + \beta \cdot \left(T_{i,k}^{n} - 273.15\right)\right] \cdot \left[\begin{array}{l} T_{i-1,k}^{n} + T_{i+1,k}^{n} + K_{\text{wp/wr}}\left(T_{i,k-1}^{n} + T_{i,k+1}^{n}\right) - \\ -\left(2 + 2K_{\text{wp/wr}}\right)T_{i,k}^{n} + \frac{1}{i-1}\left(T_{i-1,k}^{n} - T_{i,k}^{n}\right) \end{array} \right] + \\ +\beta \cdot \left[\left(T_{i-1,k}^{n} - T_{i,k}^{n}\right)^{2} + K_{\text{wp/wr}}\left(T_{i,k-1}^{n} - T_{i,k}^{n}\right)^{2}\right] \end{array} \right\}. \tag{36}$$

The term $\frac{1}{r}$ in the right-hand part of Eq. (1) is represented as $\frac{1}{(i-1)\cdot\Delta r}$ in Eq. (35). According to the requirements of FORTRAN [7, 30], the knots of the calculation mesh, which are situated on the log's surfaces, are denoted by numbers $i = 1$ and $k = 1$ along the coordinate axes r and z, respectively.

The temperature in these surface knots is calculated with the help of Eqs. (38) and (42) given below. Since Eq. (36) calculates the temperature in the knots, which are located inside the logs, i.e., in the knots with $i \geq 2$ and $k \geq 2$, the denominator of the term $\frac{1}{i-1}$ in this equation is always greater than zero.

It can be noted that the effective specific heat capacities of the log during the pointed above three ranges of its thawing process (see **Figure 1**), $c_{\text{we-1}}$, $c_{\text{we-2}}$, and $c_{\text{we-3}}$, which are unitedly represented as $c_{\text{we-1,2,3}}$ in Eq. (36), are computed according to Eq. (17) separately for each knot of the calculation mesh.

4.1.2 Presentation of the equation of the initial condition in the model

The initial condition (2) of the model of logs' thawing process obtains the following discrete finite-difference form:

$$T_{i,k}^{0} = T_{\text{w0-avg}} \tag{37}$$

where $T_{\text{w0-avg}}$ is the experimentally determined average mass temperature of the log at the beginning of the thawing process, K.

4.1.3 Presentation of the equation of boundary condition in the model along the radial coordinate

The boundary condition (3) of the logs' thawing process obtains the following final form, suitable for programming in FORTRAN:

$$T_{i,1}^{n+1} = \frac{T_{i,2}^{n} + G_{i,1}^{n} \cdot T_{\text{m}}^{n+1}}{1 + G_{i,1}^{n}}. \tag{38}$$

The variable $G_{i,1}^{n}$ in Eq. (38) is equal to

$$G_{i,1}^{n} = \frac{\Delta r \cdot \alpha_{\text{wp}}^{n}}{\lambda_{\text{w0p}} \cdot \gamma \cdot \left[1 + \beta \cdot \left(T_{i,1}^{n} - 273.15\right)\right]}, \tag{39}$$

where according to Eqs. (28) and (29)

$$\alpha_{\mathrm{wp}}^{n} = 2.56\left[T_{i,1}^{n} - T_{\mathrm{m}}^{n}\right]^{x}, \tag{40}$$

where

$$T_{\mathrm{m}}^{n} = \frac{a + c \cdot (n \cdot \Delta\tau)^{0.5}}{1 + b \cdot (n \cdot \Delta\tau)^{0.5}}. \tag{41}$$

4.1.4. Presentation of the equation of boundary condition in the model along the longitudinal coordinate

Analogously, the boundary condition (4) of the logs' thawing process obtains the following final form, suitable for programming in FORTRAN:

$$T_{1,k}^{n+1} = \frac{T_{2,k}^{n} + G_{1,k}^{n} \cdot T_{\mathrm{m}}^{n+1}}{1 + G_{1,k}^{n}}. \tag{42}$$

The variable $G_{1,k}^{n}$ in Eq. (42) is equal to

$$G_{1,k}^{n} = \frac{\Delta r \cdot \alpha_{\mathrm{wr}}^{n}}{\lambda_{\mathrm{w0r}} \cdot \gamma \cdot \left[1 + \beta \cdot \left(T_{1,k}^{n} - 273.15\right)\right]}, \tag{43}$$

where according to Eq. (27)

$$\alpha_{\mathrm{wr}}^{n} = 1.123\left[T_{1,k}^{n} - T_{\mathrm{m}}^{n}\right]^{x} \tag{44}$$

and T_{m}^{n} is calculated according to Eq. (41).

4.2 Input data for solving of the model

The numerical solving and verification of the model (1) to (4) has been realized in the calculation environment of Visual FORTRAN Professional.

Using own software package in that environment, computations were carried out for the determination of the 2D nonstationary change of t in the representative points of the logs P1 and P2, whose experimentally registered temperature fields are presented in **Figures 2** and **3**, respectively.

The initial temperature, $t_{\mathrm{w0\text{-}avg}}$; basic density, ρ_{b}; and moisture content, u, of the logs during the experiments were as follows:

- For log P1: $t_{\mathrm{w0\text{-}avg}} = -29.7$°C, $\rho_{\mathrm{b}} = 359$ kg·kg^{-1}, and $u = 1.44$ kg·kg^{-1}.
- For log P2: $t_{\mathrm{w0\text{-}avg}} = -28.0$°C, $\rho_{\mathrm{b}} = 364$ kg·kg^{-1}, and $u = 1.78$ kg·kg^{-1}.

As it was mentioned above, the duration of the freezing and duration of the subsequent thawing of the logs were equal to 50 and 70 h, respectively.

The model was solved with step $\Delta r = \Delta z = 0.006$ m along the coordinates r and z, with step $\Delta\tau = 6$ s [8, 23], and with the same initial and boundary conditions, as they were during the experimental research.

During the solving of the model, mathematical descriptions of the thermophysical characteristics of poplar sapwood with $u_{\mathrm{fsp}}^{293.15} = 0.35$ kg·kg^{-1}, $K_{\mathrm{wr}} = 1.48$, and $K_{\mathrm{wp}} = 2.88$ [7, 9] have been used.

4.3 Inverse determination of the heat transfer coefficients during solving of the model

The model (1) to (4) was solved with various values of the exponent x in Eqs. (27) and (28). The computed by the model change of t in the four representative points of the logs with each of the tested values of the exponent x during the thawing was compared mathematically with the corresponding one experimentally registered change of t in these points with an interval of 15 min.

The aim of this comparison was to determine the values of x, which ensure the best compliance between the computed and experimentally registered temperature fields in subjected to thawing logs.

As a criterion of the best compliance, the minimum average value of RSME, σ_{avg}, was used, which is equal to

$$\sigma_{avg} = \sqrt{\frac{\sum_{n=1}^{N}\sum_{p=1}^{P}\left(t_{p,n}^{comp} - t_{p,n}^{exp}\right)^2}{P\cdot(N-1)}}, \tag{45}$$

where $t_{p,n}^{comp}$ and $t_{p,n}^{exp}$ are the computed and experimentally registered temperatures in the representative points; p is the number of the representative points of the logs, $p = 1, 2, 3, 4$, i.e., $P = 4$ was inputted into Eq. (45); n is the number of the moments of the thawing process, ($n = 1, 2, 3, \ldots, N = \tau_{thaw})/(150\Delta\tau) = 252{,}000$ s/900 s = 280, because of the circumstance that the comparison of the computed values of t with experimentally registered values in the same points was made with an interval of 15 min = 900 s = $150\Delta\tau$.

For the calculation of σ_{avg}, a software program in the calculation environment of MS Excel was prepared. At τ_{thaw} = 70 h = 252,000 s, RSME has been calculated with the help of the program simultaneously for a total of $N{\cdot}P$ = 1120 temperature–time points during the thawing of each log.

It was determined that the minimum values of RSME overall for the studied four representative points are equal to σ_{avg} = 1.37°C for log P1 and to σ_{avg} = 1.34°C for log P2. These minimum values of σ_{avg} correspond to the following values of the

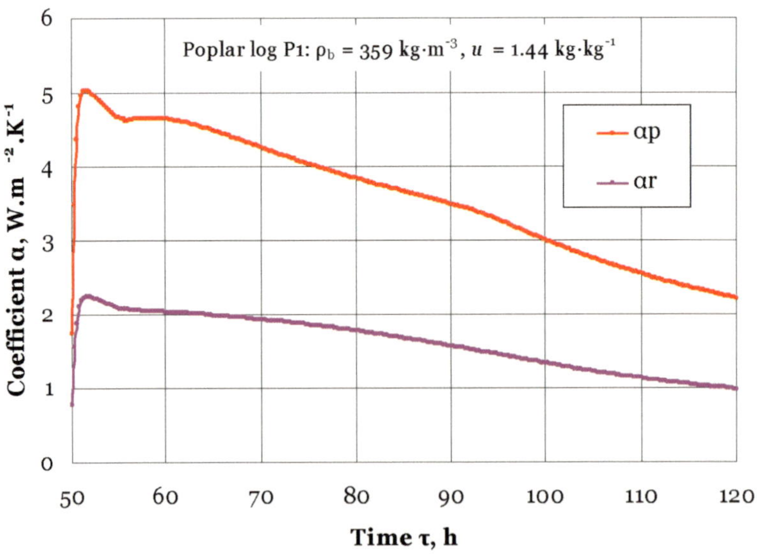

Figure 7.
Calculated change in α_{wr} and α_{wp} of the log P1 during its 70 h thawing.

exponent x in Eqs. (27) and (28), which were obtained during the solving of the inverse task, x = 0.22 for log P1 and x = 0.20 for log P2.

Figures 7 and **8** present the calculated change in α_{wr} and α_{wp} during the studied thawing process of the logs P1 and P2, respectively.

Figures 9 and **10** present the calculated change in t_m and also in the logs' surface temperature t_s and t of 4 representative points of the studied logs.

It can be seen that with the decrease of the difference between t_m and t_s during the logs' thawing, the heat transfer coefficients on **Figures** 7 and **8** gradually decrease, as follows:

- At α_{wr}: from 2.3 to 1.0 W·m^{-2}·K^{-1} for P1 and from 1.9 to 1.2 W·m^{-2}·K^{-1} for P2.
- At α_{wp}: from 5.1 to 2.2 W·m^{-2}·K^{-1} for P1 and from 4.5 to 2.8 W·m^{-2}·K^{-1} for P2.

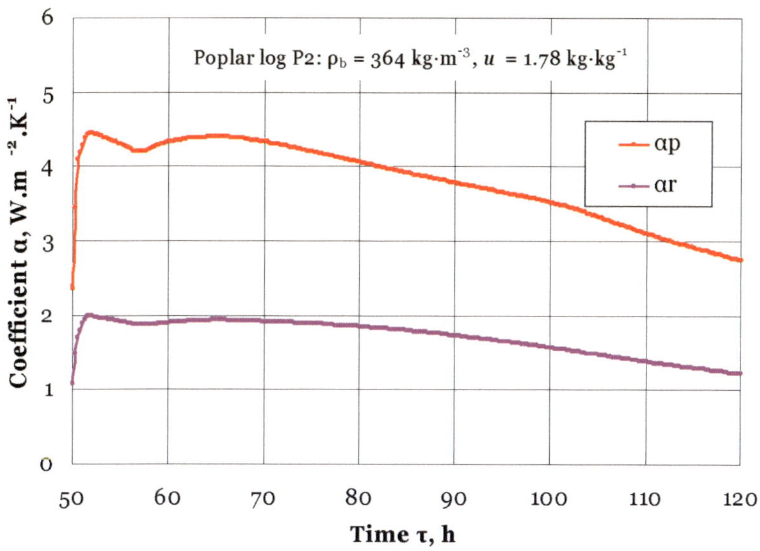

Figure 8.
Calculated change in α_{wr} and α_{wp} of the log P2 during its 70 h thawing.

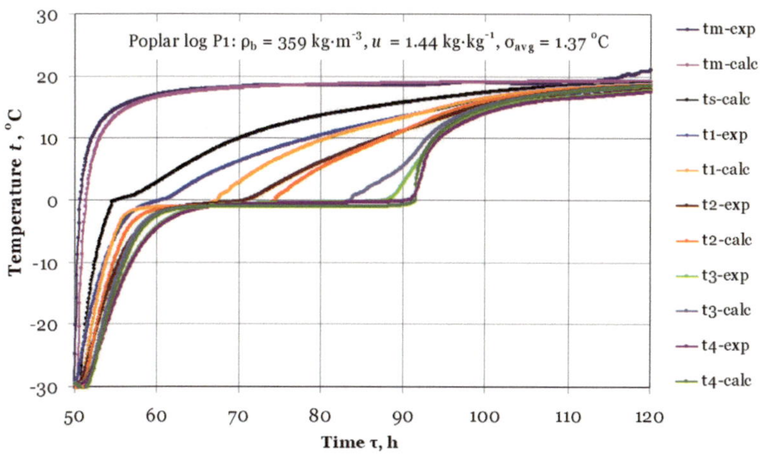

Figure 9.
Experimentally determined and calculated change in t_m, t_s, and t in four points of the log P1 during its 70 h thawing.

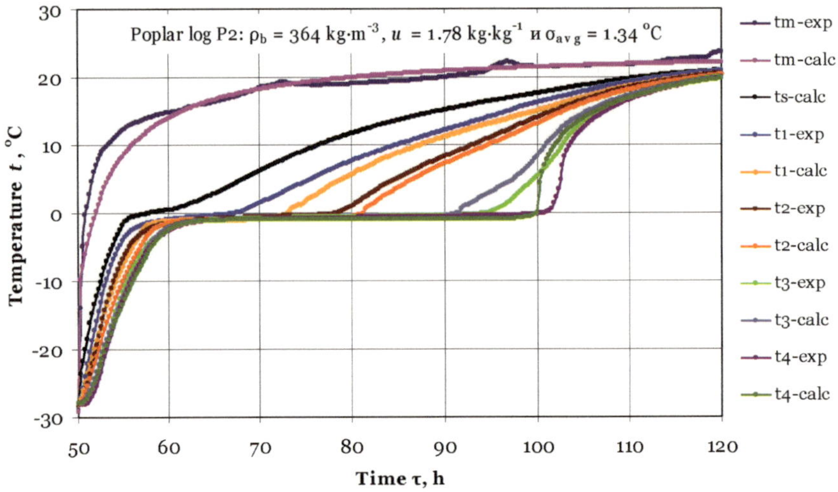

Figure 10.
Experimentally determined and calculated change in t_m, t_s, and t in four points of the log P2 during its 70 h thawing.

Using the obtained change in the heat transfer coefficients, the change in the logs' surface temperature during the thawing, t_s, has been calculated by the model (refer to **Figures 9** and **10**).

The comparison to each other of the analogical curves in **Figures 2** and **9**, and also in **Figures 3** and **10**, shows good conformity between the calculated and experimentally determined changes in the very complicated temperature fields of the studied logs during their thawing.

During our extensive simulations with the model (1) to (4), we established good qualitative and quantitative compliance between computed and experimentally determined temperature fields of logs from numerous wood species with different moisture content above the hygroscopic range [31].

The overall RSME for the studied four representative points in the logs does not exceed 5% of the temperature ranges between the minimal and maximal temperatures of each log during its thawing.

5. Conclusions

This chapter describes the creation, solving, and validation of a 2D nonlinear mathematical model for the transient heat conduction subjected to thawing frozen logs in an air environment.

The mechanism of the heat distribution in logs during their thawing has been described by a 2D equation of heat conduction at convective boundary conditions. For the numerical solving of the model with the help of explicit form of the finite-difference method, a software package has been prepared in the calculation medium of Visual FORTRAN Professional developed by Microsoft.

A validation of the model towards our own experimentally determined 2D temperature distribution in poplar logs with a diameter of 0.24 m, length of 0.48 m, and initial temperature about –30°C during their 70 h separate thawing at room temperature has been carried out.

During the validation of the model, the inverse problem has been solved for the determination of the logs' heat transfer coefficients in radial and longitudinal

DOI: http://dx.doi.org/10.5772/intechopen.93177

directions. This problem has been solved also in regard to the logs' surface temperature, which depends on the mentioned coefficients.

The following minimum values of the average RSME total for the temperature change in four representative points in each of the studied logs have been obtained:

- σ_{avg} = 1.37°C for log P1 with ρ_b = 359 kg·m^{-3} and u = 1.44 kg·kg^{-1}.
- σ_{avg} = 1.34°C for log P2 with ρ_b = 364 kg·m^{-3} and u = 1.78 kg·kg^{-1}.

During the solving of the inverse task, it was determined that the heat transfer coefficients subjected to thawing logs decrease gradually, as follows:

- At α_{wr}: from 2.3 to 1.0 W·m^{-2}·K^{-1} for P1 and from 1.9 to 1.2 W·m^{-2}·K^{-1} for P2.
- At α_{wp}: from 5.1 to 2.2 W·m^{-2}·K^{-1} for P1 and from 4.5 to 2.8 W·m^{-2}·K^{-1} for P2.

Good adequacy and precision of the model towards the results from extensive own experimental studies allow for the carrying out of various calculations with it, which are connected to the nonstationary temperature distribution in logs during their thawing in an air environment. For example, as a result of such calculations, it is possible to determine the real initial temperature of logs depending on their dimensions, wood species, moisture content, and the temperature of the air near the logs during their many days staying in an open warehouse before the thermal treatment in the production of veneer.

The information about the real value of that immeasurable parameter is needed for scientifically based computing of the optimal, energy saving regimes for thermal treatment of each specific batch of logs.

The model of the logs' thawing process can be applied also in the software for controllers used for advanced model predictive automatic control [20, 21, 32] of this treatment. The approach for solving of the inverse task of the heat transfer in this chapter could be further applied in the development and solving of analogous models, for example, for the calculation of the temperature fields during freezing or thawing processes of different wooden and other capillary porous materials.

Acknowledgements

This document was supported by the APVV Grant Agency as part of the project, APVV-17-0456, as a result of work of authors and the considerable assistance of the APVV agency.

Nomenclature

a	temperature conductivity, m^2·s^{-1}
c	specific heat capacity, J·kg^{-1}·K^{-1}
D	diameter, m
g	acceleration of gravity, g = 9.81 m·s^{-2}
Gr	Grashoff's number of similarity
L	length, m
Nu	Nusselt's number of similarity
Pr	Prandtl's number of similarity
R	radius: R = D/2, m

r	radial coordinate: $0 \leq r \leq R$, m
T	temperature, K
t	temperature, °C
u	moisture content, $kg \cdot kg^{-1}$ = %/100
w	kinematic viscosity coefficient, $m^2 \cdot s^{-1}$
x	exponent, –
z	longitudinal coordinate: $0 \leq z \leq L/2$, m
α	heat transfer coefficients between log's surfaces and the surrounding air medium, $W \cdot m^{-2} \cdot K^{-1}$
β	coefficient of the volume expansion of the air, K^{-1}
λ	thermal conductivity (for wood or air), $W \cdot m^{-1} \cdot K^{-1}$
ρ	density, $kg \cdot m^{-3}$
σ	root-square-mean error (RSME), °C
τ	time, s
φ	relative humidity, %
Δr	step along the coordinates r and z for solving of the model, m
$\Delta \tau$	step along the time coordinate for solving of the model, s

Subscripts

a	air
avg	average (for mass temperature of logs or for root-square-mean error)
b	basic (for wood density, based on dry mass divided to green volume)
bw	bound water
bwm	maximum possible amount of the bound water in the wood
comp	computed
exp.	experimental
fr	freezing
fre	end of freezing
fsp	fiber saturation point
fw	free water
i	current number of the knot of the calculation mesh in the direction along the log's radius: i = 1, 2, 3, ... , 21 = $(R/\Delta r + 1)$
k	current number of the knot of the calculation mesh in longitudinal direction of the logs: k = 1, 2, 3, ... , 41 = $(L/2/\Delta r + 1)$
m	medium (for temperature of the air environment near the logs during their thawing process)
p	parallel to the wood fibers
r	radial direction
s	surface
thaw	thawing
w	wood
we	wood effective (for specific heat capacity)
w-fr	wood with frozen water in it
w-nfr	wood with fully liquid water in it
w0p	parallel to the wood fibers at °C
w0r	radial direction of wood at °C
0	initial or at 0°C
1,2,3	1st, 2nd, 3rd (for temperature ranges of the logs' thawing process)
@	at
&	and simultaneously with this

Superscripts

n	current number of the step $\Delta\tau$ along the time coordinate during solving of the model: $n = 1, 2, 3, \ldots, N = \tau_{thaw}/\Delta\tau$
272.15	at 272.15 K, i.e., at –1°C
293.15	at 293.15 K, i.e., at 20°C

Author details

Nencho Deliiski[1*], Ladislav Dzurenda[2] and Natalia Tumbarkova[1]

1 University of Forestry, Sofia, Bulgaria

2 Technical University in Zvolen, Slovakia

*Address all correspondence to: deliiski@netbg.com

References

[1] Vorreiter L. Holztechnologisches Handbuch. Vien: Fromm; 1949. p. 2080

[2] Chudinov BS. Theoretical research of thermo physical properties and thermal treatment of wood [thesis for DSc.]. Krasnojarsk, USSR: SibLTI; 1966 (in Russian)

[3] Kollmann FF, Côté WA Jr. Principles of Wood Science and Technology. I. Solid Wood. Berlin, Heidelberg, New York: Springer-Verlag; 1984. p. 592

[4] Shubin GS. Drying and Thermal Treatment of Wood. Moscow: Lesnaya Promyshlennost, USSR; 1990. p. e337 (in Russian)

[5] Požgaj A, Chovanec D, Kurjatko S, Babiak M. Structure and Properties of Wood. 2nd ed. Bratislava: Priroda a.s; 1997. p. 485 (in Slovak)

[6] Trebula P, Klement I. Drying and Hydro-Thermal Treatment of Wood. Slovakia: Technical University in Zvolen; 2002. p. 449 (in Slovak)

[7] Deliiski N, Dzurenda L. Modelling of the Thermal Processes in the Technologies for Wood Thermal Treatment. Slovakia: Technical University in Zvolen; 2010. p. 224 (in Russian)

[8] Deliiski N. Transient heat conduction in capillary porous bodies. In: Ahsan A, editor. Convection and Conduction Heat Transfer. Rijeka, Croatia: InTech Publishing House; 2011. pp. 149-176. DOI: 10.5772/21424

[9] Deliiski N. Modelling of the Energy Needed for Heating of Capillary Porous Bodies in Frozen and Non-frozen States. Saarbrücken, Germany: Lambert Academic Publishing, Scholars' Press; 2013. p. 116. Available from: http://www.scholars-press.com//system/covergenerator/build/1060

[10] Steinhagen HP. Computerized finite-difference method to calculate transient heat conduction with thawing. Wood and Fiber Science. 1986;**18**(3): 460-467

[11] Steinhagen HP. Heat transfer computation for a long, frozen log heated in agitated water or steam – A practical recipe. Holz als Roh- und Werkstoff. 1991;**49**(7–8):287-290. DOI: 10.1007/BF02663790

[12] Steinhagen HP, Lee HW, Loehnertz SP. LOGHEAT: A computer program of determining log heating times for frozen and non-frozen logs. Forest Products Journal. 1987;**37**(11/12): 60-64

[13] Steinhagen HP, Lee HW. Enthalpy method to compute radial heating and thawing of logs. Wood and Fiber Science. 1988;**20**(4):415-421

[14] Khattabi A, Steinhagen HP. Numerical solution to two-dimensional heating of logs. Holz als Roh- und Werkstoff. 1992;**50**(7–8):308-312. DOI: 10.1007/BF02615359

[15] Khattabi A, Steinhagen HP. Analysis of transient non-linear heat conduction in wood using finite-difference solutions. Holz als Roh- und Werkstoff. 1993;**51**(4):272-278. DOI: 10.1007/BF02629373

[16] Khattabi A, Steinhagen HP. Update of "numerical solution to two-dimensional heating of logs". Holz als Roh- und Werkstoff. 1995;**53**(1):93-94. DOI: 10.1007/BF02716399

[17] Deliiski N. Modelling and automatic control of heat energy consumption required for thermal treatment of logs. Drvna Industrija. 2004;**55**(4):181-199

[18] Deliiski N. Computation of the wood thermal conductivity during

defrosting of the wood. Wood Research. 2013;**58**(4):637-650

[19] Deliiski N, Dzurenda L, Tumbarkova N, Angelski D. Computation of the temperature conductivity of frozen wood during its defrosting. Drvna Industrija. 2015; **66**(2):87-96. DOI: 10.5552/drind.2015.1351

[20] Hadjiski M, Deliiski N. Cost oriented suboptimal control of the thermal treatment of wood materials. IFAC-Papers. 2015;**48**(24):54-59. DOI: 10.1016/j.ifacol.2015.12.056

[21] Hadjiski M, Deliiski N. Advanced control of the wood thermal treatment processing. Cybernetics and Information Technologies, Bulgarian Academy of Sciences. 2016;**16**(2): 179-197. DOI: 10.1515/cait-2016-0029

[22] Deliiski N, Tumbarkova N. Numerical solution to two-dimensional freezing and subsequent defrosting of logs. In: Iranzo A, editor. Heat and Mass Transfer—Advances in Science and Technology Applications. London: IntechOpen; 2015. p. 20. DOI: 10.5772/intechopen.84706

[23] Whitaker S. Fundamental Principles of Heat Transfer. Oxford OX3 OBW: Pergamon Press; 1977. p. 574. eBook 9781483159430

[24] Kozdoba LA. Methods for Solving of Non-linear Heat Transfer Tasks. Moscow: Nauka, USSR; 1975. p. 228 (in Russian)

[25] Kanter KR. Investigation of the Thermal Properties of Wood [Thesis]. Moscow: MLTI, USSR; 1955 (in Russian)

[26] Deliiski N, Tumbarkova N. A methodology for experimental research of the freezing process of logs. Acta Silvatica et Lignaria Hungarica. 2016; **12**(2):145-156. DOI: 10.1515/aslh-2016-0013

[27] Hrčka R. Model in Free Water in Wood. Wood Research. 2017;**62**(6): 831-837

[28] Marin E, Calderon A, Delgado-Vasallo O. Similarity theory and dimensionless numbers in heat transfer. European Journal of Physics. 2009;**30**: 439. DOI: 10.1088/0143-0807/30/3/001/meta

[29] Telegin AS, Shvidkiy BS, Yaroshenko UG. Heat- and Mass Transfer. Moscow: Akademkniga; 2002. p. 456 (in Russian)

[30] Dorn WS, McCracken DD. Numerical Methods with FORTRAN IV: Case Studies. New York: John Willej & Sons Inc.; 1972. p. 451

[31] Tumbarkova N. Modelling of the freezing and thawing processes of logs and their energy consumption [PhD Thesis]. Bulgaria: University of Forestry in Sofia; 2019. p. 198 (in Bulgarian)

[32] Hadjiski M, Deliiski N, Grancharova A. Spatiotemporal parameter estimation of thermal treatment process via initial condition reconstruction using neural networks. In: Hadjiski M, Atanasov KT, editors. Intuitionistic Fuzziness and Other Intelligent Theories and their Applications. Cham, Switzerland: Springer International Publishing AG; 2019. pp. 51-80. DOI: 10.1007/978-3-319-78931-6

Chapter 5

Innovations in Heat Pump Design Using Computational Fluid Dynamics with Control Volume Method

Cemil Koyunoğlu

Abstract

Mathematical modeling of the heat pump as a result of continuity, momentum, and energy equations is obtained. To solve these equations numerically, the problem is divided by a finite number of control volumes. Then the differential equations in these control volumes integrated and converted into algebraic equations. The importance of computational fluid dynamics in Industry 4.0 applications is to make current applications more efficient in heat pump applications. In this study, the book section is composed of the application of computational fluid dynamics by the control volume method using Ansys fluent program, which will benefit readers from industry 4.0 perspective, especially in energy efficiency issues according to the volume method of controlling correct heat pump designs.

Keywords: heat pump design, industry 4.0, computational fluid dynamics, energy equations, control volume method

1. Introduction

The ever increasing demand for energy and the depletion of energy resources accelerate the search for new energy resources. The effects of global warming based on excessive fossil fuel consumption and problems in meeting the energy demand enabled the energy to become the main agenda item of the world as a current problem. In developed countries where energy is the main agenda item, frequent sessions are held on the balance of energy supply and demand. In particular, the search for cheap electricity, which the increasing population and industry needed, has increased the requirement for renewable energy resources. Hydraulic, solar, wind, and geothermal energy are important renewable energy sources because of their importance, easy-to-find, and cheap production [1–3].

At the same time, geothermal energy, which is used in the technology of soil air source heat exchanger and which is mentioned in renewable energy sources, is extensively used in topics such as cooling as well as heating homes, electricity generation, tourism, and heating greenhouses [4].

2. Soil air heat exchangers in general

In general, soil air heat exchangers passively cool or heat their environment according to the seasons in which they are used. Thermal performances of soil air heat exchangers generally vary according to pipe lengths, pipe diameters used, air inlet speeds, and number of deflectors [5].

3. Passive cooling systems

The increase in energy costs caused by the economic crises also reveals the need to reduce environmental damage by the method of recovering the heat generated. Therefore, energy-saving measures that can be taken in the main residences can be taken. The system capacities of buildings could be reduced by mechanical cooling packages.

Passive cooling is an alternative way to mechanical cooling. Heat wells, natural cooling sources as well as COP include mechanical cooling systems greater than 4. Buildings can be cooled in low energy and passive systems provided by several natural heat wells such as soil under the soil surface, utilizing ambient air.

Passive cooling systems

- Radiant cooling at night, providing a direct cooling tank for daytime use
- Night ventilation that provides direct human comfort during the day
- Comfort ventilation that directly provides human comfort daytime use
- Night ventilation aimed at cooling the building body at night
- Radiant cooling at night that supplies the cold during the day
- Direct evaporative cooling that cools the ventilation air non-mechanically
- Pool on the roof, etc. indirect evaporative cooling that provides cooling by doing can be classified as [6–8].

3.1 Soil sourced passive cooling system

It acts as a heat well especially for cooling the circulation air due to the temperature differences for a soil building. This type of energy can be used in shapes if the soil temperature is low enough. Passive cooling is possible if the building can be surrounded by soil as much as possible, provided that the wall's thermal conductivity is high, that is, uninsulated. This application is very suitable in mild winter and hot summer climates. In climates with cold winters, the method is not preferred as that will raise the heat losses. Next to the building, the soil mass beneath and sometimes above it can be considered like a natural cooling source for the building in many climatic zones. In most places with a depth of 2–3 m, soil cooler can be a source. This may not be the case for very hot regions. If the soil surface is germinated or during the daytime, dilution of the soil can be effective in using the soil as a heat source in hot regions [9, 10].

There are two known methods for ground-source passive heat source. The two methods common feature is that the soil design is provided so that evaporation is not prevented by the shading method [9, 10].

DOI: http://dx.doi.org/10.5772/intechopen.93191

In the first method, at least 10 cm thick in summer, on the soil surface, it is covered with materials such as pebble, tree, and watered [9, 10].

In the second method, water evaporation is provided from the soil surface with irrigation and summer rains. Thus, the soil temperature below is lowered and the surface temperature decreases [9, 10].

Ground-based cooling takes place in two methods, indirect and direct. Indirect contact, the thermal mass of the soil provides a decrease in indoor temperature with the soil. The precooling aspect is indirect. The circulated air temperature or water decreases thanks to the cool soil layer, so that the coolness inside the building can be used in the pipes installed underground [9, 10].

PVC pipes can be placed in the ground if the building is insulated very well as a heat exchanger. The building circulation air could be circulated to cool these pipes. Air circulation, which could be considered as a closed circuit, can also be the outside air intake. The internal air through the pipes, by circulating, buried in the ground, the air temperature could reach 10 K lower than the outside air temperature. Efficiency increases even further in lands with very high outdoor temperatures [9, 10].

4. Computational methods

4.1 Navier Stokes equations and continuity

Continuity equation and Navier-Stokes equations that can be applied to all flows are important flow equations. A conservation equation expresses the mass conservation law of fluid passing through a control volume of differential dimensions. If we apply Newton's second law to a control volume, we encounter momentum and motion conservation equations and Navier-Stokes equations. In Cartesian coordinates with isothermal constant physical properties, motion and continuity equations for a newton type and incompressible flow can be written as follows [11–17].

Navier Stokes Equations

x-dimension

$$\rho\left(\frac{\delta u}{\delta t}+u\frac{\delta u}{\delta x}+v\frac{\delta u}{\delta y}+w\frac{\delta u}{\delta z}\right)=-\frac{\delta P}{\delta x}+\rho g_x+u\left(\frac{\delta^2 u}{\delta x^2}+\frac{\delta^2 u}{\delta y^2}+\frac{\delta^2 u}{\delta z^2}\right) \tag{1}$$

y-dimension

$$\rho\left(\frac{\delta v}{\delta t}+u\frac{\delta v}{\delta x}+v\frac{\delta v}{\delta y}+w\frac{\delta v}{\delta z}\right)=-\frac{\delta P}{\delta x}+\rho g_y+u\left(\frac{\delta^2 v}{\delta x^2}+\frac{\delta^2 v}{\delta y^2}+\frac{\delta^2 v}{\delta z^2}\right) \tag{2}$$

z-dimension [11–17]

$$\rho\left(\frac{\delta w}{\delta t}+u\frac{\delta w}{\delta x}+v\frac{\delta w}{\delta y}+w\frac{\delta w}{\delta z}\right)=-\frac{\delta P}{\delta x}+\rho g_x+u\left(\frac{\delta^2 w}{\delta x^2}+\frac{\delta^2 w}{\delta y^2}+\frac{\delta^2 w}{\delta z^2}\right) \tag{3}$$

Here, all of the equations determined with the notations u, v, and w appear as the executive equation. Here, u gives the flow components x, y gives the flow components y, and z gives the flow components z. Fluid mechanics and dynamics problems are managed with this equation. For the soil air heat exchanger, this problem can be solved with various simulation software packages. Three-dimensional and two-dimensional solutions are possible. u, v, and w velocity components are variable. From other notations, P (pressure), ρ (density), and μ (dynamic viscosity) are taken constantly [11–17].

Continuity equation [11–17]

$$\frac{\delta u}{\delta t}+\frac{\delta v}{\delta t}+\frac{\delta w}{\delta t}=0 \tag{4}$$

4.2 Energy equations

The energy equation to be used for incompressible flow in Cartesian coordinates is given below in turbulent flow [11–17].

$$\left[u\frac{\delta T}{\delta x}+v\frac{\delta T}{\delta y}+u\frac{\delta T}{\delta z}\right]=\alpha\left[\frac{\delta^2 w}{\delta x^2}+\frac{\delta^2 w}{\delta y^2}+\frac{\delta^2 w}{\delta z^2}\right]+u\phi \tag{5}$$

$$\phi=2\left[\left(\frac{\delta T}{\delta x}\right)^2+\left(\frac{\delta T}{\delta y}\right)^2+\left(\frac{\delta T}{\delta z}\right)^2\right]+\left(\frac{\delta v}{\delta x}+\frac{\delta u}{\delta y}\right)2+\left(\frac{\delta w}{\delta y}+\frac{\delta v}{\delta z}\right)2+\left(\frac{\delta u}{\delta z}+\frac{\delta w}{\delta x}\right)2 \tag{6}$$

4.3 Models of turbulence

Turbulence is the irregularity of a liquid or gas in motion. Non-turbulent flow is called laminar flow. The Reynolds number determines if flow conditions are turbulent or laminar. Turbulence is one of the problems that have been handled by many scientists but no analytical solutions have been found. The molecules of a fluid with a uniform flow tend to stay as close to each other as possible and behave similarly. At the beginning of the nineteenth century, basic problems of fluids with regular fluids were solved and the foundations of fluid dynamics were laid. However, science refused to work on turbulence for a long time, seeing turbulence as an engineering problem. Turbulence modeling has an important place in computational fluid dynamics, and different numerical approaches have been developed to analyze turbulent flow [11–17].

In the DNS method called direct numerical simulation, the digital network and time resolution are at a level that can resolve the vortexes of all scales, and simulations are carried out using basic moving equations without any modeling. The fact that this method requires a lot of computational cells and time steps makes the use of DNS in academic studies limited and practically impossible [11–17].

In high Reynolds numbers, in turbulent flow, the inertial forces of the flow become more dominant than viscous forces. As a result, fluid motion becomes unstable. Velocity and all other flow properties begin to change randomly and chaotically, and the flow becomes three-dimensional. The solution of a turbulent problem is as complex as its nature, and therefore various turbulence models have been developed for use in solving turbulent problems. The developed turbulence models cannot fully define the flow. There is no single turbulence model for each flow simulation. Different turbulence models can be used for flow models with different properties. Different turbulence models have been developed for turbulent flow analysis. Some of these developed models are given below [11–17].

- Turbulence models;
- Zero equation model
- k–ε (epsilon) model
- RNG k–ε model (Reynolds normalized group turbulence model)
- k–ω (omega) model
- SST (shear stress transport) model
- The Reynolds stress model
- Omega-based Reynolds stress model
- Ansys Cfx transition model
- The large eddy simulation (LES) model
- The detached eddy simulation (DES) model
- The scale adaptive simulation model (SAS) [11–17]
- Buoyancy turbulence model

For accuracy and computational convergence accuracy, k-ε models are a good choice. Generally, this model is suitable for industrial applications with and without heat transfer for complex flows. In the k-ε models, similar to the k-ω model, two transport equations are solved, but there is a difference in the selection of the second turbulence transport variable and is frequently applied in the CFD simulations of the k-ε and k-ω models. In terms of convergence and accuracy, the calculation cost is a good choice for the k-ε model [11–17].

4.4 k-ε standard model

In the numerical solutions of the most commonly used turbulent fluids, the k-ε model is used. Diffusion ratio (ε) and turbulent kinetic energy (k) equations are given [11–17].

$$\frac{\delta}{\delta t}(\rho k)+\frac{\delta}{\delta x_i}(\rho k u_i)=\frac{\delta}{\delta x_j}\left[\left(\mu+\frac{\mu_t}{\sigma_k}\right)\frac{\delta k}{\delta x_j}\right]+G_k+G_b-\rho\varepsilon-Y_M+S_k \qquad (7)$$

and due to the distributions of ε,

$$\frac{\delta}{\delta t}(\rho\varepsilon)+\frac{\delta}{\delta x_i}(\rho\varepsilon u_i)=\frac{\delta}{\delta x_j}\left[\left(\mu+\frac{\mu_t}{\sigma_\varepsilon}\right)\frac{\delta\varepsilon}{\delta x_j}\right]+C_{1\varepsilon}\frac{\varepsilon}{k}\left(G_k+G_{3\varepsilon}G_b\right)-C_{2\varepsilon}\frac{\varepsilon^2}{k}+S_\varepsilon \qquad (8)$$

The turbulence viscosity and turbulence conductivity of the k-ε standard model can be expressed as follows [11–17].

$$k_t = \frac{\mu t C_p}{\sigma_t} \tag{9}$$

$$\mu_t = \rho C_\mu \frac{k^2}{\varepsilon} \tag{10}$$

Model constants for turbulence models are

$$C_{1\varepsilon} = 1.44\ ,\ C_{2\varepsilon} = 1.92,\ C_\mu = 0.09,\ \sigma_\varepsilon = 1.3, \sigma_k = 1.0.$$

4.5 Dimensionless parameters and heat transfer coefficients

The dimensionless parameters and heat transfer coefficients are given below are defined for the heat transfer occurring in the soil air heat exchanger (**Figures 1** and **2**) [11–17].

4.6 Heat transfer coefficients for convection

The equation below is for heat transfer from air to pipe.

$$h_a = \frac{Nu\, k_a}{D} \tag{11}$$

$$\mathrm{D} = \text{pipe diameter}\,(\mathrm{m})$$

k_a = heat coefficient for air (W/mK)

Nu = Nusselt number [11–17]

The following equation is expressed for heat transfer from pipe to ground.

$$h_s = \frac{k_s}{r_2 \ln\left(1 + \frac{\delta}{r_2}\right)} \tag{12}$$

r_2 = pipe outer diameter (m)

δ = soil thickness (m)

k_s = soils heat conduction constant $\left(\frac{W}{mK}\right)$ [11–17]

4.7 Reynolds number

Laminar to turbulent flow transition, among other parameters, relys on surface roughness, geometry of surface, free flow speed, temperature of surface, and fluid type. In the 1880s, Osborne Reynolds showed that the flow regime was based on the ratio of inertial forces to viscous forces as a result of experimental studies. The

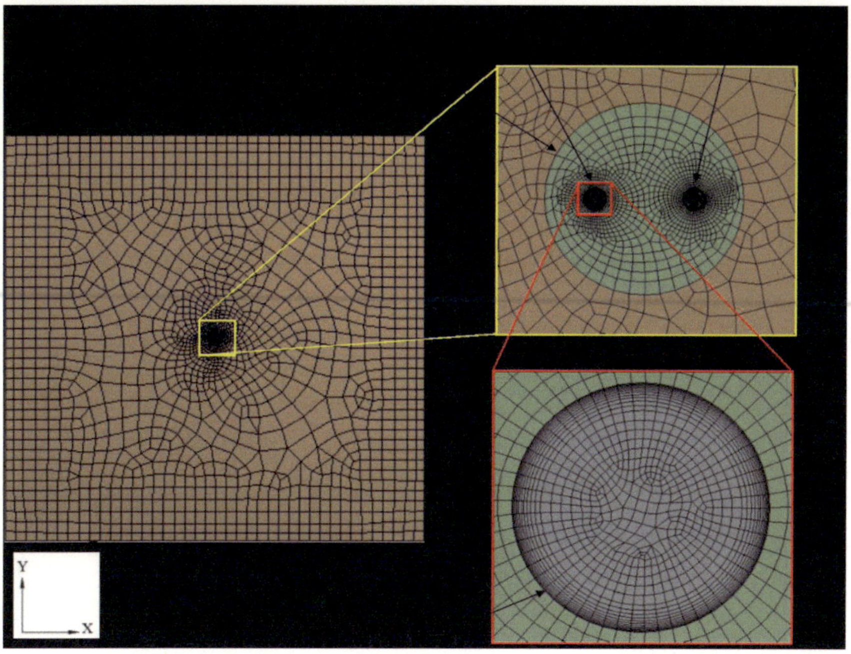

Figure 1.
Cross-sectional view of a sample domain with soil thickness [18].

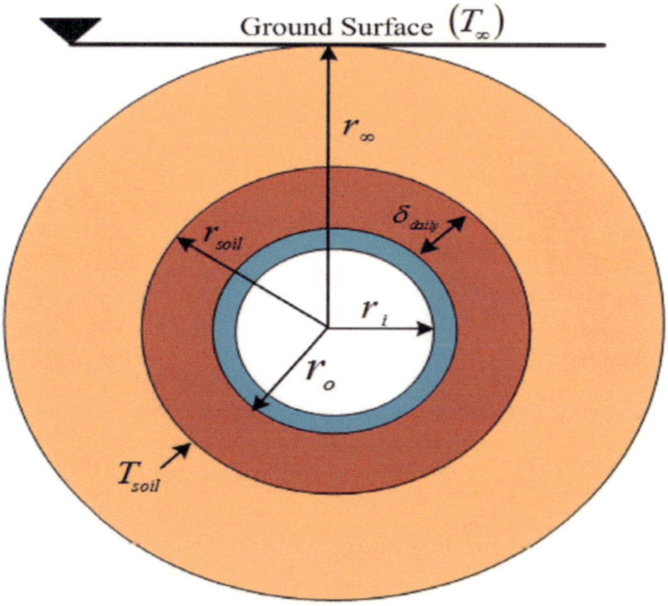

Figure 2.
A sample ground earth-air source geometry domain [19].

Reynolds number is a dimensionless group. The Reynolds number for the flow in the circular tube is expressed as follows [11–17].

$$\mathrm{Re} = \frac{\rho V_{ort} D}{\mu} = \frac{V_{ort} D}{v} \tag{13}$$

4.8 Friction factor

The friction factor in turbulent flow is expressed as follows for smooth pipes.

$$f = (0.790 \ln Re - 1.64)^{-2} \; 3000 < Re < 5 \times 10^6 \quad (14)$$

can be found from the first Petukhov explicit equation [11–17].

4.9 Nusselt number

The Nusselt number on a fluid is the result of the heat transfer recovery in that fluid layer to the ratio of transport to conduction. How effective the transport depends on the large number of Nusselt. The Nusselt number is associated with the friction factor in turbulent flow, and the sensitivity of this correlation at lower Reynolds numbers is expressed as follows:

$$Nu = \frac{(f/8)(Re - 1000)Pr}{1 + 12.7(f/8)^{0.5}(Pr^{2/3} - 1)} s \; (0.5 \le Pr \le 200) \; (3 \times 10^3 < Re < 5 \times 10^6) \quad (15)$$

is given with [11–17].

4.10 Prandtl number

Expression of thicknesses of thermal layers and velocity;

$$Pr = \frac{v}{\alpha} = \frac{\mu C_p}{k} \quad (16)$$

If given as a dimensionless parameter defined by Prandtl number [11–17]

5. Computational fluid dynamics

A numerical method based on the principle of solving basic momentum, mass, and energy equations by computer is called computational fluid dynamics (CFD) (**Figure 3**). CFD partial differential equations that can be solved in computers are converted into several algebraic equations and provide a practical and fast study on fluid dynamics. Partial differential equations can easily access many sub-data depending on the parameters of speed, pressure, and temperature distributions in the flow and these parameters by numerically solving the model expressing the flow. A model of the relevant physical problem is defined by this model, which creates basic chemical and physical principles related to flow by using CFD method, by defining this model by using fluid dynamics with various computer software, the physical and chemical principles related to fluid are defined in this model. Information about the real behavior of the problem can be obtained. This method allows the geometry of the problem to be easily created and analyzed. The emphasis on CFD is that it provides benefit from experimental studies relatively economically and from time. Computational fluid dynamics is widely used in product design and research and development today [11–17].

Many parameters related to temperature distribution of an underground reservoir, air velocity around a moving car, pressures on an airplane wing, and airflow distribution in an environment can be found using CFD. Developments

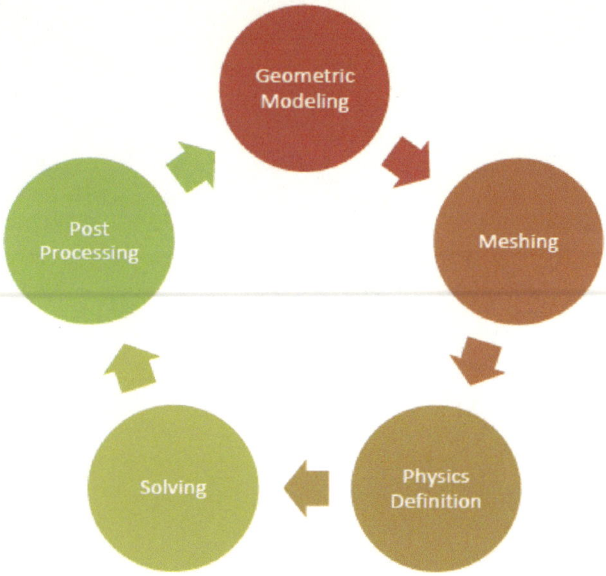

Figure 3.
Basic steps for CFD [20].

in dynamical systems and computer software have been created in the virtual environment by analyzing high turbulent flows numerically with computational fluid dynamics theory in recent years. In addition, single-phase flows, as well as multi-phase flows, have been resolved with maximum similarity. For example, the structure of harmful factors such as cavitation in pumps is examined and precautions are taken according to the results. CFD software developed to solve flux, heat, and chemical reaction problems takes place in three basic stages as solution, pre-treatment, and post-treatment [11–17].

If heat transfer is discussed with numerical method, for example, in a 3-dimensional geometry, the issues such as soil properties should be well understood due to the complexity of heat transfer. Many factors such as working fluid flow rate, soil air boundary conditions can affect the verification of the numerical method result. The following assumptions can be proposed for numerical modeling of an exemplary 3D soil air heat pump.

1. Since the model is designed in three dimensions, the average thermal properties of the ground are assumed to be constant throughout the geometry.

2. The first soil temperature defined in the model is a function of depth.

3. The effect of groundwater flow in the solid zone, which is considered as pure heat conduction, is neglected.

4. The velocity profiles of the U-shaped pipe of the ground air heat pump are equal.

Since the numerical method established is completely exposed to the external environment, the temperature is directly affected by solar radiation. When the ground surface is covered with a building, its protection from both other structures and direct sun radiation results in a low temperature fluctuation near the ground surface. For the reasons described above, the ambient temperature only represents

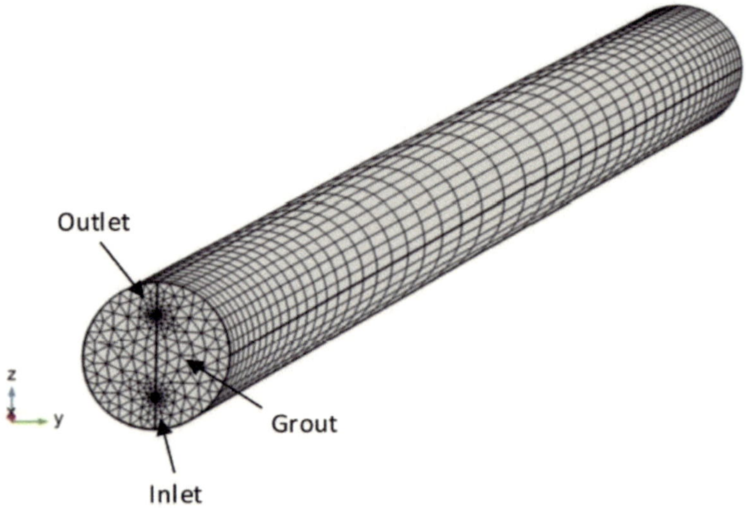

Figure 4.
A sample mesh geometry for the earth-air heat pump [21].

the floor temperature. The energy equations of the outlet and inlet pipes are derived from parameters such as the inlet and outlet angle of the working fluid of the fluid regions according to the finite volume method [11–17].

5.1 Numerical model for solution

The finite volume method, which is a numerical method used in the solution of partial differential equations, is used to solve the integral states of fluid motion equations by separating them in physical space [11–17].

For the solution to be examined, the solution must be splitted into a finite number of control volumes that do not overlap. All finite number elements are called digital networks or solution networks. Variables are generally calculated at the center of control volumes. With the finite volume method applied to very flexible solution networks, calculations are not made at the node points unlike other methods. It gives successful results in non-structural solution networks as well as structural solution networks. To be more flexible and applicable to complex geometries, mostly non-structural solution networks are preferred (**Figure 4**) [11–17].

6. Recent studies for earth-air heat pump

6.1 Earth-air heat pump study-1

In this study, the residential buildings in the Mediterranean climate describe the three parameters simulation effect on the thermal performance of the soil air source heat pump system. These three parameters are diameter of pipe, flowing air velocity, and gaps between pipes. ANSYS-CFX is used. In the simulation results confirmed by experimental data and analytical results, it was concluded that the increase of air velocity and the distance between adjacent pipes for a given pipe diameter is inversely proportional to the heat transfer for cooling. It is concluded that the soil air heat efficiency will continue even when the distance between the pipes falls from 1 to 0.5 m, with the result that it should be in the presence of 50% more soil area (**Figure 5**) [18].

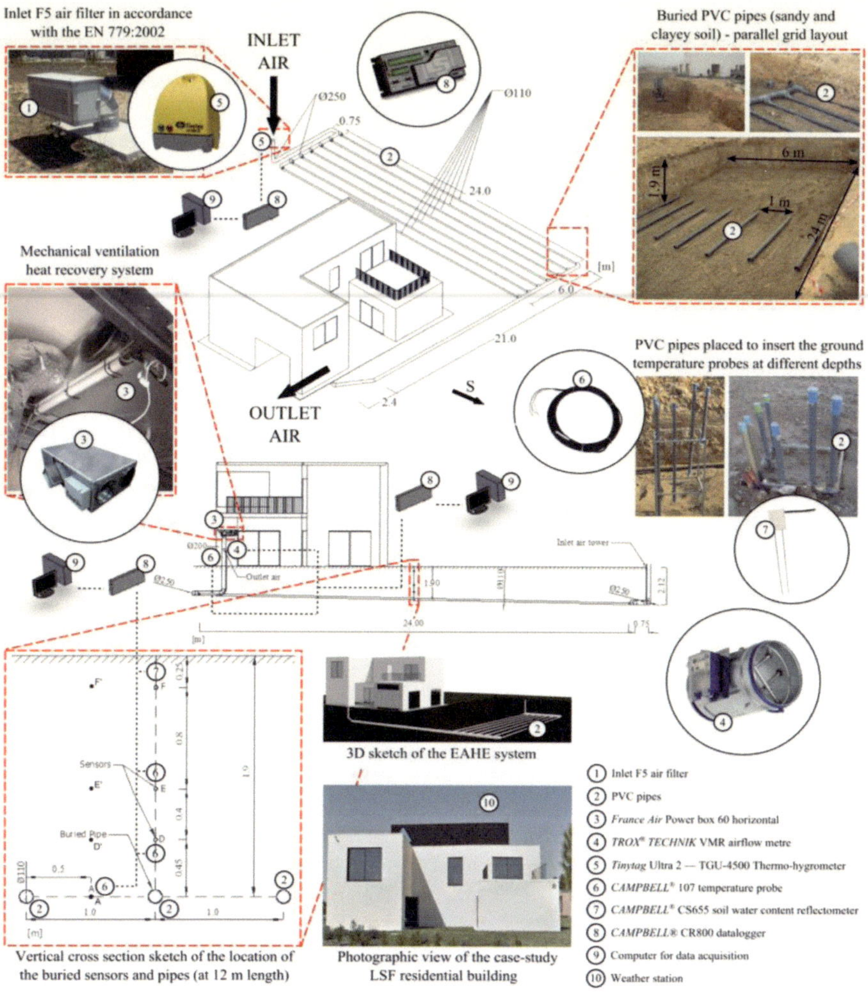

Figure 5.
Experimental scheme for the study [22].

6.2 Earth-air heat pump study-2

The need for prefabricated housing can be considered especially to compare the short-term housing needs of people who are victims of migration. In this work, a design proposal was made for a refugee house that fits the Swedish climate of the three main passive cooling and heating solutions, including the Trombe wall, the Ground air heat exchanger, and the green wall. The main purpose of combining these systems is to reduce the heating as well as cooling loads and thus reducing emissions, reducing the negative impact of the house on energy use in the environment. The prefabricated refugee house is designed to consume 180 kWh/m^2/year of energy annually. ANSYS (simulation) and TRNSYS (dynamic system modeling) software are used. According to the simulation results, 2.8 kWh/m^2/year cooling load and 7.9 kWh/m^2/year heating load were obtained. Also it is seen that the total energy consumption reached 18.4 kWh/m^2/year. 7.4 years repayment period is the pre-feasibility cost during its 25-year construction life. Main energy request is 0.032 GJ/m^2/year and CO_2 emission amount is 231.1 kg CO_2e/year. In Lund, which has an urban living laboratory in Sweden, a proof of concept has been applied to validate the simulation results through a 12-month post couple assessment and monitoring study (**Figure 6**) [19].

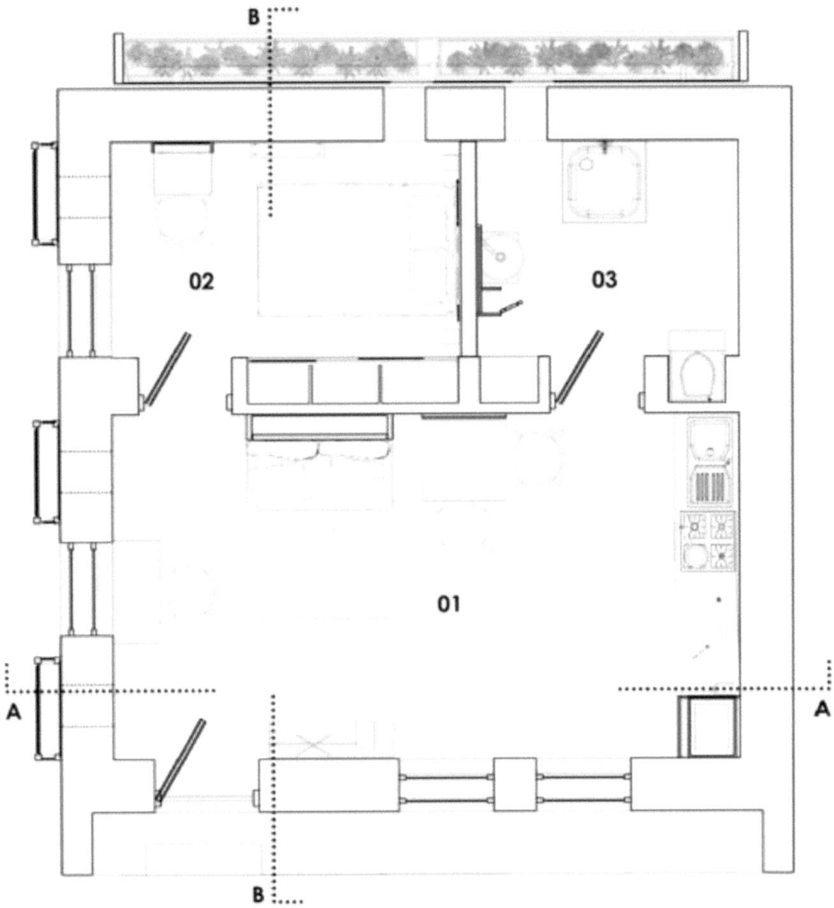

Figure 6.
A refugee building for CFD study [23].

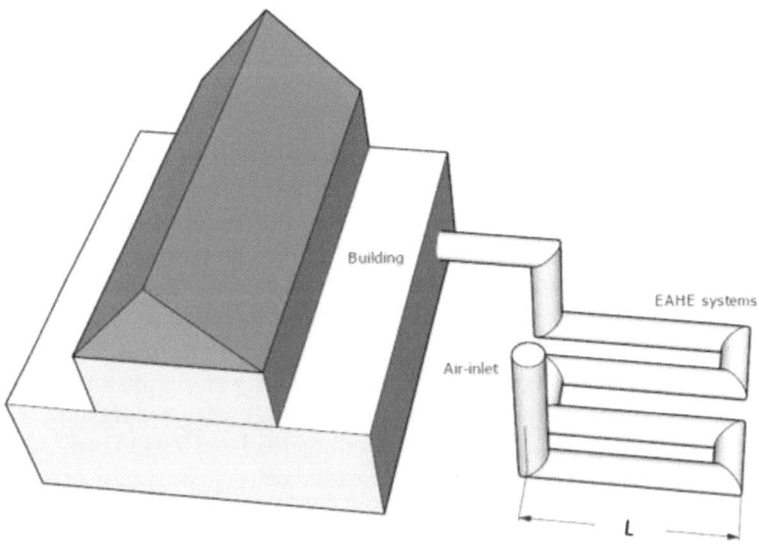

Figure 7.
An experimental domain for the study [24].

6.3 Earth-air heat pump study-3

The relationship between the cooling technology of the ground-air heat pump heat exchanger of an office building in Jinan city and the indoor heat exchange was investigated. The thermal distribution of the interior was analyzed with CFD. With the Airpak software, the distribution of the speed field, the internal temperature field, and the PMV index were obtained. In this study, energy use efficiency was also analyzed. Important conditions in the airflow design of office rooms have been determined in small temperature differences of the soil air heat exchanger. This study provides a basic reference for the soil-air heat exchanger cooling system design (**Figure** 7) [20].

6.4 Earth-air heat pump study-4

Natural and thermal ventilation behavior is evaluated as in an underground construction and determines the behavior of building components such as chimneys, tunnels, and caves in different parts of the year. With the advanced CFD model, the temperature distribution when a more realistic simulation of underground constructions is exposed to natural ventilation is provided. In every period, the role of the building components mentioned above in the arrangement of the interior changes significantly. According to the results obtained from the study, thermal stability has been provided in the cave despite the extreme energy temperatures and zero energy consumption. Floor temperature plays an important role in the regulation of natural ventilation. This is the key element in the ventilation of the building construction. Due to the lower air velocities, the ventilation shaft has no significant effect on the above situation. Adjustments and boundary conditions of advanced CFD models can play an important role in deciding the design of the energy management system and ventilation and may even be a reference model in other underground projects [25].

7. Conclusions

Computational fluid dynamics is of vital importance, particularly in determining soil air heat pumps, which are difficult to build and implement in residential buildings, especially in building energy efficiency. CFD technique is important especially in the widespread application of soil air heat pumps, which will provide less energy usage and thus increase the environmental impact.

As emphasized in the studies, for example, the three-dimensional solution of the thermal properties of a three-dimensional structure is possible only with a temporary heat transfer model. By determining a circular cross section region, it can be estimated with a rectangular geometry close to the same area. Energy balances can be established separately in the fluid and solid regions. Experimental data about the section where the liquid comes out, soil temperatures, numerical model are verified. Thermal short circuit effects between the heat transfer rate between two U pipes and the outlet thermostat temperature can be investigated. The effects of flow rate are also important. As a result of the analyzes, it can be said that the distance between the two pipes per unit soil depth gradually increases or decreases the rate of heat transfer. Numerical approaches can create effective estimates, although the soil temperature and liquid output are not stable. These studies actually reveal the value of the numerical method in evaluating the energy performance of a building or industrial facility for 1 year of energy from ground or air source heat pumps.

Conflict of interest

The author declares no conflict of interest.

Author details

Cemil Koyunoğlu
Energy Systems Engineering Department, Engineering Faculty, Yalova University, Yalova, Turkey

*Address all correspondence to: cemil.koyunoglu@yalova.edu.tr

References

[1] Amoo LM, Layi FR. 15-Climate change in developing nations of the world. In: Fagbenle RO, Amoo OM, Aliu S, Falana A, editors. Applications of Heat, Mass and Fluid Boundary Layers. Nigeria: Woodhead Publishing; 2020. pp. 437-471

[2] Whitford WG, Duval BD. Chapter 3-Characterization of desert climates. In: Whitford WG, Duval BD, editors. Ecology of Desert Systems. Second ed. USA: Academic Press; 2020. pp. 47-72

[3] Becchetti L, Bruni L, Zamagni S. Chapter 13-Growth and the environment in the era of globalization. In: Becchetti L, Bruni L, Zamagni S, editors. The Microeconomics of Wellbeing and Sustainability. USA: Academic Press; 2020. pp. 401-443

[4] Archer R. 20-Geothermal energy. In: Letcher TM, editor. Future Energy. Third ed. United Kingdom: Elsevier; 2020. pp. 431-445

[5] Yang L-H, Huang B-H, Hsu C-Y, Chen S-L. Performance analysis of an earth–air heat exchanger integrated into an agricultural irrigation system for a greenhouse environmental temperature-control system. Energy and Buildings. 2019;**202**:109381

[6] Almao N, Dopazo J, Rincón J, González E. Chapter 98 - parametric sensibility study of an indirect evaporation passive cooling system in hot and humid climate. In: Sayigh AAM, editor. World Renewable Energy Congress VI. Oxford: Pergamon; 2000. pp. 516-519

[7] Bahadori MN. 16 - Passive cooling systems in hot arid regions. In: Dixon AE, Leslie JD, editors. Solar Energy Conversion. Canada: Pergamon; 1979. pp. 461-479

[8] Fardeheb F. Natural cooling techniques in hot arid regions of developing countries. In: Bloss WH, Pfisterer F, editors. Advances In Solar Energy Technology. Oxford: Pergamon; 1988. pp. 3198-3202

[9] Givoni B. Passive Low Energy Cooling of Buildings. Canada: Wiley; 1994

[10] Santamouris M. Advances in Passive Cooling. United Kingdom: Taylor & Francis Group; 2012

[11] Chung TJ, TJA C. Computational Fluid Dynamics. United Kingdom: Cambridge University Press; 2002

[12] Versteeg HK, Malalasekera W. An Introduction to Computational Fluid Dynamics: The Finite Volume Method. United Kingdom: Pearson Education Limited; 2007

[13] Minin O, Minin I. Computational Fluid Dynamics: Technologies and Applications. Russia: IntechOpen; 2011

[14] Wendt J. Computational Fluid Dynamics: An Introduction. Berlin Heidelberg: Springer; 2008

[15] Baukal CE, Gershtein V, Li XJ. Computational Fluid Dynamics in Industrial Combustion. USA: Taylor & Francis; 2000

[16] Tu J, Yeoh GH, Liu C. Computational Fluid Dynamics: A Practical Approach. USA: Elsevier Science; 2018

[17] Murphy AD. Computational Fluid Dynamics: Theory, Analysis and Applications. India: Nova Science Publishers; 2011

[18] Vella C, Borg SP, Micallef D. The effect of shank-space on the thermal performance of shallow vertical U-tube ground heat exchangers. Energies. 2020;**13**:602

[19] Serageldin AA, Abdelrahman AK, Ookawara S. Earth-air heat exchanger thermal performance in Egyptian conditions: Experimental results, mathematical model, and computational fluid dynamics simulation. Energy Conversion and Management. 2016;**122**:25-38

[20] Nemś A, Nemś M, Świder K. Analysis of the possibilities of using a heat pump for greenhouse heating in polish climatic conditions—A case study. Sustainability. 2018;**10**:3483

[21] Janiszewski M, Caballero Hernandez E, Siren T, Uotinen L, Kukkonen I, Rinne M. In situ experiment and numerical model validation of a borehole heat exchanger in shallow hard crystalline rock. Energies. 2018;**11**:963

[22] Rosa N, Soares N, Costa JJ, Santos P, Gervásio H. Assessment of an earth-air heat exchanger (EAHE) system for residential buildings in warm-summer Mediterranean climate. Sustainable Energy Technologies and Assessments. 2020;**38**:100649

[23] Dabaieh M, Serageldin AA. Earth air heat exchanger, Trombe wall and green wall for passive heating and cooling in premium passive refugee house in Sweden. Energy Conversion and Management. 2020;**209**:112555

[24] Wengang H, Yifeng L, Yanhua L, Mingxin L. Application of earth-air heat exchanger cooling technology in an office building in Jinan city. Energy Procedia. 2019;**158**:6105-6111

[25] Porras-Amores C, Mazarrón FR, Cañas I, Villoría SP. Natural ventilation analysis in an underground construction: CFD simulation and experimental validation. Tunnelling and Underground Space Technology. 2019;**90**:162-173

Section 2

Modeling in Electronics and Engineering

Chapter 6

A Robust and Oblivious Watermarking Method Using Maximum Wavelet Coefficient Modulation and Genetic Algorithm

Surya Prasada Rao Borra, Kongara Ramanjaneyulu and K. Raja Rajeswari

Abstract

An image watermarking method using Discrete Wavelet Transform (DWT) and Genetic Algorithm (GA) is presented for applications like content authentication and copyright protection. This method is robust to various image attacks. For watermark detection/extraction, the cover image is not essential. Gray scale images of size 512 × 512 as cover image and binary images of size 64 × 64 as watermark are used in the simulation of the proposed method. Watermark embedding is done in the DWT domain. 3rd and 2nd level detail sub-band coefficients are selected for further processing. Selected coefficients are arranged in different blocks. The size of the block and the number blocks depends on the size of the watermark. One watermark bit is embedded in each block. Then, inverse DWT operation is performed to get the required watermarked image. This watermarked image is used for transmission and distribution purposes. In case of any dispute over the ownership, the hidden watermark is decoded to solve the problem. Threshold-based method is used for watermark extraction. Control parameters are identified and optimized based on GA for targeted performance in terms of PSNR and NCC. Performance comparison is done with the existing works and substantial improvement is witnessed.

Keywords: image watermarking, discrete wavelet transform, genetic algorithm, PSNR and NCC

1. Introduction

In today's world, digital media storage and its security are of the highest importance for any multimedia application. Copyright protection, proof of ownership and image authentication are some of the applications in the protection of the digital data. Watermarking Technique is one of the methods used in these applications. In the watermarking process, specific information called watermark is embedded imperceptibly into the original media object. The Watermarking algorithm is referred to as an oblivious (also called as public/blind) if the extraction can be done, just with the knowledge of watermarked image.

Quality, robustness and blindness are the three key aspects in a watermarking system. The degradation in the quality of a watermarked image should be minimal and invisible. The watermarking system should be robust enough to withstand various image watermark attacks. In applications where the original image is not available at the time of extraction, blindness is essential.

In this chapter, a robust and oblivious image watermarking scheme based on the maximum wavelet coefficient modulation is proposed.

2. Review of the related works

Watermarking process can be implemented both in spatial and transform domains. In Spatial domain, the process is simple but it is hard to achieve robustness. In transform domain, the watermarking is very secure and robust but the process is complex. Discrete Wavelet Transform (DWT), Fourier Transform (FT), Singular Value Decomposition (SVD) and Discrete Cosine Transform (DCT) are some of the popular Image transformation methods used in the watermarking algorithms. DWT based image watermarking is easy and effective when compared with the other approaches [1]. Transform coefficient selection is the most important aspect in DWT based implementation. In [2], significant wavelet coefficients are selected to embed the watermark. Wang et al. [3] proposed a watermarking method where the significant coefficients are selected based on multi-threshold wavelet coding (MTWC) and successive sub-band quantization (SSQ). Significant coefficients are selected and quantized to embed the watermark. In [4], two different watermarking algorithms were proposed. In the first method, the triplets of significant coefficients are modified based on a sequence of bits to embed the watermark. In the second method, the coefficients are divided into rectangular blocks. In each block, one watermark bit is embedded.

In [2, 5, 6], the significant coefficients which are selected from global coefficients are used and showed robustness to many image attacks. The problem is that the order of extracting the significant coefficients in the extraction process should be exactly the same as those in the embedding process. Hence, they are not suitable for blind watermarking.

W.H. Lin et al. [7] used DWT for watermarking a 512×512 grayscale image. They quantized the maximum wavelet coefficient of a variable-sized block of a selected sub-band. The watermark is a 32×16 binary image. Low embedding capacity and adjustment of the scheme parameters to satisfy some specified watermarking requirements (PSNR and NCC with attacks) are the limitations of their method.

This chapter focuses on a robust and oblivious watermarking method. In this method, local maximum coefficient in the wavelet transform domain is used for embedding a binary watermark into a grayscale original image. Third level DWT is applied to the original image and watermark is embedded in the LH sub-band. Sub-band coefficients are grouped into equal sized blocks and a watermark bit is embedded in every block. In each block, the coefficient with maximum value is either increased or decreased based on the corresponding watermarking bit. The coefficient value (maximum) is increased if the bit is 1 and it is reduced to a value slightly higher than second maximum coefficient if the bit is 0. In the extraction process, the energy of the coefficient with maximum value in every block is decreased. After the decrement, if it is still the maximum coefficient in the block, the watermark bit is 1, or else the bit is 0.

DOI: http://dx.doi.org/10.5772/intechopen.93832

The scheme is characterized by parameters to get control over the embedding and extraction process. Then, the Genetic Algorithm (GA) is used for parameter optimization. Optimization is required to satisfy the conflicting requirements of the Peak Signal to Noise Ratio (PSNR) and the Normalized Cross-correlation (NCC). Experimental results show that the proposed method is better than the existing methods [8] in terms of both PSNR and NCC.

3. Genetic algorithm

Genetic Algorithms (GAs) [9, 10] are computer-based problem-solving systems that use computational models of some of the known mechanisms in evolution as key elements in their design and implementation. GA can be described as a search heuristic that mimics the process of natural evolution. Heuristic means discovery. Heuristic methods are based on experience, rational ideas, and rules of thumb. Heuristics are based more on common sense than on mathematics. This heuristic is habitually used to generate useful solutions to improvement and search problems. Genetic algorithms belong to the larger class of organic process algorithms (EA), which generate solutions to improvement problems using techniques inspired by uncolored evolution, such as selection, crossover, acquisition, and mutation.

In a genetic algorithm, a accumulation of strings or chromosomes which encode several solutions to an optimization problem develop towards better solutions. In general, solutions are described in binary as strings of 0 s and 1 s, but other encryptions are also possible. Evolution usually originates from a group of randomly produced individuals and takes place in generations. In each generation, the suitability of every individual in the population is evaluated, aggregate individuals are randomly selected from the current grouping based on their suitableness, and adapted (with recombination and possibly random mutation) to form a new grouping. The new grouping is then used in the next process of the algorithm. The algorithm modify according to the specified resultant criteria. If the algorithm has concluded due to a extreme number of generations, an adequate solution may or may not have been reached.

A typical genetic algorithmic program requires the following:

1. Genetic creation of the solution domain

2. A fitness function to measure the solution domain

A standard delegacy of the result is as an array of bits. Arrays of other types and composition can also be used. The main attribute that makes these genetic mean favorable is that their surroundings are easily allied due to their rigid size, which serve simple crossover dealings. Variable-dimension representations may also be utilized, but crossover execution is more involved in this case. Tree-like representations are explored in genetic planning and graph-form mean are explored in organic process programming.

The fitness utility is defined over the heritable representation and explores the choice of the represented result. The fitness usefulness is always job dependent. For example, in the backpack problem, one wants to increase the total value of target that can be put in a backpack of some fixed volume. A representation of a result might be an array of fragment, where each bit represents a contrary object, and the value of the bit (0 or 1) represents whether or not the aim is in the backpack. Not all such representation is effectual, as the size of target may surpass the capacity of the knapsack. The fitness of the result is the sum of belief of all objects in the knapsack if the content is valid or 0 otherwise. In some job, it is hard or even impracticable to define the fittingness expression; in these causes, synergistic genetic algorithms are used.

Once we have got the genetic representation and the suitability function outlined, GA yield to initialize a grouping of solutions randomly, and then amend it through insistent application of the causal agent; selection, crossover, organism, and fitness evaluation. Although recollection methods that are based on the use of two rear are more "biology-inspired", some inquiry [11, 12] suggests more than two "parents" are improved to be used to re-create a good quality chromosome. Crossover and Alteration are known as the main genetic operators. It is possible to use other operators such as regrouping, colonization-extinction, or migration in genetic algorithms [13].

4. Proposed watermarking scheme

In this section, the planned scheme is represented in three sub-sections. The next piece of writing deals with the watermark embedding state, watermark dilatation is explained in advance section and the utilization of GA for determining the optimal parameters of the strategy is given in further section.

Watermark Embedding:

In the projected algorithm, a double star watermark image is integrated in a grayscale covering image. The transform in use is DWT. The embedding scheme is supported on the local maximal wavelet constant modulation.

The steps of the proposed embedding algorithm are as follows.

1. Decompose the cover image using third level DWT and obtain the sub-bands (LL_3, LH_3, HL_3, and HH_3).

2. Represent the binary watermark as a vector. Let the number of watermark bits is N_w.

3. Divide the LH_3 sub-band into N_w number of blocks.

4. Compute mean value of the maximum wavelet coefficient (MWC_{mean}) and adaptive embedding parameter (a_j) as follows:

$$\text{(a) } MWC_{mean} = \frac{1}{N_w}\sum_{j=1}^{N_w} M_j \tag{1}$$

Where,

$M_j = \max_j$, if the watermark bit is '1'.

$= \max_j \times t_1$, otherwise

$\max_j$ = maximum wavelet coefficient of the jth block.

t_1 = scaling factor

$$\text{(b) } a_j = t_2 \times \text{maximum}\left\{|avg_j|, |MWC_{mean} \times t_3|\right\} \text{ for all j} = 1 \text{ to } N_w \tag{2}$$

Where,

avg_j = average coefficient value of the jth block

t_2, t_3 are the scaling parameters

5. Modulate $\max_j$ according to the Watermark bit

for all $j = 1$ to N_w as follows:

$$\max_j^{new} = \max_j + a_j, \text{if the watermark bit is`1'}$$
$$= \sec_j + a_j \text{ otherwise} \quad (3)$$

Where,
$\sec_j$ denotes the second maximum coefficient value of the jth block.
t_3 is the scaling factor (less than 1)

6. Get the modified LH_3 sub-band by combining the modulated blocks.

7. Obtain the three-level inverse DWT using a modified LH_3 sub-band to get the watermarked image.

The parameters/scaling factors; t_1, t_2, and t_3; are used to control the value of the PSNR.

Watermark extraction:

Possibly attacked watermarked image is the only input image required for the extraction process as the scheme is an oblivious watermarking method. Parameter t_4 value is required. Even if the value of t_4 is not available, GA may be used to find its value.

Extraction of the watermark is as follows:

1. Decompose the possibly attacked watermarked image using third-level DWT and obtain the sub-bands (LL_3, LH_3, HL_3, and HH_3).

2. Divide the LH_3 sub-band into N_w a number of blocks.

3. Compute the following

$$\text{(a) } MWC_{mean}^{\circ} = \frac{1}{N_w}\sum_{j=1}^{N_w} \max_j^{\circ} \quad (4)$$

Where $\max_j^{\circ}$ denotes the maximum coefficient of jth the block.

$$\text{(b) } Mean_{block} = \frac{1}{N_w}\sum_{j=1}^{N_w} |avg_j^{\circ}| \quad (5)$$

Where, avg_j° is the average coefficient value of the jth block excluding $\max_j^{\circ}$.

4. Detect the watermark bit using the following detection rule for all $j = 1$ to N_w

$$\text{Watermark bit} = 1, \text{if } \left(\max_j^{\circ} - t_4 \times a_j^{\circ}\right) >= \sec_j^{\circ}$$
$$= 0, \text{otherwise} \quad (6)$$

Where,
t_4 is the scaling factor,

$$\overset{\circ}{a}_j = \text{maximum}\left(|\overset{\circ}{avg}_j|, |Mean_{block}|, \text{k}_1, \text{k}_2\right) \tag{7}$$

$$\text{k}_1 = \overset{\circ}{\max}_j / \overset{\circ}{MWC}_{mean} \tag{8}$$

$$\text{k}_2 = \overset{\circ}{avg}_j / Mean_{block} \tag{9}$$

$\overset{\circ}{\sec}_j$ = secondary maximum value of the jth block.
The parameter/scaling factor, t_4, is used to control the value of the NCC.

5. Optimization of parameters using GA

As spoke to in area 2, GA can be used for watermarking concern [14] dependent on the way that amazing watermarking has two opposing interest, PSNR and NCC. These two hypothesize are identified with one another and consequently the watermarking algorithmic standard spoke to above must be streamlined. Advancement movement space and the appropriateness work are spoken to as follows.

Search space: The conviction of the four estimating factors (t1, t2, t3 and t4) are the base that, if most loved appropriately, will bring about ideal unaware and lashing watermarking. It is the job of the GA to knowledge such qualities, where the GA's research space must consider all conceivable conviction for the four evaluating factors. The GA is an iterative method that accomplishes advancement in a given pursuit space utilizing the hereditary administrators (choice, multiplication, hybrid and transformation) and a wellness work as portrayed in segment 2.

The fitness function: Two common performance evaluation metrics are combined to form the fitness function, PSNR and NCC. The fitness function is formed by combining the two metrics as follows.

$$fit_l = PSNR_l + \frac{1}{P}\sum_{k=1}^{p}(NCC_{k,l} \times \alpha_k) \tag{10}$$

Where l denotes GA generation number, p denotes the total number of attacks used in the optimization process, $NCC_{k,l}$ represents NCC value with attack k and α_k represents the weighting factor for NCC. PSNR and NCC are defined by Eqs. (12) and (13).

Figure 1 shows the flow chart for the performance optimization of the watermarking scheme.

Optimization of parameters is described as follows: mutation.

Note: Steps 1 to 3 speaks to the introduction of the GA-preparing factors.

1. Define an underlying reach for all the variables (or scaling factors) utilized in the plan.

2. Specify the assortment size, hybrid rate, change rate, and various cycles.

3. Specify the end standards.

4. Write a capacity to insert a twofold watermark into the dark level spread picture following the means given in the above area. The capacity should restore the PSNR estimation of the got watermarked picture.

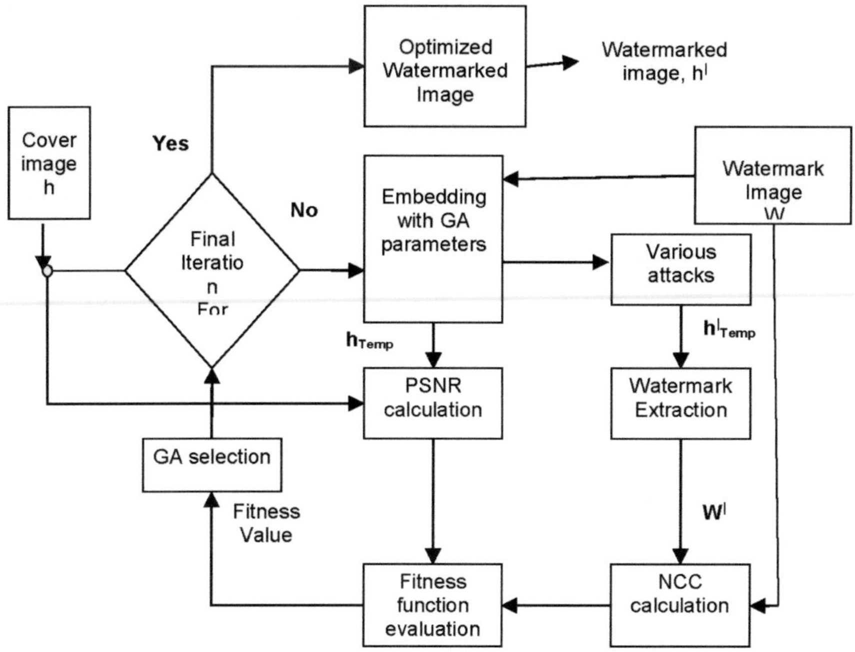

Figure 1.
Flow chart for GA based watermark embedding.

5. Write a capacity to extricate the watermark from the assaulted watermarked picture (with at least one explicit assaults) according to the technique clarified in the above segment. The capacity should restore the NCC esteem for the removed watermark.

6. Write another capacity by utilizing the boundaries of the plan, install, and separate capacities depicted in the past two stages for computing the wellness esteem. The wellness work is characterized in Eq. (10).

7. Run GA to augment the wellness work. After the end of GA, we get the ideal qualities for the boundaries.

8. Using the boundary esteems got from the past advance, ascertain the ideal estimation of PSNR for an unattacked watermarked picture and NCC values for the separated watermarks with different assaults.

9. Use the acquired ideal estimations of PSNR and NCCs with different assaults to depict the presentation of the plan.

6. Experimental results

Three different cover images are used for experimentation. They are Lena, Peppers, and Barbara (512 × 512 pixels, 8 bits/pixel) which are shown in **Figure 2** (a), (b), and (c) respectively. MATLAB 7.0 and Checkmark 1.2 [15] are used for testing the robustness of the proposed scheme. Two dimensional DWT with 'Haar' wavelet filters is used. Genetic Algorithm (GA) with a population size of 20 chromosomes, a crossover rate of 0.8, and a Gaussian mutation function (with a scale 1.0 and shrink 1.0) are used.

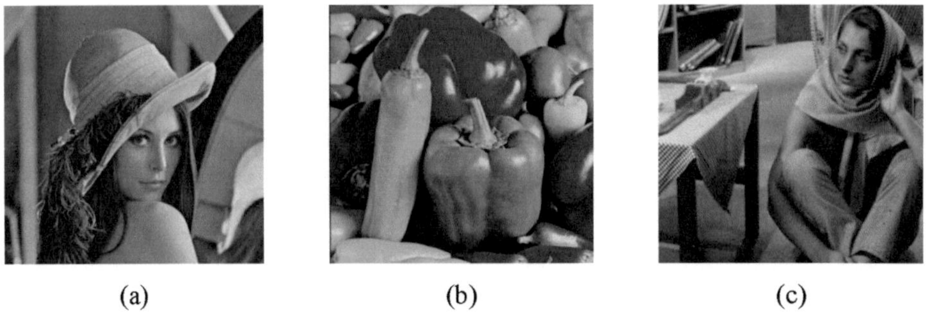

Figure 2.
Cover images of size 512 × 512 (a) Lena, (b) Peppers, and (c) Barbara.

The peak signal-to-noise ratio (PSNR) is used to evaluate the quality between an attacked image and the original image. PSNR is defined as follows:

$$PSNR = 10 \log_{10} \frac{255 \times 255}{\frac{1}{M \times N} \sum_{x=1}^{M} \sum_{y=1}^{N} [f(i,j) - g(i,j)]^2} dB \tag{11}$$

Where, M and N are the tallness and width of the picture, individually. f(i, j) and g(i, j) are the pixel esteems situated at facilitates (I, j) of the first picture, and the assaulted picture, separately. Subsequent to extricating the watermark, the standardized connection coefficient (NCC) is registered utilizing the first watermark and the separated watermark to pass judgment on the presence of the watermark and to quantify the rightness of a removed watermark.

It is characterized as

$$NCC = \frac{\sum_{i=1}^{m} \sum_{j=1}^{n} [w(i,j) - w_{mean}] \left[w^{\circ}(i,j) - w^{\circ}_{mean} \right]}{\sqrt{\left(\sum_{i=1}^{m} \sum_{j=1}^{n} [w(i,j) - w_{mean}]^2 \right) \left(\sum_{i=1}^{m} \sum_{j=1}^{n} \left[w^{\circ}(i,j) - w^{\circ}_{mean} \right]^2 \right)}} \tag{12}$$

Where, m and n are the stature and width of the watermark, individually. The images are the pieces situated at the directions of the first watermark and the separated watermark individually. The images are the mean estimations of the first watermark and the extricated watermark individually. Genetic Algorithm is executed to find the optimum values for the scaling factors of the proposed scheme. Scaling factors used in the proposed algorithm are t_1, t_2, t_3 and t_4. Scaling factors can be adjusted according to PSNR and NCC requirements. The required values (target values for GA process) must be included in the fitness function written for GA. Let the required values for PSNR and NCC are 42 and 1 respectively. PSNR depends upon the scheme parameters t_1, t_2, and t_3. NCC depends on t_4. But, PSNR and NCC are not independent. Hence, it is not possible to fix the values for both PSNR and NCC. In addition, one can specify the weights for requirements. As the required value of NCC is very small in comparison with the required PSNR, a weight 20 is used for NCC. Refer the expression shown for fitness function in the first row of **Table 1**. GA will optimize the whole process according to the requirements specified in the fitness function and produces the optimum values for PSNR, NCC, and scaling factors. We can also specify one or more image attacks against which robustness is required for the watermark. In these experiments, a JPEG attack with quality factor 40 is specified for GA.

Table 1 shows the results of GA with Lena as the cover (cover) image. Optimum values for PSNR, NCC and scaling factors (scheme parameters) after each GA generation are shown. Results are shown up to five GA generations. Hence, five sets of optimum values are available for use. The set that is more close to the requirement for the specified application can be selected. In terms of both PSNR and NCC, parameter values obtained after the fifth generation are good. Similarly, **Tables 2** and **3** show the GA results with Peppers and Barbara cover images respectively. In **Tables 2** and **3**, parameter values obtained after fourth-generation are optimum in terms of both PSNR and NCC.

Original watermark image is shown in **Figure 3(a)** and **(b)** shows the unattacked watermarked Lena. **Figure 3(c)** shows the attacked (JPEG, quality factor 40) watermarked Lena. The extracted watermark is shown in **Figure 3(d)**. Scaling factors used for watermarking are $t_1 = 0.3140$, $t_2 = 0.7962$, $t_3 = 0.8903$ and $t_4 = 0.6206$ (Refer the last row of **Table 1**).

JPEG is one of the most much of the time utilized configurations regarding the Internet and advanced cameras. The JPEG quality factor is a number somewhere in the range of 0 and 100 and partners a numerical incentive with a specific pressure level. At the point when the quality factor is diminished from 100, the picture pressure is improved, however the nature of the subsequent picture is fundamentally decreased. Changed quality variables are applied in the analyses, and the

Attack: JPEG-40
Fitness function: (42-PSNR) + 20(1-NCC)
Initial range for parameters: [0.1-1.0, 0.5-1.0, 0.1-1.0, 0.05-1.0]
Cover image: Lena

No. of generations (no. of iterations)	Fitness value	PSNR in dB	NCC	Scaling factors [t1, t2, t3, t4]
1 (20)	1.7512	41.7425	0.9253	[0.8344, 0.8784, 0.7205, 0.6015]
2 (40)	1.6931	41.4934	0.9407	[0.3313, 0.9540, 0.8266, 0.7660]
3 (60)	1.9825	42.3381	0.9178	[0.3754, 0.6596, 1.0127, 0.5832]
4 (80)	1.756	41.7370	0.9253	[0.7596, 0.8797, 0.8687, 0.6403]
5 (100)	1.5023	41.9914	0.9253	[0.3140, 0.7962, 0.8903, 0.6206]

Table 1.
Results of GA based optimization against the JPEG attack with QF = 40 (the cover image is Lena).

Attack: JPEG-40
Fitness function: (42-PSNR) + 20(1-NCC)
Initial range for parameters: [0.1-1.0, 0.1-0.6, 0.1-1.0, 0.05-1.0]
Cover image: Peppers

No. of generations (no. of iterations)	Fitness value	PSNR in dB	NCC	Scaling factors [t1, t2, t3, t4]
1 (20)	3.1412	41.8024	0.8528	[0.4017, 0.5404, 0.8020, 0.3730]
2 (40)	3.5756	42.2452	0.8371	[0.7123, 0.4546, 0.9787, 0.4052]
3 (60)	3.8528	42.1525	0.8258	[0.6213, 0.4676, 0.6829, 0.4343]
4 (80)	3.2263	41.7069	0.8493	[0.7654, 0.5576, 0.5172, 0.4459]
5 (100)	2.8405	40.8038	0.9178	[−0.8038, 0.5743, 1.0763, 0.4824]

Table 2.
Results of GA based optimization against the JPEG attack with QF = 40 (cover image is Peppers).

Attack: JPEG-40
Fitness function: (42-PSNR) + 20(1-NCC)
Parameter value ranges: [0.1-1.0, 0.4-1.0, 0.1-1.0, 0.05-1.0]
Cover image: Barbara

No. of generations (no. of iterations)	Fitness value	PSNR in dB	NCC	Scaling factors[t1, t2, t3, t4]
1 (20)	2.7381	41.4453	0.8908	[0.1757, 0.5391, 0.9408, 0.4877]
2 (40)	2.9209	41.7110	0.8684	[0.8335, 0.6549, 0.4174, 0.4410]
3 (60)	2.5027	41.6835	0.8907	[0.4936, 0.4699, 0.9824, 0.4374]
4 (80)	2.4459	41.5814	0.8986	[0.7015, 0.4967, 0.8835, 0.4220]
5 (100)	2.6055	41.6519	0.8871	[1.0284, 0.4783, 0.9497, 0.3963]

Table 3.
Results of GA based optimization against the JPEG attack with QF = 40 (cover image is Barbara).

(a) (b) (c) (d)

Figure 3.
(a) Original watermark image. (b) Watermarked Lena, PSNR = 41.9914 dB. (c) Attacked watermarked Lena with JPEG-40 attack, PSNR = 34.9652 dB. (d) Extracted watermark, NCC = 0.9253.

outcomes are appeared in **Table 4** for the three test pictures. Optimum parameter values (Fifth generation parameters for Lena, fourth-generation parameters for both Peppers and Barbara) are used for evaluation. The proposed method can detect the existence of a watermark through quality factors greater than 15. The results show that the value of NCC is greater than 0.50 for any of the three test images with JPEG quality factor greater than or equal to 15.

Other attacks like a median filter, Gaussian filter, average filter (low pass filter), sharpening filter, histogram equalization scaling, cropping, rotation, Gaussian noise, row-column blanking, row-column copying, salt and pepper noise, bit plane removal, and gamma correction etc. are also applied to the watermarked images obtained with the optimum parameters and the corresponding results are shown in **Table 5**. The proposed method can effectively resist all those attacks.

The watermarked image is rotated by some degrees to the right and then rotated back to their original position using the bilinear transformation. This is a lossy operation. In this experiment; 5, 10, 15, and 30 degrees rotations are used to test the robustness of the watermark.

The resizing operation initially reduces or increases the size of the image and then generates the image with the original size by using an interpolation technique. With this operation, the watermarked image loses some watermark information. In this experiment, initially, the watermarked image size is reduced from 512 × 512 to

JPEG quality factor (QF)	(a) Lena PSNR = 41.9914 dB t_1 = 0.3140, t_2 = 0.7962, t_3 = 0.8903, t_4 = 0.6206	(b) Peppers PSNR = 41.7069 dB t_1 = 0.7654, t_2 = 0.5576, t_3 = 0.5172, t_4 = 0.4459	(c) Barbara PSNR = 41.5814 dB t_1 = 0.7015, t_2 = 0.4967, t_3 = 0.8835, t_4 = 0.4220
	NCC	NCC	NCC
10	0.4405	0.3813	0.4767
15	0.7443	0.5087	0. 6414
20	0.8157	0. 6392	0. 7653
25	0.8781	0. 7413	0. 8441
30	0.8910	0. 8209	0. 8633
35	0.9256	0. 8363	0. 8594
40	0.9253	0. 8493	0.8986
50	0.9177	0. 9142	0. 9254
60	0.8870	0. 9219	0. 9293
70	0.9594	0. 9816	0. 9556
80	0.9890	1. 0000	0. 9853
90	1.0000	1.0000	1.0000
100	1.0000	1.0000	1.0000

Table 4.
NCC of the watermark images extracted from different watermarked images with JPEG attack [(a) Lena, (b) Peppers and (c) Barbara].

256 × 256. Later, its dimensions are increased to 512 × 512 by using bilinear interpolation.

For a low pass separating assault, a 3 × 3 veil is utilized. The middle channel is a nonlinear spatial channel which is generally used to expel commotion spikes from a picture. The watermarked picture is assaulted by middle separating with a 3 × 3 veil.

The trimming activity erases some bit of the picture. The separated watermark is as yet conspicuous significantly after 25% of trimming. In line section blanking assault, a lot of lines and segments are erased. In this examination 10,30,40,70,100,120 and 140 of lines and sections are expelled. The removed watermark indicated great comparability with the first watermark.

In succession section duplicate assault, a lot of lines and segments are replicated to the nearby or irregular areas. In this test, tenth line is duplicated to 30th column, 40 to 70, 100 to 120 and 140th line is replicated to 160th line. The separated watermark is unmistakably obvious. In bit plane evacuation assault, the least critical pieces of the watermarked picture pixel power esteems are made '0'. In gamma adjustment, the power of the watermarked picture is changed by a predefined force change. The proposed calculation is tough to bit plane expulsion and gamma rectification. The watermarked image is attacked by salt and pepper noise with a noise density of 0.001. The extracted watermark is still recognizable.

The proposed method is compared with Wang and Lin's [8], Li et al.'s [16], Lien and Lin's [17] and Lin et al. [7] methods in terms of PSNR and NCC (using the Lena as the cover image). The results of those existing methods are found in [16]. Size of the watermark image (Logo) is 32 × 16 in those methods. For comparison purposes, a watermark with the same size is embedded using GA based proposed method and obtained the results. Comparison results are shown in **Table 6** and in **Figure 4** in the graphical form. The performance of the proposed method is better than the other methods against JPEG compression and Gaussian filter attacks. But, this

Type of attack		**(a) Lena** **PSNR = 41.9914 dB** **t_1 = 0.3140,** **t_2 = 0.7962,** **t_3 = 0.8903,** **t_4 = 0.6206**	**(b) Peppers** **PSNR = 41.7069 dB** **t_1 = 0.7654,** **t_2 = 0.5576,** **t_3 = 0.5172,** **t_4 = 0.459**	**(c) Barbara** **PSNR =41. 5814 dB** **t_1 = 0.7015,** **t_2 = 0.4967,** **t_3 = 0.8835,** **t_4 = 0.4220**
		NCC	**NCC**	**NCC**
Median filter (3 × 3)		0.8751	0. 7833	0.7059
Gaussian filter (3 × 3) Variance = 0.5		0.9062	0. 9299	0.9296
Average filter (3 × 3)		0.7156	0. 7170	0.6830
Sharpening filter		0.8204	0. 7657	0.7018
Histogram Equalization		0.8432	0. 7702	0.9193
Scaling 50%		0.8299	0. 7300	0. 7475
Cropping 25%		0.5751	0. 5751	0. 5751
Gamma correction (gamma = 0.9)		1.0000	0. 8775	0. 9890
Bit plane removal (LSB)		1.0000	1.0000	1.0000
Row and column copying		0. 9443	0. 8861	0. 8900
Row column blanking		0. 6236	0. 6439	0. 6592
Gaussian noise (0.001 variance)		0.7242	0. 6124	0.7479
Salt and pepper noise (0.001)		0.9222	0. 8714	0.9130
Rotation	5 degrees	0.7074	0. 7732	0.7502
	10 degrees	0.6505	0. 7073	0.6726
	15 degrees	0.5940	0. 6591	0.6279
	30 degrees	0.5413	0. 5959	0.5759

Table 5.
NCC of the watermark images extracted from different watermarked images with various other attacks ((a) Lena, (b) Peppers and (c) Barbara).

method is slightly inferior in comparison with the methods in [7, 17] against sharpening and scaling attacks. The proposed method can detect the existence of a watermark through JPEG quality factors greater than 10. NCC value obtained against JPEG (Quality factor 10) attack with the proposed method is 0.78. But, the NCC value against the same attack for the existing methods is less than or equal to 0.34. Similarly, the proposed method is better in terms of perceptual quality (PSNR) of the watermarked image. The optimum value obtained for PSNR with the proposed scheme is 42.92 dB when 32 × 16 size watermark is embedded. Optimization is performed against JPEG, average filter, and high pass filters. The obtained parameter values are t_1 = 1.1710, t_2 = 1.1879, t_3 = 0.6047 and t_4 = 1.0058.

7. Conclusions

In this chapter, a novel and an oblivious watermarking method is proposed based on GA and using maximum wavelet coefficient modulation. A binary watermark is embedded in the third level LH sub-band of the cover image. The perceptual quality of the watermarked image is good and the watermark can effectively resist JPEG compression and various other attacks like Gaussian filter, median filter,

Attacks	Wang and Lin [8] (PSNR = 38.2 dB) NCC	Li et al. [16] (PSNR = 40.6 dB) NCC	Lien and Lin [17] (PSNR = 41.54 dB) NCC	Lin et al. [7] (PSNR = 42.02 dB) NCC	Proposed method (PSNR = 42.92 dB) NCC
JPEG (QF = 10)	NA	0.15	0.17	0.34	0.78
JPEG (QF = 20)	NA	0.34	0.61	0.67	0.90
JPEG (QF = 30)	0.15	0.52	0.79	0.82	0.83
JPEG (QF = 70)	0.57	0.63	0.97	0.97	0.99
JPEG (QF = 90)	1.00	0.78	1.00	0.99	1.00
Gaussian filter	0.64	0.70	0.84	0.88	0.93
Median filter (3 × 3)	0.51	0.35	0.79	0.90	0.87
Sharpening filter	0.46	0.38	0.88	0.97	0.83
Scaling (50%)	NA	0.35	0.79	0.88	0.81

Table 6.
Performance comparison of the proposed method with the methods of Wang and Lin's [8], Li et al.'s [16], Lien and Lin's [17], and Lin et al. [7] (using Lena as the cover image and 32 × 16 logo).

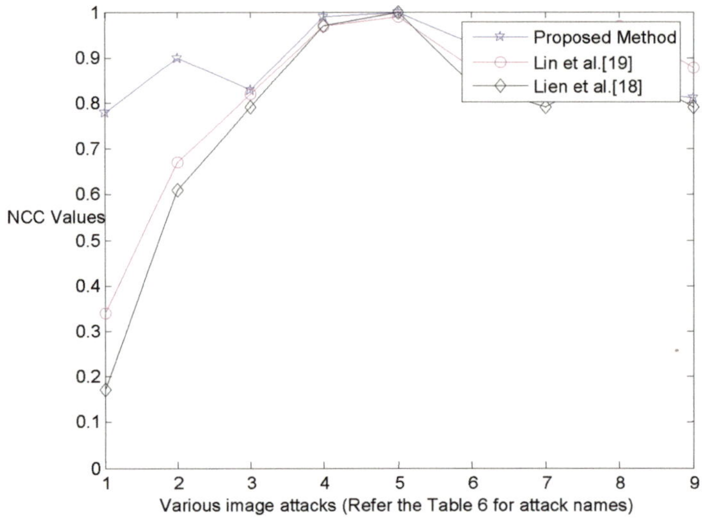

(a)

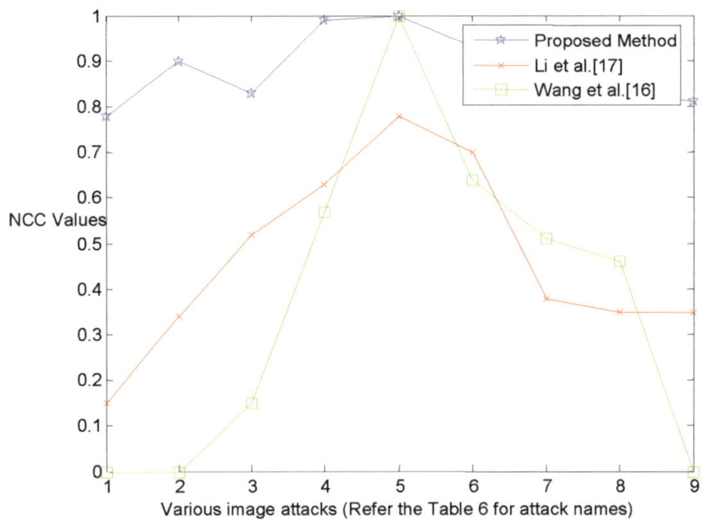

(b)

Figure 4.
Performance comparison of the proposed method with the existing methods. (a) With Lin et al. [7] & Lien et al. [17]. (b) With Li et al. [16] and Wang et al. [8].

and average filter, etc. The advantage of the proposed scheme is the effective use of GA to obtain the optimum response in terms of both PSNR and NCC. Experimental results show that the performance of the scheme is better than the existing schemes in terms of the embedding capacity, PSNR and NCC. In addition to copyright protection, the proposed scheme can also be applied to data hiding and image authentication. The flexibility of the proposed GA based scheme is also demonstrated in fixing the parameters of the scheme. Here, flexibility refers to the fixation of scheme parameters for satisfying the requirements in terms of PSNR and NCC when the input images (cover and/or watermark images) are changed.

For the scheme proposed in this chapter, watermark embedding capacity is medium. It can effectively embed 32 × 32 size watermark into 512 × 512 cover image. Hence, embedding capacity improvement is considered in the next chapter.

Author details

Surya Prasada Rao Borra[1*], Kongara Ramanjaneyulu[1] and K. Raja Rajeswari[2]

1 Prasad V. Potluri Siddhartha Institute of Technology, Kanuru, Vijayawada, Andhra Pradesh, India

2 GVP College of Engineering for Women, Visakhapatnam, Andhra Pradesh, India

*Address all correspondence to: suryaborra1679@gmail.com

References

[1] P. Meerwald and A. Uhl, "A Survey of Wavelet-domain watermarking Algorithms," Proceedings of the SPIE, Electronic Imaging, Security and Watermarking of Multimedia Contents III, pp. 505–516, 2001

[2] R. Dugad, K. Ratakonda and N. Ahuja, "A new wavelet-based scheme for watermarking images", Proceedings of the IEEE ICIP, Chicago, pp. 419–423, 1998

[3] H.J. Wang and C.C.J. Kuo,"High fidelity image compression with multi-threshold wavelet coding (MTWC)," SPIE's Annual Meeting-Application of Digital Image Processing, San Diego, pp. 383–392, 1997

[4] F. Davoine, "Comparison of two wavelet-based image watermarking schemes, " International Conference on Image Processing, Vancouver, pp. 682–685, 2000

[5] M. Hsieh, D. Tseng, and Y. Huang, "Hiding digital watermarks using multiresolution wavelet transform," IEEE Transactions on Industrial Electronics, Vol. 48, No. 5, pp. 875–882, 2001

[6] C. Temi, S. Choomchuay, and A. Lasakul, "A robust image watermarking using multiresolution analysis of wavelet," Proceedings of the IEEE ISCIT, pp. 623–626, 2005

[7] W.H. Lin, Y.R. Wang, S.J. Horng, T. W. Kao and Y. Pan, "A blind watermarking method using maximum wavelet coefficient quantization," Expert Systems with Applications, Vol. 36, No. 9, pp. 11509-11516, Nov 2009

[8] S.H. Wang and Y.P. Lin, "Wavelet tree quantization for copyright protection watermarking," IEEE Trans. Image Processing, Vol. 13, No. 2, pp. 154–165, 2004

[9] JH. Holland, "Adaptation in natural and artificial systems: an introductory analysis with applications to biology, control and artificial intelligence," Cambridge, MA: MIT Press; 1992

[10] K. Nikola Kasabo, "Foundations of Neural Networks, Fuzzy Systems, and Knowledge engineering," The MIT Press, Cambridge, Second printing, 1998

[11] A.E. Eiben, et al., "Genetic algorithms with multi-parent recombination, " PPSN III: Proceedings of the International Conference on Evolutionary Computation, The Third Conference on Parallel Problem Solving from Nature: pp. 78–87, ISBN 3-540-58484-6, 1994

[12] Ting and Chuan-Kang, "On the Mean Convergence Time of Multi-parent Genetic Algorithms without Selection, " Advances in Artificial Life: pp. 403–412, ISBN 978-3-540-28848-0, 2005

[13] Veysel Aslantas, "A singular-value decomposition-based image watermarking using genetic algorithm," International Journal of Electronics and Communications, (AEÜ), 62, pp. 386-394, 2008

[14] Ali Al-Haj and Aymen Abu-Errub, "Performance Optimization of Discrete Wavelets Transform Based Image Watermarking Using Genetic Algorithms," Journal of Computer Science, Vol. 4, No. 10, pp. 834-841, ISSN 1549-3636, 2008

[15] www.http://watermarking.unige.ch/Checkmark/

[16] E. Li, H. Liang and X. Niu, "An integer wavelet-based multiple logo-watermarking schemes, " Proceedings of the IEEE WCICA, pp. 10256–10260, 2006

[17] B.K. Lien and W.H. Lin, "A watermarking method based on maximum distance wavelet tree quantization," 19th Conf. Computer Vision, Graphics and Image Processing, pp. 269–276, 2006

Chapter 7

A New BEM for Modeling and Simulation of Laser Generated Ultrasound Waves in 3T Fractional Nonlinear Generalized Micropolar Poro-Thermoelastic FGA Structures

Mohamed Abdelsabour Fahmy

Abstract

In this chapter, we introduce a new theory called acoustic wave propagation of three-temperature fractional nonlinear generalized micropolar poro-thermoelasticity and we propose a new boundary element technique for modeling and simulation of laser-generated ultrasonic wave propagation problems of functionally graded anisotropic (FGA) structures which are linked with the proposed theory. Since it is very difficult to solve general acoustic problems of this theory analytically, we need to develop and use new computational modeling techniques. So, we propose a new boundary element technique for solving such problems. The numerical results are shown graphically to depict the effects of three temperatures on the thermal stress waves propagation. The validity, accuracy, and efficiency of our proposed theory and the technique are examined and demonstrated by comparing the obtained outcomes with those previously reported in the literature as special cases of our general study.

Keywords: boundary element method, modeling and simulation, laser ultrasonics, three-temperature, fractional-order, nonlinear generalized micropolar poro-thermoelasticity, functionally graded anisotropic structures

1. Introduction

The fractional calculus has recently been widely used to describe anomalous diffusion instead of classical diffusion, where the standard time derivative is replaced by fractional time derivative. Indeed, fractional calculus has important applications in electronics, wave propagation, nanotechnology, control theory, electricity, heat conduction modeling and identification, signal and image processing, biochemistry, biology, viscoelasticity, hereditary solid mechanics, and fluid dynamics.

Physically, according to the medium where the waves are transmitted, there are three wave types which are classified as mechanical waves, electromagnetic waves, and matter waves. Mechanical waves can travel through any medium with speed depending on elasticity and inertia and cannot travel through a vacuum. Electromagnetic waves can travel through a vacuum and do not need a medium to travel like X-ray, microwaves, ultraviolet waves, and radio waves. Matter waves are also called De Broglie waves that have wave-particle duality property. There are two mechanisms that have been proposed to explain wave generation, a first mechanism at high energy density, which leads to forces that generate ultrasound, and a second mechanism at low energy density, which generates elastic waves according to irradiation of laser pulses onto a material. The interaction between laser light and a metal surface led to great progress to develop theoretical models to describe the experimental data [1]. Scruby et al. [2] proved that the thermoelastic area source had been reduced to a surface point-source. This point-source ignores the optical absorption, the heat source thermal diffusion, and the limited side dimensions of the source. Based on point-source representation, Rose [3] introduced Surface Center of Expansion (SCOE) models which predict the major features of ultrasound waves generated by laser. Doyle [4] established that the existence of the metal precursor is due to subsurface sources which arise from thermal diffusion. According to McDonald [5], Spicer [6] used the generalized thermoelasticity theory to introduce a real circular laser source model taking into consideration spatial-temporal laser pulse design and thermal diffusion effect. The mathematical foundations of three-temperature were laid for nonlinear generalized thermoelasticity theory by Fahmy [7–12]. Fahmy [7] introduced a new boundary element strategy for modeling and simulation of three-temperature nonlinear generalized micropolar-magneto-thermoelastic wave propagation problems in FGA structures. Fahmy [8] proposed a boundary element formulation for three-temperature thermal stresses in anisotropic circular cylindrical plate structures. Fahmy [9] developed a boundary element model to describe the three-temperature fractional-order heat transfer in magneto-thermoelastic functionally graded anisotropic structures. Fahmy [10] introduced a boundary element formulation for modeling and optimization of micropolar thermoviscoelastic problems. Fahmy [11] discussed modeling and optimization of photo-thermoelastic stresses in three-temperature anisotropic semiconductor structures. Fahmy [12] proposed a new boundary element algorithm for nonlinear modeling and simulation of three-temperature anisotropic generalized micropolar piezothermoelasticity with memory-dependent derivative. This chapter differs from the references mentioned above, because it constructs a new acoustic wave propagation theory and allows the effective, efficient, and simple solution to the considered complex problems related with the proposed theory.

Recently, research on nonlinear generalized micropolar thermoelastic wave propagation problems has become very popular due to its practical applications in various fields such as astronautics, oceanology, aeronautics, narrow-band and broad-band systems, fiber-optic communication, fluid mechanics, automobile industries, aircraft, space vehicles, materials science, geophysics, petroleum and mineral prospecting, geomechanics, earthquake engineering, plasma physics, nuclear reactors, high-energy particle accelerators, and other industrial applications. Due to computational difficulties in solving nonlinear generalized micropolar poro-thermoelastic problems analytically, many numerical techniques have been developed and implemented for solving such problems [13, 14]. The boundary element method (BEM) [15–22] has been recognized as an attractive alternative numerical method to domain methods [23–26] like finite difference method (FDM), finite element method (FEM), and finite volume method (FVM) in engineering applications. The superior feature of BEM over domain methods is that it only needs to discretize the boundary, which often leads to fewer elements and easier to use. In the boundary element method (BEM) formulation, boundary integral equations involving singular integrands, the proper treatment of the singular integration has become essential in terms of numerical accuracy and efficiency of BEM. Also, some domain integrals may appear representing body forces, nonlinear effects, etc. Through our BEM solution, several approaches have been used to transform domain integrals into equivalent boundary integrals, so that the final boundary element formulation solution involves only the boundary integrals. The boundary element formulation of the current general study has been derived by using the weighted residual method [27–51]. In engineering applications, both FEM and BEM are based on the weighted residual methods with the same approximation procedure based on interpolation functions over each element to approximate the state variables distribution. Both methods differ in choosing the weighting functions. FEM as a domain method needs discretization of the whole domain, which usually leads to large systems of equations. This advantage of BEM over FEM has significant importance for modeling and simulation of thermal stress wave propagation problems which can be implemented using BEM with little cost and less input data. The solutions by BEM, like boundary thermal stress wave problems, are more accurate than by FEM, especially near the place of stress concentration. This feature is very important for our proposed theory and the technique of solving its related problems.

In this chapter, we introduce a novel theory called acoustic wave propagation of three-temperature fractional nonlinear generalized micropolar poro-thermoelasticity and we propose a new boundary element technique for modeling and simulation of laser-generated ultrasonic wave propagation problems of functionally graded anisotropic (FGA) structures which are linked with the proposed theory. Since it is very difficult to solve general acoustic problems of this theory analytically and we need to develop and use new computational modeling techniques. So, we propose a new boundary element technique for solving such problems. The numerical results are shown graphically to depict the effects of three temperatures on the propagation of thermal stresses waves. Since there are no available data for comparison with our proposed technique results, so, we replace the radiative heat conduction equations with heat conduction as a special case from our present general study. In the special case under consideration, the BEM results have been compared graphically with the FDM and FEM in the heat conduction and radiative heat conductions cases; it can be noticed that the BEM results are in a good agreement with the FDM and FEM results and thus demonstrate the validity and accuracy of our proposed theory and the technique used to solve its general problems.

A brief summary of the chapter is as follows: Section 1 introduces the background and provides the readers with the necessary information to books and articles for a better understanding of wave propagation problems in three-temperature nonlinear generalized micropolar poro-thermoelastic FGA structures and their applications. Section 2 describes the BEM modeling of the new theory and introduces the partial differential equations that govern its related problems. Section 3 outlines BEM simulation of temperature field. Section 4 discusses BEM simulation of micropolar porothermoelastic field to obtain the three temperatures thermal stress wave propagation. Section 5 presents the new numerical results that describe the thermal stress wave propagation under the effect of three-temperature on the FGA structures.

2. BEM modeling of the problem

We consider an anisotropic micropolar porous smart structure in a rectangular Cartesian system (x_1, x_2, x_3) shown in **Figure 1**, with a configuration R bounded by

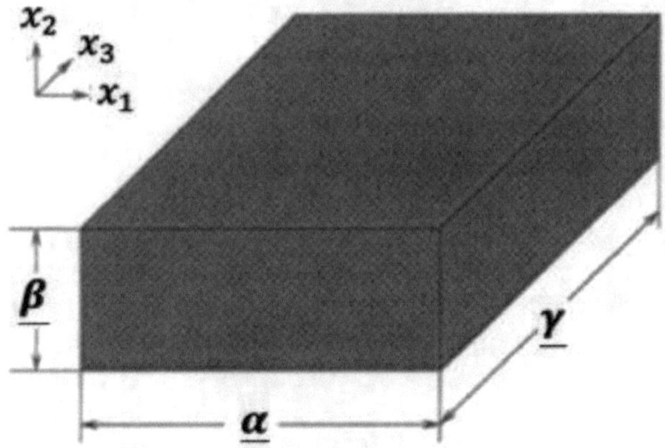

Figure 1.
Geometry of the FGA structure.

a closed surface S, and $S_i(i = 1, 2, 3, 4, 5, 6)$ denotes subsets of S such that $S_1 + S_2 = g_3 + S_4 = S_5 + S_6$. The governing equations for modeling of fractional three-temperature nonlinear generalized micropolar poro-thermoelastic problems of functionally graded anisotropic structures (FGA) can be expressed as [7].

$$\sigma_{ij,j} + \rho F_i = \rho \ddot{u}_i + \phi \rho_{\mathcal{F}} \ddot{v}_i \tag{1}$$

$$m_{ij,j} + \varepsilon_{ijk}\sigma_{jk} + \rho M_i = J\rho\ddot{\omega}_i \tag{2}$$

$$\dot{\zeta} + q_{i,i} = \mathbb{C} \tag{3}$$

where

$$\sigma_{ij} = (z \ \ +1)^m \left[C_{ijkl}\, e\delta_{ij} - A\delta_{ij}p + \breve{\alpha}\left(u_{j,i} - \varepsilon_{ijk}\omega_k\right) - \beta_{ij} T_\alpha\right] \tag{4}$$

$$C_{ijkl} = C_{klij} = C_{jikl}, \beta_{ij} = \beta_{ji} \tag{5}$$

$$m_{ij} = (x+1)^m \left[\alpha\,\omega_{k,k}\delta_{ij} + \overline{\alpha}\omega_{i,j} + \overline{\overline{\alpha}} = \omega_{\ j,i}\right] \tag{6}$$

$$\zeta = (x+1)^m \left[A u_{k,k} + \frac{\phi^2}{R} p\right] \tag{7}$$

$$q_i = (x+1)^m \left[-\overline{k}\left(p_{,i} + \rho_{\mathcal{F}}\ddot{u}_i + \frac{\rho_0 + \phi\rho_{\mathcal{F}}}{\phi}\ddot{v}_i\right)\right] \tag{8}$$

$$\epsilon_{ij} = \varepsilon_{ij} - \varepsilon_{ijk}(\chi+1)^m (r_k - \omega_k) \tag{9}$$

$$\varepsilon_{ij} = \frac{1}{2}\left(u_{i,j}1 + u_{j,i}\right) \tag{10}$$

$$r_i = \frac{1}{2}\varepsilon_{ikl}\, u_{l,k} \tag{11}$$

The time-fractional order three-temperature radiative heat conduction equations can be written as

$$D_\tau^a T_\alpha(r,\tau) = \xi\nabla[\mathbb{K}_\alpha \nabla T_\alpha(r,\tau)] + \xi\overline{\mathbb{W}}(r,\tau), \xi = \frac{1}{c_\alpha \rho \delta_1} \tag{12}$$

where

$$\overline{\mathbb{W}}(r,\ \tau)=\begin{cases}\rho\mathbb{W}_{ei}(T_e-T_i)+\rho\overline{\overline{\mathbb{W}}}_{er}(T_e-T_p)+\overline{\overline{\mathbb{W}}},\ \ \alpha=e,\ \ \delta_1=1\\ -\rho\mathbb{W}_{ei}(T_e-T_i)+\overline{\overline{\mathbb{W}}}, \qquad \alpha=i,\ \ \delta_1=1\\ -\rho\mathbb{W}_{er}(T_e-T_p)+\overline{\overline{\mathbb{W}}}, \qquad \alpha=p,\delta_1=T_p^3\end{cases} \tag{13}$$

$$\begin{aligned}\overline{\overline{\mathbb{W}}}(r,\tau)=&-\delta_{2n}\mathbb{K}_\alpha\dot{T}_{\alpha,ij}+\beta_{ij}T_{\alpha 0}\left[\mathring{A}\delta_{1n}\dot{u}_{i,j}+(\tau_0+\delta_{2n})\ddot{u}_{i,j}\right]\\ &+\rho c_\alpha\left[(\tau_0+\delta_{1n^{T_2}}+\delta_{2n})\ddot{T}_\alpha\right]\end{aligned} \tag{14}$$

and

$$\mathbb{W}_{ei}=\rho\mathbb{A}_{ei}T_e^{-2/3},\ \ \mathbb{W}_{er}=\rho\mathbb{A}_{er}T_e^{-1/2},\ \ \mathbb{K}_\alpha=\mathbb{A}_\alpha T_\alpha^{5/2},\ \ \alpha=e,i,\ \ \mathbb{K}_p=\mathbb{A}_pT_p^{3+\mathbb{B}} \tag{15}$$

The total energy is

$$P=P_e+P_i+P_p,\ \ P_e=c_eT_e,\ \ P_i=c_iT_i,\ \ P_p=\frac{1}{4}c_pT_p^4 \tag{16}$$

where we considered that $\theta=T_e+T_i+T_r$, T_e, T_i, and T_r are temperature functions of electron, ion, and photon, respectively, $\mathbb{K}_e$, $\mathbb{K}_i$, and $\mathbb{K}_r$ are conductive coefficients of electron, ion, and photon, respectively, and ρ is the material density which is constant inside each subdomain.

3. BEM simulation for temperature field

In this section, we are interested in using a boundary element method for modeling the nonlinear time-dependent two dimensions three temperature (2D-3T) radiation heat equations coupled with electron, ion, and phonon temperatures.

According to finite difference scheme of Caputo at times $(f+1)\Delta\tau$ and $f\Delta\tau$, we obtain [52].

$$D_\tau^a T_\alpha^{f+1}+D_\tau^a T_\alpha^f\approx\sum_{j=0}^{k}W_{a,j}\left(T_\alpha^{f+1-j}(r)-T_\alpha^{f-j}(r)\right) \tag{17}$$

where

$$W_{a,0}=\frac{(\Delta\tau)^{-a}}{\Gamma(2-a)},\ \ W_{a,j}=W_{a,0}\left((j+1)^{1-a}-(j-1)^{1-a}\right) \tag{18}$$

Based on Eq. (17), the fractional order heat Eq. (12) can be replaced by the following system

$$\begin{aligned}&W_{a,0}T_\alpha^{f+1}(r)-\mathbb{K}_\alpha(x)T_{\alpha,II}^{f+1}(r)-\mathbb{K}_{\alpha,I},(x)T_{\alpha,I}^{f+1}(r)\\ &\quad=W_{a,0}T_\alpha^f(r)-\mathbb{K}_\alpha(x)T_{\alpha,II}^f(r)\\ &-\mathbb{K}_{\alpha,I},(x)T_{\alpha,J]}^f(r)-\sum_{j=1}^{f}W_{a,j}\left(T_\alpha^{f+1-j}(r)-T_\alpha^{f-j}(r)\right)+\overline{\mathbb{W}}_m^{f+1}(x,\tau)\\ &\quad+\overline{\mathbb{W}}_m^f(x,\tau)\end{aligned} \tag{19}$$

where, $j = 1, 2, \ldots, F$, $f = 0, 1, 2, \ldots, F$.

Now, according to Fahmy [9] and using the fundamental solution that satisfies the system (19), the boundary integral equations corresponding to (12) without internal heat sources can be written as

$$CT_\alpha = \int_s \left[T_\alpha q^* - T_\alpha^* q\right] dS - \int_R \frac{\mathbb{K}_\alpha}{D} \frac{\partial T_\alpha^*}{\partial \tau} T_\alpha dR \tag{20}$$

Now, to transform the domain integral in (20) into the boundary, we assume that the time-temperature derivative can be approximated by using a series of known functions $f^j(r)$ and unknown coefficients $a^j(\tau)$ as

$$\frac{\partial T_\alpha}{\partial \tau} \cong \sum_{j=1}^{N} f^j(r)^j a^j(\tau) \tag{21}$$

We assume that $\hat{T}_\alpha^j$ is a solution of

$$\nabla^2 \hat{T}_\alpha^j = f^j \tag{22}$$

Thus, Eq. (20) can be written as

$$\begin{aligned} CT_\alpha = & \int_S \left[T_\alpha q^* - T_\alpha^* q\right] dS \\ & + \sum_{j=1}^{N} a^j(\tau) D^{-1} \left(C\hat{T}_\alpha^j - \int_S \left[T_\alpha^j q^* - \hat{q}^j T_\alpha^*\right] dS \right) \end{aligned} \tag{23}$$

where

$$\hat{q}^j = -\mathbb{K}_\alpha \frac{\partial \hat{T}_\alpha^j}{\partial n} \tag{24}$$

and

$$a^j(\tau) = \sum_{i=1}^{N} f_{ji}^{-1} \frac{\partial T(r_i, \tau)}{\partial \tau} \tag{25}$$

In which, the entries of f_{ji}^{-1} are the coefficients of F^{-1} with matrix F defined as

$$\{F\}_{ji} = f^j(r_i) \tag{26}$$

Using the standard boundary element discretization scheme [28], for Eq. (23) and using Eq. (25), we get

$$C\dot{T}_\alpha + HT_\alpha = GQ \tag{27}$$

where the matrices H and G are depending on current time step, boundary geometry, and material properties.

The diffusion matrix can be defined as

$$C = -\left[H\hat{T}_\alpha - G\hat{Q}\right] F^{-1} D^{-1} \tag{28}$$

with

$$\{\hat{T}\}_{ij} = \hat{T}^j(x_i) \tag{29}$$

$$\{\hat{Q}\}_{ij} = \hat{q}^j(\chi_i) \tag{30}$$

In order to solve Eq. (27) numerically, the functions T_α and q are interpolated as

$$T_\alpha = (1-\theta)T_\alpha^m + \theta T_\alpha^{m+1} \tag{31}$$

$$q = (1-\theta)q^m + \theta q^{m+1} \tag{32}$$

The time derivative of the temperature can be written as

$$\dot{T}_\alpha = \frac{dT_\alpha}{d\theta}\frac{d\theta}{d\tau} = \frac{T_\alpha^{m+1} - T_\alpha^m}{\tau^{m+1} - \tau^m} = \frac{T_\alpha^{m+1} - T_\alpha^m}{\Delta\tau^m}, \quad \theta = \frac{\tau - \tau^m}{\tau^{m+1} - \tau^m}, 0 \le \theta \le 1 \tag{33}$$

By substituting from Eqs. (31)–(33) into (27), we obtain

$$\left(\frac{c}{\Delta\tau^m} + \theta H\right)T_\alpha^{m+1} - \theta G Q^{m+1} = \left(\frac{c}{\Delta\tau^m} - (1-\theta)H\right)T_\alpha^m + (1-\theta)GQ^m \tag{34}$$

which can be written as follows [10].

$$\mathbb{a}X = \mathbb{b} \tag{35}$$

where $\mathbb{a}$ is an unknown matrix, while **X** and $\mathbb{b}$ are known matrices.

The explicit staggered predictor-corrector procedure based on communication-avoiding Arnoldi (CA-Arnoldi) method [53] due to its numerical stability, convergence, and performance [7] has been implemented for obtaining the temperature field in terms of predicted displacement field which will be explained in the next section.

4. BEM simulation for micropolar poro-thermoelastic fields

By implementing the weighted residual method, the governing Eqs. (1)–(3) can be written as

$$\int_R (\sigma_{ij,j} + U_i)u_i^* \, dR = 0 \tag{36}$$

$$\int_R (m_{ij,j} + \varepsilon_{ijk}\sigma_{jk} + V_i)\omega_i^* \, dR = 0 \tag{37}$$

$$\int_R (q_i + \dot{\zeta}_i - \mathbb{C}_i)p_i^* \, dR = 0 \tag{38}$$

in which

$$U_i = \varphi_{ij,j} + \rho F_i - \rho\ddot{u}_i - \phi\rho_{\mathcal{F}}\ddot{v}_i \tag{39}$$

$$V_i = \rho(M_i - J\ddot{\omega}_i) \tag{40}$$

where u_i^*, ω_i^* and p_i^* are weighting functions, u_i, ω_i, and p_i are approximate solutions as shown in Eqs. (4)–(11)

The boundary conditions are

$$u_i = \overline{u}_i \qquad \text{on} \, S_1 \tag{41}$$

$$\lambda_i = \sigma_{ii} n_i = \overline{\lambda}_i \qquad \text{on } S_2 \tag{42}$$

$$\omega_i = \overline{\omega}_i \qquad \text{on} \, S_3 \tag{43}$$

$$\mu_i = m_{ij} n_j = \overline{\mu}_i \qquad \text{on} \, S_4 \tag{44}$$

$$p = \overline{p} \qquad \text{on} \, S_5 \tag{45}$$

$$L = \frac{\partial p}{\partial n} = \overline{L} \qquad \text{on} \, S_6 \tag{46}$$

By integrating by parts the first term of Eqs. (36)–(38), we obtain

$$-\int_R \sigma_{ij} u^*_{i,j} \, dR + \int_R U_i u_i^* \, dR = -\int_{S_2} \lambda_i u_i^* \, dS \tag{47}$$

$$\begin{aligned} -\int_R m_{ij} \omega^*_{i,j} \, dR + \int_R \varepsilon_{ijk} \sigma_{jk} \omega_i^* \, dR + \int_R V_i \omega_i^* \, dR \\ = -\int_{S_4} \mu_i \omega_i^* \, dS \end{aligned} \tag{48}$$

$$-\int_R q \, \mathrm{p}^*_{i,i} \, dR + \int_R \dot{\zeta}_i \mathrm{p}_i^* \, dR - \int_R \mathbb{C}_i \, \mathrm{p}_i^* \, dR = -\int_{S_6} L_i \mathrm{p}_i^* \, dS \tag{49}$$

which according to Huang and Liang [54] can be expressed as

$$\begin{aligned} -\int_R \sigma_{ij,j} u_i^* \, dR + \int_R (m_{ij,j} + \varepsilon_{ijk} \sigma_{jk}) \omega_i^* \, dR + \int_R U_i u_i^* \, dR \\ + \int_R V_i \omega_i^* \, dR - \int_R q \, \mathrm{p}^*_{i,i} dR + \int_R \dot{\zeta}_i \mathrm{p}_i^* \, dR - \int_R \mathbb{C}_i \, \mathrm{p}_i^* \, dR \\ = \int_{S_2} (\lambda_i - \overline{\lambda}_i) u_i^* \, dS + \int_{S_1} (\overline{u}_i - u_i) \lambda_i^* \, dS \\ + \int_{S_4} (\mu_i - \overline{\mu}_i) \omega_i^* \, dS + \int_{S_3} (\overline{\omega}_i - \omega_i) \mu_i^* \, dS \\ + \int_{S_6} (L_i - \overline{L}_i) \mathrm{p}_i^* \, dS + \int_{S_5} (\overline{\mathrm{p}}_i - \mathrm{p}_i) L_i^* \, dS \end{aligned} \tag{50}$$

Using integration by parts for the left-hand side of (50), we have

$$\begin{aligned} -\int_R \sigma_{ij} \varepsilon^*_{ij} \, dR - \int_R m_{ij,j} \omega^*_{i,j} \, dR + \int_R U_i u_i^* \, dR \\ + \int_R V_i \omega_i^* \, dR - \int_R q \, \mathrm{p}^*_{i,i} dR + \int_R \dot{\zeta}_i \mathrm{p}_i^* \, dR - \int_R \mathbb{C}_i \mathrm{p}_i^* \, dR \\ = -\int_{S_2} \overline{\lambda}_i u_i^* \, dS - \int_{S_1} \lambda_i u_i^* \, dS \\ + \int_{S_1} (\overline{u}_i - u_i) \lambda_i^* \, dS - \int_{S_4} \overline{\mu}_i \omega_i^* \, dS - \int_{S_3} \mu \omega_i^* \, dS \\ + \int_{S_3} (\overline{\omega}_i - \omega_i) \mu_i^* \, dS - \int_{S_6} \overline{L}_i \, \mathrm{p}_i^* \, dS - \int_{S_6} L_i \mathrm{p}_i^* \, dS \\ + \int_{S_5} (\overline{\mathrm{p}}_i - \mathrm{p}_i) L_i^* \, dS \end{aligned} \tag{51}$$

By using the following elastic stress and couple stress (see Eringen [55])

$$\sigma_{ij} = \mathbb{A}_{ijkl}\,\varepsilon_{kl}, \quad m_{ij} = \mathbb{B}_{ijkl}\,\omega_{k,l} \text{ where } \mathbb{A}_{ijkl} = \mathbb{A}_{klij} \text{ and } \mathbb{B}_{ijkl} = \mathbb{B}_{klij} \tag{52}$$

Hence, Eq. (51) can be rewritten as

$$\begin{aligned}
&-\int_R \sigma_{ij}^*\,\varepsilon_{ij} dR - \int_R m_{ij,j}^*\omega_{i,j} dR + \int_R U_i u_i^*\,dR \\
&\quad + \int_R V_i\omega_i^*\,dR - \int_R q\,\mathrm{p}_{i,i}^* dR + \int_R \dot{\zeta}_i\,\mathrm{p}_i^*\,dR - \int_R \mathbb{C}_i\,\mathrm{p}_i^*\,dR \\
&\quad = -\int_{S_2} \overline{\lambda}_i u_i^*\,dS - \int_{S_1} \lambda_i u_i^*\,dS \\
&\quad + \int_{S_1} (\overline{u}_i - u_i)\lambda_i^*\,dS - \int_{S_4} \overline{\mu}_i\omega_i^*\,dS - \int_{S_3} \mu_i\omega_i^*\,dS \\
&\quad + \int_{S_3} (\overline{\omega}_i - \omega_i)\mu_i^*\,dS - \int_{S_6} \overline{L}_i\,\mathrm{p}_i^*\,dS - \int_{S_6} L_i\,\mathrm{p}_i^*\,dS \\
&\quad + \int_{S_5} (\overline{\mathrm{p}}_i - \mathrm{p}_i)L_i^*\,dS
\end{aligned} \tag{53}$$

Applying the integration by parts for the left-hand side of Eq. (53), we get

$$\begin{aligned}
&\int_R \sigma_{ij,j}^* u_i\,dR + \int_R \left(m_{ij,j}^* + \varepsilon_{ijk}\sigma_{jk}^*\right)\omega_i dR \\
&\quad = -\int_S u_i^*\,\lambda_i\,dS - \int_S \omega_i^*\,\mu_i\,dS - \int_S \mathrm{p}_i^*\,L_i\,dS + \int_S \lambda_i^*\,u_i\,dS \\
&\quad + \int_S \mu_i^*\,\omega_i\,dS + \int_S L_i^*\,\mathrm{p}_i\,dS
\end{aligned} \tag{54}$$

The weighting functions for $U_i = \Delta^n$ and $\mathrm{V_i} = 0$ along the unit vector direction e_l are as follows:

$$\sigma_{lj,j}^* + \Delta^n e_l = 0 \tag{55}$$

$$m_{ij,j}^* + \varepsilon_{ijk}\sigma_{jk}^* = 0 \tag{56}$$

The analytical fundamental solution of Dragos [56] can be written as

$$\begin{aligned}
&u_i^* = u_{li}^*\,e_l, \omega_i^* = \omega_{li}^*\,e_l, p_i^* = p_{li}^*\,e_l, \ \lambda_i^* = \lambda_{li}^*\,e_l, \\
&\mu_i^* = \mu_{li}^*\,e_l, \ L_i^* = L_{li}^*\,e_l
\end{aligned} \tag{57}$$

The obtained weighting functions for a point load $U_\mathrm{i} = 0$ and $V_i = \Delta^n$ along the unit vector direction e_1 were next used as follows:

$$\sigma_{ij,j}^{**} = 0 \tag{58}$$

$$m_{lj,j}^{**} + \varepsilon_{ljk}\sigma_{jk}^{**} + \Delta^n e_l = 0 \tag{59}$$

According to Dragos [56], the fundamental solution can be expressed as

$$\begin{aligned}
&u_i^* = u_{ii}^{**}\,e_l, \ \omega_i^* = \omega_{li}^*\,e_l, \ p_i^* = p_{li}^{**}\,e_l, \ \lambda_i^* = \lambda_{li}^{**}\,e_l, \\
&\mu_i^* = \mu_{li}^*\,e_l, \ L_i^* = L_{li}^{**}\,e_l
\end{aligned} \tag{60}$$

Using the weighting functions of (57) and (60) into (54), we obtain

$$\begin{aligned} C_{li}^{n}u_{i}^{n} &= -\int_{S}\lambda_{li}^{*}u_{i}dS - \int_{S}\mu_{li}^{*}\,\omega_{i}\,dS - \int_{S}\mathrm{L}_{li}^{*}p_{i}dS + \int_{S}u_{li}^{*}\lambda_{i}dS \\ &\quad +\int_{S}\omega_{li}^{*}\mu_{i}\,dS + \int_{S}p_{li}^{*}\mathrm{L}_{i}\,dS \end{aligned} \tag{61}$$

$$\begin{aligned} C_{li}^{n}\omega_{i}^{n} &= -\int_{S}\lambda_{li}^{**}u_{i}dS - \int_{S}\mu_{li}^{**}\,\omega_{i}\,dS - \int_{S}\mathrm{L}_{li}^{**}p_{i}dS + \int_{S}u_{li}^{**}\lambda_{i}dS \\ &\quad +\int_{S}\omega_{li}^{**}\mu_{i}\,dS + \int_{S}p_{li}^{**}\mathrm{L}_{i}\,dS \end{aligned} \tag{62}$$

Thus, we can write

$$C^{n}\mathbb{q}^{n} = -\int_{S}\mathbb{p}^{*}\mathbb{q}dS + \int_{S}\mathbb{q}^{*}\mathbb{p}^{dS+}\int_{S}\mathbb{a}^{*}p\,dS + \int_{S}\mathbb{b}^{*}\frac{\partial p}{\partial n}dS \tag{63}$$

where

$$C^{n} = \begin{bmatrix} C_{11} & C_{12} \\ C_{21} & C_{22} \end{bmatrix}, \mathbb{q}^{*} = \begin{bmatrix} u_{11}^{*} & u_{12}^{*} & \omega_{13}^{*} \\ u_{21}^{*} & u_{22}^{*} & \omega_{23}^{*} \\ u_{31}^{*} & u_{32}^{*} & \omega_{33}^{*} \end{bmatrix}, \mathbb{p}^{*} = \begin{bmatrix} \lambda_{11}^{*} & \lambda_{12}^{*} & \lambda_{13}^{*} \\ \lambda_{21}^{*} & \lambda_{22}^{*} & \mu_{23}^{*} \\ \lambda_{31}^{*} & \lambda_{32}^{*} & \mu_{33}^{*} \end{bmatrix} \tag{64}$$

$$\mathbb{q} = \begin{bmatrix} u_{1} \\ u_{2} \\ \omega_{3} \end{bmatrix}, \mathbb{p} = \begin{bmatrix} \lambda_{1} \\ \lambda_{2} \\ \mu_{3} \end{bmatrix}, \mathbb{a}^{*} = \begin{bmatrix} \mathbb{a}_{1}^{*} \\ \mathbb{a}_{2}^{*} \\ 0 \end{bmatrix}, \mathbb{b}^{*} = \begin{bmatrix} \mathbb{b}_{1}^{*} \\ \mathbb{b}_{2}^{*} \\ 0 \end{bmatrix}$$

In order to obtain the numerical solution of (63), we define the following functions

$$\mathbb{q} = \psi\,\mathbb{q}^{j}, \mathbb{p} = \psi\mathbb{p}^{j}, p = \psi_{0}p^{j}, \frac{\partial p}{\partial n} = \psi_{0}\left(\frac{\partial p}{\partial n}\right)^{j} \tag{65}$$

substituting above functions into (63) and discretizing the boundary, we obtain

$$\begin{aligned} C^{n}\mathrm{q}^{n} &= \sum_{j=1}^{N_e}\left[-\int_{\Gamma_j}\mathrm{p}^{*}\psi d\Gamma\right]\mathrm{q}^{j} + \sum_{j=1}^{N_e}\left[\int_{\Gamma_j}\mathrm{q}^{*}\psi d\Gamma\right]\mathrm{p}^{j} \\ &\quad +\sum_{j=1}^{N_e}\left[\int_{\Gamma_j}\mathrm{a}^{*}\psi_{0}d\Gamma\right]p^{j} + \sum_{j=1}^{N_e}\left[-\int_{\Gamma_j}\mathrm{b}^{*}\psi_{0}d\Gamma\right]\left(\frac{\partial p}{\partial n}\right)^{j} \end{aligned} \tag{66}$$

Equation after integration can be written as

$$C^{i}\mathrm{q}^{i} = -\sum_{j=1}^{N_e}\hat{\mathbb{H}}^{ij}\mathrm{q}^{j} + \sum_{j=1}^{N_e}\hat{\mathrm{G}}^{ij}\mathrm{p}^{j} + \sum_{j=1}^{N_e}\hat{\mathrm{a}}^{ij}p^{j} + \sum_{j=1}^{N_e}\hat{\mathrm{b}}^{ij}\left(\frac{\partial p}{\partial n}\right)^{j} \tag{67}$$

By using the following representation

$$\mathbb{H}^{ij} = \begin{cases} \hat{\mathbb{H}}^{ij} & \text{if } i \neq j \\ \hat{\mathbb{H}}^{ij} + C^{i} & \text{if } i = j \end{cases} \tag{68}$$

Thus, we can write (67) as follows

$$\sum_{j=1}^{N_e} \mathbb{H}^{ij}\mathrm{q}^j = \sum_{j=1}^{N_e} \hat{\mathrm{G}}^{ij}\mathrm{p}^j + \sum_{j=1}^{N_e} \hat{\mathrm{a}}^{ij}p^j + \sum_{j=1}^{N_e} \hat{\mathrm{b}}^{ij}\left(\frac{\partial p}{\partial n}\right)^j \tag{69}$$

The global matrix system equation for all $\boldsymbol{i}$ nodes can be written as follows

$$\mathbb{H}\mathbb{Q} = \mathbb{G}\mathbb{P} + \mathbf{a}\mathbb{i} + \mathbf{b}\mathbb{j} \tag{70}$$

the vector $\mathbb{Q}$ represents all the values of displacements and microrotations, the vector $\mathbb{P}$ represents all the tractions and couple stress vector, the vector $\mathbb{i}$ represents all the values of pore pressure, and the vector $\mathbb{j}$ represents all the values of pore pressure gradients before applying boundary conditions.

Substituting the boundary conditions into (70), we obtain the following system of equations

$$\mathbb{A}\mathbb{X} = \mathbb{B} \tag{71}$$

where $\mathbb{A}$ is an unknown matrix, while $\mathbb{X}$ and $\mathbb{B}$ are known matrices.

Now, an explicit staggered predictor-corrector procedure based on communication-avoiding Arnoldi (CA-Arnoldi) method has been implemented in (71) for obtaining the corrected displacement. Then we can get the temperature field from (35).

5. Numerical results and discussion

In order to show the numerical results of this study, we consider a monoclinic graphite-epoxy as an anisotropic micropolar poro-thermoelastic material which has the following physical constants.

The elasticity tensor is expressed as

$$C_{pjkl} = \begin{bmatrix} 430.1 & 130.4 & 18.2 & 0 & 0 & 201.3 \\ 130.4 & 116.7 & 21.0 & 0 & 0 & 70.1 \\ 18.2 & 21.0 & 73.6 & 0 & 0 & 2.4 \\ 0 & 0 & 0 & 19.8 & -8.0 & 0 \\ 0 & 0 & 0 & -8.0 & 29.1 & 0 \\ 201.3 & 70.1 & 2.4 & 0 & 0 & 147.3 \end{bmatrix} \text{GPa} \tag{72}$$

The mechanical temperature coefficient is

$$\beta_{pj} = \begin{bmatrix} 1.01 & 2.00 & 0 \\ 2.00 & 1.48 & 0 \\ 0 & 0 & 7.52 \end{bmatrix} \cdot 10^6 \frac{\text{N}}{\text{km}^2} \tag{73}$$

The thermal conductivity tensor is

$$k_{pj} = \begin{bmatrix} 5.2 & 0 & 0 \\ 0 & 7.6 & 0 \\ 0 & 0 & 38.3 \end{bmatrix} \text{W/Km} \tag{74}$$

Mass density $\rho = 7820\ \text{kg/m}^3$ and heat capacity $c = 461\text{J/kg K}$.

The proposed technique that has been utilized in the present chapter can be applicable to a wide variety of wave propagation of fractional nonlinear generalized micropolar poro-thermoelastic FGA structures problems related with the proposed theory.

The influence of three-temperature on the propagation of thermal stress waves plays a very important role during the simulation process. According to Fahmy [7], who compared and implemented communication-avoiding GMRES (CA-GMRES) of Saad and Schultz [57], communication-avoiding Arnoldi (CA-Arnoldi) of the Arnoldi [58] and communication-avoiding Lanczos (CA-Lanczos) of Lanczos [59] for solving the dense nonsymmetric algebraic system of linear equations arising from the BEM. So, the efficiency of the proposed technique has been developed using the communication-avoiding Arnoldi (CA-Arnoldi) solver to reduce the iterations number and CPU time, where the BEM discretization is employed 1280 quadrilateral elements, with 3964° of freedom (DOF).

Now, in order to assess the impact of three temperatures on the thermal stress waves, the numerical outcomes are completed and delineated graphically for electron, ion, and phonon temperatures.

Figures 2–4 show the propagation of the thermal stress σ_{11}, σ_{12}, and σ_{22} waves along x-axis for the three temperatures T_e, T_i, and T_p and total temperature T. It was noted from these figures that the three temperatures have significant effects on the thermal stress waves along x-axis through the thickness of the FGA structure.

Since there are no available results for our considered problem. So, some literatures may be considered as special cases from our considered complex problem. For comparison purposes with the special cases of other methods treated by other authors, we only considered one-dimensional numerical results of the considered problem. In the special case under consideration, the BEM results have been plotted in **Figures 5** and **6** with the results of finite difference method (FDM) and finite element method (FEM) in the two cases, namely, three-temperature (3T) theory and one-temperature (1T) theory.

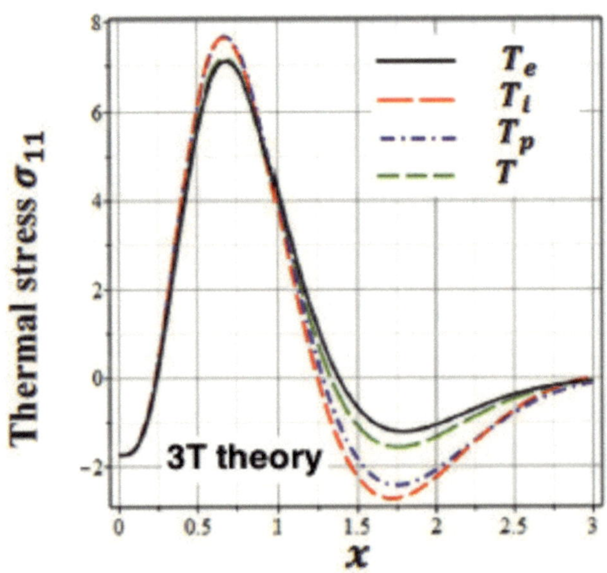

Figure 2.
Propagation of the thermal stress σ_{11} waves along x-axis for the three temperatures T_e, T_i, T_p and total temperature T.

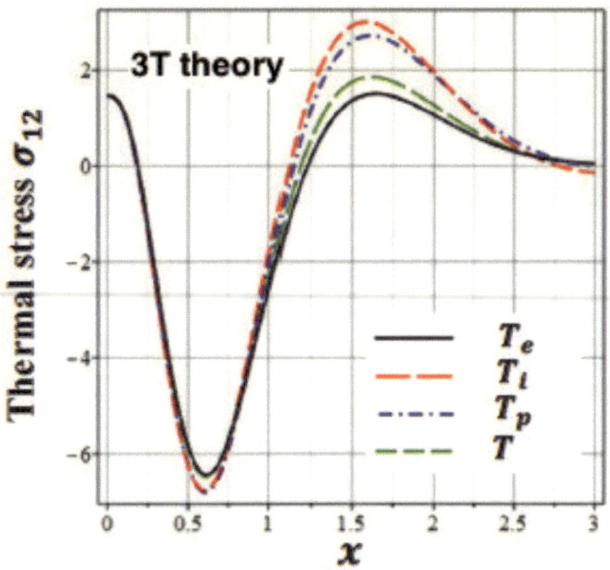

Figure 3.
Propagation of the thermal stress σ_{12} *waves along* x*-axis for the three temperatures* T_e, T_i , T_p *and total temperature* T.

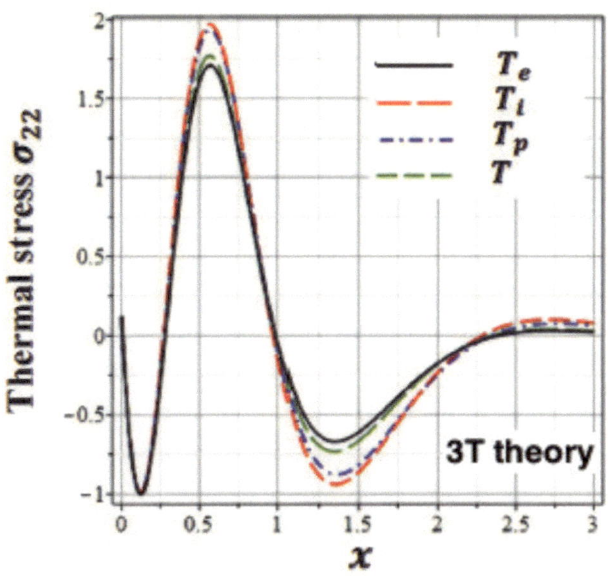

Figure 4.
Propagation of the thermal stress σ_{22} *waves along* x*-axis for the three temperatures* T_e, T_i , T_p *and total temperature* T.

Figure 5 shows a comparison of the propagation of the thermal stress σ_{11} waves for the BEM results of three-temperature (3T) radiative heat conduction theory for the BEM results with those obtained using the FDM of Pazera and Jędrysiak [60] and FEM of Xiong and Tian [61], where we replaced the 1T heat conduction theory of their work by 3T radiative heat conduction theory of our work to obtain the results. It can be noticed that the BEM results are found to agree very well with the FDM and FEM results.

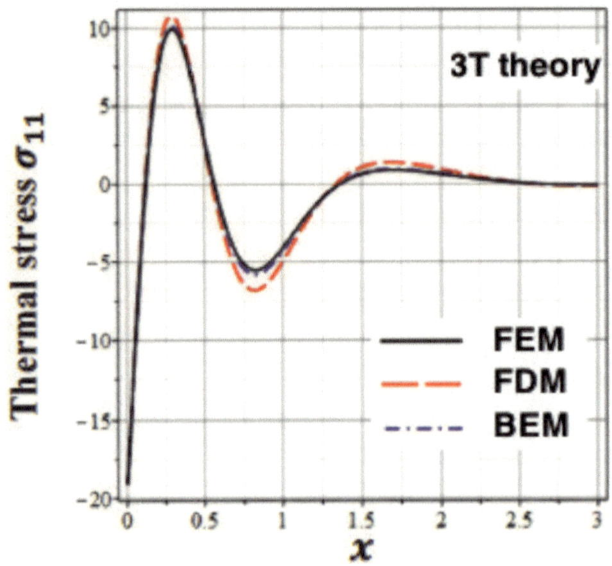

Figure 5.
Propagation of the thermal stress σ_{11} waves along x-axis for 3T theory and different methods.

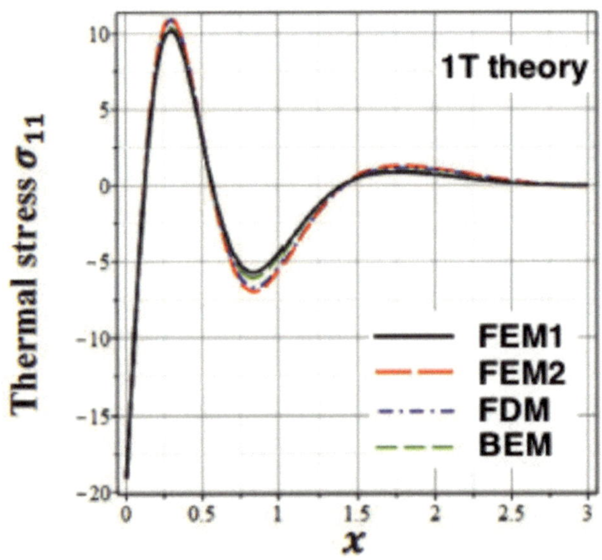

Figure 6.
Propagation of the thermal stress σ_{11} waves along x-axis for 1T theory and different methods.

Figure 6 shows a comparison of the propagation of the thermal stress σ_{11} waves for the BEM results of one-temperature (1T) heat conduction theory with those obtained using FDM of Pazera and Jędrysiak [60], FEM1 of Xiong and Tian [61], and FEM2 of COMSOL multiphysics software version 5.1, where we replaced 3T radiative heat conduction theory of our work by the 1T heat conduction theory of their work to obtain the results. It can be noticed that the BEM results are found to agree very well with the FDM, FEM1, and FEM2 results and thus demonstrate the validity and accuracy of our proposed theory and the technique used to solve its general problems.

6. Conclusion

The main purpose of this chapter is to introduce a novel theory called acoustic wave propagation of three-temperature fractional nonlinear generalized micropolar poro-thermoelasticity and we propose a new boundary element technique for modeling and simulation of ultrafast laser-induced thermal stress waves propagation problems in 3T nonlinear generalized micropolar poro-thermoelastic FGA structures which are linked with the proposed theory. By discretizing only, the boundary of the domain using BEM, where the unknowns on the domain boundary are expressed as functions depend only on the domain boundary values. Since it is very difficult to solve general acoustic problems of this theory analytically and we need to develop and use new computational modeling techniques. So, we propose a new boundary element technique for solving such problems. The numerical results are shown graphically to depict the effects of three temperatures on the thermal stress waves. Because there are no available results for comparison with the results of our proposed technique, we replace the three-temperature radiative heat conduction with one-temperature heat conduction as a special case from our present general study of three-temperature nonlinear generalized micropolar poro-thermoelasticity. In the special case under consideration, the BEM results have been compared graphically with the FDM and FEM in the two cases, namely three-temperature (3T) theory and one-temperature (1T) theory; it can be noticed that the BEM results are in a good agreement with the FDM and FEM results and thus demonstrate the validity and accuracy of our proposed theory and the technique used to solve its general problems. The numerical simulations are often faster and cheaper than experiments, and they are easily cross-platform, reproducible, relocatable, and customizable. So, the validation of the numerical simulation is of paramount importance. In this work, we implemented the explicit staggered predictor-corrector procedure based on communication-avoiding Arnoldi (CA-Arnoldi) solver due to its numerical stability, convergence, and performance as in Fahmy [10] to demonstrate the efficiency of the proposed technique. Thus, the numerical results of our proposed technique demonstrate the validity, accuracy, and efficiency of our proposed technique.

Nowadays, the knowledge of thermal stress wave propagation in three-temperature nonlinear generalized micropolar poro-thermoelastic problems associated with the ultrafast laser pulse proposed theory can be utilized by mechanical engineers in ceramic production applications and designing of boiler tubes and heat exchangers. As well as for chemists to observe the chemical reaction phenomena such as bond formation and bond breaking.

Author details

Mohamed Abdelsabour Fahmy
Faculty of Computers and Informatics, Suez Canal University, Ismailia, Egypt

*Address all correspondence to: mohamed_fahmy@ci.suez.edu.eg

References

[1] White R. Generation of elastic waves by transient surface heating. Journal of Applied Physics. 1963;**34**:3559-3567

[2] Scruby C, Dewhurst R, Hutchins D, Palmer S. Quantitative studies of thermally-generated elastic waves in laser irradiated metals. Journal of Applied Physics. 1980;**51**:6210-6216

[3] Rose LRF. Point-source representation for laser generated ultrasound. Journal of the Acoustical Society of America. 1984;**75**:723-732

[4] Doyle P. On epicentral waveforms for laser-generated ultrasound. Journal of Physics D: Applied Physics. 1986;**19**: 1613-1623

[5] McDonald F. Practical quantitative theory of photoacoustic pulse generation. Applied Physics Letters. 1989;**54**:1504-1506

[6] Spicer J. Laser Ultrasonics in finite structures: Comprehensive modeling with supportingexperiment [Ph.D. Thesis]. The Johns Hopkins University; 1991

[7] Fahmy MA. A new boundary element strategy for modeling and simulation of three temperatures nonlinear generalized micropolar-magneto-thermoelastic wave propagation problems in FGA structures. Engineering Analysis with Boundary Elements. 2019;**108**:192-200

[8] Fahmy MA. A new computerized boundary element model for three-temperature nonlinear generalized thermoelastic stresses in anisotropic circular cylindrical plate structures. In: Awrejcewicz J, Grzelczyk D, editors. Dynamical Systems Theory. London, UK: IntechOpen; 2019. pp. 1-17

[9] Fahmy MA. Boundary element model for nonlinear fractional-order heat transfer in magneto-thermoelastic FGA structures involving three temperatures. In: Ebrahimi F, editor. Mechanics of Functionally Graded Materials and Structures. London, UK: IntechOpen; 2019. pp. 1-22

[10] Fahmy MA. Boundary element mathematical modelling and boundary element numerical techniques for optimization of micropolar thermoviscoelastic problems in solid deformable bodies. In: Sivasankaran S, Nayak PK, Günay E, editors. Mechanics of Solid Deformable Bodies. London, UK: IntechOpen; 2020. pp. 1-21

[11] Fahmy MA. Boundary element modeling and optimization based on fractional-order derivative for nonlinear generalized photo-thermoelastic stress wave propagation in three-temperature anisotropic semiconductor structures. In: Sadollah A, Sinha TS, editors. Recent Trends in Computational Intelligence. London, UK: IntechOpen; 2020. pp. 1-16

[12] Fahmy MA. Boundary element algorithm for nonlinear modeling and simulation of three temperature anisotropic generalized micropolar piezothermoelasticity with memory-dependent derivative. International Journal of Applied Mechanics. 2020;**12**: 2050027

[13] Sharma N, Mahapatra TR, Panda SK. Thermoacoustic behavior of laminated composite curved panels using higher-order finite-boundary element model. International Journal of Applied Mechanics. 2018;**10**:1850017

[14] Abd-Alla AM, El-Naggar AM, Fahmy MA. Magneto-thermoelastic problem in non-homogeneous isotropic cylinder. Heat and Mass Transfer. 2003; **39**:625-629

[15] Fahmy MA. A time-stepping DRBEM for the transient

magneto-thermo-visco-elastic stresses in a rotating non-homogeneous anisotropic solid. Engineering Analysis with Boundary Elements. 2012;**36**:335-345

[16] Fahmy MA. Numerical modeling of transient magneto-thermo-viscoelastic waves in a rotating nonhomogeneous anisotropic solid under initial stress. International Journal of Modeling, Simulation, and Scientific Computing. 2012;**3**:1250002

[17] Fahmy MA. Transient magneto-thermo-viscoelastic stresses in a rotating nonhomogeneous anisotropic solid with and without a moving heat source. Journal of Engineering Physics and Thermophysics. 2012;**85**:950-958

[18] Fahmy MA. Transient magneto-thermo-elastic stresses in an anisotropic viscoelastic solid with and without moving heat source. Numerical Heat Transfer, Part A: Applications. 2012;**61**: 547-564

[19] Fahmy MA. Transient magneto-thermoviscoelastic plane waves in a non-homogeneous anisotropic thick strip subjected to a moving heat source. Applied Mathematical Modelling. 2012; **36**:4565-4578

[20] Fahmy MA. The effect of rotation and inhomogeneity on the transient magneto-thermoviscoelastic stresses in an anisotropic solid. Journal of Applied Mechanics. 2012;**79**:1015

[21] Fahmy MA. A time-stepping DRBEM for magneto-thermo-viscoelastic interactions in a rotating nonhomogeneous anisotropic solid. International Journal of Applied Mechanics. 2011;**3**:1-24

[22] Fahmy MA. A Computerized Boundary Element Models for Coupled, Uncoupled and Generalized Thermoelasticity Theories of Functionally Graded Anisotropic Rotating Plates. UK: Book Publisher International; 2019

[23] Soliman AH, Fahmy MA. Range of applying the boundary condition at fluid/porous interface and evaluation of Beavers and Joseph's slip coefficient using finite element method. Computation. 2020;**8**:14

[24] Eskandari AH, Baghani M, Sohrabpour S. A time-dependent finite element formulation for thick shape memory polymer beams considering shear effects. International Journal of Applied Mechanics. 2019;**10**:1850043

[25] El-Naggar AM, Abd-Alla AM, Fahmy MA. The propagation of thermal stresses in an infinite elastic slab. Applied Mathematics and Computation. 2003;**12**:220-226

[26] El-Naggar AM, Abd-Alla AM, Fahmy MA, Ahmed SM. Thermal stresses in a rotating non-homogeneous orthotropic hollow cylinder. Heat and Mass Transfer. 2002;**39**:41-46

[27] Brebbia CA, Telles JCF, Wrobel L. Boundary Element Techniques in Engineering. New York: Springer-Verlag; 1984

[28] Wrobel LC, Brebbia CA. The dual reciprocity boundary element formulation for nonlinear diffusion problems. Computer Methods in Applied Mechanics and Engineering. 1987;**65**:147-164

[29] Partridge PW, Brebbia CA. Computer implementation of the BEM dual reciprocity method for the solution of general field equations. Communications in Applied Numerical Methods. 1990;**6**:83-92

[30] Fahmy MA. Implicit-explicit time integration DRBEM for generalized magneto-thermoelasticity problems of rotating anisotropic viscoelastic functionally graded solids. Engineering

Analysis with Boundary Elements. 2013; **37**:107-115

[31] Fahmy MA. Generalized magneto-thermo-viscoelastic problems of rotating functionally graded anisotropic plates by the dual reciprocity boundary element method. Journal of Thermal Stresses. 2013;**36**:1-20

[32] Fahmy MA. A three-dimensional generalized magneto-thermo-viscoelastic problem of a rotating functionally graded anisotropic solids with and without energy dissipation. Numerical Heat Transfer, Part A: Applications. 2013;**63**:713-733

[33] Fahmy MA. A 2-D DRBEM for generalized magneto-thermo-viscoelastic transient response of rotating functionally graded anisotropic thick strip. International Journal of Engineering and Technology Innovation. 2013;**3**:70-85

[34] Fahmy MA. A computerized DRBEM model for generalized magneto-thermo-visco-elastic stress waves in functionally graded anisotropic thin film/substrate structures. Latin American Journal of Solids and Structures. 2014;**11**:386-409

[35] Fahmy MA. A 2D time domain DRBEM computer model for magneto-thermoelastic coupled wave propagation problems. International Journal of Engineering and Technology Innovation. 2014;**4**:138-151

[36] Fahmy MA. The DRBEM solution of the generalized magneto-thermo-viscoelastic problems in 3D anisotropic functionally graded solids. In: Proceedings of the 5th International Conference on Coupled Problems in Science and Engineering (Coupled Problems 2013); 17-19 June 2013. Ibiza, Spain; 2013. pp. 862-872

[37] Fahmy MA. Boundary element solution of 2D coupled problem in anisotropic piezoelectric FGM plates. In: Proceedings of the 6th International Conference on Computational Methods for Coupled Problems in Science and Engineering (Coupled Problems 2015); 18–20 May 2015. Venice, Italy; 2015. pp. 382-391

[38] Fahmy MA. 3D DRBEM modeling for rotating initially stressed anisotropic functionally graded piezoelectric plates. In: Proceedings of the 7th European Congress on Computational Methods in Applied Sciences and Engineering (ECCOMAS 2016); 5–10 June 2016. Crete Island, Greece; 2016. pp. 7640-7658

[39] Fahmy MA. A time-stepping DRBEM for 3D anisotropic functionally graded piezoelectric structures under the influence of gravitational waves. In: Proceedings of the 1st GeoMEast International Congress and Exhibition (GeoMEast 2017); 15–19 July 2017; Sharm El Sheikh, Egypt. Facing the Challenges in Structural Engineering, Sustainable Civil Infrastructures. 2017. pp. 350-365

[40] Fahmy MA. A computerized boundary element model for simulation and optimization of fractional-order three temperatures nonlinear generalized piezothermoelastic problems based on genetic algorithm. In: AIP Conference Proceedings 2138 of Innovation and Analytics Conference and Exihibiton (IACE 2019), 25-28 March 2019. Sintok, Malaysia; 2019. p. 030015

[41] Fahmy MA. Shape design sensitivity and optimization for two-temperature generalized magneto-thermoelastic problems using time-domain DRBEM. Journal of Thermal Stresses. 2018;**41**: 119-138

[42] Fahmy MA. Boundary element algorithm for modeling and simulation of dual-phase lag bioheat transfer and biomechanics of anisotropic soft tissues.

International Journal of Applied Mechanics. 2018;**10**:1850108

[43] Fahmy MA. Shape design sensitivity and optimization of anisotropic functionally graded smart structures using bicubic B-splines DRBEM. Engineering Analysis with Boundary Elements. 2018;**87**:27-35

[44] Fahmy MA. Modeling and optimization of anisotropic viscoelastic porous structures using cqbem and moving asymptotes algorithm. Arabian Journal for Science and Engineering. 2019;**44**:1671-1684

[45] Fahmy MA. Boundary element modeling and simulation of biothermomechanical behavior in anisotropic laser-induced tissue hyperthermia. Engineering Analysis with Boundary Elements. 2019;**101**: 156-164

[46] Fahmy MA. A new LRBFCM-GBEM modeling algorithm for general solution of time fractional order dual phase lag bioheat transfer problems in functionally graded tissues. Numerical Heat Transfer, Part A: Applications. 2019;**75**:616-626

[47] Fahmy MA. Design optimization for a simulation of rotating anisotropic viscoelastic porous structures using time-domain OQBEM. Mathematics and Computers in Simulation. 2019;**66**: 193-205

[48] Fahmy MA. A new convolution variational boundary element technique for design sensitivity analysis and topology optimization of anisotropic thermo-poroelastic structures. Arab Journal of Basic and Applied Sciences. 2020;**27**:1-12

[49] Fahmy MA. Thermoelastic stresses in a rotating non- homogeneous anisotropic body. Numerical Heat Transfer, Part A: Applications. 2008;**53**: 1001-1011

[50] Abd-Alla AM, Fahmy MA, El-Shahat TM. Magneto-thermo-elastic problem of a rotating non-homogeneous anisotropic solid cylinder. Archive of Applied Mechanics. 2008;**78**:135-148

[51] Fahmy MA, El-Shahat TM. The effect of initial stress and inhomogeneity on the thermoelastic stresses in a rotating anisotropic solid. Archive of Applied Mechanics. 2008;**78**: 431-442

[52] Cattaneo C. Sur une forme de i'equation de la chaleur elinant le paradox d'une propagation instantanc. Comptes Rendus de l'Académie des Sciences. 1958;**247**:431-433

[53] Hoemmen M. Communication-Avoiding Krylov Subspace Methods. Berkeley: University of California; 2010

[54] Huang FY, Liang KZ. Boundary element method for micropolar thermoelasticity. Engineering Analysis with Boundary Elements. 1996;**17**:19-26

[55] Eringen AC. Theory of micropolar elasticity. In: Liebowitz H, editor. Fracture. Vol. II. New York: Academic Press; 1968

[56] Dragos L. Fundamental solutions in micropolar elasticity. International Journal of Engineering Science. 1984;**22**: 265-275

[57] Saad Y, Schultz MH. GMRES: A generalized minimal residual algorithm for solving nonsymmetric linear systems. SIAM Journal on Scientific and Statistical Computing. 1986;**7**:856-869

[58] Arnoldi WE. The principle of minimized iterations in the solution of the matrix eigenvalue problem. Quarterly of Applied Mathematics. 1951; **9**:17-29

[59] Lanczos C. An iteration method for the solution of the eigenvalue problem of linear differential and integral

operators. Journal of Research of the National Bureau of Standards. 1950;**45**: 255-282

[60] Pazera E, Ędrysiak J. Effect of microstructure in thermoelasticity problems of functionally graded laminates. Composite Structures. 2018; **202**:296-303

[61] Xiong QL, Tian XG. Generalized magneto-thermo-microstretch response during thermal shock. Latin American Journal of Solids and Structures. 2015; **12**:2562-2580

Chapter 8

Interactions between Terrestrial Cosmic-Ray Neutrons and III–V Compound Semiconductors

Daniela Munteanu and Jean-Luc Autran

Abstract

This work explores by numerical simulation the impact of high-energy atmospheric neutrons and their interactions with III–V binary compound semiconductors. The efforts have focused on eight III–V semiconductors: GaAs, AlAs, InP, InAs, GaSb, InSb, GaN, and GaP. For each material, extensive Geant4 numerical simulations have been performed considering a bulk target exposed to a neutron source emulating the atmospheric neutron spectrum at terrestrial level. Results emphasize in detail the reaction rates per type of reaction (elastic, inelastic, nonelastic) and offer a classification of all the neutron-induced secondary products as a function of their atomic number, kinetic energy, initial stopping power, and range. Implications for single-event effects (SEEs) are analyzed and discussed, notably in terms of energy and charge deposited in the bulk material and in the first nanometers of particle range with respect to the critical charge for modern complementary metal oxide semiconductor (CMOS) technologies.

Keywords: radiation effects, III–V compound semiconductors, cosmic-rays, atmospheric neutrons, numerical simulation, neutron cross section, elastic scattering, inelastic scattering, nonelastic interactions, nuclear data library, Geant4

1. Introduction

The introduction of III–V high-mobility semiconductor materials into advanced CMOS manufacturing is currently envisaged as a possible "technological booster" for carrier mobility enhancement. Indeed, for nanometer-scale transistor, it will not be possible to maintain the power-performance tradeoff offered by conventional silicon-based technologies because of the transport properties of Si that are becoming a fundamental limitation for ultimate complementary metal oxide semiconductor (CMOS) [1, 2]. Several materials exhibiting higher carrier mobilities than Si are currently explored for both n-channel and p-channel transistors. Between all these materials, GaAs, InAs, InGaAs, and InP are suitable candidates for n-channel devices and GaSb and InGaSb for p-channel transistors [3–5].

In complement to their physical and electrical characterization, the exploration of the radiation response of these III–V materials is also an important concern for predicting their reliability. Several studies investigating total ionizing dose (TID) and heavy ion and laser responses of III–V MOS transistors in modern architectures, as well as the creation mechanisms of single-event effects, have been reported in literature, but relatively little work concerns their response to terrestrial neutrons [6–13]. In two recent papers [14, 15], we begun such a systematic investigation of the susceptibility to natural radiation of group IV and III–V materials exposed.

The aim of this chapter is to provide new data and metrics for this exploration via Geant4 [16, 17] numerical simulations of the radiation response of III–V binary compound semiconductors subjected to high-energy atmospheric neutrons. The study specifically focuses on eight III–V materials: GaAs, AlAs, InP, InAs, GaSb, InSb, GaN and GaP. For each material, the reaction rates for elastic, inelastic, and nonelastic events have been determined as well as the classification of all produced secondaries as a function of their atomic number, kinetic energy, initial stopping power, and range in the target bulk. Average energy and charge deposited in the bulk material and in the first nanometers of particle ranges have been also evaluated. These later quantities are important statistical metrics in the occurrence of single-event effects (SEEs [18]); they have been compared with the critical charge for various CMOS technologies (180 nm to 14 nm nodes).

The chapter is organized as follows. Section 2 presents the different compound materials studied and summarizes their main physical and electronic properties. Section 3 details the Geant4 numerical simulations conducted in the framework of this study. Section 4 presents the complete analysis of interaction databases in which all neutron-induced secondaries have been recorded for each material subjected to atmospheric neutrons. Finally, in Section 5, implications for single-event effects in CMOS based on these semiconductor materials are analyzed.

2. Semiconductor properties

III–V binary compound materials explored in this work are semiconductor alloys containing one element from group III (boron column: Al, Ga, In) and one from group V (nitrogen column: N, As, Sb) of the periodic table. **Table 1** shows the natural isotopic abundance for these six chemical elements. For example, natural gallium (^{31}Ga) consists of a mixture of two stable isotopes: 31-Ga-31 at 60.10% and 31-Ga-71 at 39.90%. Numerical simulations presented in the

Symbol	Atomic number	Nuclide	Natural abundance
Al	13	13-Al-27	100.00%
Ga	31	31-Ga-69	60.10%
		31-Ga-71	39.90%
In	49	49-In-115	95.70%
		49-In-113	4.30%
N	7	7-N-14	99.60%
		7-N-15	0.40%
P	15	15-P-31	100.00%
As	33	33-As-75	100.00%
Sb	51	51-Sb-121	57.40%
		51-Sb-123	42.60%

Table 1.
Natural abundance of nuclides related to the III–V alloys studied in this work.

III–V compound	E_g at 300K E_g (eV)	Number of atoms per cm^3 ($\times 10^{22}$)	Density (g/cm^3)	E-h pair creation energy E_{eh} (eV)
GaAs	1.42	4.42	5.32	4.8
AlAs	2.16	4.42	3.76	6.8
InP	1.34	3.96	4.81	4.5
InAs	0.36	3.59	5.67	1.8
GaSb	0.73	3.53	5.61	2.7
InSb	0.17	2.94	5.78	1.1
GaN	3.39	8.90	6.15	8.9
GaP	2.26	4.94	4.138	6.8

Partially from [19].

Table 2.
The main properties of the III–V binary semiconductors considered in this study.

following take into account such isotopic compositions for each element present in the eight studied materials.

Table 2 summarizes the main experimental values for GaAs, AlAs, InP, InAs, GaSb, InSb, GaN, and GaP bulk materials in terms of energy bandgap E_g, number of atoms per volume unit, density [19], and electron-hole pair creation energy E_{eh}. All these crystalline solids are denser than Si (2.32 g/cm^3). The following materials, GaAs, AlAs, InP, GaN, and GaP, are characterized by a bandgap larger than that of Si and, consequently, by a larger electron-hole pair creation energy (3.6 eV for Si). The other materials, i.e., InAs, GaSb, and InSb, have a bandgap clearly below 1 eV; E_{eh} values for these materials are also lower than that of Si. Finally, for GaSb and InSb, we did not find in literature an experimental value for E_{eh}; we used by default the values deduced from Klein's model [20] establishing a linear relationship between E_g and E_{eh} in semiconductor materials.

3. Geant4 numerical simulations

Geant4 simulations were carried out following a methodology used in previous works [14, 21, 22]. We considered a target of bulk material (composed of a pure material chosen between the eight binary compounds studied) with a parallelepiped geometry (surface 1 cm^2, thickness 20 μm). Each target was virtually irradiated with neutrons arriving perpendicularly to the surface and for which the energy distribution follows the terrestrial natural neutron background at sea level. This latter was chosen equal to the high-energy (above 1 MeV) neutron spectrum measured by Goldhagen et al. at sea level (New York City) [23, 24]. A total of 10^8 of incident neutrons were considered, representing the equivalent duration of 5×10^6 h of natural neutron irradiation at sea level.

Geant4 version 4.9.4 patch 01 was used for these simulations. The list of physical processes employed in these simulations is based on the standard package of physics lists QGSP_BIC_HP [25]. Other simulation details can be found in Ref. [21]. Outputs of each simulation consist in a series of files containing all the information related to the neutron interaction events in the target material. For each event, this information includes the nature and the coordinates of the vertex of the interaction, the energy of the incident neutron, the exhaustive list of secondary particles produced during the interaction, and the energy and the emission direction vector for each of these emitted particles. All these records have been post-treated and formatted into the final interaction databases (text files) following two compilation rules: (i) we eliminated in the output file (raw data) all secondaries below 1 keV of energy; (ii) we also eliminated all γ photons, π^0, e^+, e^-, and η particles, these particles being not able to deposit 1 keV of energy in the targets, which is a mandatory condition to observe single-event effects in electronics. The computational time was approximately of 3 weeks for eight parallel runs on multicore 3 GHz CPUs, the code being executed on separate cores for each material.

4. Simulation results

Table 3 gives the distributions of elastic, inelastic, and nonelastic events recorded in the different III–V compound material databases. Values for the database related to silicon are also reported for comparison. For memory, the interactions of neutrons with atomic nuclei can occur through two major mechanisms: scattering (which can be subdivided in elastic and inelastic processes) and capture (also called nonelastic) [26]. When a neutron is involved in an elastic scattering, the nature of the interacting particles is not modified; in particular the recoil nucleus is then the same as the target nucleus A or B in the case of a binary compound material AB. Similarly, during an inelastic scattering, the impacted target nucleus A or B undergoes an internal rearrangement into an excited state which eventually releases radiation. Instead of being scattered, an incident neutron may be absorbed or captured by a target material nucleus A or B. Many reactions are possible, and a large variety of particles can be emitted. This type of interaction is also called nonelastic interaction.

As evidenced by results of **Table 3**, the eight III–V materials show an interaction rate superior to the value observed for the reference case with Si even if GaSb, AlAs, and InSb show a number of interaction events, the closest from the one of Si. A single material stands out clearly from the others in terms of very high number of interactions: GaN. This result is the direct consequence of GaN crystallographic structure that leads to a number of atoms per volume unit almost double with respect to all other materials (see **Table 1**).

	Number of events (1 cm^2 × 20 μm, 5 × 10^6 h at sea level)			
Target	**Elastic**	**Inelastic**	**Nonelastic**	**Total**
Si (reference)	11,369	2048	3373	16,790
InSb	7868	6624	2574	17,066
AlAs	9246	4490	3508	17,244
GaSb	8210	6146	3298	17,654
InP	9636	5392	3218	18,246
InAs	8432	6642	3290	18,364
GaAs	8426	6374	4356	19,156
GaP	10,556	4524	4150	19,230
GaN	15,587	6349	6537	28,473

Table 3.
Number of elastic, inelastic, and nonelastic interactions induced by atmospheric neutrons in the different III–V binary compound materials obtained from Geant4 simulations.

Concerning elastic events, their proportion is clearly predominant for Si (68%), GaP, GaN (55%), AlAs (54%), and InP (53%). The sum of inelastic and nonelastic events is above 50% for GaAs (56%), InAs and InSb (54%), and GaSb (53%). For Si, this sum is only around 32%, which is lower than 40% found in previous studies [21]. The reason is that, in the present case, the minimum kinetic energy (energy cutoff) to take into account recoils and secondaries in the databases has been fixed to 1 keV, whereas this value was fixed to a higher value, i.e., 40 keV, in previous studies. According to [15], the number and, consequently, the proportion of elastic events with respect to inelastic and nonelastic events clearly depend on such energy cutoff; it is the reason why these percentages may vary.

Figure 1 shows the number n of secondary product(s) per interaction for the different materials. It is important to note that n has been evaluated after excluding γ photons, π, e^+, e^-, and η particles from the raw simulation data, as mentioned in Section 3. As a consequence, the first class of the distribution, i.e., n = 1, corresponds to single product reactions that only result in a single recoil after interaction. These reactions correspond to all elastic and inelastic events, totalized in **Table 1**. For n>2, all secondaries are produced during nonelastic interactions, with an average number of secondary products per reaction between 2.5 and 2.7 for the different III–V materials (2.6 for silicon). Note that GaN and, in a lesser extent, GaAs and GaP show the most important number of reactions for n ranging from 2 to 5. To understand these results, a more detailed analysis in terms of secondary products must be conducted.

Precisely, **Figure 2** shows the distribution of secondaries produced in the different targets of III–V binary compound materials subjected to atmospheric neutrons. Four groups of particles have been defined as a function of the atomic number Z: (i) protons, deuterons, and tritons (Z = 1), (ii) alpha particles and He-3 (Z = 2), (iii) nuclei corresponding to target atoms (named recoils #1 and #2 for binary compounds), and (iv) other nuclei (with Z different from the other three categories).

Figure 2 shows that similar distributions of these particle groups are found for all materials, GaN excepted, with approximately 20–25% of protons+alphas, 60% of recoil products constituted of target nuclei, and the remaining 15% of other nuclei. In the case of GaN, the proportion of protons and alpha particles is more important and corresponds to approximately two times the proportion observed in silicon; this result can be explained by the additional production channels of protons and alpha particles offered by the $^{14}N(n,p)^{14}C$ and $^{14}N(n,\alpha)^{11}B$ reactions [27]. Always for GaN, the combination of a high number of atoms per volume unit

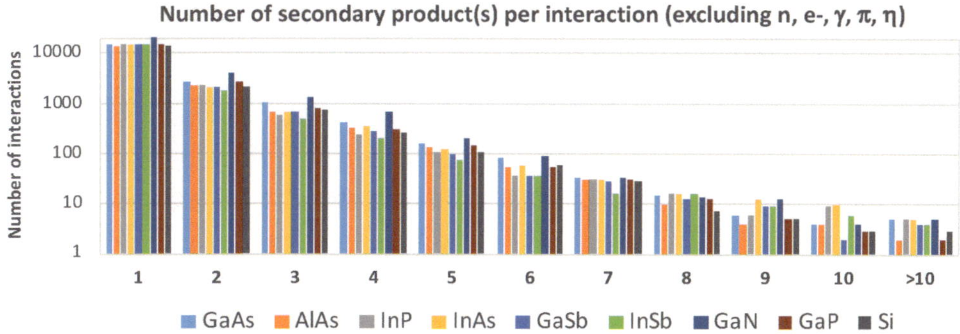

Figure 1.
Number of secondary products per interaction (after excluding γ photons, π, e^+, e^-, and η particles as explained in the text).

and the presence of nitrogen are at the origin of such a large difference with respect to other III–V materials in terms of a higher number of interactions, of secondaries produced, and of alphas and protons. In addition to **Figure 2**, **Figure 3** shows the exhaustive distribution of all secondaries produced in all materials as a function of Z. The stacked declination of the histograms is only to produce a clearer comparison

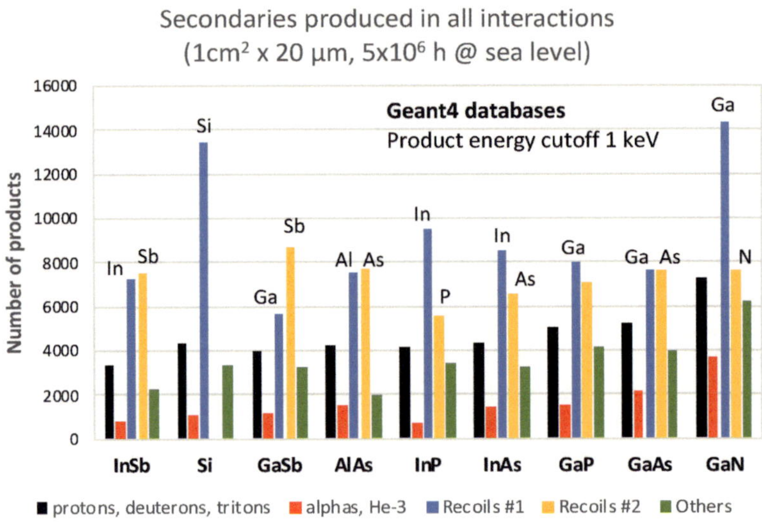

Figure 2.
Number of secondaries in the events recorded in the eight III–V material databases for the four product classes defined in the text. The nature of recoils is indicated for each material. Results for silicon are also shown for reference.

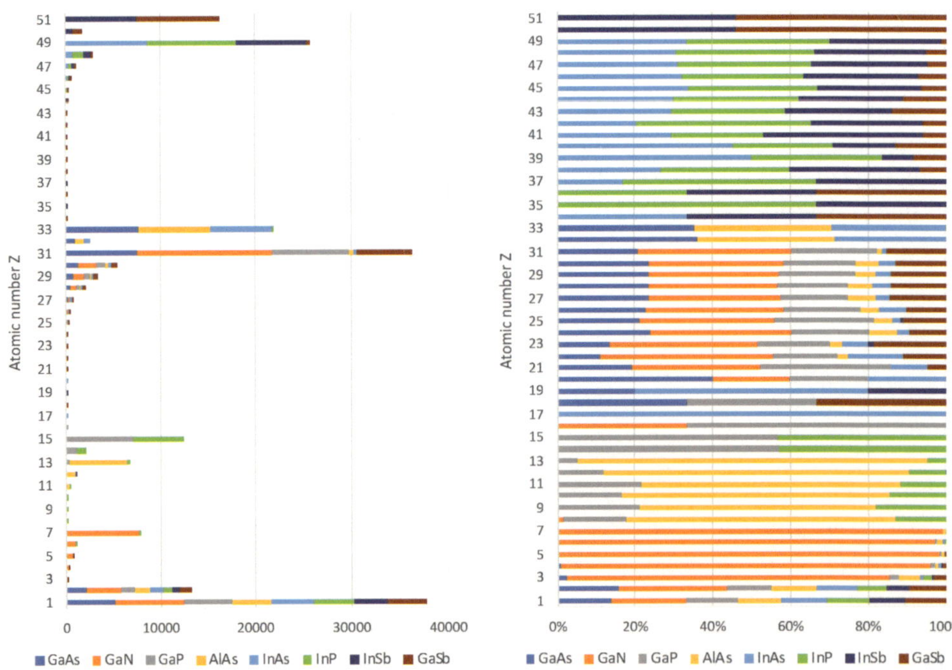

Figure 3.
Distribution in number (left) and in percent (right) of all secondaries produced in all materials as a function of their atomic number.

figure; there is of course no physical sense to add secondaries of the same Z induced by neutrons in different targets other than specifying their distribution in Z.

Figure 4 shows the energy mappings for all secondaries produced by atmospheric neutrons in the eight different targets. In these figures, each colored point corresponds to a single secondary product; the x-coordinate of the point corresponds to the energy of the incident neutron which gave birth to it; the y-coordinate corresponds to the kinetic energy of the secondary after its release at the level of the reaction vertex. The same four groups of particles as previously defined (**Figure 2**) have been considered. Such product energy mappings allow us to visually compare the contain of the different databases and to highlight similarities and differences between the atmospheric neutron susceptibilities of the eight studied materials, notably in terms of protons, alphas (GaN and GaAs as compared to InSb and InP), and recoil distributions (differences between light and heavy recoils: N, Al, and P as compared to Ga, As, In, and Sb). In **Figure 4**, we can see that all points are logically below the straight-line y = x because the maximum energy of secondary products is, at most, equal to that of the incident primary neutron.

From the data in **Figure 4**, we deduced the energy histograms in **Figure 5** for all the secondary products in the eight materials. To limit the number of curves, these histograms have been calculated for the four classes of secondaries previously defined, i.e., for protons, alpha particles, target nucleus recoils, and other ions. These energy histograms show the same information as in **Figure 4** but in a more compact and quantitative form. These curves indicate the energy domain covered for each type of particle and also the energy position of the maximum of the distributions. For recoil products, the heavier the recoil nucleus, the lower the energy of the maximum of the distribution. For protons, alphas, and other nuclei, similar distributions and energy domains are obtained (from 10^{-1} to 10^3 MeV for protons, from 1 to 10^2 MeV for alphas, from 10^{-2} to a few tens of MeV for other nuclei) for the different targets, excepted for GaN, InAs, and InSb. For GaN, an excess of low-energy protons and alphas is clearly evidenced in the range of 0.1–1 MeV; for InAs and InSb, proton distributions are narrower and only cover an energy range between 1 and 10^3 MeV.

From the above data, we deduced the linear energy transfer (LET) and range distributions of all secondary products for the different target materials. For memory, the linear energy transfer or LET of a charged particle refers to the stopping power, i.e., the energy lost by unit of length, due only to electronic collisions and expressed in MeV/(mg/cm^2) or in keV/μm. The range corresponds to the distance that a charged particle travels from its emission point through matter until it comes to rest. Both LET and range primarily depend on the type and initial energy of the particle and of the medium (i.e., the target material) in which the particle travels.

We used the popular and reference code Stopping and Range of Ions in Matter SRIM [28, 29] to perform (in batch mode controlled from a short C-code) the automatic calculation of the LET and range tables (in the range 1 keV to 10 GeV) for all possible nuclides from Z = 1 to Z = 92, which represents 2670 SRIM tables per material. A total of 2670 × 8 = 21,360 files were computed and indexed in different folders in order to be directly read from a Python code to automatically compute LET and range histograms. **Figure 6** shows the plots of SRIM tables for LET and range related to protons, alphas, and recoil products in the eight III–V materials.

The cross-combination of these SRIM data with particle types and energies listed in the different interaction databases was performed using a dedicated python script to compute (by linear interpolation of the SRIM tables) the initial LET (at product release) and the range histograms of all products, shown in **Figures 7** and **8**, respectively.

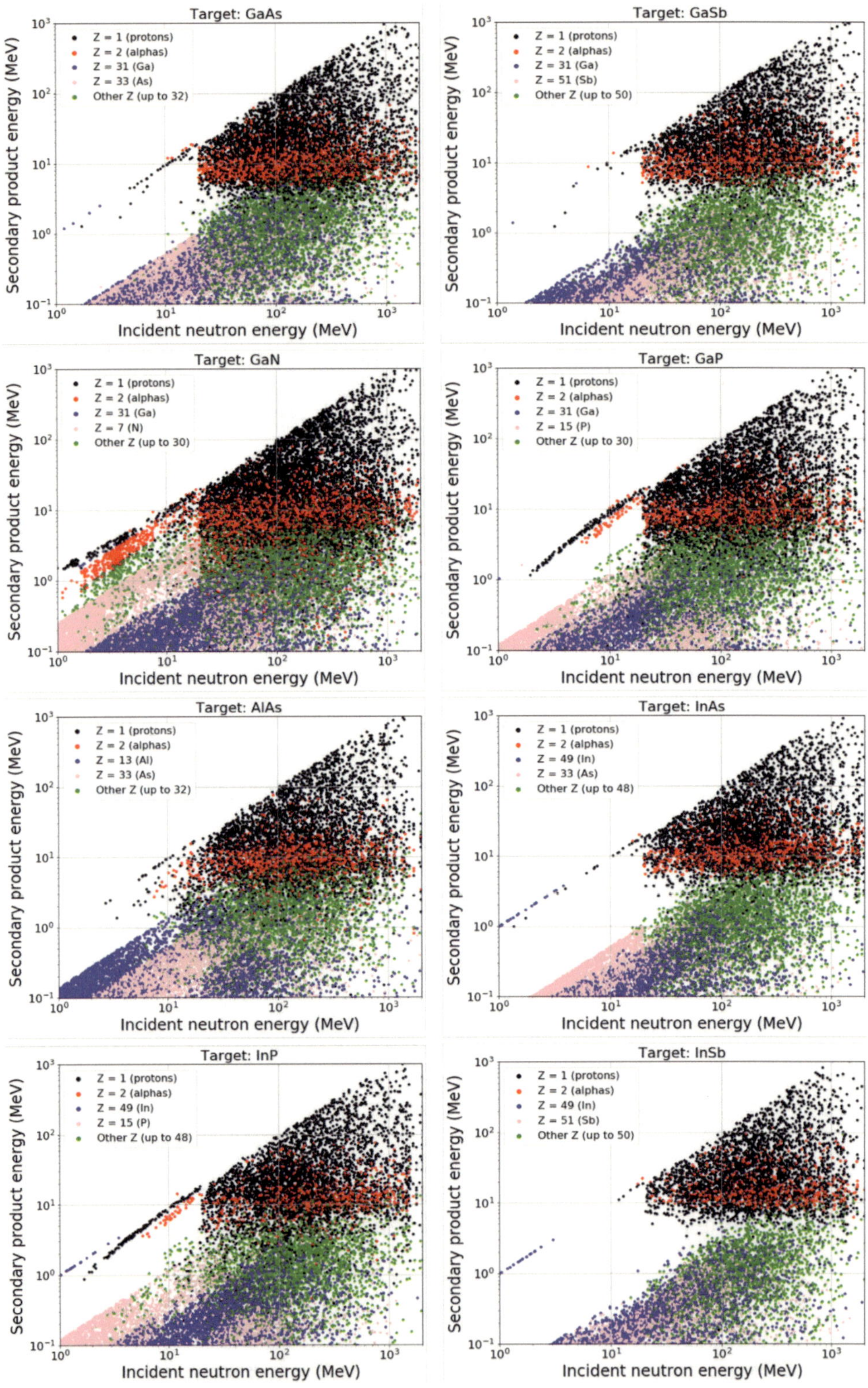

Figure 4.
Energy distributions as a function of the incident neutron energy for all secondaries produced in the events recorded in the eight III–V material databases.

DOI: http://dx.doi.org/10.5772/intechopen.92774

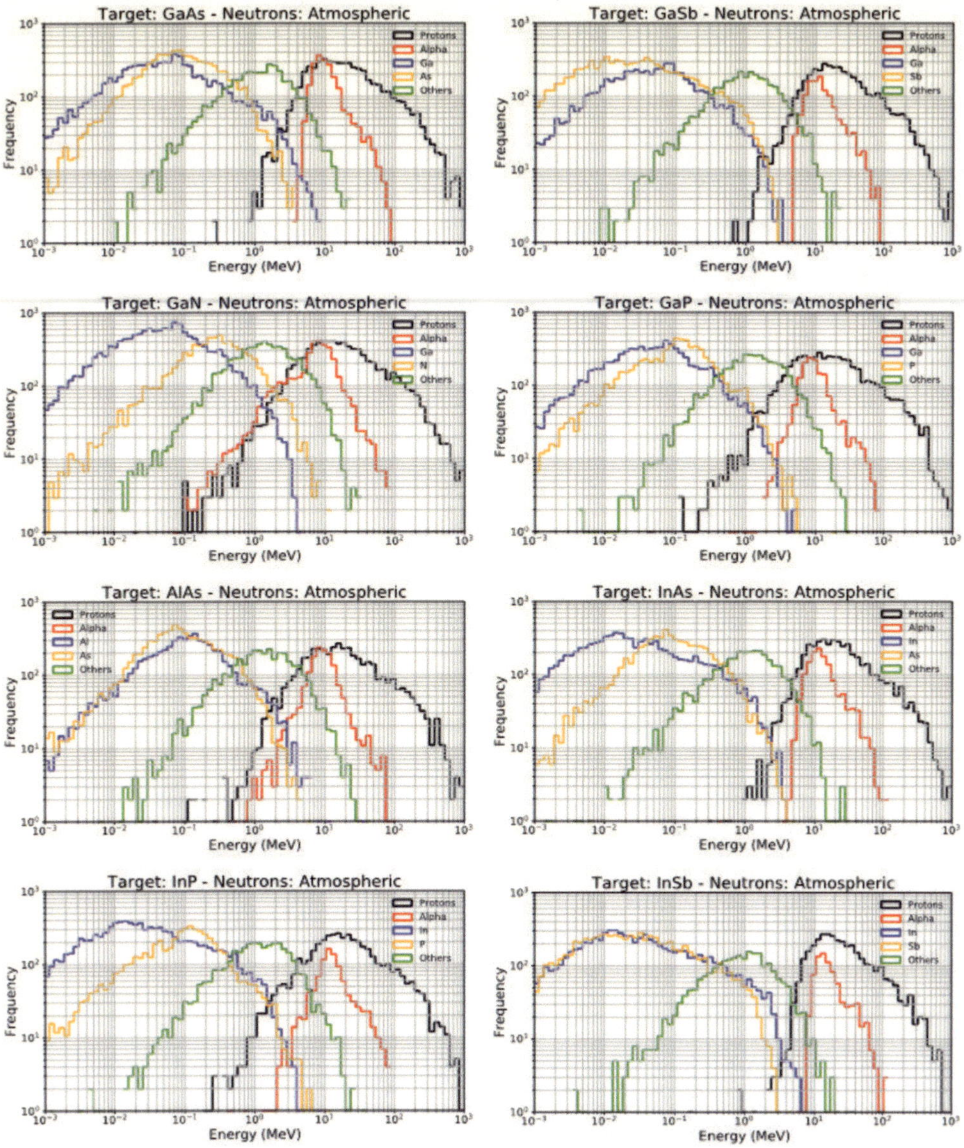

Figure 5.
Energy histograms (100 bins) of protons, alphas, target nucleus recoils, and other ions produced by atmospheric neutron interactions in the eight III–V bulk material targets.

Figures 7 and **8** logically show that the smaller the particle, the lower the initial LET, and the higher the range of the particle. Thereby protons exhibit the lowest LET values, in the interval from 10^{-3} to a few 10^{-1} MeV/(mg/cm^2) for all materials, and the highest ranges, typically from 10^{-6}–10^{-5} m to a few tens of cm. Alpha particles are characterized by intermediate values, with typical initial LET values between 0.1 and 1 MeV/(mg/cm^2) and ranges in the domain from micron to millimeter. Finally, recoil products and other nuclei exhibit the highest initial LET values, up to 10 MeV/(mg/cm^2), and the lowest ranges, from nanometer to a maximum of few tens of microns. These results strongly suggest that product recoils will play an increasing role in submicron and nanowire devices, as explored in the following.

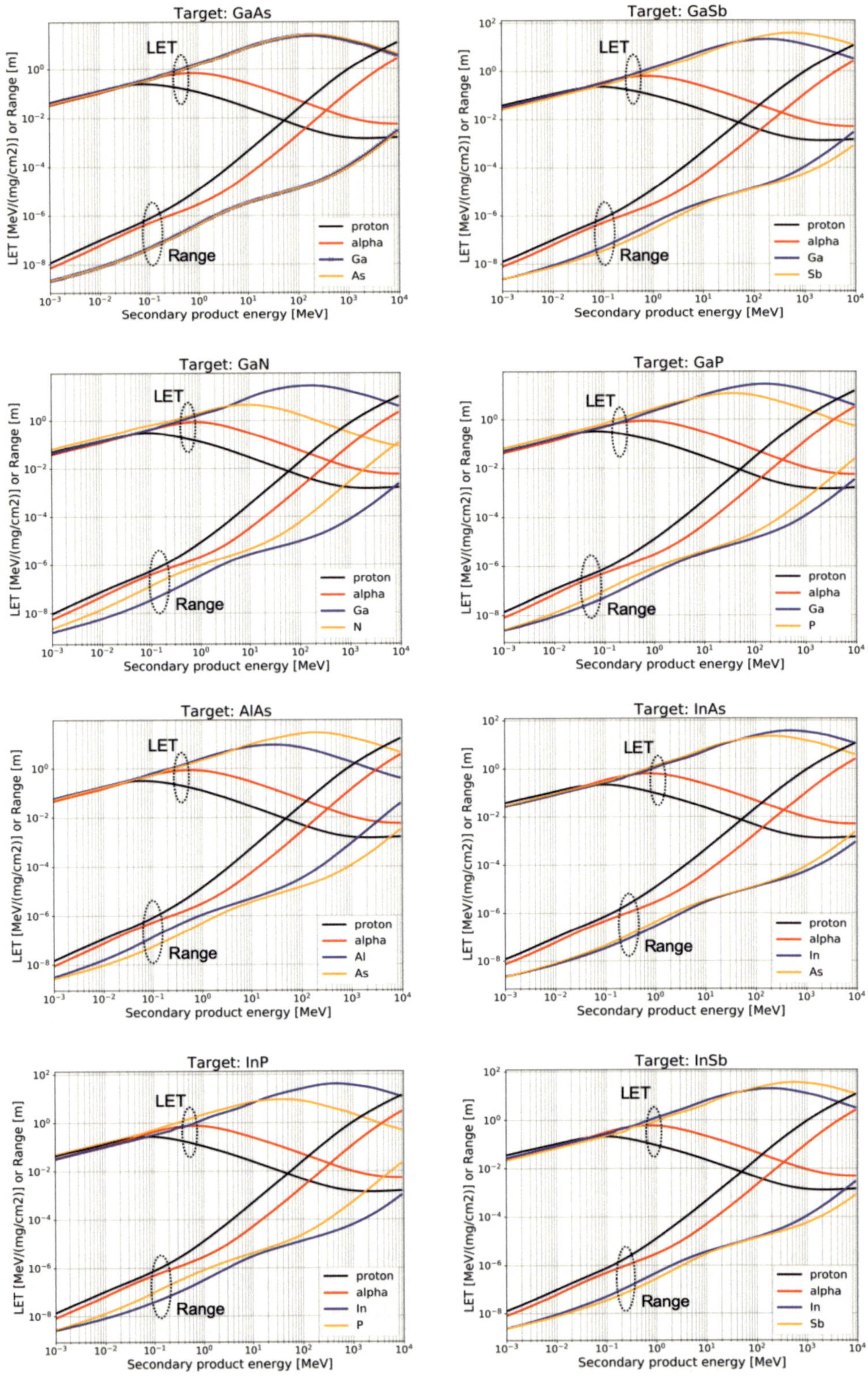

Figure 6.
Linear energy transfer (LET) and range related to protons, alphas, and recoil products in the eight III–V materials calculated with SRIM.

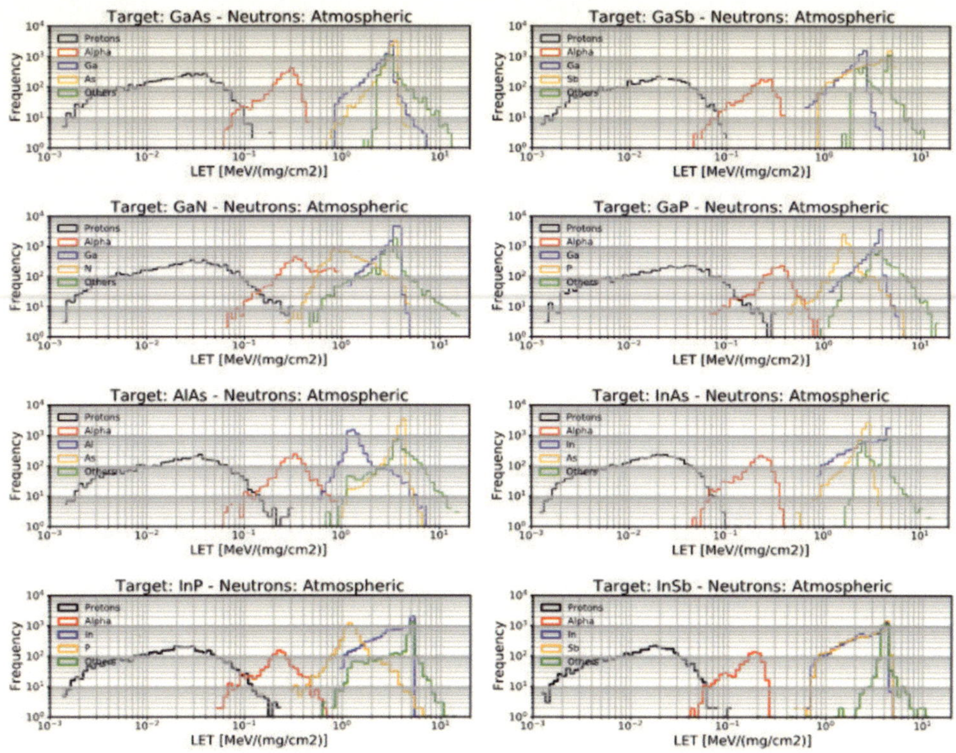

Figure 7.
Initial LET histograms (100 bins) of protons, alphas, target nucleus recoils, and other ions produced by atmospheric neutron interactions in the eight III–V bulk material targets.

5. Discussion

In complement to [15], we examine, in this last section, some consequences of the above results in terms of creation of single-event effects in electronics based on the studied III–V materials. Following neutron interactions with target nuclei and release of secondaries, the energy deposition of these secondary products in the bulk material and its conversion to free charge via the creation of electron-hole pairs are another fundamental step in the creation of SEEs.

First, we evaluated two global metrics to quantify such an energy deposition consecutive to neutron interactions in the bulk of the III–V materials: (i) the mean value of deposited energy per interaction (averaged over all events) and (ii) the corresponding amount of created electron-hole pairs. These two metrics have been evaluated, in **Figure 9**, for the different materials. The first metric, i.e., the mean energy deposited per interaction, is found to vary from around 9 MeV for Si to 14 MeV for GaAs. Atmospheric neutron interactions deposit, in average, more energy in III–V materials than in Si. This result is the consequence of a difference in the number of nonelastic interactions, which is higher in III–V materials than in Si, as shown in the following (**Figure 10** and text).

Figure 9 compares the number of e-h pairs created per interaction in the different III–V materials with respect to the value obtained for silicon (relative factor). Three groups of materials can be considered: (1) GaAs, AlAs, InP, GaN, and GaP that are found very similar to Si (relative factor close to 1 with respect to Si); (2) InAs and GaSb

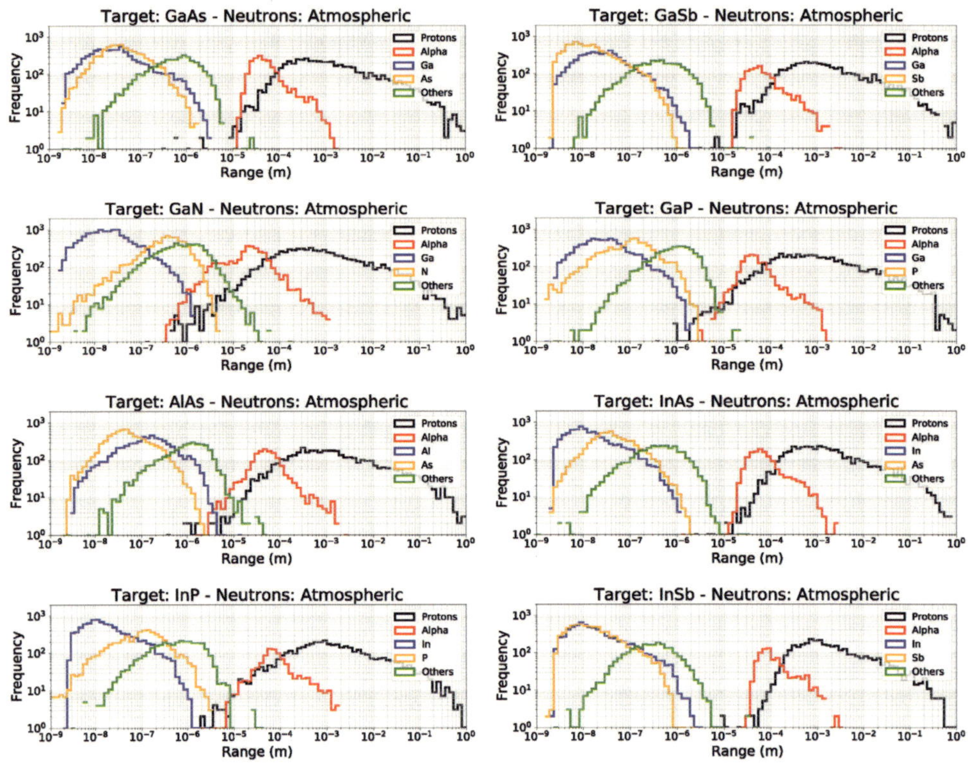

Figure 8.
Range histograms (100 bins) of protons, alphas, target nucleus recoils, and other ions produced by atmospheric neutron interactions in the eight III–V bulk material targets.

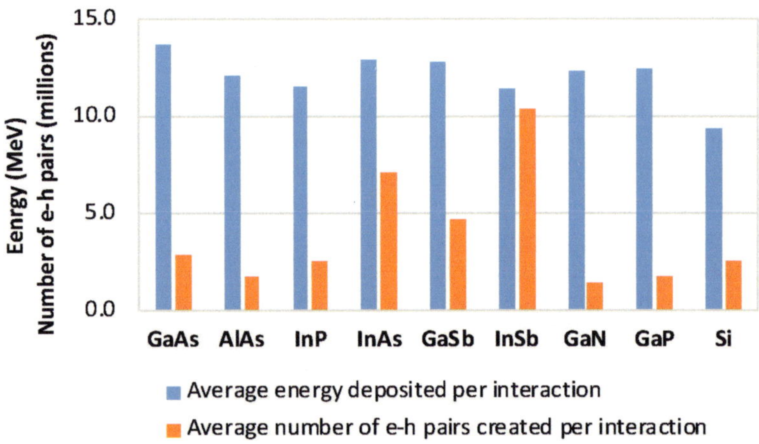

Figure 9.
Deposited energy per interaction (mean value estimated from all events) and corresponding amounts of e-h pairs created in the different III–V material targets. Values have been evaluated considering for each material the e-h pair creation energy given in ***Table 1****. Typical values for silicon are also indicated for reference.*

which exhibit a relative factor between 1.5 and 2.5; and, finally, (3) InSb characterized by the highest factor, close to 4. For the first group of materials, the higher atmospheric neutron sensitivity of these materials (which is indicated by the number of interactions) is largely compensated by a higher energy of e-h pair creation at semiconductor level, due to their large bandgap. On the contrary, for the three last materials which are lower bandgap semiconductors (see **Table 1**), their vulnerability to atmospheric

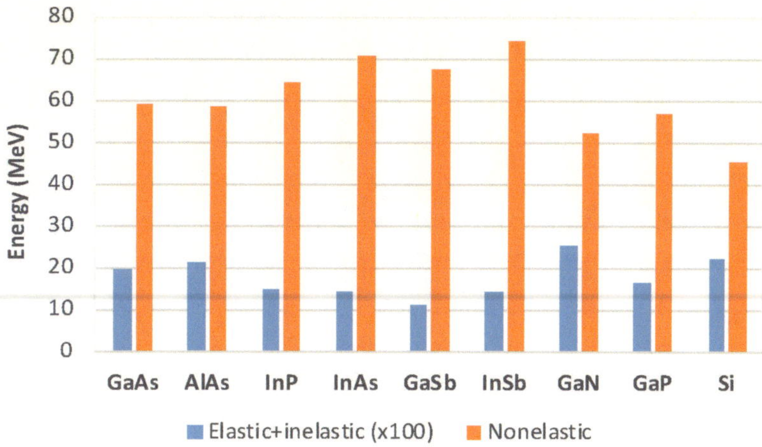

Figure 10.
Averaged values of the deposited energy per elastic or inelastic interaction and per nonelastic interaction for the different III–V material targets. For the case of elastic or inelastic interactions, values have been multiplied by a factor ×100 to be plotted on the same scale.

neutrons is finally reinforced by their electrical response level due to the relatively low values of the energy of e-h pair creation.

Global results in **Figure 9**, however, do not show important quantitative differences that exist between the respective contributions of, on the one hand, elastic or inelastic interactions and, on the other hand, nonelastic reactions, to these global values. In order to examine this particular point, we recalculated the average energy deposited per interaction. Results are shown in **Figure 10**. Elastic or inelastic interactions deposit, in average, between 0.1 MeV (GaSb) and 0.25 MeV (GaN) with a value of 0.23 MeV for Si. On the contrary, nonelastic interactions deposit, in average, more than 50 MeV for GaN and up to 75 MeV for InSb, with a comparative value of 45 MeV for Si. In other words, nonelastic interactions deposit approximately between ×200 (GaN) and ×600 times (GaSb) more energy in average than elastic or inelastic events. Because these nonelastic events are less numerous than elastic+inelastic events (see **Table 3**), this explains why the global average energies per interaction (**Figure 9**) are relatively modest, distributed between 10 and 15 MeV. But these values hide very different situations, depending on the type of interactions. Converted into electron-hole pairs, nonelastic reactions are able to deposit, in average value integrated over all the secondary tracks, charges up to a few pC, whereas elastic or inelastic reactions hardly reach values around a few fC.

In addition to the previous results, we evaluated the fraction of the total energy deposited per type of secondaries for all interaction events in the semiconductor bulks. Results are shown in **Figure 11**. Surprisingly enough, over 85% of the total energy deposited in the different III–V materials is deposited by protons, followed by alpha particles (around 10%). Other nuclei and recoil products represent less than 5%, whereas for silicon, they represent around 8% and alphas only 5%. Considering the range of protons and alphas, this result shows that the largest part of the energy is deposited far from the location of the reaction vertex.

Conversely, if we consider the fraction of the total initial LET deposited per type of secondaries for all interaction events in the different materials, we obtain results shown in **Figure 12**. For III–V material, 70% to 80% (minimum for GaP, maximum for InSb) of the total of the initial LET values corresponds to recoil products. The remaining 10% is related to other nuclei, the contributions of protons and alpha particles being negligible in this total initial LET. This signifies that recoil products

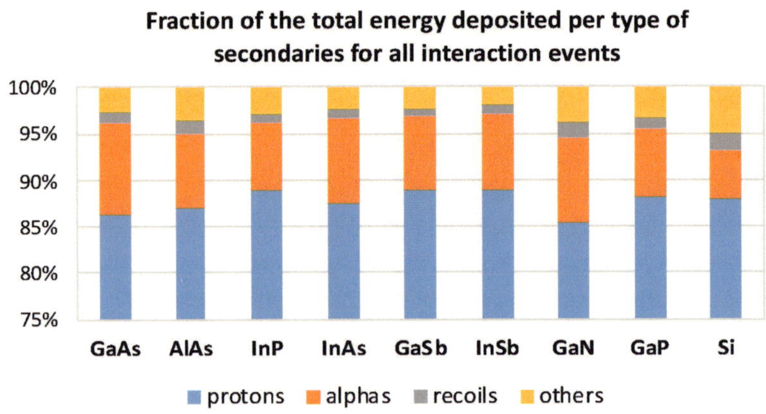

Figure 11.
Fraction of the total energy deposited per type of secondaries for all interaction events in the bulk of the studied III–V semiconductors.

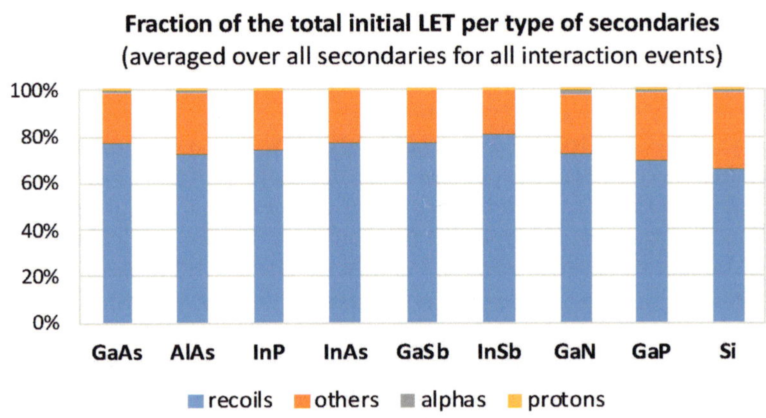

Figure 12.
Fraction of the total initial LET deposited per type of secondaries for all interaction events in the bulk of the studied III–V semiconductors.

are essentially at the origin of the charge deposited in the first (tens of) nanometers around the incoming neutron interaction point (also called reaction vertex).

To evaluate the deposited charge in the first nanometers around reaction vertex points, we derived this quantity from the initial LET of particles just after their release. Introducing E_{eh}, the energy needed for creating an electron-hole pair given in **Table 2**, and t_{Si} the thickness of the material thin layer in which the charge Q_{dep} is deposited, we obtain [13]:

$$Q_{dep}[fC] = A \times LET\left[MeV/\left(mg/cm^2\right)\right] \times tSi[\mu m] \quad (1)$$

where A is a numerical factor that only depends on the semiconductor material density ρ and on the value of E_{eh}, given in **Table 4** for all studied III–V materials and for silicon:

$$A = \frac{16,02 \times \rho\left[g/cm^3\right]}{E_{eh}[eV]} \quad (2)$$

From Equation (1), we derived an estimation of the charge deposited in the first nanometers from the reaction vertex, averaged over all secondaries for all interaction events per material. These results are shown in **Figure 13** for a distance of 10 nm. The comparison of values in **Figure 13** with the current values of the minimum critical charge for standard SRAM memory cells as a function of the technological node, reported in **Table 5**, shows that three materials, InSb, InAs, and GaSb, exhibit a charge largely superior to 0.7 fC, the minimum critical charge for the 14 nm node. On the contrary, three other material show a charge inferior to the reference value for silicon (0.36 fC), i.e., GaN, GaP, and AlAs. Finally, GaAs and InP exhibit intermediate values around 0.5 fC, also compatible with integration down to 14 nm. Finally, the comparison of these results with those of **Figure 9** suggests that integrated electronics based on InSb, InAs, or GaSb semiconductor material should be potentially more affected by neutron-induced single-event effects than those based on the other studied materials and on silicon. Of course, such a prediction will have to be verified experimentally, when devices and circuits based on these new materials for CMOS electronics will be available to be tested for radiation.

$Qdep[fC] = A \times LET[MeV/(mg/cm^2)] \times tSi[\mu m]$	
Material	**Coefficient A**
Si (for memory)	10.3
InSb	84.1
AlAs	8.8
GaSb	33.2
InP	17.1
InAs	50.4
GaAs	17.7
GaP	9.5
GaN	11.1

The numerical value of the coefficient A for this expression is indicated for the eight III–V materials (and for memory for silicon).

Table 4.
Analytical expression of the charge deposited by a particle of a given initial LET (supposed constant) in a given thickness of a given material.

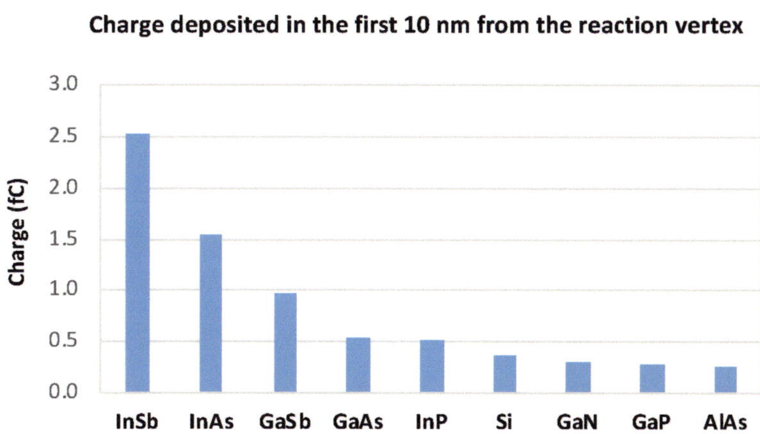

Figure 13.
Charge deposited in the first 10 nm from the reaction vertex, averaged over all secondaries for all interaction events per material.

CMOS node (nm)	180	130	90	65	45	32	22	14
Critical charge Q_{crit} (fC)	3.5	2.9	1.9	1.3	0.9	0.85	0.8	0.7

After Seifert et al. [30].

Table 5.
Minimum critical charge versus CMOS technological nodes for standard SRAM memory cells.

6. Conclusion

In conclusion, Geant4 numerical simulation was intensively used in this work as an exploration tool to anticipate the radiation response of III–V binary compound semiconductors and future electronics based on these materials (not yet available) subjected to high-energy atmospheric neutrons. Eight III–V semiconductors have been considered: GaAs, AlAs, InP, InAs, GaSb, InSb, GaN, and GaP. Simulations of bulk targets (with natural isotope compositions) exposed to sea-level neutron spectrum showed that all III–V materials exhibit more interactions than in silicon, in particular for GaAs, GaP, and GaN, the latter being a somewhat special case due to the presence of nitrogen, whose reactions with neutrons lead to an increased production of protons and alpha particles. A detailed analysis based on histograms on secondary product energy, LET, and range has been conducted, providing synthetic data about the atmospheric neutron radiation response of all these materials. We also have shown the importance of product recoils in the radiation response of ultimate CMOS electronics, due to their relative elevated masses that result in very short particle ranges and significant charge deposition within nanometer distances from the interaction points. We draw attention to the integrated electronics based on InSb, InAs, or GaSb semiconductor that should be potentially more affected by neutron-induced single-event effects than those based on the other studied materials. The current lack of experimental data in the literature forces us to consider these projections with all the precautions that we must constantly have in mind when it comes to simulation results that have not been validated experimentally.

Conflict of interest

The authors declare no conflict of interest.

Author details

Daniela Munteanu* and Jean-Luc Autran
Aix-Marseille University, CNRS, University of Toulon, Marseille Cedex 20, France

*Address all correspondence to: daniela.munteanu@univ-amu.fr

References

[1] Mauthe S et al. Monolithic integration of III-V on silicon for photonic and electronic applications. In: 76th Device Research Conference, Santa Barbara, CA. 2018. pp. 1-2

[2] Available from: https://www.zurich.ibm.com/st/nanodevices/iii-v_cmos.html

[3] Oktyabrsky S, Ye P. Fundamentals of III-V Semiconductor MOSFETs. Berlin, Heidelberg, Germany: Springer Science & Business Media; 2010

[4] Li T, Mastro M, Dadgar A, Compound III–V. Semiconductors: Integration with Silicon-Based Microelectronics. Boca-Raton, Florida, United States: CRC Press; 2016

[5] Jönsson AA, Svensson J, Wernersson L. A self-aligned gate-last process applied to All-III–V CMOS on Si. IEEE Electron Device Letters. July 2018;**39**(7):935-938

[6] Ni K et al. Single-event transient response of InGaAs MOSFETs. IEEE Transactions on Nuclear Science. 2014;**61**(6):3550-3556

[7] Gong H et al. Scaling effects on single-event transients in InGaAs FinFETs. IEEE Transactions on Nuclear Science. 2018;**65**(1):296-303

[8] Gong H et al. Pulsed-laser induced single-event transients in InGaAs FinFETs on bulk silicon substrates. IEEE Transactions on Nuclear Science. 2019;**66**(1):376-383

[9] Tsao CH, Silberberg R, Letaw JR. A comparison of neutron-induced SEU rates in Si and GaAs devices. IEEE Transactions on Nuclear Science. 1988;**35**(6):1634-1637

[10] Vu TT. Compound Semiconductor Integrated Circuits. Singapore: World Scientific; 2003

[11] McMorrow D, Melinger JS, Knudson AR. Single-event effects in III-V semiconductor electronics. International Journal of High-Speed Electronics and Systems. 2004;**14**(2):311-325

[12] H. Liu, M. Cotter, S. Datta, V. Narayanan, v Technology assessment of Si and III-V FinFETs and III-V Tunnel FETs from soft error rate perspective", International Electron Device Meeting, Institute of Electrical and Electronics Engineers. 2012, pp. 577-580

[13] Munteanu D, Autran JL. Modeling and simulation of single-event effects in digital devices and ICs. IEEE Transactions on Nuclear Science. 2008;**55**(4):1854-1878

[14] Munteanu D, Autran JL. Susceptibility of Group-IV and III-V semiconductor-based electronics to atmospheric neutrons explored by geant4 numerical simulations. In: Rao SP, editor. Numerical Simulations in Engineering and Science. London, United Kingdom: IntechOpen; 2017 Chapter 7. pp. 234-255

[15] Autran JL, Munteanu D. Atmospheric neutron radiation response of III-V binary compound semiconductors. IEEE Transactions on Nuclear Science. 2020 accepted for publication

[16] Agostinelli S et al. Geant4—A simulation toolkit. Nuclear Instruments and Methods in Physics Research Section A: Accelerators, Spectrometers, Detectors and Associated Equipment. 2003;**506**(3):250-303

[17] Allison J, Amako K, Apostolakis J, Arce P, Asai M, et al. Recent developments in Geant4. Nuclear Instruments and Methods in Physics Research Section A:

Accelerators, Spectrometers, Detectors and Associated Equipment. 2016;**835**:186-225

[18] Autran JL, Munteanu D. Soft Errors: From Particles to Circuits. Oxfordshire, United Kingdom: Taylor & Francis, CRC Press; 2015

[19] Kasap S, Capper P. Springer Handbook of Electronic and Photonic Materials. New York, USA: Springer International Publishing AG; 2017

[20] Klein CA. Bandgap dependence and related features of radiation ionization energies in semiconductors. Journal of Applied Physics. 1968;**39**:2029-2038

[21] Serre S, Semikh S, Uznanski S, Autran JL, Munteanu D, Gasiot G, et al. Geant4 analysis of n-Si nuclear reactions from different sources of neutrons and its implication on soft-error rate. IEEE Transactions on Nuclear Science. 2012;**59**(4):714-722

[22] Autran JL, Serre S, Semikh S, Munteanu D, Gasiot G, Roche P. Soft-error rate induced by thermal and low energy neutrons in 40 nm SRAMs. IEEE Transactions on Nuclear Science. 2012;**59**(6):2658-2665

[23] Gordon MS et al. Measurement of the flux and energy spectrum of cosmic-ray induced neutrons on the ground. IEEE Transactions on Nuclear Science. 2004;**51**:3427-3434

[24] Goldhagen P. Cosmic-ray neutrons on the ground and in the atmosphere. MRS Bulletin. 2003;**28**(2):131-135

[25] Geant4 version 4.9.4. Online available: http://geant4.cern.ch/collaboration/working_groups/electromagnetic/physlist9.4.shtml

[26] Rinard P. Neutron interactions with matter. Los Alamos Technical Report. 1991

[27] Chadwick MB et al. ENDF/B-VII.1 nuclear data for science and technology: Cross sections, covariances, fission product yields and decay data. Nuclear Data Sheets. 2011;**112**:2887-2996

[28] Ziegler JF, Biersack JP, Ziegler MD. SRIM—The Stopping and Range of Ions in Matter. SRIM Co.; 2008 0-9654207-1-X

[29] http://srim.org

[30] Seifert N, Jahinuzzaman S, Velamala J, Ascazubi R, Patel N, Gill B, et al. Soft error rate improvements in 14-nm technology featuring second-generation 3D tri-gate transistors. IEEE Transactions on Nuclear Science. 2012;**62**(6):2570-2577

Chapter 9

Modeling and Simulation in Microwave-Photonics Applications

Mikhail E. Belkin, Tatiana Bakhvalova, Vladislav Golovin, Yuriy Tyschuk and Alexander S. Sigov

Abstract

In this chapter, with the goal to recover an optimal mean for computer-aided modeling and simulating a newer class of microwave-photonics-based radio electronic apparatuses, a number of comparative simulation experiments for the basic microwave band electronic devices and systems using well-known software tools referred to photonic design automation or upgraded electronic design automation platforms are carried out. As a result, it is shown that exploiting the software of upgraded electronic design automation platform provides significantly better accuracy of calculations for the devices and systems of this class.

Keywords: computer-aided design, microwave photonics, radio electronic apparatus

1. Introduction

Nowadays, microwave photonics (MWP) is a relatively mature scientific and technological direction arising among radio electronic R&D society at the second half of the twentieth century in result of combining the achievements of microwave electronics and photonics techniques [1]. Initially, MWP was an area of interest for a military platform [2, 3] such as radar and electronic warfare means, but recent years, it became an object of study and development for emerging areas in the telecommunication industry [4] such as fifth-generation (5G) cellular networks. For today, MWP technology might be considered as a perspective direction of modern radio electronics for signal generation, transmission, and processing in various radio frequency (RF) circuits and systems of microwave (MW) band. Implementation of this concept will enhance the key technical and economical features and such important characteristics as electromagnetic and environmental compatibilities, immunity to external interferences.

Following this tendency, we have contributed some works referred to computer-aided design of MWP components and MWP-based devices [5–18] using two well-known software tools such as VPI Photonics Design Suite (VPI-PDS) [19] and Applied Wave Research Design Environment (AWRDE) [20]. Elaborating the direction, in this chapter, we review shortly the distinctive features of MWP technique, preselecting an optimal software to computer-aided design (CAD), a hybrid device combining microwave electronics and photonics components. After that, we highlight our last modeling and simulation results on design and optimization of advanced microwave and millimeter-wave band RF electronic facilities based on MWP technique, mainly for an access network of 5G mobile communication systems. In particular, Section 2 reviews the nature, features, and space of the MWP approach to develop advanced radio electronics apparatuses (REAs). In addition, Section 3 presents a short comparative analysis of modern computer platforms with the goal of selecting a feasible mean to design MWP-based REA. The examples for comparative computer-aided simulations of key optical and optoelectronics elements, such as laser, optical modulator, photodetector, and optical fiber, as well as based on them specific MWP devices and apparatuses for microwave-signal processing in optical range such as a delay circuit, oscillator, frequency converter, and fiber-wireless fronthaul of 5G mobile communication system, are demonstrated in Section 4. All schemes are simulated in VPI-PDS and AWRDE CAD tools. Finally, Section 5 concludes the chapter.

2. The distinctive features of MWP technique

Microwave photonics is a rather fresh interdisciplinary scientific-technical and scientific-technological direction of radio electronics and photonics, which provides an increase in the efficiency of the formation and processing of analog and digital radio signals due to their transfer to the optical range. The use of MWP in promising radio facilities for various purposes has the potential, first, from the point of view of increasing operating frequencies up to tens of terahertz, ensuring their multirange, multifunctionality, reconfigurability, and increasing speed and throughput in accordance with modern requirements. Another purpose of MWP is to improve the performance characteristics of existing REAs such as instantaneous bandwidth, electromagnetic compatibility, power consumption, reliability, resistance to natural and intentional interference, footprint, and environmental friendliness.

Generally, MWP devices are the examples of an intimate integration of photonics, microwave electronics, and planar antenna technologies for producing a complicated functional module in a multichannel analog environment. In particular, MWP technology opens the way to superwide bandwidth transmitting characteristics at lower size, weight, and power as compared with traditional electronic information and communication systems [2, 3]. For example, it is expected that this direction will find wide application in the RF equipment for accessing networks of incoming mobile communication systems with distribution in the millimeter-wave range [4, 17]. **Figure 1** demonstrates a typical MWP arrangement, where for direct and inverse transferring of MW and optical signals, two interfacing units are allocated at their bounds: MW-to-optical (MW/O) and optical-to-MW (O/MW) converters. Between the interfaces, there are various photonics processing units for transmission, switching, distribution, filtration, time delaying, amplification, and frequency conversion of microwave signals in optical domain.

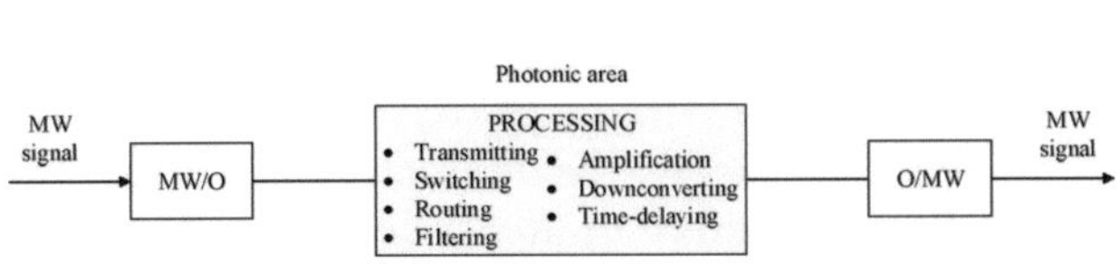

Figure 1.
A typical arrangement of MWP circuit.

3. Preselecting a feasible software to design MWP-based REAs

In the process of design, a developer of new MWP-based REA is facing a problem of choosing an appropriate software tool. As of today, the existing optical and optoelectronic CAD tools (OE-CAD) based on so-called Photonic Design Automation (PDA) platform are not developed like CAD tools intended for modeling of RF and MW circuits (MW-CAD) based on so-called Electronic Design Automation (EDA) platform that have been underway for about 5 decades. So today, to solve the problems of successful introducing MWP technique to the next-generation REAs, their individual units, and devices, there are various PDA-based CAD systems that allow creating complex models of varying difficulty. In general terms, all specialized CAD systems can be divided into a group for the structural design of optical linear and nonlinear media on various materials and a group for system modeling, in which individual devices are introduced as closed models with a set of specific characteristics.

Following it, currently, some commercial CAD systems have been developed for modeling optical and optoelectronic devices and systems based on PDA platform. The most popular representatives are VPI Photonics Design Suite from VPI Photonics, OptiSystem from Optiwave Design Software, and so on. However, our design experience in such OE-CAD systems clearly showed that they are most applicable for modeling complex apparatuses and systems, rather than individual device. In particular, the models of optical and optoelectronic components studied below are presented in the VPI-PDS tool in the form of ready-made library models with a very limited number of parameters necessary for their development. Therefore, based on this software, it is impossible to carry out detailed modeling of their functioning. For example, it is impossible to calculate a transfer characteristic in the large-signal mode taking into account introduced nonlinear distortions and also an influence of spurious elements of the input/output circuit and chip construction in the MW band.

To overcome this serious drawback, we almost 10 years ago proposed a different approach using a device-oriented MW-CAD tool [5], which was subsequently expanded in Ref. [13]. Its essence is that the optimal solution to the problem of modeling MWP components and MWP-based devices according to the criteria of accuracy and time-of-decision should be based on a rational combination of structural [in the form of an physical equivalent circuit (FEC)] and structureless models (when the response of the device is described in frequency, temporal, and spatial areas based on external input and output characteristics) of circuit elements. The effectiveness of this approach, called end-to-end multiscale design, has been confirmed experimentally, for example, when modeling optoelectronic devices with a MW passband [21]. Below, we briefly characterize both classes of CAD tools using the example of AWRDE and VPI-PDS.

3.1 Available microwave-electronic software characterization

The AWRDE is a comprehensive EDA platform for developing RF/microwave products that provide radio engineers with integrated high frequency, system, and electromagnetic (EM) simulation technologies and design automation to develop physically realizable electronics ready for manufacturing. The tool helps designers manage complex integrated circuit (IC), package, and printed-circuit board modeling, simulation, and verification, addressing all aspects of circuit behavior to achieve optimal performance and reliable results for first-pass success. The unique AWRDE tool features are the following:

- Unified design capture provides front-to-back physical design flow with dynamically linked electrical and layout design entry. Components placed in an electrical schematic automatically generate a synchronized physical layout based on libraries of standard, customized, and/or vendor-provided components.

- Design flow supports complex hierarchical projects with parameterized subcircuits for easy optimization and tuning. Circuit, system, or EM-based subcircuits can be quickly developed and used to populate larger, more complex networks common in today's RF front-end circuitry.

- Interoperability with industry-standard tools enables the exchange of design data for schematic or netlist import, bidirectional EM cosimulation, electrical or design rule check, and production-ready export. Additionally, powerful yield analysis and optimization address manufacturing tolerances for more robust designs and greater profitability.

- Customization due to the powerful application-programming interface extends the capabilities of the software using popular programming languages, providing user-defined scripts for automating common or complex tasks and custom design flows.

3.2 Available photonic software characterization

VPI-PDS sets the industry standard for end-to-end PDA comprising design, analysis, and optimization of components, systems, and networks that provide professional simulation software supporting requirements of active/passive integrated photonics and fiber optics applications, optical transmission system and network applications, and cost-optimized equipment configuration. The unique VPI-PDS tool features are the following:

- Link engineering solutions provide simple means for the cost-effective optical network configuration and offer a unified approach to control equipment libraries and engineering methodologies.

- Transmission design solutions provide professional means for investigating and optimizing system technologies and evaluating novel component and subsystem designs in a system context.

- Component design solutions provide professional means for the development and optimization of photonic ICs, optoelectronic components, and fiber-based amplifiers and lasers.

- Device simulation solution provides a versatile simulation framework for the analysis and optimization of integrated photonic waveguides and optical fibers.

3.3 Contention of the possibilities

In process of development of such MWP REAs combined microwave and photonic circuits, there was a problem to use an optimum computer product for their modeling and design. The essence is that for the accurate solution of an issue for modeling of such complicated systems containing radio engineering and optical

#	Feature	Realization	
		By MW-CAD (AWRDE)	**By OE-CAD (VPI-PDS)**
1	Analysis approach	Building blocks, 3D electromagnetic analysis	Building blocks
2	Simulation methods		
	• Linear circuits	S- and Y-matrices, equivalent circuits	S-matrices
	• Nonlinear circuits	Harmonic balance engine ALPAC, 3D planar electromagnetic simulator AXIEM modeling	S-matrices, combination of time-and-frequency domain modeling
3	Element representation		
	• Active microwave elements	Multirate harmonic balance, HSPICE, Volterra, based on measured characteristic models	Ideal or based on measured characteristic models
	• Active MWP elements	Absent	Rate equation-based, transmission line models
	• Passive elements	Lumped and distribution, microwave band specialties	Lumped, ideal
4	Possibility for calculating the key parameters of MWP circuits and links	By one-click operation	By user-created complicated schemes
5	IC layout design and analysis	Yes	No
6	Built-in design kits from the main foundries	Yes	No
7	Parameter optimization	Yes	No
8	Sensitivity analysis	Yes	No
9	Design of tolerance	Yes	No
10	Statistical design	Yes	No
11	Yield optimization routine	Yes	No
12	Built-in library of producer-specific models	Yes	No

Table 1.
Comparison of modern ME-CAD and OE-CAD tools.

elements and devices, the specialties of their functioning in both ranges must be taken into consideration. In this regard, more than 20 years ago, the conclusion was drawn that the optimal way for increasing the accuracy of MWP circuits taking into account the influence of their parasitic elements in MW band requires use of the high-power MW-CAD tool working at the symbolical level [19]. **Table 1** lists the detailed comparison of typical modern OE-CAD tool VPI Photonics Design Suite of VPI Photonics and well-known MW-CAD tool AWRDE of Cadence.

In result, the following outputs to optimally design the MWP-based REAs can be drawn out:

1. The available OE-CAD platform is most applicable for analyzing complex devices and systems, rather than their individual components, which are presented in the form of parameterized or formal library models with a very limited number of parameters necessary for accurate development of

MWP-based REAs. In particular, MW REA's passive elements such as waveguides, couplers, resonators, resistors, capacitor, and inductor represent only by ideal lumped models. In addition, calculating the key parameters of MWP circuits and links, such as large-signal transmission gain, noise figure, phase noise, intermodulation distortion, and intercept points is possible only by user-created complicated testbeds. While on MW-CAD platform, they are calculated using a 'one-click' operation.

2. From the developer's point of view, the OE-CAD platform lacks (or is just starting to appear) a large number of functions that are very useful for investigating the device under design (see items 5–12 of **Table 1**).

3. The main disadvantage of the MW-CAD platform is the lack of models of active optoelectronic components such as semiconductor lasers, photodiodes, and electro-optic modulators.

4. Our multiyear experience in CAD of MWP devices using AWRDE tool has shown that the most convenient way to introduce optoelectronic devices is to present them as a behavioral model in the form of a nonlinear physical equivalent circuit. In this circuit, the linear section is built on the basis of passive lumped or distributed components, and the nonlinear one uses sources (current, voltage, noise, etc.), the characteristics of which are based on experimental data.

4. Comparative computer-aided design

Having clarified the principal pros and cons of the two classes of software tools from the point of view of designing MWP-based REAs, in this section, we exemplify specifically the results of their comparative calculation for various devices and systems.

4.1 Calibration of optoelectronics and optical element models

To conduct accurately comparative modeling of MWP REAs, it is necessary to perform a reciprocal calibration for the models of optoelectronic and optical components. In this regard, the behavioral models in the AWRDE are initially more accurate, since they are based on experimental data. That is, the calibration consists in fitting the parameters of the VPI-PDS models so as to obtain close basic characteristics in small- and large-signal modes. Below, we present and discuss the results of model calibration for key optoelectronic and optical components, based on which a set of subsequent simulations for basic REAs will be carried out in the next subsection.

4.1.1 Semiconductor laser source

Variants of AWRDE-based semiconductor laser source (SLS) model in the form of FECs are proposed and described in detail in Refs. [5, 6, 13, 18]. On the other hand, there are more than 10 library models of SLS in VPI-PDS tool mainly based on linear or nonlinear rate equations differing in the way they are presented and in the set of input data. **Figure 2** exemplifies the result of small-signal frequency response (mod. S_{21}) simulations using AWRDE's single-carrier model [18] and VPI-PDS's "LaserRateEqSM.vtms" model. As follows from the figure, both graphs for this reciprocally calibrated optoelectronic element have a similar appearance with typical conversion losses of about 30 dB, about 3-dB rise associated with the so-called electron-photon resonance, and −3-dB direct modulation bandwidth of slightly larger than 11 GHz.

4.1.2 Electro-optical modulator

The AWRDE-based electro-optical intensity modulator (EOM) model of so-called electroabsorption type in the form of FECs is proposed and described in detail in Ref. [13]. On the other hand, there are two library models of electroabsorption modulator (EAM) in VPI-PDS tool differing in the way they are presented and in the set of input data. **Figure 3** exemplifies the result of large-signal optical spectra simulations using AWRDE model [13] and VPI-PDS's "ModulatorEA_Polynomial.vtms" model. As follows from the figure, both graphs for this reciprocally calibrated optoelectronic element have a similar appearance with approximately the same power levels of the fundamental signal and the first two harmonic distortions caused by the nonlinearity of the modulator's transfer characteristic.

4.1.3 PIN-photodiode

Variants of AWRDE-based pin-photodiode (PD) model in the form of FECs are proposed and described in detail in Refs. [7, 8, 13, 18]. On the other hand, there are only one unified model of PD in VPI-PDS tool that is ideal and handles both single-mode and multimode optical signals. **Figure 4** exemplifies the result of small-signal frequency response simulations using AWRDE model [13] and VPI-PDS's "Photodiode.vtms" model. As follows from the figure, both graphs for this reciprocally calibrated optoelectronic element have a similar appearance. However,

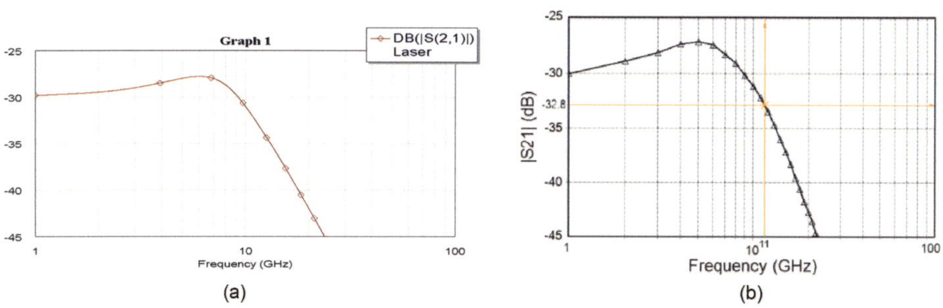

Figure 2.
Small-signal frequency response of the semiconductor laser source model by (a) AWRDE and (b) VPI-PDS.

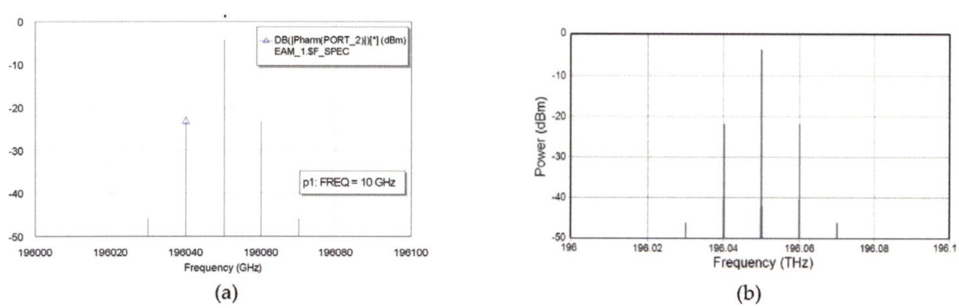

Figure 3.
Large-signal optical spectrum of the electro-optical modulator model by (a) AWRDE and (b) VPI-PDS.

using the same reference data, a −3-dB bandwidth was obtained a little more than 20 GHz for the AWRDE model and 27 GHz for the VPI-PDS model.

The most probable reason for this meaningful discrepancy is explained by the ideality of the VPI-PDS model, which does not take into account the influence in MW band of either the photodiode chip itself or the parasitic elements of its output circuit. Specifically, in order to obtain a reasonable decrease in the frequency response at higher frequencies, a library model of a low-pass filter had to be introduced at the PD model output. Effect referred to parasitic circuit elements may be clearly explained by **Figure 5**. It follows from the AWRDE graphs that a designer can realized twofold expansion of the PD's 3-dB passband (20–40 GHz) owing to the appropriate fitting of the connecting wire inductance L_w.

4.1.4 Optical fiber

In general, with the wave approach, where light is regarded as an EM wave, any optical passive element, including the optical fiber (OF), can be simulated in the same way in MW-CAD or in OE-CAD tool. Namely, in AWRDE, a segment of optical fiber of a certain length can be equivalently represented using, for example, the library model of physical transmission line with loss (TLINP). However, when constructing a realistic model of an OF, a whole set of additional effects should be taken into account, such as dispersion, reflection, scattering, nonlinearity, and ambient temperature, the influence of which can degrade the transmission characteristic. The AWRDE-based OF model in the form of FECs taking into account the above limiting factors is proposed and described in detail in Ref. [15]. On the other hand, there are as many as nine library models of multimode or single-mode OF in VPI-PDS tool differing in the way they are presented, which deteriorating factors and what set of input data are taken into account. **Figure 6** exemplifies the result of

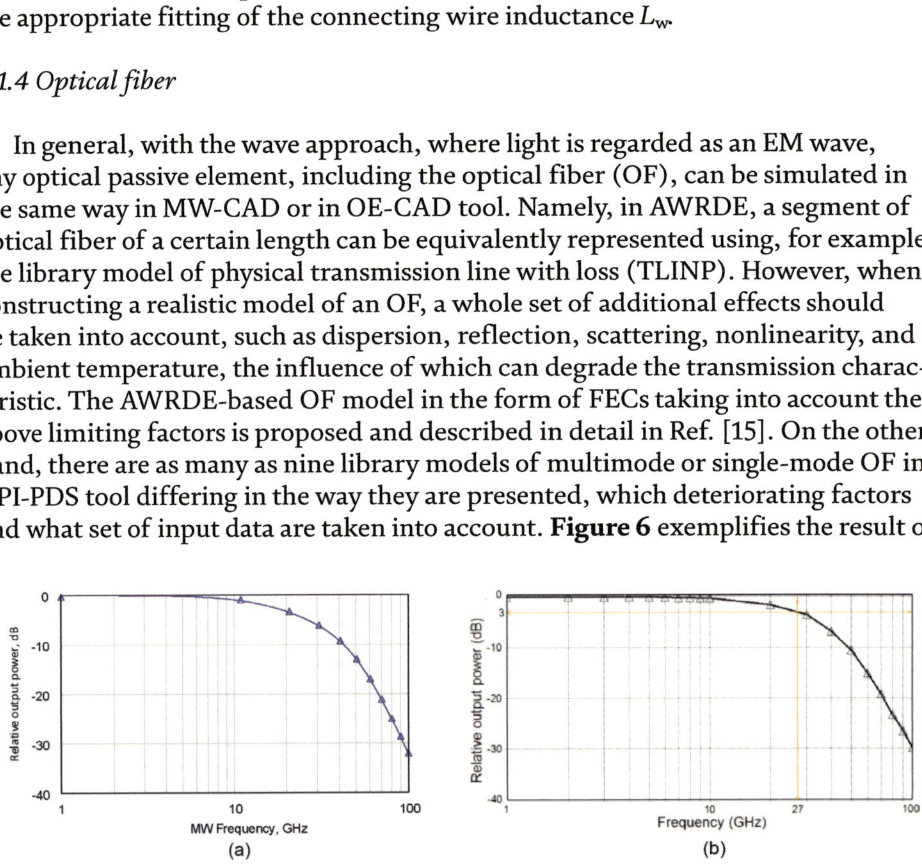

Figure 4.
Small-signal relative frequency response of the PIN-photodiode model by (a) AWRDE and (b) VPI-PDS.

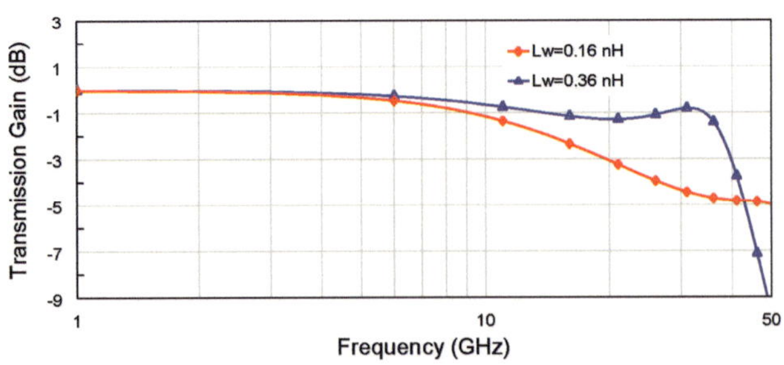

Figure 5.
Effect of the connecting wire between photodiode chip and output pad.

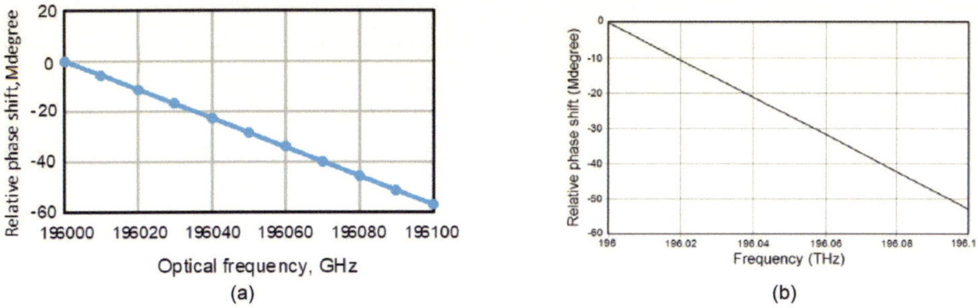

Figure 6.
Relative phase-frequency response of the single-mode optical fiber model by (a) AWRDE and (b) VPI-PDS.

small-signal phase response (arg. S_{21}) simulations using AWRDE's simplified model [18] and VPI-PDS's "UniversalFiberFwd.vtmg" model. As follows from the figure, both graphs for this reciprocally calibrated optical element have a similar appearance and the same slope.

4.1.5 Reference data for the further simulation experiments

The purpose of this subsection is to generalize the results of the reciprocal calibration for optical and optoelectronic component models in such a way as to provide unified reference data on their parameters for further studies. **Table 2** lists the common reference data for four above-considered models of SLS, EOM, PD, and OF as well as of electronic amplifier typically used after pin-PD.

4.2 Simulation examples

In this subsection, the subjects of the study are the specific microwave photonics (MWP) devices and apparatuses such as a delay circuit, oscillator, frequency converter, and fiber-wireless fronthaul of 5G mobile communication system. The tools for the comparative computer simulation are well-known commercial software AWRDE and VPI-PDS. The research takes into account some key distortion sources of the MW signal under processing such as introduced noise and nonlinear distortion of active optoelectronic elements as well as chromatic dispersion of the optical fiber. The parameters for the elements to be used are based on the data of **Table 2**.

4.2.1 MW-signal's optical delay circuit

Fiber-optic delay circuit is one of the most feasible MWP units [22]. **Figure 7** shows the block diagram of the single-channel optical delay circuit (ODC) under test including semiconductor laser that directly modulated by input MW signal, optical fiber, the length of which corresponds to the required delay time, and a photodetector, at the output of which a delayed MW signal is formed. Following it, below we will describe two models and some comparative simulation results using AWRDE and VPI-PDS tools.

4.2.1.1 Modeling in VPI-PDS

Figure 8 demonstrates the model for the simulation experiment evaluating some key quality parameters for ODC under test when transmitting continuous wave MW signals. As one can see, it contains the same ODC layout as in **Figure 7**

Parameter		Value
Semiconductor laser source	Operating current	40 mA
	Average power	8 mW
	Optical carrier	C-band (191 to 196.1 THz)
	Linewidth	1.5 MHz
	Relative intensity noise	−150 dB/Hz
	Threshold current	8.5 mA
	Slope efficiency	0.14 W/A
	Direct modulation 3-dB bandwidth	Up to 11 GHz
Electro-optical modulator (EAM)	Operating voltage	−0.6 V
	Extinction ratio	14 dB
	Slope efficiency	0.14 W/V
	Linewidth enhancement factor (α)	1.0
	3-dB modulation bandwidth	30 GHz
PIN-photodiode	Responsivity	0.7 A/W
	Dark current	100 nA
	Optical input power	<3 mW
	3-dB passband	Up to 30 GHz
Post-amplifier (if needed)	Gain	40 dB
	Noise spectral density	20×10^{-12} A/Hz$^{1/2}$
Optical fiber	Type	SMF-28e+
	Length	Up to 20 km
	Attenuation	0.2 dB/km
	Dispersion	17 e^{-6} s/m^2
	Dispersion slope	80 s/m^3

Table 2.
Reference data of elements for the further study.

consisting of the calibrated in the previous subsection library model for single-mode laser, so-called galactic model for optical fiber also including delay element, and library models for pin-photodiode and electrical post-amplifier.

4.2.1.2 Modeling in AWRDE

The layout of single-channel ODC [15] is very simple and contains (**Figure 9**) the subcircuit models of SLS, single-mode optical fiber of a corresponding length (delay ≈4.8 ns/m), and PD.

4.2.1.3 Simulation results

Figure 10 exemplifies the simulation results for ODC's group time delay (GTD), where the MW signal frequency is swapped in the range of 1–7 GHz, and the OF length is 3 m. As follows from the figure, due to the broadband of the constituent elements, the delay does not change in such a wide frequency range of modulating frequencies (almost 3 octaves). Its value coincides with high accuracy for both

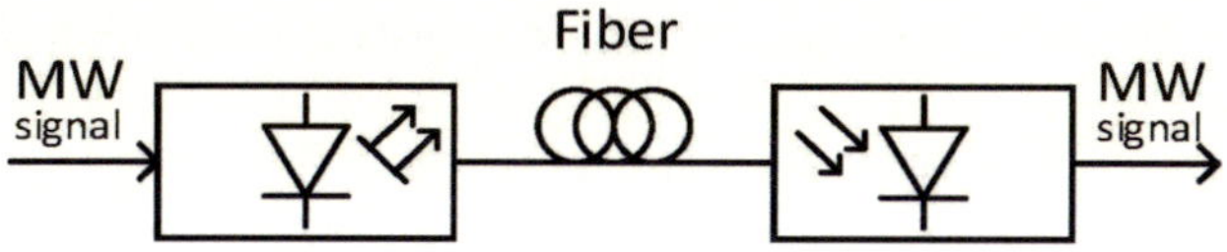

Figure 7.
Block diagram of the optical delay circuit under test.

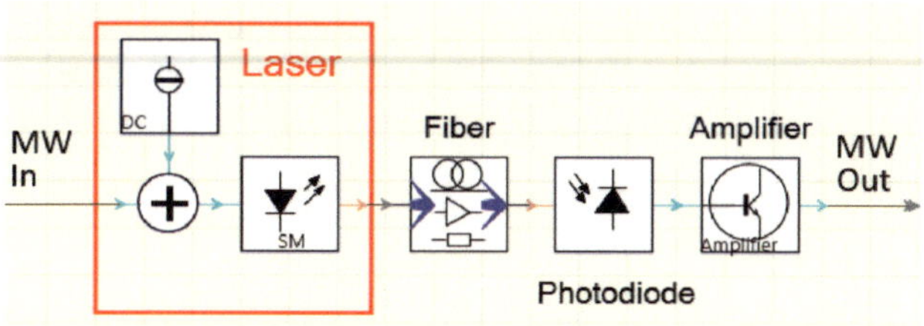

Figure 8.
VPI-PDS's model of fiber-optic delay circuit of MW signals.

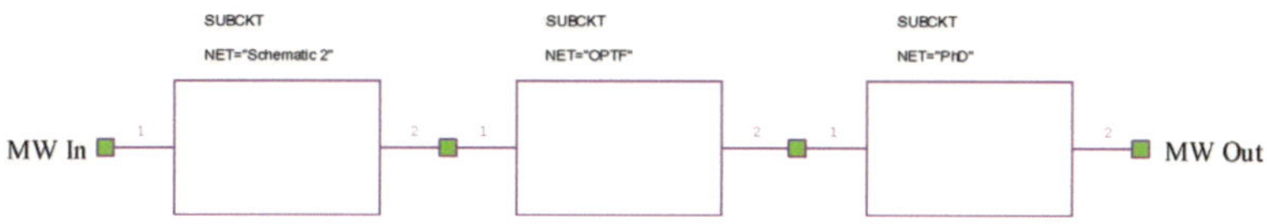

Figure 9.
AWRDE model of fiber-optic delay circuit of MW signals.

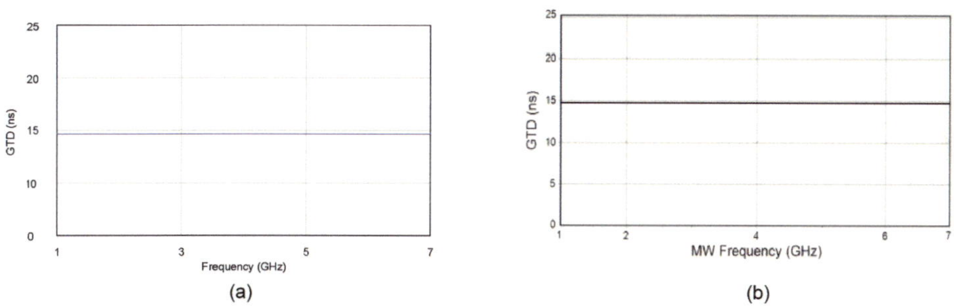

Figure 10.
Examples of the simulation results for FODC of MW signals: relative phase-frequency response by (a) AWRDE and (b) VPI-PDS.

models and is close to the above delay in a standard single-mode fiber. In addition, **Figure 11** demonstrates the large-signal amplitude characteristic of the ODC under test. As one can see from the figure, 1 dB input compression point is near −10 dBm for the both models.

The following outputs can be drawn from our study:

- The investigated optoelectronic delay circuit is a very simple device that, in contrast to the electronic analog, provides an extremely wide operating bandwidth and, thanks to the very short delay time in electro-optical and optical-electric converters and low losses in an optical fiber, an extremely wide delay range from units of nanoseconds to hundreds of microseconds.

- Both computer tools under study provide approximately the same accuracy of calculations, which coincide with the actual value of the delay in the fiber [22]; however, the AWRDE model is simpler and more flexible.

4.2.2 Optoelectronic oscillator of MW signals

Figure 12 presents the block diagram of the MW signal's optoelectronic oscillator (MW-OEO) that is another worldwide example of MWP application [23]. Generally, it contains two requisite sections: optical one and electrical one. Here, the optical section includes SLS, EOM, OF, and PD. The electrical section includes low-noise MW amplifier (LNA), band-pass filter (BPF), power MW amplifier (PA), and electrical coupler (EC).

4.2.2.1 Modeling in VPI-PDS

Following a similar approach as in our previous computation modeling, **Figure 13** shows a VPI-PDS model of MW-OEO [10]. An important specificity of this model is in taking a phase noise of SLS into consideration.

Note that due to the absence in this software the library model of optical fiber (OF) that takes into account the delay in it, the OF model in the diagram has been replaced by library models of the optical attenuator and the delay element with identical parameters.

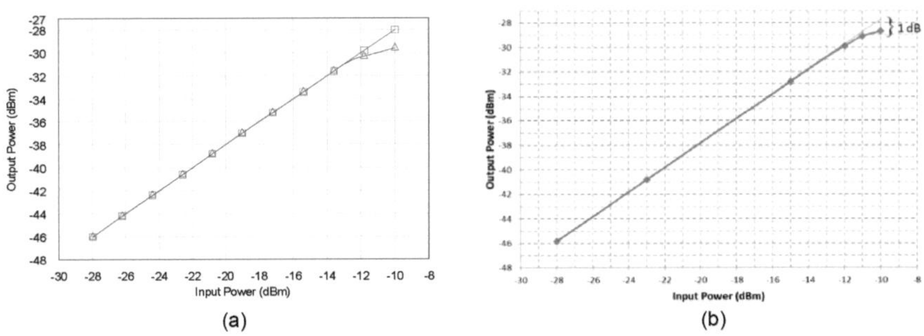

Figure 11.
Simulated large-signal power characteristic for the FODC of MW signals under test by (a) AWRDE and (b) VPI-PDS.

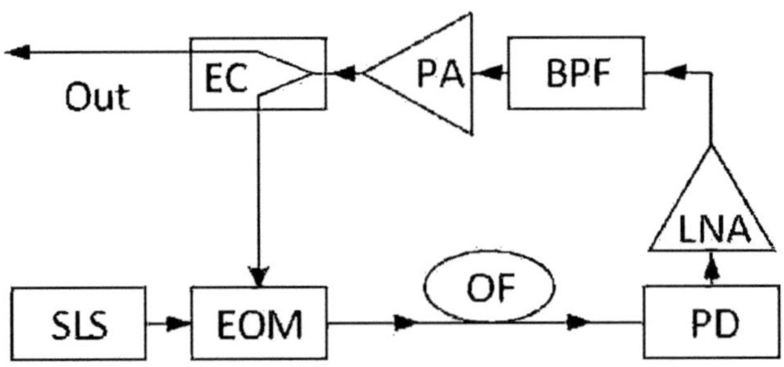

Figure 12.
Block diagram of the MW-OEO under test.

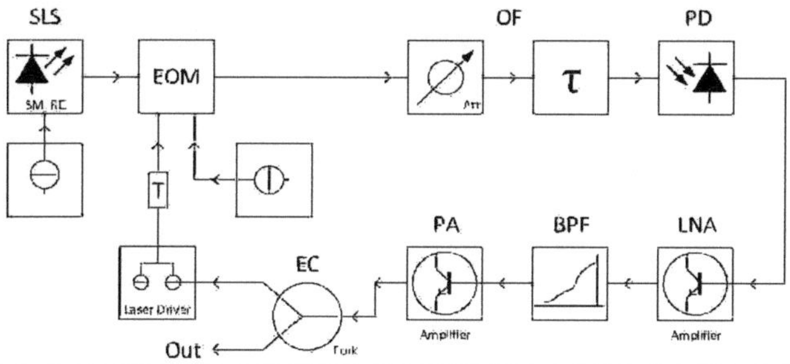

Figure 13.
VPI-PDS's model of optoelectronic oscillator of MW signals.

4.2.2.2 Modeling in AWRDE

Figure 14 represents circuit-level nonlinear model of the MW-OEO under study realized by AWRDE software. The diagram includes a chain of subcircuits (SUBCKTs) representing (from left to right): small-signal (including noise) and large-signal features of SLS (see Section 4.1.1), delay and losses of OF, nonlinear optical-to-electrical conversion feature of PD (see Section 4.1.3), gain and bandwidth of LNA, bandwidth and losses of BPF, frequency and amplitude features of PA, and couple of EC models realized by AWRDE tool. Besides, there are two service program elements mitigating self-sustained oscillation in the return path of the model: ideal DGDELAY that models an ideal, linear, frequency-dependent, digital time delay element and OSCAPROBE that initiates a large-signal oscillator simulation.

4.2.2.3 Simulation results

As an example, **Figure 15** presents phase noise characteristics for MW-OEO of 9 GHz simulated by the OE-CAD tool (black line) and by the MW-CAD tool (red curve). As one can see, there is a significant discrepancy in the simulation results at the offsets more than 100 kHz.

The following outputs can be drawn from our study:

- With small offsets from the MW carrier, the phase noise levels calculated using both software approximately coincide with each other and with experimental data [9].

- With large offsets, the discrepancy between the AWRDE-calculated and experimental data does not exceed 2 dB [9], which indicates the more validity of its model.

- To measure the phase noise of an oscillator, there is a built-in model of the noise analyzer (OSCNOISE) in the AWRDE tool, while to perform this operation in the VPI-PDS tool, it is necessary to create a complex testbed.

4.2.3 Optoelectronic frequency converter of MW signals

About 10 years ago, we proposed a simple circuit for an optoelectronic frequency converter (OEFC) of MW signals, in which the nonlinearity of a SLS's

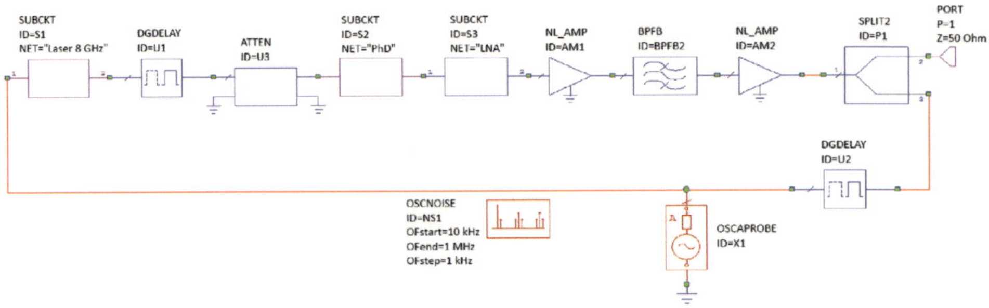

Figure 14.
AWRDE's model of optoelectronic oscillator of MW signals.

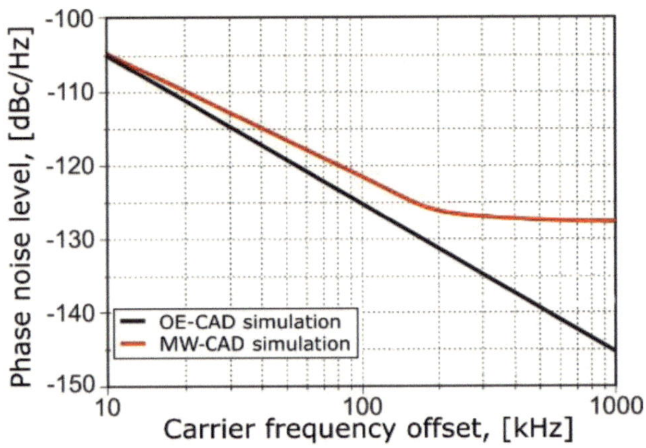

Figure 15.
Phase noise characteristics (RIN = −150 dBc/Hz).

light-current characteristic is leveraged [11]. The efficiency of this device was confirmed by modeling in VPI-PDS and experimental research at input frequencies of 1 and 1.5 GHz. Later, the operation of this device was modeled in AWRDE tool at other frequencies of the MW input signals [10]. The block diagram of the OEFC containing an electronic power combiner mixing the RF and LO MW-signals, a SLS, a pin-PD, and an electronic bandpass filter to isolate the mixing product is shown in **Figure 16**.

4.2.3.1 Modeling in VPI-PDS

Following a similar approach as in our previous computation modeling, **Figure 17** depicts a VPI-PDS model of MW-OEFC [11]. Its appearance repeats the diagram of **Figure 16** with the introduction of an electronic attenuator (El), which serves to adjust the level of MW signals at the input of the SLS.

4.2.3.2 Modeling in AWRDE

Following the above block diagram, **Figure 18** demonstrates the OEFC model under investigation in AWRDE environment. This figure includes a chain of subcircuits representing (from left to right) SLS (first three sections) and pin-PD (right sections) nonlinear models realized by AWRDE tool (see Sections 4.1.1 and 4.1.3). The laser model is presented by the FEC of the linear sections of the SLS model (S2) together with the test fixture model (S1) and nonlinear section (A1) representing

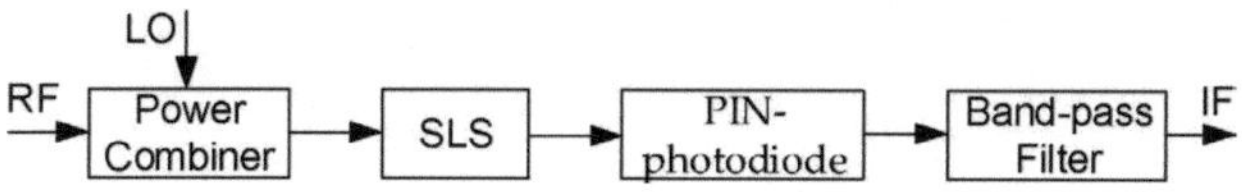

Figure 16.
Block diagram of the MW-OEFC under test.

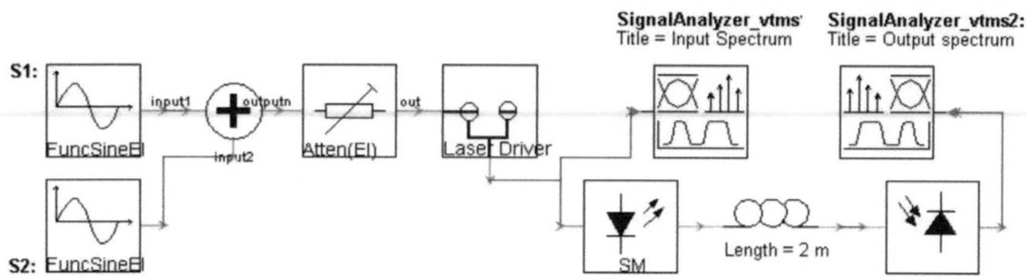

Figure 17.
VPI-PDS's model of optoelectronic frequency converter of MW signals.

AWRDE's library element LOOKUP that implements a lookup table including its measured light-current characteristic. The right section of the chain is nonlinear PD FEC model. Simulation details are reported in Ref. [10].

4.2.3.3 Simulation results

Figure 19 shows the results of simulation experiment referred to defining output spectra of the OEFC under investment by AWDE MW-CAD tool (a) and VPI-PDS OE-CAD tool (b). In both procedures, the input RF signal had a power of −20 dBm at a frequency of 1 GHz, and LO signal had a power of 6 dBm at a frequency of 1.5 GHz.

The following outputs can be drawn from our study:

- As one can see from **Figure 19(a)**, applying powerful harmonic balance method of AWRDE software resulted in output (IF) signal power near −55 dBm at a frequency of 2.5 GHz, that is, conversion gain is −35 dB. The rest of the peaks in the figure represent clearly the full output spectrum of standard microwave mixer in agreement with well-known formula $|mF_{RF} \pm nF_{LO}|$, where m and n are integers. On the other hand, **Figure 19(b)** shows a comparable result referred to conversion gain, however, a significant part of the mixing products either differs in level or is absent altogether.

- The results of simulation using the proposed AWRDE models should be closely matched to the experimental ones because their parameters are constructed on the measured characteristics of laser and photodiode.

4.2.4 Fiber-wireless fronthaul of 5G mobile communication system

In the framework of 5G's Radio-over-Fiber (RoF) concept, fiber-wireless fronthaul network (FWFN) is one of the promising ways to deliver intensive digital traffic with seamless convergence between wired optical backhaul and fiber-wireless fronthaul, which is important to keep the remote cells flexible, cost effective, and power efficient [4, 17]. The block diagram of the FWFN containing Central station (CS) and a set of Remote stations (RS) interactively connected to CS via fiber-optics links (FOL) is shown in **Figure 20**. A typical position of RS is in the

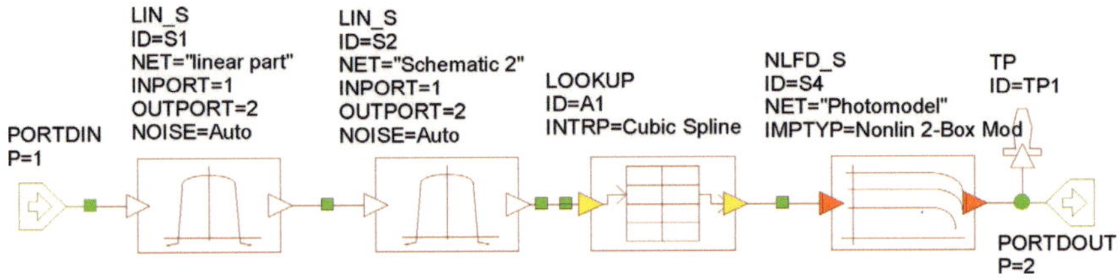

Figure 18.
Circuit-level AWRDE's optoelectronic MW-frequency converter model.

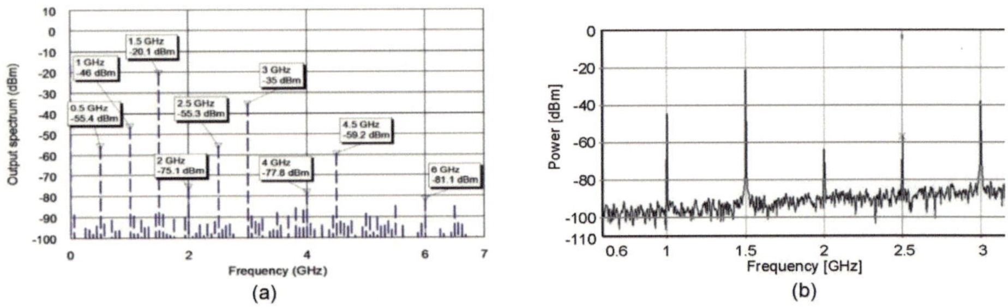

Figure 19.
Large-signal optoelectronic MW frequency converter output spectra by (a) AWRDE and (b) VPI-PDS.

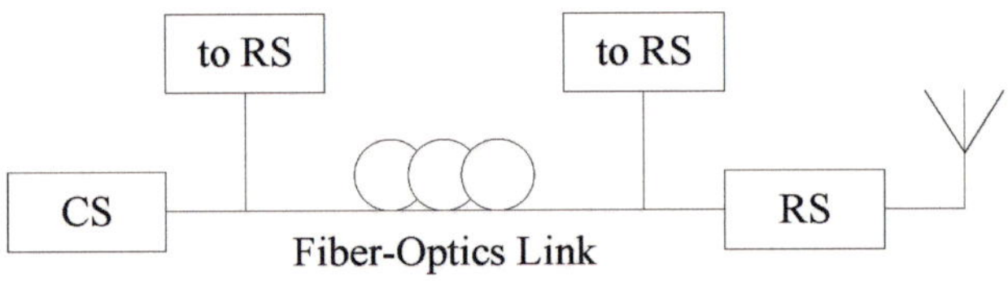

Figure 20.
Block diagram of the fiber-wireless fronthaul network under test.

center of the service area; that is, for omnidirectional covering, four phased array antennas with an azimuth of 90° would be an optimal decision [14, 16].

4.2.4.1 Modeling in VPI-PDS

Figure 21 depicts the VPI-PDS's model of downlink channel for FWFN under study that has the same block diagram as in **Figure 20**.

As one can see from the figure, there are three parts such as CS, FOL, and RS. The first one includes the set of library models imitating quadrature amplitude modulated (QAM) MW transmitter as well as the models of SLS and EOM calibrated in Section 4.1. The second one consists of the library model of polarization controller and the model of OF calibrated in Section 4.1. Finally, the third one includes the model of pin-PD calibrated in Section 4.1 as well as the set of library models imitating QAM MW receiver. A detailed description of the QAM transmitter and receiver models is given in Ref. [15].

4.2.4.2 Modeling in AWRDE

Figure 22 depicts AWRDE's model of downlink channel for FWFN under study. The model has the same arrangement as in **Figure 21** excluding the transmitting part

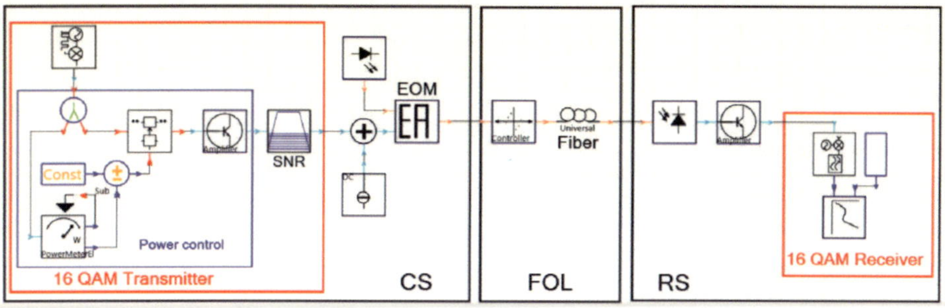

Figure 21.
VPI-PDS model of downlink channel for a fiber-wireless fronthaul network.

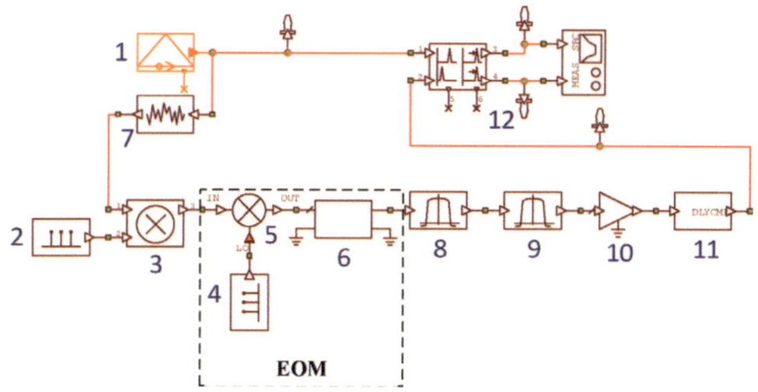

Figure 22.
AWRDE model of fiber-wireless fronthaul network. 1, QAM generator; 2, MW tone generator; 3, multiplexer; 4, quasi-optical signal generator; 5, behavioral mixer; 6, optical frequencies splitter; 7, MW noise generator; 8, model of single-mode fiber as subcircuit; 9, model of photodiode as subcircuit; 10, post-amplifier; 11, signal delay compensator; 12, vector signal analyzer.

that contains the library model of quasi-optical tone generator imitating laser carrier, the library model of multiplexer that performs the operation of upconverting signal to the optical range, and a passive subcircuit representing frequency response of the EOM under test in S2P format. Note that earlier we proposed and described in detail [13] a nonstructural nonlinear model for the EOM of the EAM type suitable for developers of local telecommunication systems based on RoF technology. However, here, its simplified model with the parameters calibrated in Section 4.1 is used.

4.2.4.3 Simulation experiment

In this section, the subject of the study is a MWP-based FWFN; the devices of study are SLS, EOM, single-mode OF, and PD, which parameters have been calibrated in Section 4.1. The tools for the computer simulation are two well-known commercial program environments such as OE-CAD VPI-PDS and MW-CAD AWRDE. The study took into account the key distortion sources of the transmitted signal: noises of the laser, chirp of the modulator, and losses and chromatic dispersion of the fiber. To eliminate the influence of nonlinear effects during modulation and signal transmission through the fiber, MW and optical signal levels were selected, so that the modulation index did not exceed 30%, and the optical power in the fiber was below 5 mW.

4.2.4.4 Reference data

Table 3 lists the common reference data for the simulation experiment.

Parameter	Value
Length of pseudo-random bit sequence	2^{15}–1
Bitrate	2.5 Gbit/s
RF carrier frequency	25 GHz
Input RF power	−11 to −26 dBm
Type of RF modulation	16-QAM
Type of optical modulation	Intensity

Table 3.
Common reference data for the FWFN under study.

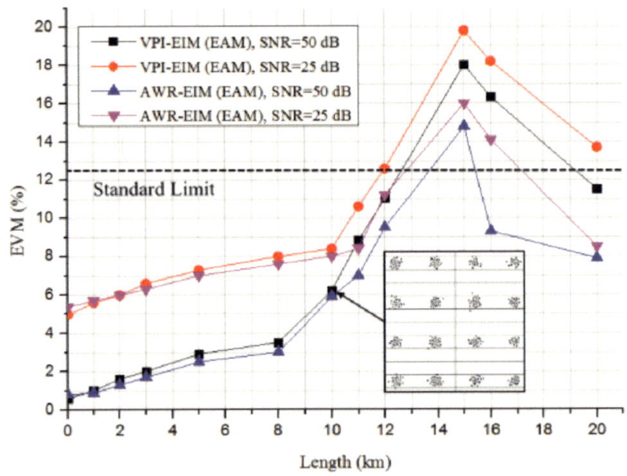

Figure 23.
EVM versus fiber length characteristics.

4.2.5 Simulation results

In preparation for the simulation experiments, the modulation index of each device under study was optimized in such a way as to ensure the maximum output MW carrier-to-noise ratio while maintaining the low-signal mode at the modulating frequency. **Figure 23** depicts an example of comparative simulation of Error Vector Magnitude (EVM) versus fiber length characteristics for the FWFN under study during transmission of 2.5 Gbit/s and 16-QAM MW signal at the frequency of 25 GHz using signal-to-noise ratio (SNR) of 50 and 25 dB. For the best vision, there is the inset in the figure showing constellation diagrams at the fiber length of 10 km. In addition, the dotted line indicates the standard limit of the EVM during transmission of the 16-QAM signal, which is 12.5%.

The following outputs can be drawn from our study:

- the EVM versus fiber length characteristics simulated by both the software closely coincide with each other at the signal-to-noise ratio of 50 and 25 dB within the FOL distance of up to 10 km and

- for longer FOL lengths, all characteristics show a peak that exceeds the standard limit, caused by the effect of chromatic dispersion [22].

5. Conclusion

The chapter is devoted to recovering the optimal principle to computer-aided design a new class of microwave band radio electronic apparatuses using microwave-photonics approach to effectively generate, transmit/receive, and process super wideband radio signals in near infrared optical range meeting minimum insertion loss of a quartz light guide. Preselecting a feasible software instrument to design MWP-based radio engineering apparatuses showed that up to date, exploiting for some decades microwave band software tools based on electronic design automation platform are preferable than relatively rudimentary software tools based on photonic design automation platform due to much more possibilities to produce the state-of-art radio engineering devices, apparatuses, and systems. In addition, the problem referred to the reasonableness and accuracy of calculations comes to the fore because in the second tool all active and passive electronic and photonic circuit elements are presented as ideal models with lumped parameters that do not take into account frequency distortion due to spurious elements and transmission lines with distributed parameters. To clear the fact and estimate the impact, a comparative modeling for four basic radio electronic apparatus designed on the microwave-photonics approach, such as optical delay circuit, optoelectronic oscillator, optoelectronic frequency converter, and 5G's fiber-wireless fronthaul link, was carried out using two widespread off-the-shelf software: VPI Photonics Design Suite (VPI-PDS) and Applied Wave Research Design Environment (AWRDE). The following outputs can be derived, which a developer should take into consideration. The advantage of the simulation in VPI-PDS software is its greater convenience and speed with acceptable calculation accuracy since the built-in library models of optoelectronic and optical components are mainly used. On the other hand, the gain of the simulation in AWRDE software is a more sophisticated and, at the same time, a more accurate characterization because their parameters are constructed on the measured characteristics of active optoelectronic components, so the results should be closely matched to the experimental ones. Our future work will focus on the upgrading already proposed models and designing new AWRDE models of devices and units for microwave photonics applications.

Acknowledgements

This work was supported by the Russian Foundation for Basic Research, Grant Nos. 17-57-10002 and 18-29-20083.

Conflict of interest

The authors declare the lack of the 'conflict of interest'.

Author details

Mikhail E. Belkin[1*], Tatiana Bakhvalova[1], Vladislav Golovin[2], Yuriy Tyschuk[2] and Alexander S. Sigov[1]

1 Scientific and Technological Center, "Integrated Microwave Photonics", MIREA—Russian Technological University, Moscow, Russian Federation

2 Sevastopol State University (SevSU), Sevastopol, Russian Federation

*Address all correspondence to: belkin@mirea.ru

References

[1] Gilbert KD, McClees HC, Lindsay PA, Paik SF. Photo-mixing experiments at X band. Proceedings of the IEEE. 1963;**51**(8):1148-1148. DOI: 10.1109/PROC.1963.2461

[2] Seeds AJ, Williams KJ. Microwave photonics. IEEE/OSA Journal of Lightwave Technology. 2006;**24**(12):4628-4641. DOI: 10.1109/JLT.2006.885787

[3] Capmany J, Novak D. Microwave photonics combines two worlds. Nature Photonics. 2007;**1**(1):319-330. DOI: 10.1038/nphoton.2007.89

[4] Waterhouse R, Novak D. Realizing 5G: Microwave photonics for 5G mobile wireless systems. IEEE Microwave Magazine. 2015;**16**(8):84-92. DOI: 10.1109/MMM.2015.2441593

[5] Belkin ME, Belkin L, Sigov AS, Iakovlev V, Suruceanu G, Kapon E. Performances of microwave-band analog signal transmission using wafer-fused long wavelength VCSELs. IEEE Photonics Technology Letters. 2011;**23**(20):1463-1465. DOI: 10.1109/LPT.2011.2162230

[6] Belkin ME, Iakovlev V. Microwave-band circuit-level semiconductor laser modeling. In: Proceedings of the 9th European Modeling Symposium on Mathematical Modeling and Computer Simulation EMS 2015, Madrid, Spain; 6-8 October 2015. pp. 1-3

[7] Belkin ME. Multiscale computer aided design of microwave-band P-I-N photodetectors. In: Gateva S, editor. Photodetectors. Croatia: InTech; 2012. pp. 231-250

[8] Belkin ME, Sigov AS. Circuit-level large-signal modeling of microwave bandwidth photodetector. In: Proceedings of the International Conference on Electromagnetics in Advanced Applications (ICEAA 2015); 7-11 September 2015; Torino, Italy. pp. 1587-1589

[9] Belkin ME, Golovin V. Microwave electronic CAD modeling of microwave-band optoelectronic oscillator based on long wavelength VCSEL. In: Proceedings of the International Conference on Microwaves, Communications, Antennas and Electronic Systems (COMCAS 2015), Tel Aviv, Israel; 2-4 November 2015. pp. 1-3

[10] Belkin ME, Tyschuk Y. Microwave electronic CAD modeling of microwave photonic devices based on LW-VCSEL mixing. In: Proceedings of the II International Conference on Microwave and Photonics (ICMAP 2015), Dhanbad, Bihar, India; 11-13 December 2015. pp. 1-3

[11] Belkin ME, Belkin LM, Loparev AV, Iakovlev V, Kapon E, Suruceanu G. Microwave-band optoelectronic frequency converters based on long wavelength VCSELs. In: Proceedings of the International Conference on Microwaves, Communications, Antennas and Electronic Systems (COMCAS), Tel Aviv; November 2011. pp. 1-6

[12] Belkin ME, Iakovlev V, Sigov AS, Tyschuk Y, Golovin V. An advanced approach to simulation of super-wide bandwidth information and communication systems combining microwave and photonic industrial technologies. In: Proceedings of the European Modelling & Simulation Symposium (EMSS2016), Cyprus; 26-28 September 2016. pp. 141-147

[13] Belkin ME, Golovin V, Tyschuk Y, Vasil'ev M, Sigov AS. Computer-aided design of microwave-photonics-based rf circuits and systems. In: Chapter 4 in Book IntechOpen RF Systems, Circuits and Components. 2018. pp. 61-81

[14] Belkin ME, Fofanov D, Golovin V, Tyschuk Y, Sigov AS. Design and optimization of photonics-based beamforming networks for ultra-wide mm Wave-band antenna arrays. In: Chapter 4 in Book IntechOpen Array Pattern Optimization. 2018. pp. 47-67

[15] Belkin ME, Bakhvalova T, Golovin V, Tyschuk Y, Sigov AS. Selecting an optimal computer software for design of microwave-bandwidth optoelectronic devices of a fiber-optics link. In: Proceedings of the European Modeling and Simulation Symposium (EMSS), Lisbon, Portugal; 18-20 September 2019. pp. 304-310

[16] Belkin ME, Fofanov D, Bakhvalova T, Sigov AS. Design of reconfigurable multiple-beam array feed network based on millimeter-photonics beamformers. In: Chapter in Book Array Pattern Optimization. Rijeka: IntechOpen; 2019

[17] Belkin ME, Bakhvalova T, Sigov AC. Design principles of 5G NR RoF-based fiber-wireless access network. In: Chapter to IntechOpen Book "Recent Trends in Communication Networks". 2019

[18] Belkin ME, Golovin V, Tyschuk Y, Sigov AS. A simulation technique for designing next-generation information and communication systems based on off-the-shelf microwave electronics computer tool. International Journal of Simulation and Process Modelling. 2018;**13**(3):238-254. DOI: 10.1504/IJSPM.2018.093104

[19] VPI Photonics Design Suite [Internet]. Available from: https://www.vpiphotonics.com/ [Accessed: 16 January 2020]

[20] Applied Wave Research Design Environment [Internet]. Available from: https://awrcorp.com/ [Accessed: 16 January 2020]

[21] Leijtens XJM, Le Lourec P, Smit MK. S-matrix oriented CAD-tool for simulating complex integrated optical circuits. IEEE Journal of Selected Topics in Quantum Electronics. 1996;**2**(2):257-262. DOI: 10.1109/2944.577373

[22] Urick VJ, McKinney JD, Williams KJ. Fundamentals of Microwave Photonics. New Jersey: Hoboken; 2015. DOI: 10.1002/9781119029816

[23] Yao XS. Opto-electronic oscillators. In: Chang WSC, editor. RF Photonic Technology in Optical Fiber Links. United Kingdom: Cambridge University Press; 2002. pp. 255-292. DOI: 10.1017/CBO9780511755729

Chapter 10

Machine Health Monitoring and Fault Diagnosis Techniques Review in Industrial Power-Line Network

Saud Altaf and Shafiq Ahmad

Abstract

The machinery arrangements in industrial environment normally consist of motors of diverse sizes and specifications that are provided power and connected with common power-bus. The power-line could be act as a good source for travelling the signal through power-line network and this can be leave a faulty symptom while inspection of motors. This influence on other neighbouring motors with noisy signal that may present some type of fault condition in healthy motors. Further intricacy arises when this type of signal is propagated on power-line network by motors at different slip speeds, power rating and many faulty motors within the network. This sort of convolution and diversification of signals from multiple motors makes it challenging to measure and accurately relate to a certain motor or specific fault. This chapter presents a critical literature review analysis on machine-fault diagnosis and its related topics. The review covers a wide range of recent literature in this problem domain. A significant related research development and contribution of different areas regarding fault diagnosis and traceability within power-line networks will be discussed in detail throughout this chapter.

Keywords: fault diagnosis, machine health monitoring, signal processing, industrial power-line network, artificial intelligence, wireless sensor network

1. Introduction

This chapter presents a critical literature review analysis on machine-fault diagnosis and related topics. Most of the contents are extracted from doctoral thesis of the first author of this chapter [1]. The review covers a wide range of recent literature in the problem domain and is classified into the following groups:

- Existing signal processing techniques
- Feature extraction methods
- Existing fault diagnosis methods
- Propagation of fault signals in industrial power-line network

- Fault type diagnosis using wireless sensor networks (WSNs) within industrial machinery networks

- Identified shortcomings in electric current fault diagnosis research

A significant related contribution, and development of these areas, namely fault diagnosis and traceability within power-line networks will be discussed in detail throughout this chapter.

2. Signal processing techniques

In order to collect useful data from targeted physical assets, various fault diagnosis techniques are used in real environments. Machine condition monitoring data include vibration, electric current, temperature and pressure or environmental data.

There are more studies on isolated machine fault diagnosis [1–5] than multiple motors' signal fault diagnosis [6, 7]. Raw data acquired from sensors were pre-processed before being used for further analysis. Errors caused by background noise, human factors and sensor faults need to be eliminated and appropriate features need to be calculated, selected and/or extracted for further fault diagnosis. Once a number of features are obtained, feature-selection methods need to be employed to identify the most effective features to facilitate the fault diagnosis process [7].

2.1 Feature extraction techniques

For accurate fault diagnosis, data must be turned into information before knowledge can be acquired. To turn waveform data into information, fault condition indicators (features) are extracted and/or selected from the acquired signals. Reliable features generally have the following characteristics [8, 9]:

- Inexpensive computational measurement

- Understandable in physical terms

- Mathematically properly definable

- Insensitive to unnecessary variables

- Uncorrelated with other domain features

After acquiring the spectrum data, different types of signal processing methods have been utilised to extract useful feature information and interpret signal waveform data for further fault diagnosis purposes in motors. Most feature extraction techniques can be divided into three groups, as shown in **Figure 1**:

2.1.1 Time-domain feature

Time-domain methods are based on the statistically characteristic behaviours of the waveform signal in time. The most prominent and simplest features in time-domain analysis are root mean square (RMS) and crest factor (CF) of the signal [10]. Other most frequently used features are variance, kurtosis, standard deviation

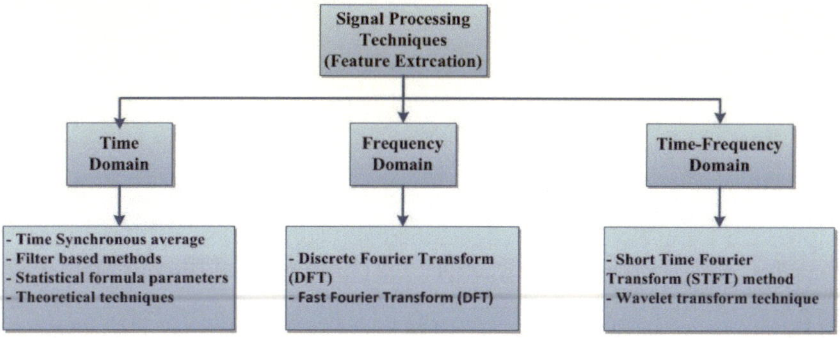

Figure 1.
Overview of common feature extraction techniques.

and skewness. These features are based on the distribution of signal samples with time series random variables also called moments or cumulate. In most constituent moments, the probability density function (PDF) can be broken down into parts, because any change in the signal could alter the behaviour of the PDF and would change the cumulate. Therefore, observing this circumstance can provide useful diagnostic information.

Some other time-domain feature extraction techniques discussed in [10–13] include demodulation and adaptive noise cancelling, filter-based and stochastic techniques. One of the shortcomings of the time-domain feature extraction technique is a lack of visible symptoms of faults particularly when a fault is at an early phase. The technique may be useful when short-duration features are extracted from the signal [12].

RMS is one of the most significant time-domain features and is very efficient in distinguishing any imbalance, related fault in industrial rotating equipment. However, it cannot normally identify explicit failing components. It is also not sensitive enough to detect incipient machinery fault [12]. RMS is the measure of the power content of a waveform and can be expressed as follows:

$$RMS = X_{rms} = \sqrt{\frac{\sum_{n=1}^{N} f^2 S(n)}{\sum_{n=1}^{N} S(n)}} \tag{1}$$

where, f=frequency value; and $S(n)$=spectrum for n^{th} sample of waveform from failing components, that is $n = 1, 2, 3, \ldots, n$.

Crest factor (CF) is expressed as a percentage of the peak level of an input signal to RMS level. However, signal peaks in the time domain lead to change in the CF value dynamically [14]. CF can be useful for the detection of impulse vibration changes. CF is defined as:

$$CrestFactor = CF = \frac{Amp_{\max}}{X_{rms}} \tag{2}$$

where, $Amp_{\max}$ is the maximum value of amplitude in signal.

Other significant time-domain features can be calculated by the following equations:

$$Kurtosis = kur = \frac{\frac{1}{n}(X_{rms})^4}{X_{rms}} \tag{3}$$

$$Variance = \sigma^2 = \frac{1}{2}P(X_{rms})^2 \tag{4}$$

$$Skewness = ske = \frac{P(X_{rms})^3}{X_{rms}} \tag{5}$$

where P indicates the expected value of the function.

An approach using NN has been developed and considers signal vibrations to be input features [15]. They use genetic algorithm [15] to extract the most considerable input features for fault diagnosis contexts. When doing this, six input features are selected from a large set of possible available features. Pineda et al. [16] discussed the major disadvantage of cost for vibration monitoring that require access to the machine.

2.1.2 Frequency-domain feature

Frequency-domain features are capable of overcoming the weaknesses of time-domain analysis. Frequency-domain methods are based on the information that a localised fault is produced by a periodic waveform signal, along with distinctive frequency points and features.

When frequency-domain features are used for fault symptom detection, some changes in frequency-domain parameters may indicate the existence of faults, because diverse faults have different spectrums in the frequency domain. Frequency-domain parameters can be also used for early detection of machine faults and failures [17]. Therefore, such indices can be used to perform fault diagnostics processes.

Fast Fourier transform (FFT) is one of the most commonly used techniques in the frequency domain [18]. The FFT, which is a fast algorithm for discrete Fourier transform (DFT), can easily transform a signal into the frequency domain. If it is difficult to analyse a signal in the time domain, it is easier to transform and analyse it in the frequency domain [17].

To enhance the results of spectrum analysis, several types of frequency filter, side-band structure analysis, demodulation and descriptive representation methods are often used [19]. Different types of frequency spectra, such as power spectrum and high-order spectrum, have been developed. The most traditional way of producing a power spectrum is by using a DFT, but some additional methods can also be used, such as the maximum entropy technique. The following parameters in the frequency domain are commonly used as fault indicators for diagnostics [20].

$$Sideband\_peakvalue = Pv = \max|i(j)| \tag{6}$$

$$Frequency\_Centre = FC = \frac{\sum_{n=1}^{N} f.S(n)}{\sum_{n=1}^{N} S(n)} \tag{7}$$

$$Mean\ Square\ Frequency = \mathrm{MSF} = \frac{\int_0^{+\infty} f^2 p(f)\partial f}{\int^{+\infty} p(f)} \tag{8}$$

$$Root\ Mean\ Square\ Frequency = \mathrm{RMSF} = \sqrt{\frac{\int_0^{+\infty} f^2 p(f)\partial f}{\int^{+\infty} p(f)}} \tag{9}$$

$$\text{Standard deviation Frequency} = SDF = \sqrt{\frac{\sum_{n=1}^{n} (f - f_c)^2 S(n)}{\sum_{n=1}^{n} S(n)}} \tag{10}$$

where, f represents frequency value in cycles per second (Hz); P = number of poles; n_s = synchronous speed in revolutions per minute (RPM); n_r = motor speed in RPM; n = total number of samples; $Amp_{\max}$ = maximum value of amplitude in signal; $i(j)$ = series of signals for $j = 1,2,3, \ldots ,N$ and N is the number of data points in the signal; and $S(n)$ = spectrum for nth sample value, i.e. $n = 1,2,3, \ldots ,n$.

Camps et al. [20] present the measurement of the instantaneous supply frequency for the diagnosis of two electric machines with rotor asymmetries [21]. The technique of instantaneous frequency is used based on the extraction of fault components (RMS, crest factor, etc.) associated with the frequency side bands and the assessment of the instantaneous supply frequency. Furthermore, in case of failure of this technique, the neural network is described in [22] to solve the rotor asymmetries-related faults.

Furthermore, authors [22] suggest further improvements in their previously introduced methodology for the detection of rotor asymmetries and eccentricities for the detection of double-faults rotor asymmetry and eccentricity. They used slip and speed as frequency-domain features on a single isolated motor for fault diagnosis. But in this research, other features are not considered that shows some side bands related to other faults.

Moreover, another relevant study is introduced in [23] that is quite similar with the work discussed in [22]. A critical analysis of temporal lateral side fault component for physically pattern evaluation is presented, with amplitude and frequency values to ends with the proposition method.

The technique proposed in [24] is structured on the extraction of the side-band fault component, and its comparison with the simulated pattern computed in the previous study. It also introduces a method for the quantification of the fault, dividing the spectrum of the fault component of the start-up signal. Mróz et al. [25] introduced a systematised methodology and extended it theoretically to any type of induction machine fault, in which its fault components are a function of the slip, providing a practical guide for the application of the methodology.

2.1.3 Time-frequency domain

Time-frequency methods have the ability to describe machinery fault signatures in both time and frequency domains when the signal is non-stationary [4]. The traditional time-frequency technique uses the time and frequency distributions that signify the energy of the signal in two dimensions.

Short-time Fourier transform (STFT) is the most commonly used distribution technique when the signal is in a non-stationary state [5]. STFT is an enhanced form of Fourier transform (FT). In this technique, the target signal is converted into small windows. After choosing the width of the window function, this is multiplied and shifted with the signal segment to produce concise non-stationary signals. Based on the same procedure, FT is then applied at each segment to obtain the STFT of the signal. This shows the changing behaviour of the frequency spectrum with time value. STFT gives a constant resolution at all necessary frequency points.

Another new time-frequency domain technique is wavelet transform, which overcomes the shortcomings of STFT. This technique is also used to analyse the signal in a non-stationary state with time values. Wavelet transform provides multi-resolution at different frequency levels.

A comparison of FFT, STFT and continuous wavelet transform (CWT) methods [9–11] is summarised in **Table 1**.

2.2 Fault diagnostic methods

Different fault diagnosis techniques have been applied for single and multiple fault diagnosis in industrial machinery systems. The four main types are signal-based, model-based, knowledge-based and hybrid methods [8]. Further classifications of these methods are presented in **Figure 2**.

2.2.1 Signal-based methods

Signal-based methods are largely dependent on signal processing methods for fault diagnosis. Usually, these techniques require pre-identified circumferences. Signals are dependent on features. Once the signal or features pass outside their boundaries, an abnormal situation may be happening [23]. There are many methods available that are based on signal analysis, such as vibration analysis, MCSA, axial flow (AF), torque analysis, noise monitoring and impedance of inverse sequences.

Techniques	Faults diagnosed	Advantages	Disadvantages
FFT [6]	• Broken rotor bar fault • Short winding fault • Air gap eccentricity • Bearing faults	• Suitable for high load conditions • Easy to implement • Good for visualisation fault symptoms	• Lost time information • Not effective in light load condition
STFT [7]	• Broken rotor bar fault • Bearing faults	• Fast speed • Suitable for varying load conditions	• Analyse signal with fixed sized window • Poor frequency resolution
Wavelet transform [8, 9]	• Broken rotor bar fault • Short winding fault • Bearing faults • Load fault	• Fast speed • Suitable for varying load and light load conditions • Excellent low time and frequency resolution for low-frequency side-band components	• Absence of phase information for a complex-value signal • Poor directionality • Shift sensitive for input-signal, causes an unpredictable change in transform coefficients in time.

Table 1.
Comparison between FFT, STFT and CWT.

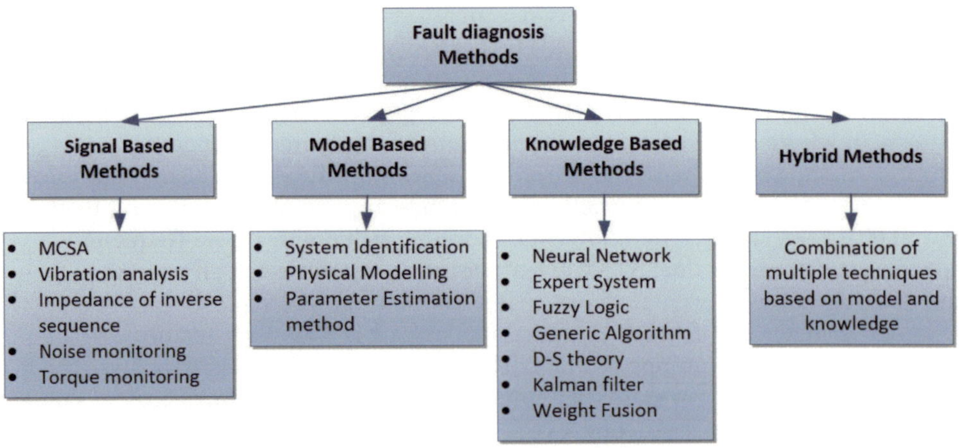

Figure 2.
Classification of different fault diagnosis methods [1].

Most mechanical faults in high-speed rotating machines lead to increase in vibration levels. The largest sources of vibration and noise in electric machines are the radial forces due to the air-gap field. Vibration monitoring is an effective and efficient approach to providing condition indicators for machine health management [24]. Vibration-based diagnostics is the best method for fault diagnosis, but needs expensive accelerometers and associated wiring. This limits its use in several applications, especially in small machines where cost plays a major factor in deciding the condition monitoring method. And this limitation becomes more complex when the diagnosis is based on multiple motors that are running in parallel with much noise.

Some studies [22–25] discussed the multi-motor faults detection methods using vibration analysis when motors are running in isolation from the system. Different signal processing techniques were used for feature extraction. These studies compared different features in time and frequency domain using ANN, but they never observed the different behavioral conditions of multiple motors that simultaneously running within same power-line.

In recent years, the stator current monitoring, well recognised as MCSA, has become the focus for many researchers in both academia and the industry. It can provide an indication of motor condition similar to the indication provided by other monitoring methods (e.g., vibration), without any need to access the motor [14]. In most electrical machine applications, the stator current is usually measured for motor protection. When the motor is being controlled by drive, measuring the current becomes integral to the drive apparatus, which makes it available at no cost. There are three main methods through which captured current data can be analysed for fault detection using current signature analysis. These are: frequency spectral analysis; negative-positive and zero-sequence current components; and Park's vector representation of the three-phase electric current [15].

Different authors [23–26] in recent years have discussed multiple-motor faults detection using MCSA method, but they isolated motors from the system. Author [26] introduced, in a concise manner, MCSA for the diagnosis of abnormal mechanical and electrical conditions that specify, or may cause, a failure of multiple induction motors, but analyse through separation of the system. The MCSA utilises the results of signal analysis of the stator electric current for the detection of broken rotor bars, air-gap eccentricity and other component damage. Another research [27] discussed fault diagnosis using MCSA on multiple motors simultaneously, but they diagnose a single fault and noise level in each motor. However, in this research, the authors did not focus much on uncertainty management due to the complexity of different faulty signals.

A comparison of MCSA, vibration and other methods [13–17] is summarised in **Table 2** as follows.

2.2.2 Model-based methods

Model-based fault diagnosis techniques are normally dependant on the dynamic system model. The model-based methods of an industrial system benefit from the actual system and model output. A comparison can be made between the simulation and actual data outputs and, therefore, through visualisation, the condition of a motor can be ascertained. Dynamic models can be developed using physical modelling, system identification and parameter estimation methods. The most significant problem with the model-based methods is that the accuracy of the developed model describes the behaviour of the diagnosis system [28]. Modelling uncertainty happens from the unfeasibility of obtaining knowledge from monitoring process when the system is running in a noisy environment.

Normally, model-based methods have also been used to collect the dynamic response of systems under normal and fault conditions, by different authors [25–28], but on motors isolated from systems. A general architecture of the model-based method is shown in **Figure 3** as follows.

Typically, model-based methods can be divided into two parts: residual generation and decision-making. A fault diagnostics structure is presented in **Figure 3**. In the first portion of the diagram, process models in healthy and faulty conditions are compared with actual process measurements to produce continuation that describes the present condition of the development. In the second portion, the decision-making process is done based on the residual results. In both parts of fault diagnosis, it applies separate models that can be based on data, knowledge-based or a combination of both analytical models. The residual generation in the fault diagnostics system is normally based on model and pre-defined process outputs, but residuals can be generated through different methods where model parameter features are estimated from process measurements.

2.2.3 Knowledge-based methods

Knowledge-based model strategies usually implement human brain-like knowledge of the process for machine fault diagnosis. In real-time fault diagnostic practices, the human professional expert could be an engineer who applies and operates the diagnosis process, having good knowledge about the strategies and methods of diagnosing multiple motor faults. The knowledge-based methods also work on expertise, like engineers, to diagnose the fault in a motor system when the signal is

Methods	Required measurement	Faults diagnosis	Advantages	Disadvantages
MCSA	Stator electric current	• BRB • Air-gap eccentricity • Stator electric current fault	• Non-sensitive • Low cost	• Limited to some fault conditions at no-load • Frequency levels vary with motor size
Vibration analysis	Accelerometers and associated wiring	• Bearing fault • Other mechanical faults	• Available in many configurations • Integrate to velocity output	• Sensitive to mounting techniques and surface conditions • One accelerometer does not fit all applications
Torque harmonics analysis	Two stator electric current and voltage	• BRB • Mechanical faults in small load • Stator winding fault	• Non-sensitive • Good for mechanical faults detection	Not accurate in short circuit-related faults diagnosis
Axial flow	Axial flow	• Air-gap eccentricity • BRB • Stator current fault	• Cheap solution	• Non-invasive • Not good for dynamic condition
Impedances of inverse sequence	Two stator voltage and electric current values	• Stator winding fault	• Initial faults detection • Non-intrusive	• Needs high measurement accuracy

Table 2.
Summary comparison of MCSA, vibration and other methods.

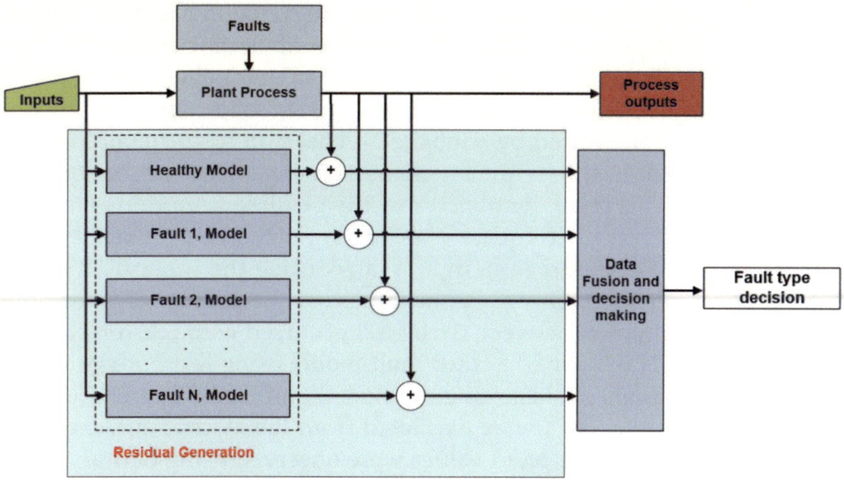

Figure 3.
Architecture of model-based methods.

in a dynamic condition. These methods can be very useful to reduce the percentage of uncertainty when signals are in complex form.

Many studies have been presented in the research area of fault diagnosis using isolated induction motors based on different techniques [28]. The artificial neural network (ANN) has been perhaps the most commonly used artificial intelligence technique in motor condition monitoring and fault diagnosis, due to its excellent pattern recognition ability and ability to recognise fuzzy and indefinite signals. ANN has the following special characteristics, enabling many applications in information fusion and fault diagnosis [29]:

- The neural network has the ability to gain new knowledge, similar to the way human beings acquire their knowledge. The learning process is implemented by continuous adjusting of the weight values among the neurons

- A neural network can be a multi-input and multi-output system (MIMO). This structure demonstrates that neural networks can handle complicated multiple object problems, like multiple faults in a machine

- The neural network processes the information in a parallel way, similar to the way humans process complicated information. This special feature indicates that neural networks can fuse information from different sources simultaneously and naturally

- The knowledge in a trained neural network is stored in a distributed way, by means of a set of weights. This also resembles the way the knowledge is stored in human memory

- A neural network has good fault tolerance performance. This property mainly originates from its parallel structure and distributed information storage system

ANN is reported in the literature as being a knowledge-based technique for single/multiple motor fault diagnosis. These studies perform the diagnoses by mapping different fault symptoms in an isolated motor to produce a diagnosis decision.

Authors [30] presented a diagnosis system based on ANN on machines isolated from system, which applies the RMS measurements of electric current, voltage and speed to train the ANN in diagnosis of motor rotor faults. Voltage faults are only identified in a steady-state condition, not in a dynamic-load condition.

Another study was presented by Shoba [30], based on the influence of the rotor fault on electric current in the frequency domain, using ANN in a steady-motor operating condition. This study demonstrated the possible symptoms of significant frequency components on the frequency spectrum related to a broken rotor bar fault. These symptoms are used as an input matrix using the supervised ANN architecture. The proposed technique concluded that the process of rotor fault diagnosis and discrimination between each fault occurred with reasonable accuracy.

Another author [31] presented a rotor fault model using fast Fourier transform (FFT) and the supervised ANN learning method. Significant features (RMS, crest factor, highest magnitude, etc.) were extracted from the electric current spectrum and all possible high peak side-band values were observed using neural network (NN). The back propagation neural network (BPNN) algorithm is applied for training to detect a rotor fault on a single motor. To introduce complexity to the model, they injected some noisy signals into the healthy spectrum to obtain a reliable and intelligent NN.

Zhou et al. [32] carried out the work on fault diagnosis using four layers of feed forward neural network (FFNN) for identification of broken rotor bar and eccentricity faults. They noted that the accuracy in fault detection was 86–92 %, depending on NN architecture, classification method and number of classified samples. The best NN structure [$11 \times 13 \times 11 \times 2$] was proposed from different architectures, using the Levenberg Marquardt (LM) algorithm with 92.11 % accuracy in classification.

Most fault diagnosis studies based on ANN using isolated motors have been successful. But in the case of a distributed network, this may create confusion through multiple similar motor faults in a network, due to non-linear manipulation of the signal. This sort of complexity and mixture of signals from multiple sources make it difficult to measure and precisely correlate the fault to a given machine or fault type. To overcome this confusion, a distributed ANN approach is used in this research to identify the fault type and location within a motor network on the basis of significant motor features.

2.2.4 Hybrid methods

As each method for fault diagnosis has its own limitations, a combination of several approaches may become a good option. Several different authors have proposed combined techniques such as neuro-fuzzy [27], neural network and Bayesian interface [28] and DS theory with expert system [29]. A hybrid system called generic integrated intelligent system architecture was proposed for equipment monitoring, fault diagnosis and maintenance [30]. The system integrated different AI techniques such as fuzzy logic and neural network.

A hybrid method [31] was developed that used neural networks to estimate an engine's internal health, and generic algorithms to detect and estimate sensor bias. The method had the advantage of a non-linear approximation facility provided by neural networks, and advances the system robustness in measuring uncertainty through the combination of generic algorithms within the application.

2.3 Propagation of fault signal in industrial power-line network

In an industrial power-line network, when a faulty wave signal propagates within the main power-line, it shows a strong relationship between the electric current and voltage waves with certain impedance characteristics [32]. The given input impedance of the multiple connected electric motors has been an interesting parameter, mainly in the closeness of the grid frequency (50/60 Hz) [33]. The importance of input impedance at a higher signal frequency level has gained attention due to the universal usage of available motor variable speed drives. The fast switching between the different phases of power semiconductors of the inverter injects different signals with high energy contents and a large frequency spectrum into the motor feeder cable. Due to the injection of the spectrum into the power-line network, it can generate electromagnetic emission, invertor problems and damage the insulation winding of induction motors. The presence of these complications is related to the impedance discrepancy between the motor and industrial feeder cable. As discussed earlier, the induction motor acts as a termination impedance when transmitting signals into an industrial low-voltage distribution network between the power-line and motor network. The high-frequency signal characteristics of the induction motor may affect the influence of the high-frequency characteristics of the main power-line path.

Induction motors within power-line network depend on several factors based on input impedance. In supplying the grid, different frequencies propagate close to the supply frequency and change the behaviour of different motor characteristics due to the injection of electric current signals into the induction motor terminals through stator winding. In this case, the input impedance may rely on the leakage induction, magnetisation inductance of the stator coils resistance and mechanical torque load of the induction motor [33]. At high levels of frequency, the input impedance of induction motors may be affected due to capacitance and leakage inductance. Furthermore, due to the skin effect, all resistances of induction motors increase, depending on frequency points.

There are a number of approaches that describe the propagation of fault signals throughout the power-line network. But power-line communication (PLC) is a widely used strategy in the industrial power system to transfer transmission control messages through the power line network. PLC technology uses the power lines for signal propagation. Frequencies in the range of 30–500 kHz have been utilised in the industry for PLC communication [34]. These ranges of frequency are considered sufficient to be isolated from the normal operation of the power system. The available impedance characteristics of a power transmission-line are presented as the ratio between the electric current and voltage of the travelling waves with an infinite spectrum length.

The fault signal may manifest within the electric current of different motors through the main power-line. It can be suffered from attenuation factor due to power-line characteristics and show faulty impedance pattern at the junction points of motors connections. The propagation delay between the multiple paths of the signal can result in disturbance of the signal. Therefore, attenuation is a very significant factor because it decides the signal strength as a function of distance; therefore, it plays an important role in validating the locations of faulty motors with in the power-line network. Continuous propagation of signal impedance in power-line becomes a combination of the inductance, resistance and parallel capacitance of the transmission line [35].

Several studies have been presented [32–35] about implementation of the PLC concept in power-lines for fault diagnosis. The propagating frequency of PLC channels is higher than the fault signature frequency and is useful in estimating the attenuation level over transmission lines. However, the calculation method combines with some technical approaches to develop a fault and attenuation pattern. For the authenticity of the fault signal within power-line network, different measuring points would be a better approach to diagnosing the origin of a fault generator.

2.4 Industrial fault diagnosis using wireless sensor networks

Several WSN solutions for industrial machinery have been developed and reported on from commercial organisations [32, 33] or individual researchers [34, 35]. Most of these solutions only use the WSN for data acquisition and transmitting signals. Feature extraction and data fusion tasks are then performed on a central computer. Upon sensor data acquisition, feature extraction and fault diagnosis is another tactic capable of diffusing raw data that can scale down the number of features and save node power. But most of these solutions are based on isolated motors. Industrial wireless sensor network (IWSN) for motor fault diagnosis and condition monitoring needs to consider the high-power system requirements of industrial processes and the distinctive available characteristics of motors [34]. Some industrial processes are very important, such as high sampling rate, quick data transmission rate and reliability of data. However, there are constraints in IWSN, such as computational ability, limited radio bandwidth and battery energy. Thus, limitations exist between the high system requirements of electrical machine fault diagnosis and the resource constraints feature characteristics of IWSN.

Some recent literature focuses on the application of IWSN in machine condition monitoring and fault diagnosis, pumping fault diagnosis, manufacturing machines, smart grids, power plants and structural health monitoring. Ref. [34] presents electric current and vibration-based data acquisition for monitoring rotating machinery in power plants. They present a sensor-level data fusion algorithm to diagnose the condition of isolated machines. A comparison result has been performed between available fused and healthy data by using wireless nodes. A time-series data judgement and task-level fusion algorithm was introduced to reduce power and bandwidth needs.

The authors, in [35], introduced a diagnosis solution using electric current and vibration signature data acquisition system for observing rotating machinery at power plants. The diagnosis system monitors the motor vibration and stator electric current signatures from two different motors. Node-level feature extraction techniques were implemented and a neural network classification method used for training and uncertainty management. Decision-level fusion was implemented at the node coordinator. The training was executed in offline mode in an efficient manner, and the BRB and eccentricity fault states have to be detected manually at two experimental motors by applying different load levels.

2.5 Shortcomings in existing fault diagnosis research

The current harmonics present in the motor electric current are mainly created by machine asymmetries and vibrations from machine faults. The reliability of signal-processing techniques depends upon a good understanding of the electric and mechanical characteristics of the machine in both a healthy and faulted state under different loading conditions. The following shortcomings were identified on the basis of information discussed in the literature review:

- Most of research has been effectively tested on isolate motors to diagnose its current condition and performance by comparing healthy and faulty motors characteristics. Limited research has been done on distributed multi-motor signature analysis where all motors are part of the system and propagate a faulty signal over the network.

- Some limitations have been perceived in implementing diagnosis in a distributed motor network, with confusion between different similar machine fault symptoms in the power-line network, and lack of accuracy in the analysis system due to the existence of non-linear interference from industrial noise signals.

- There has been only limited research on the effect of load variations on the amplitudes of fault frequency components under healthy and faulty conditions. The majority of the studies only consider a full-load case, with limited research considering partial-load cases. To detect faults and estimate fault severity in machines, using characteristic fault frequencies, it is important to examine the variability in their amplitudes with other effects than load and fault severity. This area has had limited research on machine condition monitoring.

- Few studies have focused on the detection of multiple faults, that is, the combination of broken rotor bars and eccentricity faults under varying loading conditions.

- The majority of studies considered only the stator electric current as a diagnostic medium to detect different faults in induction motors. Only a few researchers have proposed using an instantaneous network power signal as a diagnostic medium to detect rotor-related faults under different load conditions. The use of instantaneous power to detect other major faults in the machines (eccentricity, shorted turn and misalignment) and multiple faults (combinations of different faults) under varying loading condition has not been reported in previous research.

- Insensitivity to and independence of operating conditions in the power-line network system.

- Utilisation of the neural network technique on distributed industrial motor networks has not been reported in previous research where the signal propagation process could change the pattern behaviour of each neighbouring motor and create a confusion in identifying the actual source of fault indices.

- To date, distributed signature analysis using WSN with sensor-level data fusion, based on multiple motors that are propagating signals into the power-line network, is a relatively unexplored topic where all motors send their respective features, data to central computer for fault diagnosis.

Based on the above-identified shortcomings, the focus of this research was to diagnose multiple faults when all motors operating are part of system and propagating a faulty signal over the network can create confusion between different similar motor faults symptoms in the power-line network. To overcome this confusion, ANN was utilised in identification of fault indices within a network when faulty signals manifest into healthy signals from other motors. Finally, wireless sensor-level data fusion was implemented using an Arduino development kit to improve efficiency and accuracy in decision-making when all motors are operating in parallel.

3. Conclusions

This chapter has covered a variety of different topics, as well as several particular techniques, algorithms, approaches and methods. The literature was mainly categorised into three major themes: fault propagation and diagnosis in power-line network; data fusion and wireless sensor networks. The following conclusions were drawn from the literature review:

- Machinery fault diagnosis has been too reliant on single information sources of data, especially electric current or vibration data. The use of multiple information sources for fault diagnosis from multiple connected motors within the same power-line has not been well addressed and is an unexplored area.
- Correct feature extraction and selection increase the performance of a network and reduce the network input dimensions and training time.
- Consideration of multi-parameter data-fusion techniques can play a vital role in improving system performance, such as in accuracy, reliability and robustness.
- Deployment of the WSN in industrial-machinery fault diagnosis can improve its efficiency and reliability, and reduce the chances of uncertainty in management of complex data.

Based on the above concluding points, the scope for this research was limited to the significant utilisation of available advanced techniques and approaches for feature extraction and motor fault diagnosis using WSN.

Acknowledgements

- The authors would like to thank AUT University and Ministry of Science and Innovation, New Zealand for funding the research.
- The authors extend their appreciation to the Deanship of Scientific Research at King Saud University for funding this work through research group No. (RG-1438-089).

Conflict of interest

The authors declare that there is no conflict of interest regarding the publication of this book chapter.

Author details

Saud Altaf[1*] and Shafiq Ahmad[2*]

1 School of Engineering, Computer and Mathematical Sciences, Auckland University of Technology, New Zealand

2 Department of Industrial Engineering, King Saud University, Saudia Arabia

*Address all correspondence to: saltaf@aut.ac.nz and ashafiq@ksu.edu.sa

References

[1] Altaf S. Smart sensor network organization: Sensor data fusion and industrial fault traceability [thesis]. Auckland University of Technology; 2015. Available from: http://hdl.handle.net/10292/9271

[2] Altaf S, Soomro M, Mehmood M. Fault diagnosis and detection in industrial motor network environment using knowledge-level modelling technique. Modelling and Simulation in Engineering. 2017;**2017**:1-10. DOI: 10.1155/2017/1292190

[3] Altaf S, Al-A A, Hosseini HG. Fault signal propagation in a network of distributed motors. In: Proceedings of the 2014 IEEE 8th International Power Engineering and Optimization Conference (PEOCO '14); March 2014, Langkawi, Malaysia. pp. 59-63. DOI: 10.1109/PEOCO.2014.6814399

[4] Subramanian S, Ghouse F, Natarajan P. Fault diagnosis of batch reactor using machine learning methods. Modelling and Simulation in Engineering. 2014;**2014**:1-14. DOI: 10.1155/2014/426402

[5] You L, Fan W, Li Z, Liang Y, Fang M, Wang J. A fault diagnosis model for rotating machinery using VWC and MSFLA-SVM based on vibration signal analysis. Shock and Vibration. 2019; **2019**:1-16. DOI: 10.1155/2019/1908485

[6] Bing H, Zhao Y, Pang L, Zhao M. Research on fault diagnosis model of rotating machinery vibration based on information entropy and improved SVM. E3S Web of Conferences. 2019; **118**:02036. DOI: 10.1051/e3sconf/201911802036

[7] Jiang L, Yin H, Li X, Tang S. Fault diagnosis of rotating machinery based on multi-sensor information fusion using SVM and time-domain features. Shock and Vibration. 2014;**2014**:1-8. DOI: 10.1155/2014/418178

[8] Ayhan B, Chow M-Y, Song M-H. Multiple discriminant analysis and neural-network-based monolith and partition fault-detection schemes for broken rotor bar in induction motors. IEEE Transactions on Industrial Electronics. 2006;**53**(4):1298-1308. DOI: 10.1109/tie.2006.878301

[9] Altaf S, Mehmood MS, Soomro MW. Advancement of fault diagnosis and detection process in industrial machine environment. Journal of Engineering Sciences. 2019;**6**(2):d1-d8. DOI: 10.21272/jes.2019.6(2).d1

[10] Shahriar MR, Ahsan T, Chong U. Fault diagnosis of induction motors utilizing local binary pattern-based texture analysis. EURASIP Journal on Image and Video Processing. 2013;**2013**(1). DOI: 10.1186/1687-5281-2013-29

[11] Diagnosis of broken bars fault in induction motors. Fault Diagnosis of Induction Motors. 2017:367-429. DOI: 10.1049/pbpo108e_ch8

[12] Kim Y-H, Youn Y-W, Hwang D-H, Sun J-H, Kang D-S. High-resolution parameter estimation method to identify broken rotor bar faults in induction motors. IEEE Transactions on Industrial Electronics. 2013;**60**(9):4103-4117. DOI: 10.1109/tie.2012.2227912

[13] Edomwandekhoe K, Liang X. Current spectral analysis of broken rotor bar faults for induction motors. In: Proceedings of the 2018 IEEE Canadian Conference on Electrical & Computer Engineering (CCECE). 2018. DOI: 10.1109/ccece.2018.8447776

[14] Xu BQ, Tian SH. A detection method for broken rotor bar fault in induction motors based on SVD combined MUSIC with extended Prony.

Applied Mechanics and Materials. 2014; **707**:333-337. DOI: 10.4028/www.scientific.net/amm.707.333

[15] Pandarakone SE, Mizuno Y, Nakamura H. A comparative study between machine learning algorithm and artificial intelligence neural network in detecting minor bearing fault of induction motors. Energies. 2019;**12**(11):2105. DOI: 10.3390/en12112105

[16] Pineda-Sanchez M, Riera-Guasp M, Antonino-Daviu J, Roger-Folch J, Perez-Cruz J, Puche-Panadero R. Instantaneous frequency of the left sideband harmonic during the start-up transient: A new method for diagnosis of broken bars. IEEE Transactions on Industrial Electronics. 2009;**56**(11): 4557-4570. DOI: 10.1109/tie.2009.2026211

[17] Ameid T, Menacer A, Talhaoui H, Harzelli I. Broken rotor bar fault diagnosis using fast Fourier transform applied to field-oriented control induction machine: Simulation and experimental study. The International Journal of Advanced Manufacturing Technology. 2017;**92**(1–4):917-928. DOI: 10.1007/s00170-017-0143-2

[18] Magno M, Sigrist L, Gomez A, Cavigelli L, Libri A, Popovici E, et al. SmarTEG: An autonomous wireless sensor node for high accuracy accelerometer-based monitoring. Sensors. 2019;**19**(12):2747. DOI: 10.3390/s19122747

[19] Kia S. Monitoring of wound rotor induction machines by means of discrete wavelet transform. Electric Power Components and Systems. 2018; **46**(19–20):2021-2035. DOI: 10.1080/15325008.2018.1562647

[20] Barusu M, Sethurajan U, Deivasigamani M. Non-invasive method for rotor bar fault diagnosis in three-phase squirrel cage induction motor with advanced signal processing technique. The Journal of Engineering. 2019;**2019**(17):4415-4419. DOI: 10.1049/joe.2018.8242

[21] Keskes H, Braham A. Recursive undecimated wavelet packet transform and DAG SVM for induction motor diagnosis. IEEE Transactions on Industrial Informatics. 2015;**11**(5): 1059-1066. DOI: 10.1109/tii.2015.2462315

[22] Camps Echevarría L, Llanes Santiago O, Campos Velho H, Silva NA. Fault Diagnosis Inverse Problems. Cham: Springer International Publishing AG; 2018. DOI: 10.1007/978-3-319-89978-7

[23] Gertler J. Fault Detection and Diagnosis in Engineering Systems. [S.l.]: CRC Press; 2019. DOI: 10.1201/9780203756126

[24] Antonino-Daviu J, Riera-Guasp M, Pons-Llinares J, Park J, Lee S, Yoo J, et al. Detection of broken outer-cage bars for double-cage induction motors under the startup transient. IEEE Transactions on Industry Applications. 2012;**48**(5):1539-1548. DOI: 10.1109/tia.2012.2210173

[25] Boughrara K, Takorabet N, Ibtiouen R, Touhami O, Dubas F. Analytical analysis of cage rotor induction motors in healthy, defective, and broken bars conditions. IEEE Transactions on Magnetics. 2015;**51**(2): 1-17. DOI: 10.1109/tmag.2014.2349480

[26] Mróz J, Poprawski W. Improvement of the thermal and mechanical strength of the starting cage of double-cage induction motors. Energies. 2019; **12**(23):4551. DOI: 10.3390/en12234551

[27] Martinez J, Belahcen A, Arkkio A. Broken bar indicators for cage induction motors and their relationship with the number of consecutive broken bars. IET

Electric Power Applications. 2013;**7**(8): 633-642. DOI: 10.1049/iet-epa.2012.0338

[28] Guo H, Liu M-K. Induction motor faults diagnosis using support vector machine to the motor current signature. In: 2018 IEEE Industrial Cyber-Physical Systems (ICPS). 2018. DOI: 10.1109/icphys.2018.8390701

[29] Qing-Feng Z, Shao-Wei G, Zong-Xiang C, Lu-Sheng G. Motor bearing faults diagnosis using modified empirical mode decomposition and bi-spectrum. In: 2018 13th IEEE Conference on Industrial Electronics and Applications (ICIEA). 2018. DOI: 10.1109/iciea.2018.8398043

[30] Шавкун ВМ. Diagnostics of electric transport traction electric machines. Eastern-European Journal of Enterprise Technologies. 2014;7(67):48. DOI: 10.15587/1729-4061.2014.20196

[31] Shoba P, Arivuselvam B. Induction motor conditional monitoring using wireless sensor network. Applied Mechanics and Materials. 2014;**626**: 95-100. DOI: 10.4028/www.scientific.net/amm.626.95

[32] Cheng Y, Liu Q, Wang J, Wan S, Umer T. Distributed fault detection for wireless sensor networks based on support vector regression. Wireless Communications and Mobile Computing. 2018;**2018**:1-8. DOI: 10.1155/2018/4349795

[33] Lu S, Zhou P, Wang X, Liu Y, Liu F, Zhao J. Condition monitoring and fault diagnosis of motor bearings using undersampled vibration signals from a wireless sensor network. Journal of Sound and Vibration. 2018;**414**:81-96. DOI: 10.1016/j.jsv.2017.11.007

[34] Huang J, Chen G, Shu L, Zhang Q, Wu X. WSNs-based mechanical equipment state monitoring and fault diagnosis in China. International Journal of Distributed Sensor Networks. 2015; **11**(11):528464. DOI: 10.1155/2015/528464

[35] Bergmann NW, Hou L. Machine condition monitoring with industrial wireless sensor networks. Industrial Wireless Sensor Networks. 2017:23-45. DOI: 10.1201/b14072-2

Chapter 11

Semiconductor Device Modeling and Simulation for Electronic Circuit Design

Samira Shamsir, Md Sakib Hasan, Omiya Hassan, Partha Sarathi Paul, Md Razuan Hossain and Syed K. Islam

Abstract

This chapter covers different methods of semiconductor device modeling for electronic circuit simulation. It presents a discussion on physics-based analytical modeling approach to predict device operation at specific conditions such as applied bias (e.g., voltages and currents); environment (e.g., temperature, noise); and physical characteristics (e.g., geometry, doping levels). However, formulation of device model involves trade-off between accuracy and computational speed and for most practical operation such as for SPICE-based circuit simulator, empirical modeling approach is often preferred. Thus, this chapter also covers empirical modeling approaches to predict device operation by implementing mathematically fitted equations. In addition, it includes numerical device modeling approaches, which involve numerical device simulation using different types of commercial computer-based tools. Numerical models are used as virtual environment for device optimization under different conditions and the results can be used to validate the simulation models for other operating conditions.

Keywords: device modeling, physics-based model, empirical modeling, TCAD device simulation, SPICE model

1. Introduction

Researchers are devoting their time and efforts on the development of efficient and high-speed device models as the requirement for faster, smaller circuits and systems are becoming more and more stringent. These models take into account semiconductor devices such as MOSFETs and analyze the device features through rigorous testing and optimization of the device characteristics. The device models are developed employing various mathematical calculations and simulation processes before being adopted into practical circuit and system-level simulation steps. This book chapter takes a deeper dive into different types of semiconductor device modeling and simulation techniques by leveraging their full potential.

To understand the characteristics of a device, analytical modeling is performed under various environmental and operating conditions by varying the device parameters. Physics-based analytical models are developed by analyzing the behaviors of a device based on the fundamental physics by solving rigorous mathematical equations governing the underlying device physics. This enables selection of optimal device features and predictability of the device operation under various conditions to simulate its performance in electronic circuits and systems. Although this type of modeling provides accurate results, the calculation scheme is not fast enough for higher level analysis tools including circuit simulators such as SPICE. For fast calculation of device characteristics, empirical models are commonly used. Empirical modeling is a computer-based modeling scheme involving experimental data. Unlike analytical modeling approach, this specific technique depends on simulation of device behavior by implementing mathematically fitted equations. This results in a trade-off between the accuracy of device models and the computational speed. Empirical modeling of a device plays a leading role in circuit simulation using tools such as SPICE, which is a general-purpose analog electronic circuit simulator. It has the capability to analyze and predict the device behavior in a circuit design by solving a combination of theoretical and empirical models. However, to explore full potential of a device in implementing efficient circuits, researchers are dedicating much time in implementing numerical models using commercial device simulators such as technology computer-aided design (TCAD) tools. Numerical modeling optimizes the characteristics of a device by simulating the device in virtual environment. This type of modeling of a device involves solutions to a set of coupled partial differential equations. The core concept of this type of modeling involves analyzing various mathematical techniques to provide a realistic solution for predictability and operation of the device. Creating virtual environment under different conditions to simulate various device features and characteristics enables researchers to achieve a grasp on the functionality of a certain device and its characteristics in circuit environment.

2. Physics-based and empirical compact modeling for circuit simulation

2.1 Physics-based models

Physics-based models are developed by simplifying coupled nonlinear partial differential equations that describe the physics of the semiconductor devices. These models need to be robust, accurate, and computationally efficient and are often preferred in analog and RF circuit design. Although modern industry standard models often have some empirical fitting parameters, their core is usually physics-based and most parameters have some physical significance. Since these models try to capture the essence of underlying physics, they usually have better scalability and predictive power compared to their empirical counterparts.

2.1.1 Types of physics-based models

Physics-based compact models can be divided into several subcategories. The most widely used models in industry are BSIM3 [1] and BSIM4 [2]. These models are threshold-based, source-referenced, characterized by inversion charge proportional to overdrive voltage, and use interpolation between strong and weak inversion. In addition, some empirical fitting parameters are used in these models to cover wide bias, geometry, and temperature ranges.

Surface potential-based models such as PSP [3] and HiSIM [4] have recently emerged as other important physics-based compact modeling paradigms. PSP was developed as a collaboration between Gildenblat et al. and Philips corporation and is characterized by both inversion charge and drain current being computed from the surface potential φ_s. This is a symmetric and body-referenced model whose core idea rests upon the symmetric linearization of surface potential, which provides an efficient solution for surface potential with 10 pV accuracy.

Another approach is known as inversion charge-based model such as EKV named after its founders (Enz-Krmmencher-Vittoz) [5] and ACM (Advanced Compact model) [6]. EKV was originally developed at CSEM and EPFL at Switzerland and has found use in low-power and RF integrated circuit (IC) design due to some of the shortcomings of BSIM-based models in these applications. It is a body-referenced and symmetric model based on channel charge linearization. There is also a companion model for hand analysis.

In addition to these popular choices, there are other models such as, analytical model for ballistic field-effect transistors [7], MIT Virtual Source model [8] etc. Although these models are not used in industry, they involve a relatively small set of parameters with strong physical significance and can provide useful insight into the underlying physical phenomena of nanoscale transistors.

2.1.2 Brief overview of previous works

A number of works have been performed over the years on physics-based modeling of transistors. Gummel in [9] developed a model based on finite difference method for solving model equations to provide information about internal parameters such as potential and electric field distribution along with the terminal characteristics. This approach was modified in [10] using a new discretization technique for ensuring convergence. Building upon Scharfetter-Gummel algorithm, Slotboom [11] proposed a new model using two new artificial variables for linearization of differential equations facilitating implementation in computer-aided design (CAD) programs.

Early pioneers of device modeling include Pao and Sah who came up with the classic double integral drain current expression and explored different characteristics of transistor action [12, 13]. However, these formulas are computation intensive and CAD implementation requires a simplified model. Brews in [14] proposed a charge sheet model that assumes the inversion layer to be a conducting plane of zero thickness.

As the transistors kept getting smaller, the significance of subthreshold leakage conduction became apparent and the authors in [15] explored basic charge equation to derive a model that covers conduction mechanism from subthreshold to strong inversion. A one-dimensional model reported in [16] incorporates the dependence of subthreshold conduction on drain voltage, substrate bias, and temperature. The effect of terminal voltages on subthreshold conduction was captured in another model proposed by Taylor [17], which also explored the potential adverse two-dimensional effects on drain conductance. Later, Taylor unified the existing short- and long-channel models into an analytical model in [18]. Moreover, with the increasing use of MOSFETs in the domain of analog circuit design, there has been a growing need for a better small signal CAD models. Liu et al. presented a first-order and a second-order large-signal MOSFET models and derived corresponding small-signal models where the parameters are associated with bias condition and process technology [19].

Several researchers have explored the effect of electric field, doping density, and temperature on carrier mobility. Arora et al. developed an analytical expression of carrier mobilities in silicon as a function of doping concentration and temperature based on experimental data and modified Brooks-Herring theory of mobility [20]. Masetti et al. explored the dependence of carrier mobility on dopant concentration in silicon [21]. Later, Reggiani et al. proposed a unified model that combines mobility dependence on multiple factors such as doping, temperature, and electric field

[22]. Another major contribution was the development of a universal expression for carrier generation and recombination, which was independently reported by Hall [23] and Shockley-Read [24] in 1952. Carrier lifetime is the most important parameter affecting the rate of generation-recombination and its dependence on temperature and electric field was analyzed by Schenk in [25].

The first-generation CAD models refer to the three built-in models (Level 1, 2, and 3) in the SPICE2 program [26]. Sheu et al. developed CSIM (Compact Short-channel IGFET Model) [27] and later improved and converted it into its now-famous successor called "Berkeley Short-channel IGFET Model" (BSIM) [28]. This was the beginning of the second generation of SPICE models. Technical considerations underlying the evolution of these models will be explored in greater detail in Section 2.5.

2.2 Empirical model

Empirical modeling is an alternative to physics-based modeling, which is used for rapid and accurate circuit simulation. The basic methodology is to take experimental or simulated device data as input and then create a model capable of accurately reproducing the complex nonlinear behavior of the semiconductor devices under different operating conditions using some sort of special functions such as Black-Box model or table look-up models. Usually, these methods are flexible and can be applied to different types of transistors [29].

2.2.1 Types of empirical models

The most commonly used empirical models utilize look-up table and quadratic or higher order polynomials for interpolation between data points. The data can be obtained from TCAD simulations or experimental results. Some simulators internally use table look-up methods for faster simulation. Currently, there are some mixed-device circuit simulators, which can generate table look-up models from TCAD simulations for carrying out circuit simulation. These methods can have some serious drawbacks such as wiggles in I-V characteristics, nonphysical negative resistances, limited applicability in exponentially varying regions of operation resulting from the use of low-order polynomial interpolation, inability to accommodate changes in temperature and geometry, limited capability for modeling statistical variation and noise, and lack of predictive capabilities for future technologies.

Another method involves using special functions such as hyperbolic tangent in an ingenious way to match the shape of experimental data. Parameters tend to be fitting coefficients but they may have some sort of first-order physical significance. A different approach, known as Black-Box modeling, leverages sophisticated numerical packages that take arbitrary sets of data and automatically generate some form of mathematical model that best fits the supplied data. This approach has mostly been confined to complex interconnect structures and system-level modeling. The boundary between physics-based and empirical models has gradually become fuzzier in recent years since most modern industry standard physics-based models now have some empirical content.

2.2.2 Brief overview of previous works

The table look-up method was implemented for digital circuit simulation in the timing simulator MOTIS [30], which was used to obtain timing information on the propagation of signals through circuits. Rofougaran et al. reported a FET model consisting of a main look-up table, along with a coarse 3-D sub-table for including substrate effects and another table for interpolating between different channel lengths [31]. This was used to resolve some of the limitations faced by analytical models in capturing short-channel effects. Another table-based method was used in [32] to address the requirements of analog circuit design, which demands greater accuracy in reproducing small-signal parameters, large-signal nonlinearities, subthreshold conduction, body effects, and bias-dependent capacitances.

Meijer proposed an n-dimensional model with first-order continuity in [33] where each table model could replicate the DC I-V characteristics of two basic physical device models, namely, the Ebers-Moll model for bipolar transistor and the GLASMOST model for MOSFET with higher accuracy and faster simulation time compared to physics-based compact models. Bourenkov et al. implemented ingeniously combined exponential and polynomial interpolation into a blending function to accurately evaluate drain current in the moderate inversion region [34]. The user can choose among several available interpolation schemes based on speed, memory, and accuracy requirement and the scheme worked well for DC, transient, and AC analyses. Root et al. used table data to develop non-quasi-static FET models for RF simulation [35]. In these models, the characteristics of GaAs FET devices were determined by state functions, which define nonlinear relationships for the three-terminal lumped elements. An array of s-parameters, measured over a wide range of terminal biases, is used to determine state functions, which dictate the characteristics of GaAs devices.

Yanilmaz et al. extended Bernstein approximation technique to multidimensional variation diminishing interpolation and modeled DC I-V and Q-V characteristics of a MOSFET [36]. An important attribute of this model is the preservation of continuity and monotonicity, which are important for convergence in Newton-Raphson algorithm commonly used in most modern circuit simulators. Similarly, the authors in [37] have used Lagrange interpolation and Bernstein approximation techniques for modeling multi-gate SOI transistors. Shima et al. employed monotonic piecewise cubic interpolation on stored table data obtained from a 2-D TCAD simulator to evaluate operating points of MOS transistors [38]. Authors in [39] used a tableau-style quadratic spline formulation that ensured the continuity of the model function and its derivative and proposed a new data-compression method for efficient storage of coefficients. The authors in [40] have used multidimensional linear and cubic spline interpolation methods for modeling SOI four-gate transistor (G4FET).

2.3 CAD model for SPICE

2.3.1 Criteria for a good SPICE model

A comprehensive list of attributes of a good CAD model for circuit simulation can be found in [41]. In this section, a brief discussion on the most salient features of an excellent compact model is presented. To design analog and mixed analog/digital circuits effectively, CAD models have to meet some basic requirements based on I-V characteristics, charges, leakage currents etc.; should provide continuous results that must have physical sense; should meet the requirement for intrinsic and extrinsic effects; and should provide accurate prediction for temperature range of interests etc. In addition, the model must have criteria for any combination of channel length and width values from the minimum specified upward bound and should provide a flag when it is used outside the limit of validity. Finally, and perhaps most importantly, a compact model must be computationally efficient, sufficiently accurate, and numerically robust.

2.3.2 Model formulation

The model developers need to satisfy certain criteria beyond model simulation. The general considerations include choice of parameters [42], choice of references [43], choice of modeling expressions [44], out of range behavior [42], charge versus capacitance formulation [45], and non-quasi-static analysis [46]. Furthermore, there are two important points, namely the choice of smoothing function and the judicious use of conditionals, which are the topics of the following discussion.

Smoothing function is an important tool to build a single expression by combining several expressions. Sometimes it is hard to model a device with general expressions for different regions of operation. The resultant single expression from smoothing function can be used for all the regions. However, the smoothing functions reveal particular expression in particular regions while maintaining continuity at boundaries between regions.

For example, the traditional MOSFET drain current, I_{DS} with an abrupt transition from non-saturation to saturation operation at a drain-source voltage, V'_{DS} can be written as shown in the following equation [42],

$$I_{DS} = \frac{W}{L}\mu C'_{ox}\left[(V_{GS} - V_{TH}) - \frac{\alpha}{2}V_{DS,eff}\right] \tag{1}$$

$$\text{where, } V_{DS,eff} = \begin{cases} V_{DS}, & V_{DS} \leq V'_{DS} \\ V'_{DS}, & V_{DS} > V'_{DS} \end{cases}$$

where μ is the mobility, W and L are the channel width and length respectively, C'_{ox} is the oxide capacitance, V_{TH} is the threshold voltage, V_{GS} is the gate-source voltage, and α is a fitting parameter. Now, rather than using two conditional terms for $V_{DS,eff}$, the equation can be simplified and converted into a single expression using smoothing function. The following equations are based on [47, 48],

$$V_{DS,eff} = V'_{DS} - 0.5 * \left[V'_{DS} - V_{DS} - \delta + \sqrt{(V'_{DS} - V_{DS} - \delta)^2 + 4\delta V'_{DS}}\right] \tag{2}$$

and

$$V_{DS,eff} = \frac{V_{DS}}{\left[1 + \left[\frac{|V_{DS}|}{V'_{DS}}\right]^A\right]^{1/A}} \tag{3}$$

Here δ and A are fitting parameters. **Figure 1** shows how these functions make the transition region smooth and conserve higher order continuity. Similarly, other functions are used for smooth transition between weak- and strong-inversion [49].

Sometimes, it is hard to maintain perfectly smooth model without using any conditionals. For efficiency, conditional models are used to include or exclude block models that are turned on or off by using different model parameters [47]. For example, let us consider the following common limiting function:

$$y = \frac{1}{A}\ln\left[1 + \exp(Ax)\right] \tag{4}$$

This function asymptotically approaches zero for large negative x and approaches x for large positive x. But it may cause a numeric overflow for large positive x, which can be solved using the following equivalent conditional equation:

$$y = \begin{cases} \frac{1}{A}\ln\left[1+\exp\left(Ax\right)\right], x \le 0 \\ x + \frac{1}{A}\ln\left[1+\exp\left(-Ax\right)\right], x > 0 \end{cases} \quad (5)$$

2.3.3 Evolution of different generations of CAD models for SPICE

The "Simulation Program with Integrated Circuit Emphasis" (SPICE) was developed in the Electronics Research Laboratory at the University of California, Berkeley in 1973 [50]. However, the real popularity of SPICE comes after the release of SPICE 2 in 1975, which included three first-generation MOSFET models for the first time [51]. The first-generation compact models for MOSFET include Level 1, Level 2, and Level 3 models. The second-generation models are BSIM, BSIM2, and HSPICE Level 28. The third-generation models include Level 7, Level 48, BSIM3, and other advanced models. The following section presents the chronological progression from the Level 1 model to Level 3 and finally to BSIM models.

Level 1 model: This first SPICE model for MOS transistor, published in 1968, is often referred to as the Shichman-Hodges model [52]. It is the simplest compact model that is only accurate for long-channel (more than ~10 μm) MOSFETs with uniform doping. This threshold voltage-based model assumes that, when the gate-to-source voltage, V_{GS}, is greater than or equal to the threshold voltage, V_{TH}, then the carrier concentration at the surface under the gate oxide gets inverted in polarity with respect to the substrate. The threshold voltage, V_{TH} as expressed in Eq. (6), is a function of the body effect parameter, γ, the potential difference between the source and the substrate, V_{BS}, and the bulk potential, $2\phi_p$ [53]. In Eq. (6), V_{TO} represents the threshold voltage when V_{BS} = 0.

$$V_{TH} = V_{TO} + \gamma\left(\sqrt{2\phi_p - V_{BS}} - \sqrt{2\phi_p}\right) \quad (6)$$

In this model, the MOSFET operation is divided into three regions. When $V_{GS} < V_{TH}$, the drain-to-source current, I_{DS}, is zero. This is called the cutoff region. When $V_{GS} > V_{TH}$, the MOSFET is turned on. In this state, if the drain-to-source voltage,

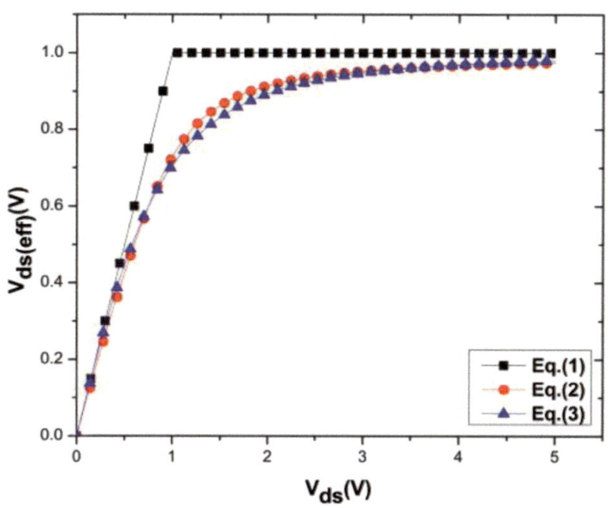

Figure 1.
Illustration of two smoothing functions for ensuring higher order continuity of the model as shown in Eq. (1-3). (Here, V'_{DS} =1V, δ =0.1 V, A=2).

$V_{DS} < V_{GS} - V_{TH}$, the device is said to be in the linear region and if $V_{DS} > V_{GS} - V_{TH}$, then the device is operating in the saturation region. The drain current, I_{DS} in linear and saturation regions is expressed in Eqs. (7) and (8), respectively [53],

$$I_{DS} = K_P \frac{W}{L - 2X_{jl}} \left(V_{GS} - V_{TH} - \frac{V_{DS}}{2} \right) V_{DS}(1 + \lambda V_{DS}) \tag{7}$$

$$I_{DS} = \frac{K_P}{2} \frac{W}{L - 2X_{jl}} (V_{GS} - V_{TH})^2 (1 + \lambda V_{DS}) \tag{8}$$

In Eqs. (7) and (8), the term, X_{jl}, refers to the lateral diffusion in source and drain regions, W is the channel width, and K_P is the conduction parameter. The effective channel length is then given by *(L−X$_{jl}$)*, where, *L* is the actual channel length. The term *(1+λV$_{DS}$)* introduces an empirical correction of the conductance in the saturation region, where λ represents the channel length modulation parameter. These five parameters, K_P, V_{TO}, γ, λ, and $2\phi_p$, characterize the model and can be directly specified in SPICE simulation or can be calculated from physical device parameters including substrate doping, substrate permittivity, gate oxide capacitance, and thickness.

Level 2 model: The Level 1 model does not include the effect of channel dimensions on the threshold voltage. However, the experimental data show that when the channel length is small enough to be comparable with the source and the drain depletion regions, then the relationship between the channel dimension and the threshold voltage is no longer negligible. John E. Meyer addressed this effect along with some other second-order effects to provide a more accurate model for smaller sized devices, which is considered as the Level 2 model [54]. The threshold voltage V_{TH} is modified in this model, as shown in Eq. (9), by introducing a change in the body effect parameter, γ, as shown in Eq. (10) [53],

$$V_{TH} = V_{FB} + 2\phi_p + \gamma' \sqrt{2\phi_p - V_{BS}} + \frac{\epsilon_s \delta \pi}{4C'_{ox} W} \left(2\phi_p - V_{BS} \right) \tag{9}$$

$$\gamma' = \gamma \left[1 - \frac{X_j}{2L_{eff}} \left(\sqrt{1 + \frac{2W_S}{X_j}} + \sqrt{1 + \frac{2W_D}{X_j}} - 2 \right) \right] \tag{10}$$

where V_{FB} represents the flat-band voltage (the amount of applied gate voltage when the channel region and the substrate have the same amount of carrier concentration of the same polarity), ε_s is the substrate permittivity, δ is the width-effect parameter, C'_{ox} is the oxide capacitance, X_j represents the doping depth in the source and the drain regions, W_S and W_D are the depletion widths at the source and the drain regions, respectively. W_S and W_D both are functions of the substrate bias and the bulk potential. Level 1 model also assumes that the fixed charge in the depleted channel region is independent of the channel-to-substrate voltage. This assumption becomes erroneous for large V_{DS}, as a result of the significant difference of the depletion widths between the drain and the source regions. Taking this effect into account, the drain current, I_{DS} expression in the linear region is modified, as presented in Eq. (11), which gives current values close to those of the Level 1 model for smaller V_{DS}.

$$\begin{aligned} I_{DS} = & \frac{K_P}{(1 - \lambda V_{DS})} \frac{W}{(L - 2X_{jl})} \left\{ \left(V_{GS} - V_{FB} - 2\phi_p - \frac{V_{DS}}{2} \right) V_{DS} \right. \\ & \left. - \frac{2}{3} \gamma \left[\left(V_{DS} - V_{BS} + 2\phi_p \right)^{1.5} - \left(-V_{BS} + 2\phi_p \right)^{1.5} \right] \right\} \end{aligned} \tag{11}$$

The drain voltage in the saturation region is expressed in Eq. (12). The drain current in the saturation region is obtained from Eq. (11) at $V_{DS} = V_{D,sat}$. A significant modification from Level 1 is the variation of the drain current with γ even if $V_{BS} = 0$. The drain-to-source voltage at saturation can be expressed as,

$$V_{D,sat} = V_{GS} - V_{FB} - 2\phi_p + \gamma^2\left[1 - \sqrt{1 + \frac{2}{\gamma^2}(V_{GS} - V_{FB})}\right] \tag{12}$$

The Level 2 model offers other modifications including nonzero drain current in the weak-inversion region when $V_{GS} < V_{TH}$, and voltage-dependence of K_P, reflecting the change of the carrier mobility with the gate and the drain voltages.

Level 3 model: The basic equations of the Level 3 model were proposed by Dang in 1979 [55]. This model can successfully predict the characteristic of a device with a channel length down to 2 μm. In the linear region, the drain current expression of Level 2 is simplified in this model by using the Taylor series expansion, as expressed in Eq. (13),

$$I_{DS} = \beta\left(V_{GS} - V_{TH} - \frac{1 + F_B}{2}V_{DS}\right)V_{DS}; F_B = \frac{\gamma F_S}{2\sqrt{2\phi_p - V_{BS}}} + F_n \tag{13}$$

The short-channel effect influences the empirical parameters, F_S and β, while the narrow channel influences another fitting parameter F_n. Level 3 uses a hypothesis, similar to Level 2, in formulating the threshold voltage. The threshold voltage proposed in Level 3 is presented in Eq. (14). However, the influence of the difference in the depletion width between the source and the drain regions, at higher V_{DS}, is now empirically expressed with the parameter, σ.

$$V_{TH} = V_{FB} + 2\phi_p - \sigma V_{DS} + \gamma F_S\sqrt{2\phi_p - V_{BS}} + F_n\left(2\phi_p - V_{BS}\right) \tag{14}$$

This model handles the gate voltage dependence of the surface mobility, μ_s, and the drain-to-source electric field dependence of the effective mobility, μ_{eff}, in a simpler way, as expressed in Eq. (15), by using the mobility modulation parameter, θ.

$$\mu_s = \frac{\mu}{1 + \theta(V_{GS} - V_{TH})}; \mu_{eff} = \frac{\mu_s}{1 + \mu_s\left(V_{DS}/v_{max}L_{eff}\right)} \tag{15}$$

In Eq. (15), the term v_{max} is the velocity limit reached by the carrier when $V_{DS} = V_{D,sat}$. The Level 3 version of the saturation voltage $V_{D,sat}$ is presented in Eq. (16).

$$V_{D,sat} = \frac{V_{GS} - V_{TH}}{1 + F_B} + \frac{v_{max}L_{eff}}{\mu_s} - \sqrt{\left(\frac{V_{GS} - V_{TH}}{1 + F_B}\right)^2 + \left(\frac{v_{max}\,L_{eff}}{\mu_s}\right)^2} \tag{16}$$

BSIM1 model: To bring higher accuracy in modeling shorter channel devices (down to 1 μm), the Berkeley Short Channel IGFET Model 1 (BSIM1) was introduced in 1987 [28]. Similar to Level 2 and Level 3 models, this model incorporates both the strong- and weak-inversion components of the drain current. However, unlike the previous models, BSIM1 used numerical approximation for modeling the dependence of the drain current on the substrate bias to speed up the simulation process. An automated parameter extraction program was designed to extract the model parameters. BSIM1 incorporates an improved formulation of short-channel effects to deal with short-channel devices. To enhance the scalability of the model, several fitting parameters are introduced for each of the model parameters. However, this model offers no significant improvement in scalability and due to a large number of fitting parameters, it has failed to gain popularity among circuit designers.

BSIM2 model: BSIM2 was developed in 1990 for submicron devices by improving some aspects of BSIM1 including model continuity, output conductance, and subthreshold current [56]. It employs cubic spline to achieve smoother transition between weak- and strong-inversion and between linear and saturation regions. BSIM2 uses more parameters for improved accuracy but the model has not solved the issue regarding the difficult parameter extraction process. The user still cannot get a set of parameters that are valid for a range of device sizes and has to deal with many sets of model parameters, each covering a limited range of device geometries.

BSIM3 model: BSIM3 was developed in 1994 from a coherent quasi-two-dimensional analysis of the MOSFET by addressing these issues of previous models [49]. To ensure good scalability, this model explicitly considers the effect of device size and process variation. The second version, BSIM3v2, was released with better accuracy and scalability than the previous version. However, this second version still suffers from the discontinuity, such as negative conductance and glitches in transconductance over drain current versus gate voltage plot at the boundary of weak- and strong-inversion regions. The third version, BSIM3v3.0, was introduced to eliminate all the shortcomings of the previous versions [57]. The significant distinction of BSIM3v3.0 is the introduction of the single-equation approach and prediction-ability that enabled statistical analysis [58]. The improvement of this third version of BSIM3 continued to three consecutive subversions, from BSIM3v3.0 to BSIM3v3.2 to incorporate significant developments including the introduction of a new charge-capacitance model considering the quantization effect, improved threshold model, substrate current model, and non-quasi-static model [59].

BSIM4 model: BSIM 4 was released in 2000 to support sub 130-nmm CMOS technologies and the growth of high-speed analog, mixed-signal, and RF integrated circuits [60]. A significant addition is a holistic noise model for the channel thermal noise and induced gate noise [61]. An intrinsic input resistance model is used to obtain accuracy at high-frequency operation. It also introduces a charge layer thickness model incorporating novel quantum effects [62]. Moreover, it includes the first model that takes into account the drain leakage current resulting from direct-tunneling [63]. Other improvements include pocket implant effect, layout-dependent factors including mechanical stress and well-proximity and enabled modeling of high-k metal-gate stacks and non-silicon materials.

BSIM-bulk model: There have been recent efforts to combine the best features of BSIM4 and EKV models. This has resulted in the newest addition to the Bulk MOSFET model from BSIM group and is named BSIM-bulk (formerly known as BSIM6). In contrast to its threshold voltage-based predecessors, BSIM-bulk is a charge-based and body-referenced model, which passes the symmetry test for DC and AC, correctly predicts harmonic slope, and exhibits accurate results for RF and analog simulations [64]. In addition, bulk charge effect has been modeled analytically to improve the model accuracy for transconductance and output conductance [65]. There is also a new NQS (non-quasi-static) model effective up to the millimeter wave regime.

2.4 Modeling of novel transistors and emerging devices

To continue the advancement of semiconductor industry beyond the imminent demise of Moore's Law, researchers all around the world have been exploring new technologies and consequently, a multitude of novel devices have emerged in recent years. This book chapter has been focused mainly on the development of compact models for bulk MOSFET. These models have been modified and extended for several novel transistors. For example, for SOI (silicon-on-insulator) devices, PSP-based model [66] and BSIM-based model [67, 68] have been reported. From the BSIM group, BSIM-IMG model for independent multi-gate MOSFET operation [69] and BSIM-CMG for common multi-gate transistor, that is, FinFET have been developed [70].

In addition to different nanoscale transistors, the lessons learned during development of different generations of compact models have also been successfully used to model many emerging devices such as metal-oxide-based resistive random-access memory (RRAM) devices [71, 72], insulator-metal-transition devices [73], biomolecular memristors [74] and memcapacitors [75] etc.

3. Device simulation

For any newly developed semiconductor device, different parameters need to be optimized before the device model can be adopted for practical circuit applications. However, with rapid development of new device and process technologies, optimization of semiconductor manufacturing processes guided by experimental approach becomes very time-consuming and expensive. As an alternative, device simulation can allow optimization of the device parameters in a virtual environment in a fast and cost-effective way to verify the device models for a newly developed semiconductor technology. In general, the tools used for numerical device simulation include three major components: (i) simulation of the fabrication process, (ii) simulation of the device characteristics, and (iii) simulation of the device for circuit applications. **Figure 2** shows the basic hierarchy of process, device and circuit

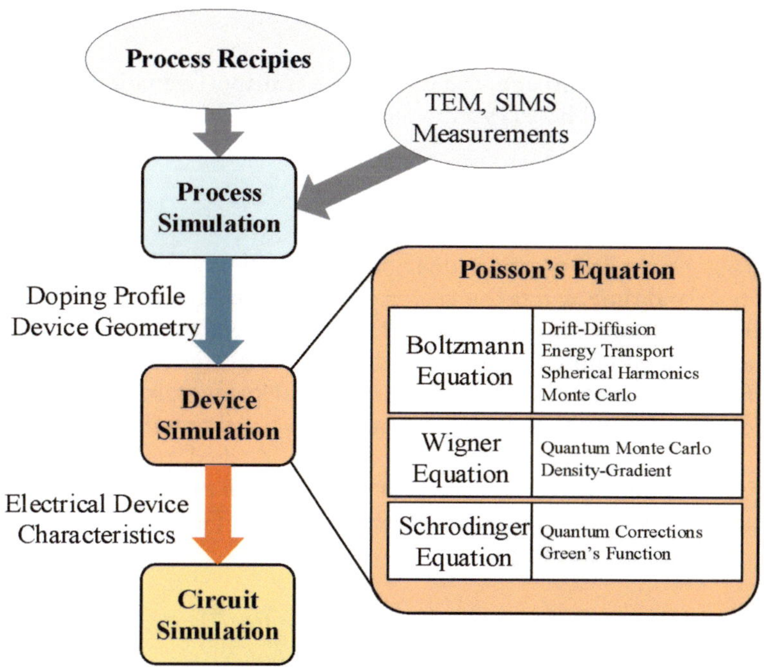

Figure 2.
Hierarchy of process, device, and circuit simulation.

simulation. Process simulation is closely coupled to the original device simulation because the behavior of the fabricated device is significantly related to the overall processing steps. Process simulation is implemented by mimicking the original device fabrication steps that include several lithography steps as well as ion implantation, diffusion, annealing, and oxidation steps. This simulation is based on the measurement of doping profile using secondary ion mass spectroscopy (SIMS), topography provided by transmission electron microscopy (TEM), the process recipe, and the lithography masks. Simulation of the device characteristics is based on the overall geometry of the device coupled with the simulated profile from the process simulation. This part of the simulation mainly focuses on the device output and transfer current-voltage (I-V) characteristics, capacitance-voltage (C-V) characteristics, or frequency response. The compact model intended to be used for the circuit simulation can be developed based on the output of the process and device simulation data optimized using different device parameters in TCAD tools.

3.1 Formulation of device simulation models

Semiconductor device simulation usually follows two different approaches such as semiclassical approach and quantum mechanical formulations. In the semiclassical approach, Boltzmann transport equation is used to model the carrier transport in the semiconductor devices by developing the drift-diffusion model along with the energy transport model. The solution of Boltzmann transport equation is usually obtained from doping profile of the device structure. The electrostatic potential, which depends on the dopant profile, is obtained from the Poisson's equation. In order to incorporate quantum mechanical transport phenomena in the modern device models, Boltzmann transport equation is coupled with Schrödinger equation and Wigner function [76, 77]. Device simulation using the classical approach is discussed in next section, which is then followed by a discussion of the quantum mechanical approach.

3.1.1 Device simulation using semiclassical approach

In the semiclassical approach, the Boltzmann transport equations to describe the transport of electron and holes in a device can be written as,

$$\frac{\partial f}{\partial t} + \boldsymbol{v}.\nabla_r f - \frac{q\boldsymbol{E}}{\hbar} \bullet \nabla_k f = Q(f) \tag{17}$$

where $f(r,k,t)$ stands for carrier distribution, which is a function of space, r, momentum, k, and time, t; $\boldsymbol{v}$ is the velocity; and $\boldsymbol{E}$ is the electric field. $Q(f)$ denotes the collision operator as a function of the carrier distribution that takes into account different scattering phenomena of the particle in the presence of impurities, phonon, interfaces, and scattering from other sources. However, solving the equation in this form can be computationally intense and thus usual practice is to solve it by applying approximate methods. One such method is called method of moments, which yields a set of differential equations as a function of time and space after multiplying a weight function with each term [78, 79]. The definition of the moments of the distribution function is written as,

$$\langle \Phi \rangle = \frac{1}{4\pi^3} \int \Phi f(r,k,t) d^3k \tag{18}$$

The drift-diffusion model can be obtained, by applying the method of moment in the Boltzmann transport equation. For the derivation of the drift-diffusion model, the first two moments such as $\Phi_0 = 1$ and $\Phi_1 = \hbar k$ of the distribution function are multiplied and integrated over k space. The integral of the collision operator Q can be approximated by applying macroscopic relaxation time (RTA) along with further simplification using the relationship of parabolic dispersion. Using this method, the following set of differential equations for the drift-diffusion model can be obtained,

$$\nabla.J_n = qR + q\frac{\partial n}{\partial t} \tag{19}$$

$$\nabla.J_p = -qR - q\frac{\partial p}{\partial t} \tag{20}$$

$$J_n = qn\mu_n E + qD_n \nabla n \tag{21}$$

$$J_p = qp\mu_p E - qD_p \nabla p \tag{22}$$

where J is the current density, R is the net recombination rate, n and p are the concentration of electron and hole, respectively, μ is the mobility, E is the electric field, and D is the diffusion coefficient. These set of equations for the drift-diffusion model combined with the Poisson's equation build the basic platform for the semiconductor device simulation. The charge transport in the semiconductor device with respect to the electrostatic potential is obtained by using the Poisson's equation as given by,

$$\nabla \bullet (\varepsilon_s \nabla \varphi) = q(n - p - N_D - N_A) \tag{23}$$

where φ is the electrostatic potential, ε_s *is* the dielectric permittivity, and N_D and N_A are the doping concentration of donor and acceptor atoms, respectively.

3.1.2 Device simulation using quantum mechanical approach

The basic simulation model using the semiclassical approach does not consider the quantum mechanical properties present in the semiconductor device. However, with the continuous reduction of the device size and due to the dual wave-particle nature of electron, quantum mechanical effects in the semiconductor devices have become significant and thus need to be incorporated in the model. There have been several procedures developed to formulate the quantum mechanical transport in modern electronic devices. **Figure 3** shows a flow chart representing the relationships among the relevant formulation of quantum models including Schrödinger equation, transfer-matrix, density matrix, Green's functions, Wigner function, and path integral approaches [80].

One of the most common ways to incorporate the quantum mechanical effect with the already developed semiclassical model involves coupling of Boltzmann transport equation with Schrödinger equation inside a self-consistent Schrödinger-Poisson loop. In this approach, the carrier concentration and the electrostatic potential are obtained by using Schrödinger equation and Poisson equation, respectively, in several iterations until a self-consistent solution is obtained. Boltzmann transport equations are then solved using the derived carrier concentration [81].

Another approach involves using the Wigner function along with Boltzmann transport equation to derive Boltzmann-Wigner equation [82],

$$\frac{\partial f}{\partial t} + v.\nabla_r f - \frac{q}{\hbar}\sum_{\alpha=0}^{\infty}\frac{(-1)^{2\alpha}}{4^{\alpha}(2n+1)!}\nabla_r^{2n+1}V(r) \bullet \nabla_k^{2n+1} f = \left(\frac{\partial f}{\partial t}\right)_C \tag{24}$$

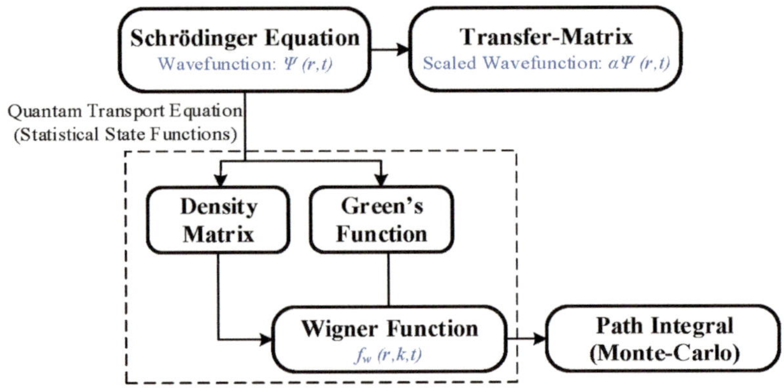

Figure 3.
Flow chart illustrating the formulation of the quantum mechanical transport.

where V denotes an external potential. This equation can be reduced to the classical Boltzmann equation by considering the term $\alpha = 0$. On the other hand, considering $\alpha = 1$ results in the density-gradient model as given by [83, 84]

$$\frac{\partial f}{\partial t} + \frac{\hbar \bullet k}{m^*} \nabla_r f - \frac{1}{\hbar} \nabla_r \left(V(r) - \frac{\hbar^2}{12m^*} \nabla_r^2 \ln(n) \right) \nabla_k f = \left(\frac{\partial f}{\partial t} \right)_C \tag{25}$$

where m^* is the effective mass of the carrier. By using this equation, the quantum drift-diffusion model can be obtained in a similar way by applying the method of moments described in the previous section [85].

$$n = N_c \exp\left(\frac{E_f - E_c - \Lambda}{k_B T} \right) \tag{26}$$

$$J_n = -\mu_n k_B T \nabla n - \mu_n n \nabla (E_c - k_B T \ln N_c + \Lambda) \tag{27}$$

$$\Lambda = -\frac{\gamma \hbar^2}{12m^*} \left(\nabla^2 \ln n + \frac{1}{2} (\nabla \ln n)^2 \right) = -\frac{\gamma \hbar^2}{6m^*} \frac{\nabla^2 \sqrt{n}}{\sqrt{n}} \tag{28}$$

where γ and Λ are used as correction factors, E_f and E_c are the Fermi level and the conduction energy band respectively, k_B is the Boltzmann constant, and T is the temperature. The implementation of the density-gradient model represents local quantum effect, which is in many cases more convenient to implement in a numerical device simulator than Schrödinger-Poisson equation that depends on nonlocal quantities [86–90]. This is due to the fact that for most numerical simulations, the overall device structure is divided into infinitesimal meshes and the electrical properties are then numerically calculated considering propagation along the meshes. However, there have been some studies that show that although this approach is suitable to model the carrier concentration of the inversion layer of the MOSFET, it fails to model the tunneling currents, which represent other important quantum mechanical effects present in modern devices [85]. Application of nonequilibrium Green's function is another approach to formulate quantum system that has non-vanishing boundary conditions for Schrödinger equations. However, the solution of the Green's function quantum transport equation is very complex and several assumptions and approximations are applied to simplify the derivation [91, 92] and the carrier concentration can be calculated as,

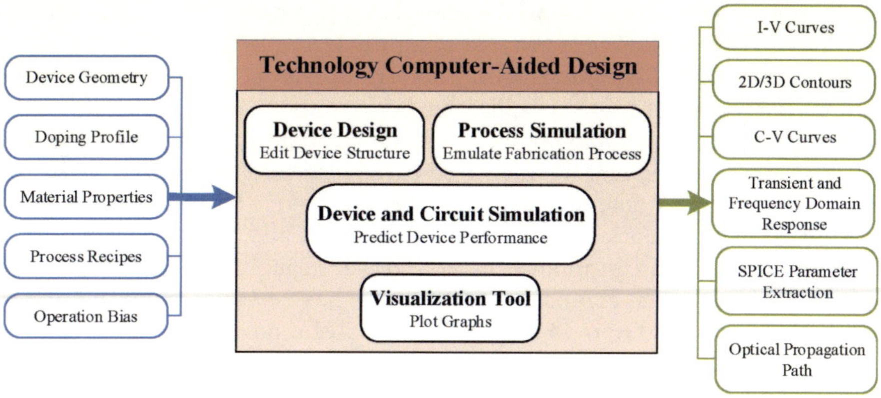

Figure 4.
Principle tools inside TCAD device simulation suites with input and output files.

$$D = \frac{m^* k_B T}{2\pi^2 \hbar^2} \int A(E) \ln\left(1 + \exp\left(\frac{E_f - E_c}{k_B T}\right)\right) dE \tag{29}$$

3.2 TCAD device simulation

The numerical models described in the previous section are very computationally intensive and iterative in nature. For this reason, device simulation is usually performed using technology computer-aided design (TCAD) tools, which can provide excellent predicting capability of the device properties allowing virtual prototyping and optimization [93–95]. Most of the modern TCAD packages consist of several tools to implement device processing, device design, parameter extraction, device and circuit simulation, and data visualization as shown in **Figure 4**. Several of these tools can be combined together based on designer preference in order to study the impact of any single step on the overall system performance. Among these, the process simulation tool creates a virtual environment to emulate the original fabrication and processing recipes that allow the process engineer to study each processing step on the device characteristics and thus facilitate fine tuning of their recipe to optimize the device performance. Electrical, thermal, and optical properties of semiconductor devices are analyzed using another dedicated tool for device simulation. Most TCAD device simulation tools implement finite element methods and some of them have the capability to extract SPICE model parameters for implementation in circuit applications. Physical equations and material properties are incorporated for better prediction while considering the convergence speed. The simulated data are stored in a standard format, which can be represented by the visualization tools for further analysis.

4. Conclusion

In the era of rapid development of device technology and electronic circuit design, semiconductor device modeling plays a vital role. To build sophisticated electronic circuits, one needs to take a deeper dive into understanding the features and the characteristics of the device through various modeling techniques. In this chapter, different approaches of device modeling for electronic circuit design have been discussed. To understand the behavior of any type of device, the first and foremost approach is to understand the underlying physics for the device operation. Physics-based analytical models provide accurate description of a device formulation using mathematical equations with different operating parameters. However, with the development of more complicated device structure, this type of technique is becoming more complex and computationally inefficient. To achieve a computationally efficient process, empirically fitted parameters are introduced in the original physics-based equations. In order to predict the device behavior in a circuit application, SPICE simulation with efficient, accurate, and robust device model becomes essential. With continuous research breakthroughs and introduction of new physical phenomena, compact device models have evolved from the first-generation Level 1 model to more sophisticated BSIM models. The newly developed device models include a number of device parameters not only to describe the fundamental device characteristics but to include other secondary phenomena that have become significant with continuous device scaling and modification. In addition to the development of efficient device models for wide range of circuit applications, it is also important for device simulation to optimize the fabrication parameters, prior to actual processing. This is to keep pace with the rapid development of newly emerging devices. This book chapter attempts to provide a brief overview of different aspects and methods for device modeling and simulation for electronic circuit design.

Author details

Samira Shamsir[1]*, Md Sakib Hasan[2], Omiya Hassan[1], Partha Sarathi Paul[2], Md Razuan Hossain[2] and Syed K. Islam[1]

1 Department of Electrical Engineering and Computer Science, University of Missouri, Columbia, MO, USA

2 Department of Electrical Engineering, The University of Mississippi, MS, USA

*Address all correspondence to: sshamsir@mail.missouri.edu

References

[1] Cheng Y, Hu C. MOSFET Modeling & BSIM3 User's Guide. Boston, MA: Springer Science & Business Media; 1999

[2] Liu W, Hu C. BSIM4 and MOSFET Modeling for IC Simulation. Singapore: World Scientific; 2011

[3] Gildenblat G, Li X, Wu W, Wang H, Jha A, Van Langevelde R, et al. PSP: An advanced surface-potential-based MOSFET model for circuit simulation. IEEE Transactions on Electron Devices. 2006;**53**(9):1979-1993

[4] Miura-Mattausch M. The Physics and Modeling of MOSFETs: Surface-Potential Model HiSIM. Singapore: World Scientific; 2008

[5] Enz CC, Vittoz EA. Charge-Based MOS Transistor Modeling: The EKV Model for Low-Power and RF IC Design. New York: John Wiley & Sons; 2006

[6] Galup-Montoro C, Schneider MC, Cunha AIA, de Sousa FR, Klimach H, Siebel OF. The advanced compact MOSFET (ACM) model for circuit analysis and design. In: IEEE Custom Integrated Circuits Conference. San Jose; 2007

[7] Rahman A, Guo J, Datta S, Lundstrom M. Theory of ballistic nanotransistors. IEEE Transactions on Electron Devices. 2003;**50**(9):1853-1864

[8] Khakifirooz A, Nayfeh OM, Antoniadis D. A simple semiempirical short-channel MOSFET current–voltage model continuous across all regions of operation and employing only physical parameters. IEEE Transactions on Electron Devices. 2009;**56**(8):1674-1680

[9] Gummel HK. A self-consistent iterative scheme for one-dimensional steady state transistor calculations. IEEE Transactions on Electron Devices. 1964;**11**(10):455-465

[10] Scharfetter DL, Gummel HK. Large-signal analysis of a silicon read diode oscillator. IEEE Transactions on Electron Devices. 1969;**16**(1):64-77

[11] Slotboom JW. Iterative scheme for 1 – and 2 – dimensional D. C. – transistor simulation. Electronics Letters. 1969;**5**(26):677-678

[12] Sah CT. Characteristics of the metal-oxide-semiconductor transistors. IEEE Transactions on Electron Devices. 1964;**11**(7):324-345

[13] Pao HC, Sah CT. Effects of diffusion current on characteristics of metal-oxide (insulator)-semiconductor transistors. Solid State Electronics. 1966;**9**(10):927-937

[14] Brews JR. A charge-sheet model of the MOSFET. Solid State Electronics. 1978;**21**(2):345-355

[15] El-Mansy YA, Boothroyd AR. A new approach to the theory and modeling of insulated-gate field-effect transistors. IEEE Transactions on Electron Devices. 1977;**24**(3):241-253

[16] Troutman RR. Subthreshold design considerations for IGFET's. IEEE Journal of Solid-State Circuits. 1974;**9**(2):55-60

[17] Taylor GW. Subthreshold conduction in MOSFET. IEEE Transactions on Electron Devices. 1978;**25**(3):337-350

[18] Taylor GW. A unified device model for a short-channel MOSFET. In: IEEE 39th Annual Device Research Conference. 1981

[19] Liu S, Nagel LW. Small-signal MOSFET models for analog circuit design. IEEE Journal of Solid-State Circuits. 1982;**17**(6):983-998

[20] Arora ND, Hauser JR, Roulston DJ. Electron and hole mobilities in silicon as a function of concentration and temperature. IEEE Transactions on Electron Devices. 1982;**29**(2):292-295

[21] Masetti G, Severi M, Solmi S. Modeling of carrier mobility against carrier concentration in arsenic-, phosphorus-, and boron-doped silicon. IEEE Transactions on Electron Devices. 1983;**30**(7):764-769

[22] Reggiani S, Valdinoci M, Colalongo L, Rudan M, Baccarani G, Stricker AD, et al. Electron and hole mobility in silicon at large operating temperatures. I. Bulk mobility. IEEE Transactions on Electron Devices. 2002; **49**(3):490-499

[23] Hall RN. Electron-hole recombination in Germanium. Physical Review. 1952;**87**(2)

[24] Shockley WT, Read WT Jr. Statistics of the recombinations of holes and electrons. Physical Review. 1952;**87**(5):835

[25] Schenk A. A model for the field and temperature dependence of Shockley-Read-Hall lifetimes in silicon. Solid State Electronics. 1992;**35**(11): 1585-1596

[26] Vladimirescu A, Liu S. The Simulation of MOS Integrated Circuits Using SPICE2. Electronics Research Lab. Berkeley: University of California; 1980

[27] Sheu BJ, Scharfetter DL, Poon HC. Compact Short-Channel IGFET Model [CSIM]. Electronics Research Lab., College of Engineering, Berkley: University of California; 1984

[28] Sheu BJ, Scharfetter DL, Ko PK, Jeng MC. BSIM: Berkeley short-channel IGFET model for MOS transistors. IEEE Journal of Solid-State Circuits. 1987; **22**(4):558-566

[29] Hasan MS, Shamsir S, Shawkat MS, Garcia F, Islam SK. Multivariate regression polynomial: A versatile and efficient method for DC modeling of different transistors (MOSFET, MESFET, HBT, HEMT and G4FET). International Journal of High Speed Electronics and Systems. 2018;**27** (03n04):1840016

[30] Chawla B, Gummel H, Kozak P. MOTIS-An MOS timing simulator. IEEE Transactions on Circuits and Systems. 1975;**22**(12):901-910

[31] Rofougaran AR, Furman B, Abidi AA. Accurate analog modeling of short channel FETs based on table lookup. In: Proceedings of the IEEE 1988 Custom Integrated Circuits Conference. Rochester, NY; 1988

[32] Rofougaran A, Abidi AA. A table lookup FET model for accurate analog circuit simulation. IEEE Transactions on Computer-Aided Design of Integrated Circuits and Systems. 1993;**12**(2): 324-335

[33] Meijer PB. Fast and smooth highly nonlinear multidimensional table models for device modeling. IEEE Transactions on Circuits and Systems. 1990;**37**(3):335-346

[34] Bourenkov V, McCarthy KG, Mathewson A. MOS table models for circuit simulation. IEEE Transactions on Computer-Aided Design of Integrated Circuits and Systems. 2005;**24**(3): 352-362

[35] Root DE, Fan S, Meyer J. Technology independent large signal non-quasi-static FET models by direct construction from automatically characterized device data. In: 21st European Microwave Conference. Stuttgart, Germany; 1991

[36] Yanilmaz M, Eveleigh V. Numerical device modeling for electronic circuit simulation. IEEE Transactions on Computer-Aided Design of Integrated Circuits and Systems. 1991;**10**(3): 366-375

[37] Hasan MS, Rahman T, Islam SK, Blalock BB. Numerical modeling and implementation in circuit simulator of SOI four-gate transistor (G4FET) using multidimensional Lagrange and Bernstein polynomial. Microelectronics Journal. 2017;**65**:84-93

[38] Shima T, Tamada H, Luong R, Dang M. Table look-up MOSFET modeling system using a 2-D device simulator and monotonic piecewise cubic interpolation. IEEE Transactions on Computer-Aided Design of Integrated Circuits and Systems. 1983;**2**(2):121-126

[39] Barby JA, Vlach J, Singhal K. Polynomial splines for MOSFET model approximation. IEEE Transactions on Computer-Aided Design of Integrated Circuits and Systems. 1988;**7**(5):557-566

[40] Hasan MS, Islam SK, Blalock BJ. Modeling of soi four-gate transistor (G4FET) using multidimensional spline interpolation method. Microelectronics Journal. 2018;**76**:33-42

[41] Tsividis Y, McAndrew C. Operation and Modeling of the MOS Transistor. New York: Oxford University Press; 2011

[42] McAndrew CC. Practical modeling for circuit simulation. IEEE Journal of Solid-State Circuits. 1998;**33**(3):439-448

[43] Bendix P, Rakers P, Wagh P, Lemaitre L, Grabinski W, McAndrew CC, et al. RF distortion analysis with compact MOSFET models. In: Proceedings of the IEEE 2004 Custom Integrated Circuits Conference (IEEE Cat. No. 04CH37571) 2004 Oct 6. Orlando, FL, USA; 2004. pp. 9-12

[44] Iniguez B, Moreno EG. A physically based C_∞-continuous model for small-geometry MOSFET's. IEEE Transactions on Electron Devices. 1995;**42**(2):283-287

[45] Cirit MA. The Meyer model revisited: Why is charge not conserved? (MOS transistor). IEEE Transactions on Computer-Aided Design of Integrated Circuits and Systems. 1989;**8**(10):1033-1037

[46] Machida K, Navarro D, Miyake M, Inagaki R, Sadachika N, Ezaki T, et al. Efficient non-quasi-static MOSFET model for both time-domain and frequency-domain analysis. In: Digest of Papers. 2006 Topical Meeting on Silicon Monolithic Integrated Circuits in RF Systems. San Diego, CA; 18 Jan. 2016

[47] Liu W, Jin X, Chen J, Jeng MC, Liu Z, Cheng Y, et al. BSIM3v3. 2.2 MOSFET Model. Users' Manual. Berkeley: University of California; 1999

[48] Joardar K, Gullapalli KK, McAndrew CC, Burnham ME, Wild A. An improved MOSFET model for circuit simulation. IEEE Transactions on Electron Devices. 1998;**45**(1):134-148

[49] Huang JH, Liu ZH, Jeng MC, Hui K, Hu C. BSIM3 Manual Ver. 2.0; Berkeley: University of California; 1994

[50] Nagel L, Pederson DO. SPICE (simulation program with integrated circuit emphasis). Berkeley: Electronics Research Laboratory, College of Engineering, University of California; 1973

[51] Nagel LW. SPICE2: A computer program to simulate semiconductor circuits [Ph.D. dissertation]. Berkeley: University of California; 1975

[52] Shichman H, Hodges DA. Modeling and simulation of insulated-gate field-effect transistor switching circuits. IEEE Journal of Solid-State Circuits. 1968;**3**(3):285-289

[53] Massobrio G, Antognetti P. Semiconductor Device Modeling with SPICE. New York: McGraw-Hill; 1993

[54] Meyer JE. MOS models and circuit simulations. R.C.A. Review. 1971;**32**:1

[55] Dang LM. A simple current model for short-channel IGFET and its application to circuit simulation. IEEE Transactions on Electron Devices. 1979; **26**(4):436-445

[56] Jeng MC. Design and modeling of deep-submicrometer MOSFETs [Ph.D. Dissertation]. Berkely: University of California; 1990

[57] Cheng Y, Chan M, Hui K, Jeng M, Liu Z, Huang J, et al. BSIM3 Version 3.1 User's Manual. Vol. 97. Berkeley: University of California; 1995. Memorandum No. UCB/ERL M

[58] Chen JC, Hu C, Wan CP, Bendix P, Kapoor A. ET based statistical modeling and compact statistical circuit simulation methodologies. In: International Electron Devices Meeting. Vol. 8. Technical Digest; 1996. pp. 635-638

[59] Liu W, Jin X, Chen J, Jeng MC, Liu Z, Cheng Y, et al. BSIM 3v3. 2 MOSFET Model Users' Manual. Berkeley: University of California; 1998

[60] Liu W, Jin X, Cao KM, Hu C. BSIM4. 0.0 MOSFET Model Users' Manual. Berkeley: Department of Electrical Engineering and Computer Sciences, University of California; 2000

[61] Jin X, Ou JJ, Chen CH, Liu W, Deen MJ, Gray PR, et al. An effective gate resistance model for CMOS RF and noise modeling. In: International Electron Devices Meeting. 1998

[62] Liu W, Jin X, King Y, Hu C. An efficient and accurate compact model for thin-oxide-MOSFET intrinsic capacitance considering the finite charge layer thickness. IEEE Transactions on Electron Devices. 1999; **46**(5):1070-1072

[63] Cao KM, Lee WC, Liu W, Jin X, Su P, Fung SK, et al. BSIM4 gate leakage model including source-drain partition. In: International Electron Devices Meeting. Technical Digest; 2000. p. 2000

[64] Gupta C, Goel R, Agarwal H, Hu C, Chauhan YS. BSIM-BULK: Accurate compact model for analog and RF circuit design. In: 2019 IEEE Custom Integrated Circuits Conference (CICC). San Jose; 2019

[65] Gupta C, Agarwal H, Goel R, Hu C, Chauhan YS. Improved modeling of bulk charge effect for BSIM-BULK model. IEEE Transactions on Electron Devices. 2019;**66**(6):2850-2853

[66] Wu W, Li X, Gildenblat G, Workman GO, Veeraraghavan S, McAndrew CC, et al. PSP-SOI: An advanced surface potential based compact model of partially depleted SOI MOSFETs for circuit simulations. Solid-State Electronics;**53**(1):18-29

[67] Su P, Fung SKH, Tang S, Assaderaghi F, Hu C. BSIMPD: A partial-depletion SOI MOSFET model for deep-submicron CMOS designs. In: Proc. of the IEEE Custom Integrate Circuits Conference. San Jose; 2000

[68] Chan M, Su P, Wan H, Lin CH, Fung SK, Niknejad AM, et al. Modeling the floating-body effects of fully depleted, partially depleted, and body-grounded SOI MOSFET. Solid State Electronics. 2004;**48**:969-978

[69] Lu DD, Dunga MV, Lin CH, Niknejad AM, Hu C. A multi-gate MOSFET compact model featuring independent-gate operation. In: 2007 IEEE International Electron Devices Meeting. 2007. pp. 565-568

[70] Dunga MV, Lin CH, Niknejad AM, Hu C. BSIM-CMG: A compact model for multi-gate transistors. In: FinFETs and Other Multi-Gate Transistors. Springer, Boston, MA; 2008. pp. 113-153

[71] Amer S, Hasan MS, Rose GS. Analysis and modeling of

electroforming in transition metal oxide-based memristors and its impact on crossbar array density. IEEE Electron Device Letters. 2017;**39**(1):19-22

[72] Chen PY, Yu S. Compact modeling of RRAM devices and its applications in 1T1R and 1S1R array design. IEEE Transactions on Electron Devices. 2015; **62**(12):4022-4028

[73] Amer S, Hasan MS, Adnan MM, Rose GS. Spice modeling of insulator metal transition: Model of the critical temperature. IEEE Journal of the Electron Devices Society. 2018;7:18-25

[74] Hasan MS, Najem JS, Weiss R, Schuman CD, Belianinov A, Collier CP, et al. Response of a memristive biomembrane and demonstration of potential use in online learning. In: IEEE 13th Nanotechnology Materials and Devices Conference (NMDC). Portland; 2018

[75] Najem JS, Hasan MS, Williams RS, Weiss RJ, Rose GS, Taylor GJ, et al. Dynamical nonlinear memory capacitance in biomimetic membranes. Nature Communications. 2019;**10**(1): 1-11

[76] Sano N, Hiroki A, Matsuzawa K. Device modeling and simulations toward sub-10 nm semiconductor devices. IEEE Transactions on Nanotechnology. 2002;**1**(1):63-71

[77] Yu Z, Dutton RW, Kiehl RA. Circuit/device modeling at the quantum level. IEEE Transactions on Electron Devices. 2000;**47**(10):1819-1825

[78] Blotekjaer K. Transport equations for electrons in two-valley semiconductors. IEEE Transactions on Electron Devices. 1970;**17**(1):38-47

[79] Stratton R. Diffusion of hot and cold electrons in semiconductor barriers. Physical Review. 1962;**126**(6):2002

[80] Biegel BA. Quantum electronic device simulation [PhD dissertation]. Stanford University; 1997

[81] Pacelli A. Self-consistent solution of the Schrodinger equation in semiconductor devices by implicit iteration. IEEE Transactions on Electron Devices. 1997;**44**(7):1169-1171

[82] Jensen KL, Ganguly AK. Numerical simulation of field emission and tunneling: A comparison of the Wigner function and transmission coefficient approaches. Journal of Applied Physics. 1993;**73**(9):4409-4427

[83] Ancona MG, Yu Z, Dutton RW, Voorde PV, Cao M, Vook D. Density-gradient analysis of MOS tunneling. IEEE Transactions on Electron Devices. 2000;**47**(12):2310-2319

[84] Ancona MG. Equations of state for silicon inversion layers. IEEE Transactions on Electron Devices. 2000; **47**(7):1449-1456

[85] Hohr T, Schenk A, Wettstein A, Fichtner W. On density-gradient modeling of tunneling through insulators. IEICE Transactions on Electronics. 2003;**86**(3):379-384

[86] Asenov A, Slavcheva G, Brown AR, Davies JH, Saini S. Increase in the random dopant induced threshold fluctuations and lowering in sub-100 nm MOSFETs due to quantum effects: A 3-D density-gradient simulation study. IEEE Transactions on Electron Devices. 2001;**48**(4):722-729

[87] Brown AR, Asenov A, Watling JR. Intrinsic fluctuations in sub 10-nm double-gate MOSFETs introduced by discreteness of charge and matter. IEEE Transactions on Nanotechnology. 2002; **1**(4):195-200

[88] Connelly D, Yu Z, Yergeau D. Macroscopic simulation of quantum mechanical effects in 2-D MOS devices

via the density gradient method. IEEE Transactions on Electron Devices. 2002; **49**(4):619-626

[89] Matsuzawa K, Takagi SI, Takayanagi M, Tanimoto H. Device simulation of surface quantization effect on MOSFETs with simplified density-gradient method. Solid State Electronics. 2002;**46**(5):747-751

[90] Wettstein A, Schenk A, Fichtner W. Quantum device-simulation with the density-gradient model on unstructured grids. IEEE Transactions on Electron Devices. 2001;**48**(2):279-284

[91] Datta S. Nanoscale device modeling: the Green's function method. Superlattices and Microstructures. 2000;**28**(4):253-278

[92] Datta S. The non-equilibrium Green's function (NEGF) formalism: An elementary introduction. In: Digest. International Electron Devices Meeting. IEEE; 2002. pp. 703-706

[93] Dutton R, Antoniadis D. Process simulation for device design and control. In: IEEE International Solid-State Circuits Conference. Vol. 22. Digest of Technical Papers; 1979. pp. 244-245

[94] Rafferty CS, Pinto MR, Dutton RW. Iterative methods in semiconductor device simulation. IEEE Transactions on Electron Devices. 1985;**32**(10): 2018-2027

[95] Dutton RW. Modeling and Simulation for VLSI. In: International Electron Devices Meeting. IEEE; 1986. pp. 2-7